HIGHER THAN THE EA

Stephen Venables is best known as the mountaineer who in 1988 became the first Briton to climb Everest without oxygen – one of many pioneering expeditions around the world. He began climbing while at Oxford in the early 1970s, and has written eight books about his mountain travels, winning the Boardman Tasker Prize, the King Albert Medal and the Grand Award at the Banff International Mountain Literature Festival. He has also appeared in several television documentaries and worked on two IMAX movies – appearing in Shackleton's Antarctic Adventure and writing *Alps – Giants of Nature*. His most recent book, *Ollie*, was a *Sunday Times* bestseller. He was President of the Alpine Club in the year of its 150th anniversary. He lives in Bath with his wife and son.

Higher Than the Eagle Soars was the winner of the Mountain Literature Award at the Banff International Mountain Literature Festival, 2007.

'In a refreshing antidote to climbing disaster stories, Venables tells how his early adventures led him to summit Mount Everest without oxygen in 1988. He relishes the tactile pleasure of hands on rock and the aesthetic beauty of mountains – and reminds us that climbing is not all about suffering and toil' Tarquin Cooper, *Daily Telelgraph*

'The story of his descent after a night spent at the top is . . . both harrowing and deeply moving' *Sunday Times*

'Venables has produced an engaging account of his achievements that allows the reader to vicariously experience the majesty, grandeur and terrifying challenges presented by some of the world's greatest peaks . . . An intimate, yet epic, account' *Traveller*

HIGHER THAN THE EAGLE SOARS

A Path to Everest

STEPHEN VENABLES

arrow books

Published by Arrow Books 2008

1 3 5 7 9 10 8 6 4 2

Copyright © Stephen Venables 2007

The right of Stephen Venables to be identified as the author of this work has been
asserted by him in accordance with the Copyright, Designs and Patents Act, 1988

First published in Great Britain in 2007 by
Hutchinson

Arrow Books
The Random House Group Limited
20 Vauxhall Bridge Road, London SW1V 2SA

www.rbooks.co.uk

Addresses for companies within The Random House Group Limited can be found
at: www.randomhouse.co.uk/offices.htm

The Random House Group Limited Reg. No. 954009

A CIP catalogue record for this book
is available from the British Library

ISBN 9780099505440

The Random House Group Limited supports The Forest Stewardship Council
(FSC), the leading international forest certification organisation. All our titles are
printed on Greenpeace approved FSC certified paper carry the FSC logo. Our
paper procurement policy can be found at www.rbooks.co.uk/environment

Typeset by Palimpsest Book Production Limited,
Grangemouth, Stirlingshire

Printed in the UK by CPI Bookmarque, Croydon, CR0 4TD

To my many climbing partners over the years. Thank you for your companionship and thank you for helping to keep me alive.

Parapismus was the name the Ancient Greeks gave to the high snow peaks of the Hindu Kush. The word derives from the Persian *uparisena*, meaning 'the peaks over which the eagle cannot fly' and could apply aptly to all the great ranges of Central Asia which have given me so much pleasure over the last thirty years.

Contents

Illustrations

Dave Wilkinson descending from recce, Kunyang Kish, 1980. (SV)
Dave Wilkinson on Jatunhuma I, Peru, 1982. (SV)
Finsteraarhorn North-East Face, Day Two, 1983. (SV)
Finsteraarhorn North-East Face, Day Three, 1983. (SV)

Second Section

Kishtwar-Shivling – the vision in 1979. (SV)
Kishtwar-Shivling first ascent, Day Four. (SV)
Kishtwar-Shivling first ascent, Day Five. (RR)
Siachen Indo-British Expedition 1985 – team photo. (SV)
Rimo I – Victor Saunders at fourth bivouac. (SV)
Rimo I – Victor Saunders at highpoint. (SV)
Camp on Shelkar Chorten Glacier. (SV)
Victor Saunders and Henry Osmaston researching peni-tentes. (SV)
Dave Wilkinson on Terong River ropes. (SV)
Dick Renshaw with the Gujars, Kishtwar, 1983. (SV)
Final camp in Mountains of the Moon, 1986. (SV)
Phil Bartlett on Snow Lake, 1987. (SV)
Phil Bartlett and Duncan Tunstall battling spindrift. (SV)
Rosie at Ferntower Road. (SV)
Reading party at Camp Two on Shishapangma, 1987. (SV)
Luke Hughes on Hinterstoisser Traverse, 1986. (SV)
Luke Hughes at Shishapangma highpoint, 1987. (SV)
View down Webster's Wall, Everest Kangshung Face, 1988. (SV)
Ed Webster on crevasse rope bridge, Everest 1988. (SV)
Paul Teare camping at Pethang Ringmo, Everest, 1988. (EW)
The author returning to South Col, Everest, 1988. (EW)
The author and Robert Anderson returning to South Col, Everest 1988. (EW)
The author with frostbitten nose, Everest, 1988. (PT)
Ed Webster with frostbitten fingers, Everest, 1988. (PT)

Pasang, Kasang and Angchu celebrate success of Everest, 1988. (SV)
Ed, Mimi, Stephen and Robert final photo at Advance Base, Everest, 1988. (JB)

Photo Credits

PB	Philip Bartlett
JB	Joseph Blackburn
ND	Norman Dockeray
LG	Lindsay Griffin
DL	David Lund
RR	Richard Renshaw
PT	Paul Teare
RV	Richard Venables
SV	Stephen Venables
EW	Ed Webster

Maps

Acknowledgements

When I first wrote about our Everest adventure nearly twenty years ago, the late Bradford Washburn's magnificent map of the mountain had still not appeared. Now, with the help of Brad's artistry I have corrected some of the heights quoted in my original account, *Everest Kangshung Face*. I have also benefited from reading Ed Webster's own version of our expedition, *Snow in the Kingdom*, which made me aware of several details I had previously overlooked. There is no such thing as a definitive account of an expedition, and in any case Everest appears here rather differently, as the surprise culmination of a long personal journey. Nevertheless, I am glad to have removed some inaccuracies and, perhaps, to have got a little closer to the real essence of our Tibetan adventure.

The Everest climb would not have been possible without the support of corporate sponsors such as Rolex, who had the faith to back our improbable plans. Likewise the 1985 Siachen expedition, made possible by the generous support of Grindlays Bank, and the Shishapangma expedition, sponsored by ICI and Eric Hotung. Many other organisations and individuals have also contributed generously over the years to my travels, but I would like most of all to thank the Mount Everest Foundation and the international committee of the British Mountaineering Council who continue, year after year, to support the kind of exploratory ventures which we seem to enjoy in Britain.

I would like to thank Phil Bartlett, Geoffrey Grimmett, Marianne Meister and Béatrice Rozier for their advice on the manuscript. Many thanks, also, to Phil Bartlett, Joseph Blackburn, Lindsay Griffin, Luke Hughes, David Lund, Joe

McGorty, Dick Renshaw, Paul Teare and Ed Webster for allowing me to use their photographs. And to my godfather, Norman Dockeray and my father, Richard Venables, who had no choice in the matter; I wish they were still alive to see their photos in print. And to Reginald Piggott who resists the tyranny of the computer and still draws his beautiful maps by hand. Vivienne Schuster, my agent, and her assistant at Curtis Brown, Stephanie Thwaites, were their usual efficient, nurturing, encouraging selves, as were the wonderful team at Hutchinson: Neil Bradford, Aislinn Casey, James Nightingale and my fellow mountaineer and editor, Tony Whittome. To all of them, a big 'thank you'.

Prologue

South Col

Frosted tent fabric sparkles in the light of a torch beam where Ed sits hunched beside me in the cramped dome. He spoons a mouthful of noodles from a plastic measuring jug. I slurp my own tepid spoonful, which tastes vaguely of chicken. Or prawns. Or perhaps tomato. What does it matter? It is purely functional, fuel for the job, a last attempt to stoke the furnace for the long journey ahead.

We have moved beyond the world of sensual pleasure. Up here, nearly five miles above sea level, there is no finesse: all that matters is survival. And yet I feel a great surge of excitement, even pleasurable anticipation. For six weeks this mountain has been everything. It has been our life. We have been consumed totally by this wild, crazy, beautiful odyssey. It has been hard, hard work. But it has also been pleasurable work, creative work: our very own new route up the great Kangshung Face. We have defied the sceptics and surprised ourselves. And now we're here, on the South Col, the first people ever to get here from Tibet. And today, tonight, we are setting off on the final leg of our journey to the top of the world.

Robert is in the other tent a few yards away, but Paul has gone. He had to leave this morning – kind, wise, irreverent, funny Paul. He didn't feel well and decided that the only safe thing to do was to go back down. When he said goodbye there were tears in his eyes. But he did the right thing: outstay your welcome here, at almost eight thousand metres, and cerebral oedema – fluid on the brain – can kill you very quickly.

So now there are just three of us. Ed and I hear an occasional rustle from Robert's tent, but we are busy with our own preparations. Meal finished, we work methodically through a series of chores, focused totally on the mundane detail which can make the difference between life and death. Gloves, mittens, over-mitts, spare mitts, spare torch-bulb. Water bottle topped up with laboriously melted snow, then stowed deep inside five layers of clothing. A thick pasty layer of sun cream smeared over nose and cheeks, ready for the blazing solar radiation which will hit us in seven hours' time. Then the slow ritual of preparing feet: smoothing socks, pulling on pre-warmed inner boots, lacing outer boots loosely, trying not to constrict circulation; finally, panting with the exertion, zipping giant foam-soaks over the top of boots.

We hardly talk because talking wastes breath, and here every scrap of breath is a hard-won prize, a gleaning from the thin air. Since we arrived here yesterday evening I have got better at it: I've quelled the panic, learned how to regulate the lungs' rhythm, letting my diaphragm work the bellows. I feel more confident, particularly now that the wind has dropped and is no longer flapping the frozen tent fabric. Everything is silent, peaceful, calm.

I unzip the tent door and crawl out into the darkness. Then stand up to look around, feeling the air bite sharp and cold on my face. We had hoped our summit bid might coincide with a full moon, but tonight we have only the stars. Against their faint glimmer I can just make out the black solidity of Lhotse, the world's fourth-highest mountain. Turning round the other way, the sky is blocked by the closer, foreshortened bulk of Everest – the final pyramid, the last stage of our journey.

I pull back a mitten to check my watch. Ten-thirty p.m. Robert has now emerged from his tent. Or at least his legs have, swaddled in bulging goose down, unwieldy boots resting on the snow crust. The rest of his body is still slumped inside the tent, trying to find the energy to sit up and clamp crampons – those vital ice-gripping metal spikes – to his boots. I struggle with my own, cold steel searing through flimsy inner gloves, numbing my fingers in seconds, so that I have to retreat into our tent and rejoin Ed, huffing and puffing my fingers back to life. In the end it is Ed – kind, patient Ed – who leans over, panting with the exertion, and completes the fiddly job for me.

At eleven o'clock we are all ready to leave. Ed produces a length of rope, purple in the torchlight. He knots the middle and clips it to a loop around his waist. Robert ties into one end, and I take the other. Then we set off into the darkness. My muffled ears can only just discern the squeaking crunch of boots on snow and the rustle of nylon and those sounds are almost drowned by the closer rasp of my own breath. Everything is reduced to this organism, this body, this miraculous construct of muscle and bone and coursing blood, so fragile and vulnerable, sustaining this consciousness – this *me*, with all my dreams and hopes and fears and interconnected threads of memory.

Soon it will be midnight. And then the dawn of a new day. The most beautiful sunrise I will ever have seen. It could be my last sunrise: tomorrow could be the day I die. Or it could be the day I stand on top of the world. I still don't know whether I am capable of it. But how wonderful to have this chance to find out. What a privilege to be here, on this famous stage, playing out the final scene of our story. What a treat. I hardly dare to believe that it is really happening. Who could have imagined that I would end up here? Who could have guessed that that shy, timid, skinny boy would ever set foot on a mountain at all? How could *I* have known that so many months and years of my life would be spent doing this – trespassing so brazenly in this vertical starlit landscape, choosing such a perverse path, forsaking all those other myriad pleasures? But that path has brought its own special rewards. And pleasures. Yes – real pleasure. And, in a strange, unpredictable, serendipitous sort of way, it has led inexorably to this moment, as though all those other adventures were a preparation for this greatest adventure of all.

Chapter One

Norwood Hill

Mountaineers are expected to explain themselves. Why the suffering? Why the perverse flirtation with danger? Why the repeated heartache and separation – the endless partings, with their recurrent threat of no return? Why? And, even if we can answer those questions, then how on earth did we get into this crazy pastime in the first place – what was the blinding flash on the road to Damascus? But all I can offer by way of initiation is a glimmer on the road to Bangor.

It was a summer's evening in 1963 and we had driven all the way up from London, singing songs most of the way, as we always did on long car journeys, my father improvising harmonies to old favourites like 'Green Grow the Rushes, O', his loud bass competing with the familiar thrum of the Volkswagen's rear engine. Twilight was falling as we entered the cleft of the Ogwen Valley but in the gloaming I could just make out the mountainside looming over the road – immense heathery slopes riven by gullies; battlements of dark rock veined white with quartz; boulders tumbled wantonly across the most elemental landscape I had ever seen. I was nine and I just knew that I wanted to be up there, amongst those rocks.

Perhaps that was the moment when the seed was sown; but I don't think the course of a life can ever be explained so simply. The influences are far more richly layered, contradictory and subliminal than that; and in any case, the mountains have only been one strand – albeit a vital one – in my life. So, even if that Snowdonia discovery was a key moment, I want first to go back to the beginning, to where I came from, starting with my Scottish great-grandfather.

William Ogilvie was one of eleven children born into a prosperous Dundee family. In the summer of 1875, during a year spent travelling round the Continent with his mother and some of his brothers and sisters, he visited Zermatt and did some climbing there. He seems to have been an adventurous type, for after training at Edinburgh University to be a civil engineer he sailed in 1886 to Valparaíso, to take up a post working on, amongst other projects, the trans-Andean railway. His young sweetheart, Rotha, refused to sail with him to Chile, assuming that he would soon come back to her. He did eventually return, but in the meantime he met and married a German woman who bore him five children. The family returned to Britain at the turn of the century and right at the end of his life, after his first wife had died, Willy did finally marry Rotha, when he was seventy. Of his successful children, one son became a surgeon, the other a university don. Both were knighted. One of the three daughters married the Anglo-Irish novelist Joyce Cary; the eldest girl, Florence, married an ordained schoolmaster who loved the verse of Shelley, despite the poet's atheism. His name was Malcolm Venables.

My father Richard was the youngest of Malcolm and Florence's six children and grew up at Harrow School, where Malcolm was an English teacher and housemaster until forced to resign in 1942 on the pretext of wartime economies. Malcolm then became a parish priest in Somerset and might have ended his life there in obscurity if it hadn't been for a surprise letter from Clement Attlee announcing his royal appointment as a canon – and later Precentor responsible for music – at St George's Chapel, Windsor. I still retain a glimmer of a memory of a visit to Windsor Castle before Grandfather died in 1957 – tantalisingly sketchy images of waking early in a strange room with bare floorboards … glimpses of battlements through a high window … aunts coming to quieten me and my younger brother lest we disturb our rather moody grandfather. Granny didn't die until I was eighteen and we used to see her about once a year. She was tall and gentle, and smelt of powder and fur; and she was very generous, giving us her Blüthner grand piano – and her violin – when she claimed she was too old to play them any more.

My other grandfather, Granchie, the splendidly named John Gower Meredith Richards, was actually only *half* Welsh – his English mother was a descendant of the Victorian sculptor Sir Richard Westmacott – but there was something unmistakably Celtic about his dark good looks. His three brothers were all scientists – a botanist, an entomologist and a physician – but he bucked the trend by reading Greats at Oxford, then going to the Sorbonne where he wrote short stories, became a fluent French speaker and fell in love with a beautiful young woman called Nina. Nina's mother was a Russian émigré opera singer whose husband, a Polish-Jewish violinist, had long since done a bunk, leaving her to raise her daughter alone in a tiny flat. The daughter married Gower and moved to London, where Gower earned his living as a schoolteacher and later as a schools inspector, before joining the Ministry of Food during the Second World War. They had just one child, my mother, Ann.

I never knew my grandmother Nina. By all accounts she was a flamboyant extrovert, who loved to sing, performing at every possible occasion and embarrassing my hockey-playing tomboy mother with her foreign accent. Nina was devastated when her own mother, my great-grandmother, died alone and penniless in Paris during the war, unreachable behind the fortress walls of the German occupation. Yet despite that, and her Jewishness, when Nina went to work in Berlin after the war as a translator, fluent in Russian, German, French and English, she wrote to Gower that seeing the misery and destruction all around her it was impossible to hate the Germans. After returning to England she was badly burned in a domestic accident and died a few days later in hospital.

Nina died at the end of 1949 when my mother was away

in the Alps on a skiing holiday, paid for with the exhibition she had just won for her first term's work at Oxford. Later that academic year she met my father, a second-year undergraduate, who spent his time sailing, fly-fishing, playing cricket and singing. The next time my mother went on a university ski trip she took Richard with her. Before he graduated with his third-class degree they became engaged and my mother, daughter of a Welsh agnostic liberal and a Jewish bohemian, was taken to Windsor Castle to meet her prospective father-in-law, The Reverend Malcolm Venables, a pillar of the Anglican establishment, who almost certainly thought the name Lloyd George was synonymous with the devil.

It seems an unlikely marriage, but I like the idea of opposites joined, dissonance resolved. I was proud, as a child, to learn about my mongrel roots and the diverse enthusiasms of my relatives; and yet, despite the Celtic element, I have always thought of myself as English. And European. And inescapably middle-class.

When I was eighteen months old my parents bought their first house – a dilapidated seventeenth-century cottage in a Surrey hamlet called Norwood Hill, within commuting distance of the London advertising agency where my father was an account executive. My brother Mark was born here, at Roundabout Cottage, in January 1956, just after we moved in. As my parents liked to go skiing at least every other year, they staggered babies at two-year intervals. Philip followed in 1958 and Cangy in 1960. Lizzie was a late surprise in 1966.

Early memories include playing in the muddy lane by the farm next door. Walking down the hill to Chantersluer, where I once fell off the Armstrongs' pony, catching my foot in the stirrup and being dragged at high speed, head bouncing along a concrete path, as the pony bolted for its stable. Falling in the Norfolk Broads, aged four, watching curiously the vertical clay bank as I slipped underwater. Afternoon walks at home, shuffling alongside a pramload of younger siblings, stopping perhaps at the village post office. Driving to the little town of Horley where Stapleys the grocer's smelt of cheese and coffee,

Dulwich, 1956 – in godfather Norman Dockeray's garden

and men in brown aprons wrapped provisions in paper parcels. Balancing upright on my first bike, wobbling triumphantly round the lawn on a misty, smoky autumn evening. The acetic-acid smell of the glue hardener in the garage, where we got under the feet of our father who was always busy, always making things – sailing boats, bookcases, tables, toy houses. Lying in bed at night, listening to the melancholic drone of propeller engines as the planes came in to land at the new airport at Gatwick.

The idea that I might actually fly in aeroplanes myself seemed preposterous. Ours was quite an inward life, with no television and not much radio, and I was woefully ignorant about the outside world. The Cuban missile crisis passed me by completely and a year later, when the children in my class told me one morning that Kennedy had been shot, I asked, 'Who's Kennedy?' Likewise the news of Churchill's final, fatal stroke, overheard at a petrol station in January 1965 on the way back from a London visit to *Toad of Toad Hall*: only then, at nearly eleven, did I finally register Omdurman, the Boer War, the North-West Frontier, Munich, Dunkirk and the last heroic stand of the Empire in Britain's 'finest hour'.

By now we had moved half a mile to a bigger house. It was

9

a shoddily converted stable block but there were tantalising remnants of the demolished Victorian mansion it had once served and, as we hacked and burned through acres of brambles, we unearthed remains of heated greenhouses, brick paths and old apple orchards. We had space to roam, trees to climb, fields and woods to explore. It was a secure, comfortable childhood. We all went to a local private school where about half the children were boarders and, bicycling back each afternoon, I thought how lucky we were to be at home with our parents.

High Trees School may have been private but it was not grand. Lessons were taught in old wooden huts smelling of cedar pencil sharpenings and chalk. On frosty winter mornings the windows were opaque with swirling fern patterns and we had to shake numb hands in time with our table reciting, waiting for the paraffin stove slowly to warm the room. Our headmaster, John Norsworthy, combined high educational ideals with splendid eccentricity. Science and current affairs might have been neglected, but he assumed that any vaguely intelligent child should be introduced to Bach and Wordsworth as a matter of course and should participate enthusiastically when he decided to put on a Purcell opera. One year his nephews and nieces gave him for his birthday a baby goat, Seamus, which grew rapidly to the size of a small cow. Neighbours would report glimpsing at twilight a huge malevolent yellow-eyed beast charging headlong through the Surrey woods, dragging on a tether its master – a devout lay preacher – dressed in a black cassock.

When I was six I attended my first football game, gawky in baggy shorts and steel-studded boots, lurking uncomprehendingly at the end of the pitch next to a boy who for some reason best known to himself had taken up position between two white posts, announcing that he was the 'goldie'. At home that evening I reported proudly to my mother, 'One time the ball came flying straight towards my head, but I just managed to duck in time.' I never really came to terms with team games and in the gym I resented Mrs Buzzoni's endless ball-patting exercises, when I longed to be vaulting the box and climbing the neglected wall bars.

Holidays were different. Several summers in succession we went to the seaside. I loved leaping off sand dunes, traversing cliffs and exploring the great blowhole on the headland above Trevone Bay. And I loved going out from Padstow harbour, trolling for mackerel and bass with bearded Captain Lombard, or casting a spinner from the rocks at the mouth of the estuary, or clutching the jib sheet as the sailing dinghy skimmed the waves.

I loved the wild power of the sea and perhaps I might have become a sailor if the mountains hadn't interrupted during the summer of 1963. In August we camped beside a Scottish loch, and on the way north we stayed with some friends in the Lake District. I was allowed to join the adults on a walk up Crinkle Crags. I loved all the ritual of it: the restorative thermos flask, the map and compass in the swirling mist, the smell of peat and moss, the brief excitement of climbing bald rock on the 'Bad Step' immortalised in one of Wainwright's classic pen-and-ink drawings. Then in September came North Wales and that first twilit glimpse of the Glyder mountains as we drove the final stretch to Bangor to stay with my great-uncle Paul and his family. He was Professor of Botany at the university and on the Sunday afternoon he took us up past the great chasm of the Devil's Kitchen to potter barefoot in the bogs above, pointing out all the different red, yellow and green sphagnums and showing me my first carnivorous sundew plant. Later that week we walked up Snowdon, which I suppose was my first real summit.

This was also the year when Mark and I were first taken skiing. The anticipatory thrill of Advent was intensified by busy preparations in the workshop as our father stripped down second-hand skis, repainting the wooden soles, polishing and sharpening the screw-on metal edges, and adjusted bindings, fitting cables and straps to our leather boots with their exotic shiny lace-hooks and cleated rubber soles. Philip and Cangy were packed off to stay with friends and on Boxing Day the rest of us caught the evening ferry to Dunkirk, continuing by road across northern France to Basel, and on for a second long day's drive to the Engadine Valley in the far eastern corner of Switzerland.

Four years running we made that epic journey and by the fourth trip only baby Lizzie, out of the five of us, was left at home. Twice the car's dynamo packed up near Arras. Once the windscreen was smashed two hundred miles short of Dunkirk on the return journey, during an afternoon of horizontally driven sleet. Black ice, freezing fog and the wilful perversity of French signposting all added a sense of challenge. Our father occasionally cursed, blaming it all on Charles de Gaulle, but we children were content in our sleeping bags, comforted by the steady drone of the engine, only dimly aware of the sudden rumble of cobbled streets in yet another obscure town somewhere on the Marne.

It was always thrilling to reach the Alps, but nothing could ever beat the anticipation of that first journey in 1963, after two days finally coming over the crest of the Julier Pass and looking down across the white mountainside to the twinkling lights of St Moritz. Our parents disliked the glitzy resort and all it stood for, and we stayed in a tiny village called Brail further down the valley. Arriving late that first night, Mark and I had to be dissuaded from putting skis on straight away; we went reluctantly to bed but we were up again at dawn, floundering happily in the snow outside the chalet.

We skied mainly at the village of Zuoz, which had two ski lifts. In later years we went increasingly to the big runs above St Moritz and Pontresina. And that was how I saw my first real glaciated mountains. And my first avalanche, spilling, tumbling, cascading with strangely silent power down the great buttressed face of Piz Palu. I don't think I imagined actually *climbing* these huge peaks; I just liked being amongst them, content simply to enjoy the rush of air as I sped down prepared pistes. One afternoon on the way back to Brail, we stopped to watch the bobsleighs hurtling down the terrifying Cresta Run and my mother said, 'Maybe one day you'll do brave things like that . . . or climbing the North Face of the Eiger.'

'What's the Eiger?'

'Oh – it's that huge mountain wall where all those climbers died in the 1930s.'

I was a rather timid child, and I wasn't at all sure that I would ever attempt anything so brave. Nevertheless I did, one summer in the Rhinog mountains in Wales, enjoy setting myself little climbing problems on the scattered boulders of Harlech grit. It was 1966 and we were all staying at a cottage called Nantcol, complete with three-weeks-old Lizzie and our black Labrador bitch and her latest batch of puppies. Grandfather Gower and his second wife Maud came to stay and one morning I walked with them up to Llyn Hywel. This exquisite little tarn was far enough for them but I asked if they would mind waiting while I continued to the summit of Rhinog Fach.

'What, up there! Are you sure you should?' asked Maudie. 'Will you be all right?'

'Yes, I'll be careful.'

'Oh well, darling, I suppose so; we'll watch you.'

And I was away, racing up the steepening slope, loving the urgent intensity of it, grappling with rock and heather, feet balanced wide, hands searching, testing, grasping, my whole being absorbed totally in the finding of the route, the solving of the puzzle, thrilling to the deepening view down to the lake, now far beneath my feet. And then the glorious surprise of the summit – so broad and flat and smooth after all that rocky steepness. I lay there for ten minutes, soaking up the warmth and the smell of heather and the companionship of a lone kestrel hovering silently beside me in the powder-blue sky.

Three weeks later I was back at school, for my last year at High Trees, struggling to concentrate on simultaneous equations and the Latin subjunctive as I stared wistfully at the newly swelling curves of Susan Whillock's tunic-clad body and dreamed impossible fantasies of love requited. At Easter she left, and I consoled myself with the thrill of singing in the *Messiah*, my father conducting the tiny village choir in Charlwood church, and, showman that he was, also doing the baritone solos. That summer I worked hard for the Common

Entrance exam, getting reasonable marks in most subjects. I even managed to win a couple of races on Sports Day and, hoping to draw me out of my shell a little, John Norsworthy gave me the lead part in the school play that he had written. On television – for the first time in years we had a working set at home – I watched the news of Israel's Six-Day War, trying to make sense of history unfolding. Later that summer we all watched the first global satellite transmission, which included the Beatles recording 'All You Need is Love', live in London. A few weeks later the *Sergeant Pepper* album was released. Even in our rural Surrey backwater there was an optimistic buzz in the air. My father was now a company director, with a bigger salary, so that this year we went twice abroad, spending our summer holiday in Brail, walking, fishing, cooking sausages on fires and, for one brief day, going rock-climbing.

It was my mother's idea to sign up for a day's collective course with a guide from Pontresina. She and I met the rest of the group early in the morning and followed the guide up through resinous pine woods to a cluster of boulders, where we practised standing on tiny rock nubbins, jamming hands in cracks, grasping side-pulls . . . defying gravity. As the only child, I was pleased to outperform two rather earnest young German men who scrabbled ineffectually in their natty tailored breeches; and after lunch I was thrilled to tie for the first time onto a rope and take my turn following a full pitch of about thirty metres up a steep crag. I looked up the mountainside to further crags and an enticing, jagged ridge soaring to a summit, and assumed that we would be going up there.

But no. Not a bit of it. It was three o'clock in the afternoon and the guide announced that the day's course was finished. The lack of a summit was disappointing, but I had enjoyed my gentle induction and made a mental note to take this game further when the chance arose.

In September 1967 I started at boarding school. The intention had always been to follow in my father's steps to Marlborough, where he had been incarcerated during the war, but at the last moment my mother baulked at the long pre-M25 drive from Surrey and suggested the closer establishment of Charterhouse, near Godalming. Ever since Robert Graves's damning account of the school in *Goodbye To All That*, it had had a reputation for oppressive philistinism, but my father was persuaded that things might have changed in fifty years and agreed to give it a try. And so, one warm afternoon, as the first apples and conkers began to fall, I arrived amongst the hundred and forty or so new boys to take hesitant steps into the place which would be my second home for the next four and a bit years.

Brushing my teeth the first evening, trying to look inconspicuous in my brand-new woollen dressing gown, I was startled by a gaggle of older boys barging into the washroom and asking eagerly, 'Are you Venables?'

'Yes.'

'Any good at football?'

My hopes wilted. Everyone had assured me that it wasn't compulsory to be sporty at this place. Now I had only been here two hours and already I was being harangued about football. 'What do you mean?' I asked.

'Aren't you related? You know – Our Tel . . . Terry Venables. Tottenham Hotspur.' And as they chanted, 'Ter-ry, Ter-ry' I blinked myopically and contorted my face into what I hoped was a nonchalant smile, pretending that I had heard of this tiresome man who was apparently the most famous footballer in the country.

In fact I escaped lightly, only having to play football once a week for my first two years, and not at all after that. Cricket – the game I would love to have played if I had not been so totally inept – was only forced on me for my first summer term, one afternoon a week; and because the Yearlings in my house were the best in the school, I was never called on to bowl or bat, and only rarely touched the ball at all, whilst fielding on the far perimeter, enjoying the smell of freshly mown grass and the summery whisper of a light breeze amongst the beech leaves.

During my first term I was delighted when the head of the art department, Ian Fleming-Williams, showing new boys round studio, took us into a room full of books and records and announced, 'You have as much right to come and sit on these sofas and listen to these records as the head of school.' I warmed to that note of gentle subversion. Only much later did I discover that he was a scholarship-winning artist in his own right, as well as being a world expert on Constable. His colleagues – the seventy or so masters who made up 'Brooke Hall' – were an eclectic bunch; most of them worked extremely hard and between them they amassed an impressive range of talents and enthusiasms.

And the boys – that lumpen mass of adolescents corralled so unnaturally onto a few acres of prime Surrey real estate? Of course there was the occasional bully or boorish slob. But there were also many I admired for their brains and talents. And I think that in the late 1960s the stultifying conformity which can make adolescent life so hard was nowhere near as relentless as it has now become. Mavericks and eccentrics were tolerated, even cherished. No one complained when my beloved Brahms roared from my record player, competing with the Jimmy Hendrix, Bob Dylan and Stones numbers pulsating through the studies of my house, Gownboys.

Music was the great escape. My violin teacher, Geoffrey Ford, was incisive, encouraging and always funny. My piano teacher, Jean Mabbott, took me on a magical journey, introducing the boundless landscape of the Beethoven sonatas, daring me to risk everything in the leaping octaves of Brahms's rhapsodies. Aged fourteen, I returned one evening to house from my first orchestra rehearsal chattering excitedly about the glorious surge of a tune I had just discovered in 'Rachimoskythingamy'; we were accompanying an older boy from my house rehearsing Rachmaninov's Second Piano Concerto. Earlier that year, singing for the first time with a big choir and orchestra, I was electrified by the thud of the bass drum in Verdi's *Dies Irae*, overwhelmed by the arching structure of the *Requiem*, transfixed by the soprano solo soaring ethereally over the whole massed choir and orchestra at the dazzling climax of *Libera Me.*

It was all new and exciting. Likewise the rapid induction into art and literature and the arcane wonders of medieval history – a crash course through the highlights of European civilisation. And in case that all sounds horribly earnest, I had my moments of rebellion, enjoying the occasional illicit cigarette amongst the leafy boughs on Northbrook playing fields, or climbing illegally at night on the school's irresistible Victorian Gothic rooftops, rousing our housemaster, John Phillips, to fine displays of disciplinary wrath which never quite concealed his private amusement. The following term, deterred from climbing, we went caving instead, crawling through a manhole cover into a fascinating warren of forbidden cellars. Needless to say, we were caught and punished again.

There was an older boy, Claude Wreford-Brown, who was a real climber and who occasionally showed off his smooth-soled rock-climbing shoes on the arched gateway of Gownboys Tower. By the time I was working for A levels he had already left and was accompanying the American climber Rick Sylvester up a new route on Yosemite's gigantic granite wall, El Capitan. Another possible subliminal influence was George Mallory, the Charterhouse schoolmaster who had died close to the summit of Everest in 1924. Every day, walking through the cloister to music school, I passed his memorial plaque, alongside that of another Charterhouse master, Wilfrid Noyce, who had died much more recently in the Pamir mountains, and whose *Climber's Fireside Book* was given to me for my fourteenth birthday. Both men had been fine natural climbers and both had been unapologetic romantics, lured by the mystical qualities of wild mountain country. While I had no particular ambition yet to be 'a mountaineer' – and certainly no desire for a premature death – I think that at a subconscious level I did hope that perhaps I might follow their steps, at some unspecified future date.

In the meantime I kept reasonably fit by running. Most mornings during my first year I was up before first bell, running my way through an endless backlog of punishments. The dawn start became a habit and, even after I learned to avoid punishments, I often got up voluntarily to do a couple of miles before breakfast, determined to excel in the annual cross-country race. For a while I also enjoyed that wonderfully idiosyncratic game, fives, playing regular doubles until the other three boys in the group tired of my dyspraxic incompetence. I also loved tennis. And I had the occasional camping trip with the Scouts – the only permitted alternative to the military CCF. But school on the whole was an indoor business, with the freedom of the holidays set aside for the outdoors.

In August 1968 we camped with our old friends the Pellys beside Loch Ewe, in Wester Ross, and for the first time in my life I handled the world's most beautiful climbing rock, Lewisian gneiss, scrambling around the craggy shoreline, occasionally scaring myself with the possibility of a big ankle-snapping fall. The following year we went back to Switzerland and the year after that to the ancient volcanic domes of the Auvergne. That holiday was preceded by an exchange, Mark and I staying with friends in Paris related obliquely to my mother's Russian-French ancestors. The Potiers had a small house in the Forest of Fontainebleau and did a bit of climbing. One Sunday afternoon they took Mark and me to climb on the sandstone boulders which have been a playground for generations of Parisian climbers. Mark, I think, was indifferent. I loved it, and insisted on going back every afternoon, on one occasion, with the eldest Potiers boy, Vincent, managing briefly to get stuck on top of the famous Eléphant boulder, while Vincent's mother tried unsuccessfully to loop a rescuing rope over the top. We managed eventually to slither back down to the ground.

The following summer in Norway, camping beneath the immense Jostedal Glacier, I longed to be cutting steps in the ice and gazed covetously at smooth granite walls looming out of turquoise fjords. Back in Surrey I telephoned a boy in the village called Jonathan Watkins. He was two years younger than me, just fifteen, but was reputed to be a climber. His ambitions included a plan to read the whole of *War and Peace* whilst floating on a lilo on Snowdon's Llyn d'Arrdhu, and hitch-hiking to Kathmandu. And he played the violin. He seemed to have the right approach to life, so I asked if he would take me climbing.

We drove over to the Sussex–Kent border to do some routes on the sandstone rocks at Stone Farm and later that autumn we went to the more extensive Harrison's Rocks. I bought my first pair of 'PAs' – close-fitting shoes with smooth high-friction rubber soles, invented by the Parisian mountaineer Pierre Allain. For Christmas my parents gave me a climbing waistbelt, steel karabiner and standard forty-metre length of polypropylene rope – unsuitable for leading, but quite adequate for 'top-roping' on the little sandstone cliffs of South-East England. I never managed the harder routes at Harrison's, but succeeding on even the easier ones was immensely satisfying. Even more satisfying, in a grim, brutal sort of way, were the natural chimneys at High Rocks, where you thrutched, squirmed and grunted your way up between frictionless walls of dank mossy stone.

In December 1971 I finished at Charterhouse. Apart from spells of homesickness I had generally enjoyed my time there, aware, I think, how incredibly lucky I was to be given all the possibilities of a richly endowed public school. Doors had been opened, interests nurtured, horizons stretched by other boys cleverer and more talented than me. True, I was socially inept and didn't have any real friends, but at least I had discovered that I could work hard and manage on five hours' sleep a night if necessary, greedy to do all the things I wanted to do. In my final year I had particularly enjoyed the school's traditional endurance test, the 'Fifty Miles March', walking the sixteen-hour journey alongside a boy called Martin Winter, reciting manic Ginsberg protest poems through the long night, and finally hobbling home through the silent streets of Godalming as the milkmen started their pre-dawn rounds. After a blissful two-hour soak in a hot bath, I had spent the rest of the day on a frenetic round of concerts and music competitions, riding my endorphin high. Now, in my last term, I enjoyed a final glut of music and painting, rather resentfully making some additional time to mug up my British and European History and Latin translation for the Oxford entrance exam, which I assumed somewhat arrogantly that I would pass. Luckily I did, because every other university I applied to turned me down.

And so I walked out into the real world, with nine months to fill before going up to Oxford. During the winter I did odd bits of voluntary work at various hospitals and hostels in Bermondsey; then, in April, a few days before my eighteenth birthday, I flew to Israel to work on a kibbutz. After landing at Tel Aviv I took a bus up the coast road and, as instructed, got out at a stop a few miles north of the city. The bus disappeared towards Netanya and alone in the darkness I shouldered my rucksack and started walking up an empty lane flanked by black cypresses.

Something clicked loudly behind the trees. My scalp prickled as I imagined terrorists lurking with guns. I walked faster. The clicking continued. My throat tightened, but I forced myself to keep walking. Then at last there was a gap in the cypress trees and in the dim starlight I glimpsed the harmless sprinklers flicking spray across the fields. A few minutes later I reached the lights of the kibbutz, found a Swiss volunteer called Ruedi working the night shift in the plastics factory, and he took me to the little hut which would be my home for the next few weeks.

I had dreamed of picking lemons and oranges, but most of my time at Yakum was spent washing up in the kitchen and clearing tables in the dining room – the *haderochel*. At first I was annoyed to find myself terribly homesick and I considered doing a bunk, running back to England. But I stuck it out, and became gradually quite fond of the place, working in the mornings and spending afternoons reading, practising the piano or swimming in the Mediterranean nearby. In the mornings we were usually up at five, working for an hour and a half before breakfast. And what breakfasts! I was only just eighteen and still growing, and I feasted rapturously on yogurt and honey, olives, cheese, sour cream, eggs, bread, marmalade, cheese, coffee and huge succulent Jaffa oranges.

Word got around that I played the piano and occasionally I accompanied a violinist called Edith during her leaves from the army; but most of the resident 'kibbutzniks' were quite aloof, self-contained, even a little dour. Or at least that's how they seemed to a very gauche eighteen-year-old. Nearly all of them were Ashkenazi Jews from Europe. The kibbutz had been founded in 1947, and it was sobering to think that most of the adults who ran the place were people who had somehow survived or escaped the Holocaust, bringing with them a legacy of unimaginable horror. No wonder they seemed brittle.

My hut was shared with a Japanese volunteer called Yoshito. I liked his courteous reserve and found him cheerfully inscrutable until the night of 30 May 1972, when Japanese terrorists ran amok with machine guns and grenades at Tel Aviv airport nearby, slaughtering twenty-four people on behalf of the PFLP. For a few days afterwards my room-mate was profoundly depressed and apologetic for what his countrymen had done.

On the whole, though, we volunteers lived in an isolated bubble, enjoying an easy existence under a hot Mediterranean sky. By saving up free days and the few shekels we were paid each week it was possible to go off on trips around the country. For the first time I experienced the dusty, spicy smell of the Orient, walking through the old city wall of Jerusalem one Friday evening, then going to find a quiet corner to lay my sleeping bag on the Mount of Olives. On a longer trip I hitch-hiked to Bethlehem and Beersheba, then down through the Negev Desert to Eilat, where I snorkelled in the Red Sea, goggling at impossibly iridescent fish amongst pale fingers of coral. Then, after waiting twelve hours for a lift, I hitched back north, dropping below sea level on the long hot road past the saline wastes of Sodom and Gomorrah, to the Dead Sea. I wanted to see Masada, but the cable car had closed for the night, so I rushed up the zigzag path on foot, reaching the summit plateau as the sun was setting over the Judaean desert. Wandering amongst the two-thousand-year-old ruins, I was glad to have this summit to myself, to ponder on those brave harassed Jews making their last suicidal stand against the Romans.

Back at Yakum I feasted ravenously in the *haderochel* and managed to emerge slightly from my introspective shell, getting more friendly with the other volunteers. One balmy night during the kibbutz's twenty-fifth anniversary celebrations, as klezmer music blended with the cicadas' chirruping in the olive trees, a lissom girl from Stockholm called Aneli threw her arms round my neck and kissed me passionately on the mouth. It was blissful, but later I ran away – earnest, cautious fool that I was – because I didn't think that I was really in love with her. What a waste. The next day I left for the north with another Swedish girl, called Rita, and Tom, a swaggering New Yorker keen to get into Rita's sleeping bag, and keen to climb Mount Hermon. We were turned back by troops on the Golan Heights and never made it to the snows of Hermon, but we did spend a memorable evening as guests of a Druze family, sleeping on their flat roof, and sharing a huge breakfast with them the next morning. Like most of the Palestinians we met, the Druze seemed far more hospitable than their frenetic Israeli overlords.

I left the other two in Galilee, to make my way alone down the Jezreel Valley and back to Yakum – I never discovered how Tom fared in his quest with Lovely Rita. A couple of weeks later I said my goodbyes, gave Aneli one final regretful hug, shouldered my rucksack and set off back down the avenue of cypress trees to get the bus to the airport. I planned to join my family and the Potiers in the Alps, but first I wanted to see something of southern Europe, hitch-hiking from Athens and doing the whole journey for fifteen pounds, determined to save some spare cash for the Alps, in case I needed to hire a guide.

*   *   *

Standing at the roadside on the outskirts of Athens, I was crippled by an overwhelming loneliness, ashamed at my failure to live up to the ideal of adventure. But later that day a German woman stopped in a Mercedes and took me to Delphi. We walked round the enchanting oracular ruins. I gazed wonderingly at the rocks of Parnassus and then we continued, driving past a huge plain filled with grey-green olive trees, soft in the evening light. We sped on over mountains and she asked if I would like to see the monasteries at Meteora and would I like to stay with her and her friend at her house in Trikala? So instead of a roadside sleeping bag I had dinner and a bottle of wine, and a comfortable bed for two nights, and a companionable guide as we visited the monasteries perched on their crazy towers of pebbly conglomerate. Later, in the evening, we joined a black-cloaked priest friend of my hostess, drinking pungent ouzo in the shade of a plane tree while storks chattered noisily at their nest on the church tower.

I continued alone to Thessalonika and the Halkidiki peninsula, getting a boat to the monastic enclave of Mount Athos, where I refused childishly to have my shoulder-length hair cut, and so was unable to stay with the monks and explore further.

Eastward and onward to Istanbul, for a first glimpse of Asia and a brief exploration of that city's encrusted layers of faded imperial glory. I had grandiose plans for the Balkans but loneliness and the homing instinct kept me moving straight up through Bulgaria and Yugoslavia, never deviating from the main road. On a misty July evening, as some kind person drove me through the mountain meadows of Slovenia, I felt that I was home: this was the Alps, the Europe that I knew. I spent two days in Venice, salivating over the restaurants I couldn't afford and settling instead for the spiritual succour of Bellini's serene *Sacra Conversazione* altar pieces. Then onward again to a grassy verge in Bergamo where the police came at midnight to wake me rudely, shining their headlights on my sleeping bag and telling me to move on.

Which I did, heading now up the shore of Lake Como, where a genial local gent picked me up in his little Fiat and exclaimed 'Bello, bello' as we drove higher into the mountains of the Bregaglia.

'Si – bello,' I agreed, neck craning to look up at romantic granite spires.

'Bello, bello' he repeated, this time patting my bare bronzed knee and smiling at me indulgently. I finally twigged and asked if he would put me out at Chiavenna. He did, most graciously, with no hard feelings; pointing to my skinny frame he handed me a thousand-lire note, telling me to go and get a pizza.

The following morning it was a Dutchman who befriended me, driving me all the way across the Alps to Basel, where I was going to visit an old family friend, Rosie Reinhardt. As he put me down in Basel the Dutchman said hopefully, 'You must come and stay with me in Amsterdam when you have time off from Oxford. Stay as long as you like. Come alone or bring a lover if you want – a boy or a girl – I don't mind.'

And so ended my first big overseas adventure. But as I went in search of a tram to take me to Rosie's mother's house on the outskirts of Basel, I was impatient to start the next adventure; because, after a few days in Switzerland, we were going to drive over to France and join my family in the Vallée de Freissinières, close to where the Potiers were spending their summer holidays. The valley was just on the edge of the Dauphiné mountains – the Massif des Oisans – and Monsieur Potier, Jean Pierre, was, I hoped, going to take me on my first alpine climb.

Chapter Two

Alpine Initiation

The great day started hideously with a rough hand on my shoulder, wrenching me from dreams at four o'clock in the morning. The air was thick with the smell of musty blankets. Bunks creaked with the weight of human bodies shifting reluctantly, glimpsed in random flashes of torchlight. Downstairs we sat on benches, forcing down bread, jam and coffee, delaying our exit into the darkness. It was my first 'alpine start'.

Well, actually, it was my second. A few days earlier, with a guided 'collective' of about ten people, I had walked up to a high pass from another hut; but today was to be my first real alpine *climb*, with Jean Pierre. Unprepared to take sole responsibility for me, he had hired a guide. My share of the fee came to eighteen pounds sterling – the remains of what I had saved through my ascetic hitch-hiking from Athens – and I was determined to enjoy the fruits of this huge investment; so I was disappointed, as we followed the guide into the first grey glimmer of dawn, to find that the snow underfoot was not properly frozen, and to see above us tatters of cloud obscuring the dwindling stars.

We stopped for a moment. Jean Pierre conferred with the guide, then turned to me. The weather looked unpredictable and a storm might be coming. Would I mind if we didn't do the proposed route – a long buttress leading to the summit of

Les Agneaux? The guide was suggesting a shorter rock climb but a harder one – the traverse of a little pinnacle called the Pointe des Cinéastes.

I never discovered the origin of the peak's cinematic name, but, for all its obscure briefness, it was a magnificent climb. We went 'arrow' fashion: the guide would lead a section or 'pitch', then the two of us would follow more or less simultaneously, reeled in on separate ropes. The rope tugged insistently, forcing me to move quickly, the cleated soles of my new alpine boots moving swiftly over slightly damp granite. After just half an hour we reached the crux pitch, where you had to step across onto tiny holds, reach up and pull through a little overhang. 'Yes!' I thought, as I glanced down at patterns of rock dropping into the mist and tried to hold the moment, relishing the flex and tension, the spring of the upward reach, the swirling space beneath the feet: 'Yes, this it!' A moment later I joined the other two at the ledge above, where they were anchored to a steel peg. 'Vous grimpez bien,' said the guide. 'Oui, très bien,' reinforced Jean Pierre. 'Ce n'était pas un passage facile, hein?'

It *had* been tricky, but not overwhelmingly so, and I didn't want it to be over. Until, a few minutes later, snow started to dust the rock and my hands turned numb. In the absence of gloves, I pulled on a spare pair of socks, but they soon got soaked. Moaning with the pain of hot-aches, I shuffled quickly along the final traverse to the summit, glad that someone else was in charge, eager to get back down to easy ground.

But then the clouds blew over, the sun came out and the whole world glittered; numb fingers returned to life and brief discomforts were forgotten instantly. To our south, beyond the turquoise ice towers of the Glacier Blanc, there was a great wall of dark rock veined with pale fresh snow – a magnificent succession of north faces, all of them over three thousand feet high, culminating in the summits of Mont Pelvoux, the Pic Sans Nom and the wonderfully savage Pic du Coup de Sabre. Beyond that I could just see the mighty Ailefroide, whose north-west face had first been climbed in the 1930s by the legendary Giusto Gervasutti. It was all so beautiful, so austere, so richly overlaid with epic tales of great struggles. I wanted it all, now, for myself. Wanted to be balancing, pulling, edging, hooking, grasping my way up those walls, sleeping out on those tiny ledges, living in that vertical world. But for the moment that was all pure fantasy and I had to content myself with the reality of returning to the hut by nine in the morning, pleased to have done my first alpine climb, but wishing that I had got a bit more for my hard-saved eighteen pounds.

Before going up to Oxford that autumn, I borrowed the family Fiat 600 to chug up from Surrey to North Wales and stay for the first time in nine years at the Bangor house of my botanical great-uncle Paul. He and Ann were away, but their daughter, Sally, was looking after the house, along with a friend of hers from Leeds University. They were both two years older than me and seemed scarily intellectual. I spent the days driving into Snowdonia, desperate to climb. As the only climber I knew, Jonathan Watkins, was now back at school, I had to roam alone, contenting myself with easy scrambles like the Snowdon Horseshoe and Glyder Fach's Bristly Ridge, the latter on the classic circuit over Tryfan and the Glyders, which I did on a misty afternoon, navigating by compass to find the correct way down off the sphagnum bog where we had botanised nine years earlier.

Emerging from the cloud, zigzagging down past the Devil's Kitchen, I began to stare covetously at the Idwal Slabs – the traditional heartland of British rock climbing. As I reached the foot of the slabs some climbers were just packing up to leave. They seemed to be the usual bearded types – curt and unlikely to be impressed by a callow public-school boy keen to embrace the rock. In any case I would have been far to shy to approach them.

They left and I lingered, studying the rock, eyeing up the obvious slanting gash of 'Ordinary Route'. It was only graded 'Diff' – difficult for its 1897 pioneers but now right at the easy end of the climbing spectrum – and even if it was running with water the holds were too big for that to be a problem. So, once the beards had disappeared from sight, I started up the route, delighting in the fluid ease of it as I raced up three hundred feet of tilted rock, wishing that I could get my hands on something steeper and harder.

In desperation, two days later I telephoned the National Mountaineering Centre and asked how much it would cost to hire a guide for a day. Ten pounds, they said. It was cheaper than the Alps, but still a lot of money. I dithered for a moment, then asked them to book me someone.

The next morning, in one of the lay-bys set into the dry-stone wall which keeps the sheep off the Llanberis Pass road, I met Brede Arkless. She was Irish and, yes, she had red hair. And she had a freckly, round, wide-open sort of face, with a smile that was warm and friendly, but with a hint of indomitable strength. Years later I met her again in the Alps, where she spent the summers guiding, earning enough money to support all her many children who lived with her on the campsite. But now, back in September 1972, she was in Snowdonia, giving me my first day's climbing in the Llanberis Pass.

From the road the crags seemed disappointing – mere incidents on the hillside, dwarfed by the summits of the Glyders – but after the quick panting walk up scree slopes the cliff of Carreg Wasted actually reared up with satisfying abruptness. I asked if I should put on PAs – my nimble rock shoes – but Brede said I would be fine in big boots. So I had to concentrate hard to place clumping cleated edges on the curious angular ripples of our first route, *Wrinkle*. From the top we descended a gully, then started up another route, *Crackstone Rib*. On the second pitch, as Brede led out left-wards, stepping on minuscule nubbins, dancing lightly above a magnificently profiled overhang, I suddenly recalled the photo in my *Penguin Book of Mountaineering*. 'Yes,' she said when I joined her at the end of the pitch, 'it's an absolute classic.' At the top we sat for a moment in the September sunshine, looking across the Pass, and she pointed out the darker, smoother, steeper cliffs of Cyrn Las. But for today I was kept on the sunny south-facing side. After lunch we walked along to another cliff to fight up a brutal steep cleft called *Goat Crack* and then follow the elegant ramp of *Nea*, named after its author Nea Morin, French mother-in-law of Charles Evans, who had led the first ascent of Kanchenjunga in 1955.

I wanted to carry on until dark, but Brede had children to feed so I thanked her for my four routes and drove back to Bangor. Back at home in Surrey, I spent two weeks tractor driving for the farmer father of my friend John Lory, roto-vating stubble fields to earn some much-needed cash, then set off with Jonathan Watkins for a weekend on the sea cliffs near Swanage. Jonathan had proper climbing gear and we took it in turns to lead routes up the smaller cliffs. It was thrilling to do my first lead, trying to find secure crack placements for nuts – slotting in the alloy wedges, and clipping the rope to them with karabiners. I longed unrealistically to attempt the vertical fifty-metre-high cliffs of Boulder Ruckle, but Jonathan wisely kept me on the smaller cliffs. Even there, on one steep little 'Very Severe' called *Freda*, I managed to get myself thoroughly frightened, fingers of one hand clinging grimly to a limestone edge while the other hand fumbled with a succession of nuts, desperate to find the right size and clip the rope before gravity triumphed.

That private battle with fear and weakness – trembling close to the edge of one's ability but ultimately winning control, surging through to the top of the cliff on a wave of elation – was intoxicating. As were the gentler moments, where the climbing was a kind of vertical dance, each move a delight. Not to mention the sun and the waves and the scent of clifftop flowers in the salt air. I loved it, just as I loved the harsher mineral smell of the high mountains and dreamed of the biggest mountain faces in the world. I hoped that at university I would find the people to help make it happen.

The notice advertising an introductory evening with the Oxford University Mountaineering Club was unpromising, inviting me to turn up to a lecture theatre in the Inorganic Chemistry

Laboratory. It was the *In* bit I found so incongruous – a bit like being invited to a Christian Union meeting at the Department for Atheist Studies. I couldn't help feeling that something as richly creative as mountaineering ought at least to be graced with an *Or*ganic lab.

The guest lecture was by a mountaineer called Alan Rouse. I assumed that I was coming to listen to some venerable sage and was surprised to find a callow youth only just down from Cambridge, accompanying his slides of hard alpine climbs with a relentlessly understated commentary. Where, I wondered, was all the passion? And the adventure?

Of course I had blundered in head first, making instant assumptions. Alan Rouse, I soon discovered, was an outstanding mountaineer, bursting with talent, physical and intellectual. As for my fellow OUMC members, some of them, even at university, were pioneering hard new rock climbs and making early repeats of some of the hardest routes in the Alps. Most tended to be scientists, fluent in a language that I, having only studied science cursorily for two years, barely understood; and many of them were destined for distinguished careers in academic research or medicine. They just wore their intellect lightly.

I hardly got involved in the club during my first year. Living in one of the world's most beautiful cities, with just eight weeks a term to enjoy it, I baulked at the thought of long drives to the Peak District or North Wales. In any case, I was very busy, singing, playing in the university orchestra and plunging recklessly into the world of undergraduate theatre. I also tried, a bit half-heartedly, to grasp the academic possibilities on offer. Having insisted, against all advice, that I should read English, not History, I had to try and justify my obstinacy. Needless to say the experts were proved right and my fantasy of immersing myself in critical analysis of the literary canon was never really fulfilled. My two tutors that year, Christopher Tolkien and John Bayley, made encouraging noises but never quite disguised their boredom as I read out my plodding essays.

Playing music and working on shows was much more fun.

The really good people were already staking out their territory, laying the ground for successful professional careers. Peter Phillips was conducting his embryonic Tallis Scholars, Andrew Mariner playing the clarinet divinely, Jane Glover conducting a Cavalli opera for which I laboured as deputy stage manager. In the Playhouse, Oz Clarke was serenading Maria in *West Side Story* and Mel Smith was clowning in the Revue. Compared to the introverted world of the mountaineers, all that showy talent was intoxicating and, even if I was never going to act, I enjoyed the camaraderie of the production team and the incomparable excitement of curtain-up on a first night.

In the summer term I allowed myself foolishly to get involved in four shows, so barely made it to a single tutorial and left vital Old English revision until the night before Honour Moderation exams. Unfortunately I went to a party that evening, drank too much and on returning to my room fell instantly asleep, only waking up at eight-thirty the next morning, with half an hour left to revise.

The Anglo-Saxon papers were a disaster. I tried to redeem myself by staying awake for the next sixty hours, popping caffeine pills and working solidly through two consecutive nights, garnering scraps of literary memory to eke out the nineteenth- and twentieth-century papers; but it was too little, too late. I gained a Pass in Mods, which is a polite way of saying 'Fail'. When I telephoned John Bayley to ask which papers had been most disastrous, he stammered cheerfully, 'Well, I sh-should imagine that they were probably, er, a-a-*all* pretty disastrous.'

It was the first time in my life that I had failed a major exam and it was humiliating; but luckily it wasn't going to affect my final degree. And it certainly wasn't going to stop me climbing. Between the musical and theatrical dabbling, I had continued to read about the mountains, devouring books by famous climbers like Diemberger, Buhl, Bonington, Bonatti and Roberts. During Christopher Tolkien's lectures on the Norse sagas I had, by way of lateral association, fantasised about virtual climbs up the pale crystalline granite rising out of the

Norwegian fjords. And, during the Easter vacation, I had climbed my own very real, very tactile granite, on the Hebridean island of Arran.

Jonathan Watkins was going there on a school geography trip and suggested that I go up with him a week early, for some rock-climbing. My ever-forbearing parents agreed to lend us the Volkswagen minibus, and the canoe, so that brother Mark and an old friend, Anthony Pelly, could come too and paddle while Jonathan and I climbed.

I now had my very own eleven-millimetre-diameter kern-mantel rope – a proper climbing rope with a bright red sheath, the 'mantel' protecting the silky, stretchy, longitudinal fibres of the inner core, the 'kern'. And the other bits and pieces to go with it – the nuts, tape slings and karabiners into which the rope would be clipped protectively as I balanced masterfully up an immense sweep of gorgeously sculpted rock. Or so I imagined, until, on the way to Arran, we attempted a very easy climb in the Lake District called Middlefell Buttress. First I misread the guidebook and failed to get off the ground. When I did eventually find the correct route, sleet began to sweep up Langdale. By the time I was halfway up the pitch my hands were frozen, clawing ineffectually at glassy holds. I was cold and terrified and I hated all mountains.

On Arran we carried tents up into the wild boggy sweep of Glen Sannox, only discovering later that we had chosen the windiest spot on the entire island. For our first climb Jonathan and I chose a difficult route on a forbidding bastion with some unpronounceable Gaelic name. I attempted to edge out onto a sloping ledge above a terrifying void, unsure of whether I was on the correct route or not, until Jonathan called me back and insisted on a sensible retreat. But at last, two days later, the dream, the vision, was finally realised.

It was a frosty morning, with ice droplets jewelling the heather beside the stream, but as we crossed the saddle leading over to Glen Rosa the south face of Cir Mhor was already glowing in the spring warmth – a magnificent sculpture of overlapping armoured plates, a giant granite armadillo basking benevolently in the sunshine. The *South Ridge Direct* is about a thousand feet long and is graded Very Severe. We alternated leads up the lower slabs, until Jonathan led the famous S-shaped crack. Then we sat, tied side by side on a ledge, and ate our sandwiches. Then it was my turn to lead the crux Y crack above, stepping up tentatively at first, pointed rubber toes testing quartz crystals, fingers feeling sideways, exploring the crack. I locked off one hand and reached down with the other to remove one of my brand-new hexagonal wedges from my waistbelt, then wiggled it into the crack, giving it a sharp tug to lock it firmly in place, then clipping a karabiner into its tape loop and clipping the rope into the karabiner, pleased with its promise of security.

After all the faltering starts and disappointments, at last I was enjoying the sensation of a craftsman at work, totally absorbed. I moved my feet higher, reached up, placed another protecting nut, then stretched up to the arms of the Y, spread-eagled wide, savouring the outward lean of the wall and the rope falling away beneath me, then daring myself to commit for the final upward reach, over the top and onto the broad slab above, where I placed an anchor and brought up Jonathan.

South Ridge Direct was sheer pleasure all the way. Quite different, on a cold afternoon with sleet threatening, was the flared, leaning chimney of *West Flank Route*. It was a thuggish struggle, with numb hands jammed feverishly into a crack full of lacerating crystals. The wounds took weeks to heal, but the elation was instantaneous as we completed the route, zigzagging through overlaps on the upper slabs. In those days all harder Scottish rock climbs were graded simply Very Severe. In England and Wales, this was a medium grade, clearly defined; here it encompassed a vast spectrum of difficulty from medium to desperate, deliberately confusing ignorant Sassenachs. Years later, when Scotland began to adopt the more informative grading system from south of the border, I was childishly gratified to see *West Flank Route* upgraded two full levels to E1: one of my very first rock climbs was actually an Extreme lead.

* * *

In July, after the Mods exam debacle, I set off for the Alps with Dave Luscombe, a small, rather earnest bespectacled Yorkshireman who had just finished his second year at Oxford studying physics. Our chauffeur was David Mills, a medic several years older than us, who owned a mini-van. A week before departure he ploughed the Mini into a tree and turned the wreckage into a luxury kennel for his dogs. For us he found a slightly larger Morris Minor van, into which we piled our climbing gear and ourselves, driving first to Nuits St Georges to collect a case of burgundy from a winemaker friend of David's, and then to Val d'Isère to meet David's wife, David's mother and David's local swimming-instructor friend, in whose house we stayed.

It rained every day and David seemed relieved that the mountains were 'out of condition'. I read *Anna Karenin*, wondering if we would ever go climbing. But at last, after a week's indolence, we continued to the Dauphiné Alps – the same massif where I had had my little debut the previous summer. A liberal plastering of new snow thwarted our ambitions, but we did finally do a gorgeous rock climb up a spire called the Aiguille Dibona.

Dave Luscombe and I stumbled up a couple of other easy climbs, then we all drove over to Switzerland, to the Arolla Valley, for some more easyish climbs. In those days there were few introductory alpine courses. As for hiring local guides, as I had done briefly with Jean Pierre, the cost would have made that impossible. So we learned on the job, getting ropes tangled, stepping into half-concealed crevasses, getting lost, gaining experience through trial and error. It's a good way to learn, taking your turn at the sharp end of the rope right from the start – provided that none of your mistakes is terminal.

I was nineteen, fit and keen. Dave was equally keen, but moved very slowly in a medium where speed is of the essence. As for our insouciant elder, David Mills – he was delightful company but rarely set foot on a mountain if he could help it. It seemed that everyone was restraining me, frustrating my dreams; so one morning, in a fit of misanthropy, I sneaked off out of the tent at three a.m. to do a climb on my own.

A few days earlier I had spotted an attractive ice face on a peak called the Blanche de Perroc. The guidebook graded it TD–. Très Difficile was the second-hardest alpine grade but the minus sign reduced slightly the seriousness of what I was intending. I gobbled some breakfast, then set off up the path through the pine woods, climbing fast, panting impatiently, stomach still rumbling from the previous evening's mix of fire-charred potatoes and Drambuie. The path zigzagged through the forest and out onto open meadows, dewy in the dawn light. Then I left the path to traverse across scree and boulders to the tongue of a little glacier, where I stopped, removed my rucksack and took out the tools for the job.

The crampons were a pair of Grivels, unchanged almost since they were invented in the 1930s – each one a steel frame shaped something like an elongated H, with the long strokes following roughly the shape of the boot sole, and a hinge on the middle crossbar. From the long sides of the H six looped prongs bent upward to grip the leather boot welt, with metal rings providing fittings for straps buckled over the top of the boot. A further ten prongs, sharpened spikes, bent downward to grip underfoot; but most critical of all were the front ends of the H's two long strokes – the sharpened prongs which projected beyond the toe of the boot for kicking directly into the ice, flexing slightly as they strained to the force.

At home the Charlwood blacksmith had heated the steel, bending the softened frames to fit my boots. Now I was thrilled to be using the crampons in earnest for the first time. I pulled the buckles tight, put my rucksack back on, slipped my gloved right hand through the wrist-loop of my ice axe, and then I was away, steel crunching on gritty ice, striding impatiently up the glacier. The angle increased and soon I was 'front-pointing' up a forty-five-degree slope, delighting in the rhythm of it all, savouring the geometric sweep of white ribs and runnels, picking the line with the firmest, hardest snow. It steepened to fifty degrees. And then to perhaps fifty-five degrees, so that when my arm was held horizontal to the slope my body was standing fully upright, perched on those points of steel. Here the snow had sloughed off, leaving bare ice, which I had to traverse rightwards to gain the upper, easier snowfield.

In 1973 it was already common practice to ice climb with two axes, but for the moment I could only afford one – an alloy tool made by the famous Scottish climbing inventor Hamish MacInnes – so on this steep traverse, determined to maintain three points of contact, I had to cut holds for my left hand, curling gloved fingers over each new chipped edge, holding myself steady while my right hand swung the axe to secure another anchor point for the next rightward crab move. I could see red rock through the translucent ice. At one point the 'skin' was only two inches thick, with air between it and the rock, so I could cut perfect holds for my left hand, curling my fingers into proper handles; but the fragility of the detached carapace was worrying. I glanced down past my feet, contemplated briefly the three-hundred-metre drop to the foot of the face, then resolved to ignore it.

The concentration was total. For those few minutes all life was reduced to this intense, precise contact between ice, steel and fingers. And then I allowed myself an inward giggle as the traverse ended and I was again kicking easily in firm snow, rushing up the top snowfield, watching the ridges at either side converge until I stepped out onto the final sharp white point and sat, deliriously happy, revolving slowly on my snowy perch, gazing out over the whole of the Western Alps, gulping in across the valley the legendary, unique silhouettes of the Dent Blanche, the Weisshorn, the Matterhorn . . . and hazy in the far west the pale looming bulk of Mont Blanc.

It wasn't the North Face of the Eiger, but it was my first proper ice climb and I was thrilled. Less thrilling was the descent of the rocky west ridge, where I foolishly took a short cut, resulting in several dead ends and an interminable stumble through a waterless wasteland of tottering boulders, my head ringing in the midday heat. But what relief to emerge finally and wander down through an alpine idyll of shady pines and fresh-cut hay. And to be congratulated, not castigated, when I joined the others back at the campsite at two o'clock that afternoon. They were setting off for the Vignettes Hut – a spectacular eyrie perched high on the other side of the valley. After a couple of hours' rest I set off to join them, slogging for another three hours up to the hut, where David Mills's friends were planning a snowy romp up the Pigne d'Arolla.

Dave Luscombe and I set off at first light the next morning to do battle with a pile of tottering rubble on a peak called Petit Mont Collon, which did little to improve our partnership. But when we returned to the valley at nine o'clock that night and the other David said he was driving round to Zermatt the next day, we couldn't resist the chance to finish on a high note – by climbing the Matterhorn.

The most relentlessly branded mountain in the world proved actually to be an anticlimax, disappointing after my rapturous morning three days earlier on the Blanche de Perroc. We were far too slow and only reached the summit in the afternoon. The descent was interminable and when night fell we were still about one hour above the hut. At Dave's correct insistence we stopped and I experienced my first unplanned bivouac, sitting on a rock, shivering through the night, gazing longingly down at the lights of the cosy hut a few hundred feet below us. And so, quivering with cold near the foot of the Matterhorn, I ended my first alpine season.

Back in Oxford for my second year, I had a large room in a quiet corner of New College by the old city wall, next door to a man called Nicky Spice, whose superior piano-playing introduced me to Chopin's greatest composition, the last Ballade. From the back desk of the university orchestra's second violins, rehearsing each Monday evening in Wren's Ashmolean Theatre, I discovered the equally spacious, arching structure of Elgar's First Symphony. And I was busy directing an early play by Tom Stoppard called *Enter a Free Man*. I didn't know much about directing, but I had a good cast and production team, who all knew what they were doing, and I grew very fond of them, pleased at having made this thing happen. On the week of the show the audiences laughed in all the right places and full houses turned in a small profit. That was the fifth week of term. During the seventh week I was busy at the playhouse, as a very harassed and rather untechnical 'technical director' for Thomas Kyd's *The Spanish Tragedy*. And at the end of that week, exhausted after the midnight get-out from the theatre, but desperate for air and light, determined not to lose touch with the visceral reality of climbing, I rose early on the Sunday morning to join the mountaineering club on the coach to Bristol.

Climbing in the Avon Gorge is like climbing nowhere else on Earth. A major trunk road roars along the foot of the cliff, beside the oily brown effluvium of the Avon, and most of the climbs are man-made – the pink and grey stone blasted, prised and chipped from the Clifton Downs by Victorian quarrymen. That Sunday, the last day of November 1973, it all looked very forbidding under a dank sky, with the temperature hovering barely two degrees above freezing. But I managed to climb competently, leading a near-novice called Pierre up the classic *Piton Route*.

Pierre seemed to cope well, so I asked him if he would like to try something a little harder. I had never knowingly climbed a 'Hard Very Severe' but this seemed as good a time as any to try; so we walked up the road to *Suspension Bridge Arête*, scrabbling up a steep brambly slope to the foot of the cliff which buttresses the Clifton end of Brunel's elegant bridge. I checked that Pierre was tied on securely, then tied the other end of the rope to my waistbelt and started up the route. The rock here was natural, unquarried limestone, almost vertical, dimpled, wrinkled and calcified by millions of years of acidic rain, with an occasional hole through which you could thread a sling to clip in the rope for protection as you pondered the next moves.

The crux of the route is a chimney where the trick is to stay on the outside, feet bridged wide on the walls each side, keeping the body in balance. But I got too deep inside, squirming and slithering, hands reaching high, greedy for holds, cold fingers trembling with the strain, fumbling, dithering, fiddling in desperation to get a protecting alloy nut secure in a pocket. My hands were numb but my body was sweating with the effort, one outstretched leg juddering like a sewing machine, threatening to shake the foot off its hold. In the end I gave up on placing protection, lunged higher, grabbed a handhold, and then found a rusty old steel piton, into which I clipped the rope to protect the next teetering moves. I escaped from the chimney, the angle relented and I swarmed up the final wall in a joyful rush. Few things could beat this surge of elation: I had managed, I had coped, I had triumphed over weakness, and all I had to do now was bring up Pierre.

Rather than go round the corner to a tree, I decided to belay – to anchor myself – right at the edge, where I hoped to communicate above the noise of the traffic. That was my big mistake.

In those days when the range of alloy wedges was fairly limited, we usually carried in addition a few steel pitons and a hammer. At the back of my ledge there was a horizontal hairline crack and in my woeful ignorance I thought that a single knife blade of chrome molybdenum steel, hammered one and a half inches into this crack, would make a sufficiently secure anchor. I tied myself into the peg, pulled up the slack rope below me and, when it came tight, shouted to Pierre to climb. I held the rope firmly round my waist, with a twist round my anchoring left hand. I was annoyed at forgetting my belay gloves, but thought that as the only fall I would have to hold would be the steady strain of the second man on a tight rope – not the whipping jerk of a leader fall – I would be fine.

I *would* have been fine if Pierre, struggling out of the chimney onto the vertical right wall, had not neglected to unclip the rope from the ancient rusty piton. Spreadeagled on the right-hand wall, unable to reverse his moves, he realised too late that the rope was no longer tight above him but running down and across through the piton in the chimney. Several metres above him, I wondered what was happening. I could hear him grunting and shouting on the wall below me, but I couldn't see over the edge. The shouting got more urgent, so I braced my legs, grasping the rope tight in my left hand.

There was another shout and then a violent tug, yanking me forward and ripping the rope through my hands. I tried to grip tighter, braking with the left hand, but my knees were buckling and I was being pulled towards the edge, my feet sliding on loose rock chippings. As the belay yanked tight I heard the bright metallic ring of steel jolting from rock and I flew outward, over the edge, face down, staring into the blurred green-brown confusion of roadside brambles a hundred feet below, where I was about to die.

I woke about a minute later to find myself not splattered dead amongst the brambles but miraculously alive, dangling beside a ledge thirty feet above the ground. There was an acrid smell of melted nylon and the first hint of pain where the rope had burned raw grooves into the fingers of my left hand. As I pulled myself onto the ledge, I realised that my left shoulder was dislocated; my right leg had seized up, stiff and swollen at the knee, stabbing with pain every time I tried to move it. The steel knife blade dangled uselessly from my waist. Pierre, thank God, was unhurt, below me. He had come to a halt only two or three feet short of the ground. Above us the rope was stretched in a taut inverted V, suspended high on the cliff from a single fulcrum – the rusty old piton in the chimney.

Battered and shivering, I sat on my ledge for a couple of hours while Bristol's official cliff-rescue unit tried farcically to lower a stretcher on a motorised winch. In the end they admitted failure and allowed two kind climbers to get me swiftly, competently down to the ambulance, where the BBC cameras were waiting. Furious at this humiliation, I cursed and gesticulated at the television cameras, my old black and white jumper immediately recognisable to all the friends who saw me on the *Nine O'Clock News* that night and reported to my parents that their eldest son had fallen down the Avon Gorge.

*   *   *

Pierre never came on another OUMC meet, but he did insist on giving me fifteen pounds to cover the cost of a new rope. He – and everyone – was generously forgiving. I was young and I mended fast, helped by a week of intensive physio-therapy after Christmas. Ted Heath's government might have been crippled by power shortages and the three-day week, and the nation might be in turmoil, but the only effects of my accident were a slightly misshapen right knee, lifelong scars on the fingers of my left hand, and a healthy new understanding of belaying techniques.

I put the mended knee to its first big test during the Easter vacation, climbing the snow-smothered ramparts of Ben Nevis's *Tower Ridge*. A couple of weeks later, in North Wales, I got to know a tousle-headed mathematician called David Lund who agreed to climb with me in the Alps that summer. By way of bonding we spent one May weekend on a Lake District meet, doing amongst other things the classic *Troutdale Pinnacle Superdirect*. Descending elated from Black Crag, intoxicated by the bluebell scent and the sappy shimmer of young birch leaves against Derwent Water, I felt gloriously, indestructibly alive, greedy to embrace all life's possibilities.

Late that evening, back in Oxford, I went round to St John's College to sort out the week's rehearsal schedule with Nicholas Lowton, director of a joint St John's/New College production of *Threepenny Opera*, whose cast included a puppyish long-haired Tony Blair as one of the gang at Mr Peachum's brothel. I was the stage manager and I was loving Weill's plangent, sardonic harmonies, loving the buzz of a team working towards a performance. Nicholas and I finished the schedule, then just sat and talked. At some point I played through a whole Beethoven sonata, badly, on his piano. We talked more – about plays and music and about the transcendent day I had just spent in the Lakes. And we worked our way contentedly through a bottle of gin. At about three-thirty in the morning I climbed through a window into a secluded courtyard garden and lay down on my back to stare happily at the fading stars.

I awoke, dewy, cold and shivering, to the sound of gruff

voices. 'Who is he? Ain't one of our grads. Where d'yer reckon 'e's come from?' My eyes opened a crack and registered the morning light. Then, silhouetted against the sky, the dark suits and bowler hats of three college porters standing over me. I had fallen asleep in the private Fellows' Garden.

St John's forgave my trespass. New College was less forgiving of my academic failings. At the end of that term I was summoned to the exquisite Warden's Lodgings above New College Lane, and ushered into the panelled study of Sir William Hayter, a former British ambassador to Moscow. 'I have alarming reports about your work,' he began, without niceties. 'Dr Buxton says that you have only produced one diminutive essay all term. Mrs Jones says that she hasn't seen you at all since Easter. I trust that you will be spending the long vacation doing some serious study.'

I mumbled apologies and didn't mention my summer alpine plans. John Buxton had already agreed to write a reference letter supporting my application for a travel grant from the Sandy Irvine Fund, established as a memorial to the young Oxford mountaineer who died on Everest in 1924:

Dear Sirs
    Stephen Venables shows little aptitude for academic work, so he might as well spend the summer climbing. He recently injured himself falling off a cliff in Bristol, so I should imagine that some alpine training would be a very good idea.
    Yours sincerely
    John Buxton

So I went to the Alps, first on a family holiday, traversing the Pigne d'Arolla with my mother and youngest brother Philip, then hitching over to the Bregaglia in eastern Switzerland to meet Jonathan Watkins and David Lund. On our first climb, the Pioda, we were caught out at night on the summit, shivering under a nylon sheet, praying that we wouldn't get a direct hit as thunder crashed all around us. After that trial by fire

Jonathan decided that alpine climbing was not for him. I was tempted to follow him home, but stuck it out with David and other partners, doing several routes in the Bregaglia, and later the Mont Blanc massif, clocking up more experience but never – despite succeeding on Ricardo Cassin's famous north-east face of the Badile – quite assuaging the hunger for bigger, harder, wilder climbs.

In my final year at Oxford I sank into a morass of self-indulgent depression, falling miserably and unilaterally in love with a girl called Susan at the Polytechnic. Nicholas Lowton and Jim Hayward, another friend from the *Threepenny Opera*, with whom I shared a flat, were not doing Finals that year and were happily busy with shows, while I was trying to salvage something from the wreckage of my academic career so that I could at least leave Oxford with a Third. Occasionally, in a slump of solipsistic despair, I would seek oblivion with a bottle of whisky, waking late the following day to the sound of the factory hooter across the road, announcing the lunch break of people in the real world who had already done a whole morning's work.

I grew fond of Yeats's early poems. Their Celtic melancholy seemed to fit my mood, until a don at St Catherine's called Michael Gearin-Tosh pointed out that the later poems are much, much better. Gearin-Tosh was a flamboyant teacher – Lytton Strachey without the beard, as Alan Bennett put it – and he also introduced me to Synge and Beckett and O'Casey and helped me get to grips with the dense imagery of T. S. Eliot's *Ash Wednesday*. He also pointed out that, whatever I did or didn't decide to do in the future, it might at some stage prove useful to have a degree. And so, at last, I began to do some real study and stopped feeling so pathetically sorry for myself.

Meanwhile, the dreams of great climbs sustained me. I even dared, with an ex-Oxford climber called Bill Stevenson, to mention the possibility of attempting the North Face of the Eiger. And in the Easter vacation I went again to Ben Nevis for the annual 'President's Meet'.

The President – may his soul rest in peace – had not actually invited me into the cosy inner sanctum of the stone hut beneath the cliffs. So I slept outside, sharing a tent in the snow with David Lund and the delightfully cuddly Sîan Pritchard-Jones. Each evening we cooked our meal on the Primus stove and each morning we used the stove to thaw out frozen leather boots for another day's climbing. It was a week of pure enchantment, with the whole North Face of Ben Nevis encrusted white, gleaming under a powder-blue sky.

We battled up the frozen parallel walls of *Glover's Chimney*. I led teeteringly up the right-hand start to *Italian Climb*, calf muscles quivering as my bendy old crampon points flexed in the vertical blue ice. David and I hooked our way up the subtly 'mixed' slopes of rock and snow on *Observatory Ridge*, which leads direct to the ruins of the celestial viewing station that once stood on Ben Nevis's summit. The conditions were so perfect that, running back down the broad easy chute of *Number Four Gully* afterwards, I suddenly left David and the others, kicking urgent steps back up to the left, traversing to an icy cleft called *Green Gully*, eager to cram in one more route before the day ended.

I don't know why I had to squeeze in this extra route, while the others were content to call it a day. Perhaps I just expected more from life? Perhaps I was greedy? But it seemed right to follow my instinct, trusting my confidence, seizing the experience while it was there. I relished the fearful intensity, the total self-reliance, moving alone between beetling rock walls, hooking my way up the blue ice, which was easy at first but which then bulged outwards, so that my face was pressed close to the glassy surface. This vertical dance, unhindered by trailing ropes, was a glorious liberation. At a purely physical level it was its own reward.

But as I pulled out through the finishing cornice, I realised that there was another, more serendipitous, reward. It was barely an hour since I had last stood on the summit, but this time the view, which before had been merely beautiful, was transformed into something visionary, summit snow glowing with unearthly intensity against the stormy blue of the Great

Glen, with a thousand different coloured shafts of light shining down onto Loch Linnhe and the distant Hebridean islands stretching far, far out to the west.

I was on a roll and the next morning when a complete stranger called Dave, from Edinburgh, appeared outside our tent asking if anyone was free to do *Zero Gully*, I said 'Yes, please.' When it was first climbed by Hamish MacInnes and his team in 1957 *Zero Gully* had been way ahead of its time and even in 1975 this Grade V ice climb still had a reputation. And it had still not, despite some famous near-fatal attempts, had an Oxford ascent. In the hut the club's two superstars, Roger Everett and Phil Bartlett, were getting the measure of my ambition, and were wondering whether the crazy Venables might be plotting a solo attempt on *Zero*; so they emerged straight after breakfast and headed rapidly towards the gully. I followed in hot pursuit with Dave-from-Edinburgh. By the time we reached the foot of the gully, Phil and Roger were a couple of hundred feet higher, sending down a steady torrent of ice particles. We were just getting organised ourselves when a scruffy-looking youth with a jersey full of holes and a head full of wild curly hair turned up and asked if we had a bit of wire to mend his crampons.

'Are you doing *Zero* too?' he queried.

''Fraid so.'

'Damn. Oh well, I'll have to do *Point Five* and come back for this one tomorrow. I've just made a bet that I can hitch from Leeds, solo *Zero* and *Point Five*, and hitch back to Leeds, all in forty-eight hours.'

And so for the first time I met the hugely ambitious Alex MacIntyre, who would soon become one of the world's greatest Himalayan climbers, showing the rest of us the way to the future.

But that Friday morning there was no thought of the Himalaya: just the immediacy of *Zero Gully*, which was bigger, steeper and altogether more monumental than *Green Gully* – so much so that at one point my crampon points popped and I found myself hanging free from my axes (I did now own a tool for each hand), while I kicked my feet back into contact with the ice. *Zero* made an exhilarating finish to a glorious week and that night I was invited to join the elite in the cosy fug of the hut.

During my final summer term, I got to know that elite a bit better. Roger Everett climbed brilliantly, had a First in biochemistry, and had just started a life's career in genetic research. Phil Bartlett, a physicist by training and a philosopher by inclination, played the violin, loved debate and climbed with a trembling nervous energy underpinned by bold assurance. Andy Brazier was less of a virtuoso but, alone amongst us, he took brilliant photos. Geoffrey Grimmett was a fine oboist, Olympic fencer, combative conversationalist and world expert in Probability Theory. And there were others, including a second-year historian called Paul Beney, who loved Bob Dylan and P. G. Wodehouse, and climbed like a dream. Once, briefly, I had the chance to climb with him.

It was the last weekend before starting Finals, and I decided to escape on a club meet to the Lake District, throwing my *Selected Wordsworth* into the rucksack as a token gesture at last-minute revision. Sorting out climbing partners at the traditional Friday-evening stop at The Hollies transport café just off the M6, I found myself paired unexpectedly with Paul. It was a perfect June weekend and it was thrilling to climb with someone so fluent on the rock: like accompanying an intuitive musician, or returning the serves of a good tennis player, I managed to rise to the occasion, moving with a new confidence, even leading one of the 'extremes' we did, *Gimmer String*. That was one of three Langdale routes we did on the Sunday; on the Saturday we climbed on the stunning Esk Buttress, high on the flanks of Scafell, swapping leads on three classic lines all first climbed on the same day in 1962 – *Red Edge*, *Black Sunday* and *Central Pillar* – routes to leave me buzzing for several days afterwards, reinvigorated for the final marathon of Finals, sitting nine papers – three hours and three essays per paper – spread over five days.

I surprised everyone by getting a Second, not a Third; but

I missed the result being published in *The Times* because I had already gone, away to the Alps, brimming with hopes of great climbs. Geoffrey Grimmett and Paul Beney gave me a lift out, driving through the night and reaching Snell's Field, the unofficial summer residence of the British climbing fraternity in Chamonix, the following afternoon. We soon found friends amongst the squalid cluster of tents and polythene shelters, and caught up on the gossip. David Lund and another OUMC member, Will Tapsfield, were just off to the Mer de Glace, hoping to climb the East Face of the Grepon the next day. They kindly invited me along. Despite the sleepless overnight drive and my general lack of fitness, it was too tempting to resist, so I quickly packed my rucksack, pulled on climbing boots, and headed off for the start of the long zigzag trail through the forest to Montenvers. As I left, Paul laughed, 'You're mad, Venables.'

It was the last time I saw him. Two days later he was dead.

Chapter Three

Christmas in the Super Couloir

It was a hot day, heavy with suppressed electricity. Tired from the Grepon climb, I rose late. At lunchtime we wandered over to the Biolet campsite on the other side of Chamonix to visit three other Oxford climbers including Dave Luscombe, with whom I had climbed in 1973; but they were away on a climb. Purple clouds were massing and as we returned to Snell's Field thunder exploded on the invisible summits hanging over the valley. I wondered how Dave's team was faring; and feared for some of the others: Phil Bartlett and Roger Everett on the West Face of the Dru; Paul Beney and Geoffrey Grimmett on the North Ridge of the Aiguille du Peigne. But like most afternoon storms this one blew over and soon the trampled grass of Snell's Field was glistening in bright sunshine. The aiguilles would be running with water, but at least our friends would have a chance to dry out by nightfall. We relaxed. Until someone arrived from Chamonix to say that there had been an accident on the Peigne.

It was Andy Brazier – responsible elder-statesman Andy – who set off immediately into town to find out more. I was preparing supper, chopping onions, when he returned an hour later and announced simply, 'Paul's been killed on the Peigne'.

Paul and Geoffrey had turned back that afternoon when electricity began to buzz on the fixed steel pitons; like all the aiguilles, the Peigne was a potential lightning conductor and they hadn't wanted to be near the summit if there were a direct hit. They had teamed up with two other climbers who were also retreating, sharing their ropes to save time, abseiling efficiently, rope length by rope length. On this particular abseil the two strangers had gone first. Then Paul had followed. He had been hanging on the double ropes when the tape sling they were looped through sliced over a sharp edge on the anchoring block of granite, sending him falling to his death.

All that evening we sat around in dazed silence. Geoffrey was brought down by helicopter and appeared briefly at the campsite. Too shocked to say anything meaningful, hiding behind the mundane, I just asked him if he would like some food; but he was about to go and have supper with John Wilkinson, an Oxford don who lived in Chamonix and acted as an unofficial guardian, watching over the OUMC. I didn't seem to have the emotional language to offer real comfort and when Geoffrey reappeared briefly the next day, I didn't like to pry or dwell on details. Instead, I just kept returning privately, over and over again, to my own imagined replay of Paul's face – startled, incredulous – as he suddenly fell away, dropping through the air.

Death was something I had barely experienced. Grandfather Gower had died eight years earlier, my father's mother more recently; I had been sad, of course, and I still missed them, particularly Gower because he had died when I was fourteen, just as I was really starting to appreciate him. But their deaths – one from a stroke, one from cancer – had been in the normal order of things: that was what happened to old people. But this sudden, brutal, visceral obliteration was utterly different. It was only three days ago that we had been talking through the night as Geoffrey drove us across France; only two days since Paul had said goodbye, smiling that gently sardonic grin of his at my crazy enthusiasm, when I set off for the Grepon. I replayed a recent day in the Avon Gorge, climbing a Bonington route called *Mercavity*, while Paul and Geoffrey crossed our line on the great traverse of *Equator*, Paul leading all the way with such effortless confidence. I wished selfishly that I had had a chance to know him better; wished that there had been more occasions like those two enchanted days in the Lake District; wished that I could have hitched more rides on his quiet talent. Wished that, like some of the others, I had met his sisters and parents at their house in Edale, on the edge of the Peak District. Wished that they were not having to suffer this brutal loss.

The grief of parents was the hardest thing to face: that was what really rammed home the destructiveness of our pursuit. And, as if the death of one son did not cause enough misery, we later discovered that Paul's parents were not the only ones grieving at home.

It was eleven days after the accident that someone noticed a brief column-filler in a British newspaper, announcing that three Oxford climbers had been reported missing on Mont Blanc. We suddenly remembered a stranger coming round after the storm to ask if we knew the three climbers who had been on the Brenva Ridge that day. They had been having difficulties – late in the evening, on the final ice cliffs, after the storm blew over – and he had lent them an ice screw. He rather wanted it back. Did we know where they were? We hadn't been sure at the time who the climbers were, but now it suddenly made sense: it must have been Dave Luscombe and the other two at the Biolet, who had been out when we called on the day of the storm.

We rushed over to the other campsite and our fears were confirmed immediately. The tent was unchanged. Nothing had been touched for eleven days. At the Gendarmerie de Haute Montagne the blue-breeched officers confirmed that the three young Britons had never returned from the Brenva Ridge. During an extensive helicopter search the rescue team had found a rucksack and other scraps of gear amongst the avalanche debris and cavernous crevasses at the foot of the face, but no bodies. It had been too dangerous to search inside the crevasses, but they had had to assume that all three climbers had fallen down the huge Brenva Face and been killed, their bodies buried in the glacier ice.

So four Oxford climbers – not one – had died that after-noon. Again, there was the horrible imagining of what it might have been like . . . the three climbers tired at the end of a long day, buffeted by the storm, trying to find somewhere to bivouac amongst the ice cliffs . . . roped together, searching for some-where to make a secure anchor . . . one of them slipping, perhaps . . . the others plucked from the slope, sliding, turning, bouncing . . . flung brutally down that huge precipice. I thought about Dave Luscombe, remembered his mild apologetic manner and generosity, and, too late, felt twinges of remorse for all my irascible impatience two years earlier.

By a cruel quirk of fate – it seemed almost revenge for stolen pleasures – one of the other two, John Weatherseed, had, like Paul, been with me on that recent idyllic Saturday on Esk Buttress, in the Lake District, the weekend before my Finals. He was a Second Year, but now he would never be doing Finals. A couple of days later his parents came out to Chamonix and took the cable car up to the Aiguille du Midi, to look across to the Brenva Face and see where their son had died and try bravely to understand what special beauty had drawn him there. John's father appeared one evening amongst the shabby tents of Snell's Field to say hello and see if anyone could drive the dead climbers' car back to Britain. As we stood in an awkward semicircle, offering clumsy sympathy, I felt that we were all guilty: we had conspired in this perverse game that had destroyed his son. It was we – all of us, encouraging each other, reinforcing each other's dreams and ambitions – who had stolen his child. But the father was completely without bitterness, never once criticising, never blaming: just wishing us luck with the rest of our alpine season.

The day Paul died my immediate reaction was to think that I should go home. This careless snuffing-out of a life was so shocking, its repercussions so destructive, that I couldn't imagine wanting to continue. And perhaps if, like Geoffrey, I had been the one who had actually witnessed the accident, I would have packed it all in as he did. But I *hadn't* been there;

so I was cushioned, protected from visceral reality, able – once the initial shock had passed – to revive the mountaineer's protective self-deception: even though every rational cell in my brain knew that this could have been me, I was prepared to be duped into pretending that I could be more careful, more lucky. Of course, if I stopped for a moment to consider the evidence I knew that I too might die; and of course that possibility was frightening. But I had always known that anyway: I had already made the decision to accept that hypothetical possibility.

So, two days after Paul's death I went back up into the mountains, hoping to exorcise the horror. Having turned up in Chamonix on spec, with no fixed partner, I walked up alone to the hut above La Tour, slept briefly in a clearing amongst boulders, then at midnight got up by torchlight to cross the glacier and climb a famous ice route, the North Spur of the Aiguille du Chardonnet. Alone in the dark, conscious of the growing drop beneath my feet, I should perhaps have been frightened, but I wasn't. Cautious, yes; wary, yes; but also bold and precise, confident that I was in my element, pleased to be up there, witnessing that first russet glimmer behind familiar dark velvet silhouettes.

Pleasure was reaffirmed and now I was committed to staying – for nine weeks in the end – on a shoestring budget, living off the cheapest food from the supermarket, avoiding expensive tickets for trains or cable cars, bivouacking outside rather than sleeping in huts, doing the whole season for £140 including return travel from England. At times it was deeply frustrating. At one stage it rained almost non-stop for a fortnight. Bill Stevenson, with whom I had hatched grandiose plans including the North Face of the Eiger, came out from England, accompanied me heroically up the magnificent Nant Blanc Face of the Aiguille Verte, but returned to Snell's Field with a high temperature to discover that he had glandular fever.

End of that partnership. Next I teamed up with a loquacious Brummy architect called Bob Milward. Tired of Chamonix rain, we hitched east through Italy to the Dolomites, to pitch our tent beneath the Sella Towers, revelling in a whole new world of vertical limestone rising out of flowery meadows.

Our biggest summit in this Austrian-Italian region of the South Tirol was the Langkofel or Sassolungo – the Long Rock – but our biggest test of nerve was the celebrated *Micheluzzi* route on the South Face of Piz Ciavazes. On a fine sunny morning we romped delightedly up the lower section of gorgeously solid, rough-textured limestone. Most parties only climb the lower tier, then traverse off easily at a huge ledge called the Gamsband. Purist that I am, I was determined to climb all the way to the top, so we continued on the rarely climbed upper tier. The rock here was dull brown, slightly loose and dusted with earth. There were virtually no signs of Micheluzzi – or anyone else for that matter – ever having been here. At one point Bob could find nothing to anchor to, so we just had to keep moving together, linked irrevocably by our fifty metres of rope. Bob eventually found a dubious old piton and tied in to that. I set off up the next pitch, clipping the rope into another shaky old peg after five metres, then continuing into the unknown, committing to ever steeper, flakier rock with no sign anywhere of a crack for a peg or a nut. Eventually, I climbed into a dead end. I knew that if I continued any higher I would fall off. My only hope was to reverse the previous moves until I could traverse left to what seemed more hopeful terrain.

My mouth was sticky-dry, my forearms ached and my fingers were beginning to uncurl. My big leather boots – in those days we never took light rock shoes to the Alps – were trembling on dusty nubbins. From my waist the rope hung clear, twenty metres to the shaky peg runner. If I fell it would almost certainly rip, as would the token belay where Bob's upturned face watched anxiously. We would be catapulted two hundred metres down to the Gamsband, bounce off that and tumble another three hundred metres to the boulders at the foot of the face.

Of course I was frightened. But there was also a kind of elation, as I lowered my body, looking down between my legs, focusing on precise detail, reaching down with that outstretched boot toe, searching, testing, then weighting the hold, bringing down the other foot, then the right hand, then the left from its pinch grip, unclenching to relieve the taut quivering muscle between thumb and forefinger, before grasping a lower hold, thrilling to the vital contact between skin and rock.

It was all so beautifully simple: make the moves correctly or die. There was no random external threat from an avalanche, or a failing nylon sling, or a burst tyre on the motorway, or insidious fatal cancer ... it was all in my control.

I teetered down for several moves and at last reached easier ground, where I could stand in balance and shake out my trembling hands.

'That looked exciting,' shouted Bob.

'Sorry ... I think I should be further left.'

'Yes – see if you can find any of those nice little iron men.'

There wasn't a peg in sight, but just as I had run out the full rope length I finally found a good crack where I could hammer in one of our own, thrilling to the sweet ring of steel bedding deep between solid walls of stone.

Later that afternoon, coiling the rope on the huge flat top of the Ciavazes escarpment, I felt pleased that we had climbed the entire route, complete with dodgy upper band – had climbed our way out of danger. Had coped. Had passed the test. It was good, just occasionally, to have to fight your way out of a corner. Perhaps if I had been born thirty years earlier and had been forced to fight for real, as a soldier, in a proper cause, I might have exhausted all desire for risk. But growing up in what was probably the most privileged, cosseted generation the world had ever known, I seemed to relish these moments of artificial struggle.

Back in Chamonix, worn down by more unsettled weather, Bob's patience ran out and he set off home. Snell's Field was now almost empty and I moved into the de luxe polythene shelter under the big pine tree, equipped luxuriously with tables and sofas requisitioned from some rubbish tip. Here, eking out dog-eared books and bottles of cheap wine, the season's rump of climbers hung on, still hoping, as the days shortened and the snow began to settle below the tree line, to realise unfulfilled dreams.

Amongst the washed-up remnants there was a very tall genial man called Lindsay Griffin. He had been at Oxford before me, but his reputation had lived on. With Roger Everett he had made the third ascent of a famous climb pioneered by Chris Bonington and friends, high on Mont Blanc – the Right-Hand Pillar of Brouillard. On another occasion, after climbing a new winter route on Mont Blanc du Tacul, Lindsay had survived an epic descent in a prolonged blizzard, leading his companion for days through a labyrinth of crevasses on the Bossons Glacier. He had come uncomfortably close to dying during that winter ordeal and had lost parts of several toes to frostbite, but now, a year and a half later, he was back, rehabilitating himself with a vengeance, enjoying a long summer break from his day job as a researcher in laser physics.

He would emerge from his tent late in the morning, wandering into the polythene kitchen for a mug of tea, Marks & Spencer pyjamas flapping round the long legs which had once triple-jumped for England's junior athletics team. Nowadays he moved with slow deliberation, pausing for hours at a time to chat enthusiastically about esoteric valleys and summits in every corner of the Alps. He found the mountains endlessly fascinating and in his secret black book he kept copious notes about remote unrepeated rock climbs in Italy, weather conditions in Himachal Pradesh, addresses in Kenya, unclimbed summits in Bolivia, glacier pilots in Alaska . . . He could be wary and reserved; but also hugely charming, courteous and funny – at ease in any company. He loved what he was doing, and that boundless enthusiasm was very attractive.

Lindsay had had a busy season, working his way through an ambitious, eclectic selection of alpine climbs, burning off a series of partners in the process. Keen for more action, he signed me on as his new apprentice. I felt thrilled and flattered. Here at last was someone older, better and more experienced than me, who seemed to share some of the same dreams and aspirations.

For my initiation he decided to take me to the Vanoise massif. 'You know that North Face route on the Grande Casse . . . John Wilkinson did the first British ascent a couple of years ago. I've always fancied having a look at it.' I waited humbly while the master rummaged in his tent for the right food and gear, pulling out unique exhibits of home-sewn clothing and stowing them in the inevitable mini-van. Then we got in too and limped round to the south side of Mont Blanc, arriving late that afternoon at the village of Pralognan. By the time we had walked up to somewhere near the foot of the Grande Casse, the mist had descended and darkness was encroaching. As we stumbled around crepuscular mounds of moraine debris, trying to work out where exactly we were, eventually settling down on some boulders to brew up tea and lie down to sleep, I wondered if this was standard Griffin practice. I later discovered that it was entirely normal.

At dawn the mist lifted and we found our north face. And climbed it. For most of the way we moved quickly together, unroped. Then, just below the summit, where the snow and ice lay thin over slaty rock, Lindsay announced that we would rope up. 'I think I'll lead this bit,' he said.

'Of course,' I answered, slightly taken aback. Before I had always been the leader, or at least the lead had been shared, and I wasn't used to someone else taking charge. But I managed to shrug off that pique. Lindsay was just being cautious, climbing for the first time with a new partner on precarious terrain. In any case, he was much more experienced than me. He was the boss.

We reached the summit of the Grande Casse, descended carefully and drove back north until Lindsay's van died somewhere near St Gervais, leaving us to hitch the last few kilometres back to Snell's Field. The weather deteriorated again, I ran out of money and patience, and on a cool autumn morning I packed my rucksack for the last time and headed for home. The summer's tally of climbs hadn't come anywhere close to my expectations, but I had had some good moments. And I had enjoyed my outing with Lindsay. We seemed to get on well and, before I walked out to the road to hold out my thumb, he said that we must do more climbs together in the future.

But what future? Other than that vague promise of adventure, there were few bright reflections as I stared into the murky pool of my still-unlived life, searching for ideas. Unlike most of my Oxford contemporaries, I had no career lined up, other than the promise of a seasonal summer job on the stage crew at Glyndebourne Festival Opera. That would start in April 1976. In the meantime, I felled trees stricken by Dutch Elm disease, decorated houses and did odd bits of carpentry around Norwood Hill, whilst paying my parents a contribution to household expenses.

I also bought my first camera. On Piz Ciavazes, Bob Milward had asked me to take some pictures with his little Olympus. I had enjoyed framing the shots as he climbed towards me, a red figure dancing on a tilted golden stage. One day, perhaps, all this climbing and travelling might amount to something – might be a story to tell – and I would want photos to illustrate it. And, anyway, it was a chance to get back to making pictures, recapturing the pleasure of drawing and painting which had filled so many afternoons at school.

After Christmas a letter arrived from Lindsay suggesting a week's Scottish winter climbing during his February half-term: his research funding had packed up and he was now teaching at a secondary school in Kendal. Half-term coincided with abysmal weather and all we achieved was getting thoroughly soaked in some sodden gully on Ben Nevis, then retreating to the disused distillery in Fort William to take shelter amongst some abandoned filing cabinets before limping back to Kendal in Lindsay's latest car. The Lake District was marginally kinder, allowing us one or two rock climbs, including the classic *Praying Mantis* on Goat Crag. The birches glowed magenta in soft winter light and the rock was dappled jade. I scrabbled fiercely and proudly up the initial crack, then watched humbly as Lindsay followed, looking just like a praying mantis himself, all arms and legs, prehensile, deliberate, balanced delicately on invisible holds, stretched wide across the cliff and avoiding completely the loathsome crack where I had squandered so much energy.

But a few weeks later I did better in North Wales. I was at the cliffs of Tremadoc, climbing with a stranger who pointed me up one of the classic routes of the great master Joe Brown – *First Slip*. It was one of those days when everything flows. Balancing up an open corner, feet and palms smeared against smooth walls, clinging joyfully to nothingness, I felt invincible. So, I thought, why not try *the* Brown classic, *Vector*? Right now!

And so I found myself teetering off the famous 'flat-topped spike' onto the tiniest holds, hunching up under an overhang, then stepping across space, right toe reaching high onto the slanting wrinkles of the gorgeously lichened Ochre Slab, which hangs in space, tilted over the void. Then more fearful teetering past an ancient ring piton, hands thrust desperately into the crack above, feet walking up the slab in a flurry of blind faith. Then the surge of relief at reaching the belay, crouched amongst jumbled roofs. Then the final pitch, dancing leftwards through a sea of overhangs, marvelling at the genius of the man who had found this secret passage and had had the boldness to commit himself to the sinew-stretching reach up that final precarious groove.

'So, how did you enjoy the greatest Welsh rock climb?' asked Lindsay when I met him in Chamonix a few days later. He had just arrived with a friend called Dave Wilkinson – a hugely enthusiastic alpinist whose name was familiar from the climbing magazines. I had hitched out through France, complete with my skis. At Macon, standing beside the road, hoping for a lift before nightfall, I had suddenly heard someone shout 'Stephen', and looked round to see Vincent Potier, totally out of context, three hundred kilometres from Paris, in the one provincial town where he happened to be studying ceramics. I had spent the night with him and his girlfriend, enjoying food and company, heartened by that extraordinary coincidence. The omens seemed good and the 'meteo' was promising continued high pressure over the Alps. It was time for my first winter alpine climb.

Winter was what had first brought me to the Alps. Winter, with its columns of ice encrusted on the village fountain where the black-dressed old ladies came to fill their pails each morning. Winter, with its pungent smell of cow manure, sharp in the clear air, outside the shingled stables. Winter, with its bare tree limbs frosted thick beside the steaming river. Winter, with the mountains silent and pristine beneath the heavy whiteness.

But that was playing and skiing as a child in the Engadine. To climb right up into the heart of those mountains seemed impossibly heroic. Reading the accounts by the great alpinists like Hermann Buhl and Walter Bonatti only intensified that sense of awe. Likewise the more recent magazine reports from British climbers who were starting to emulate the Continental masters. It seemed a masochistic game, with laborious approaches, slogging through snowdrifts on snowshoes or skis, then teetering for days up sunless walls, making little progress in the short daylight hours, shivering through interminable bivouacs. Masochistic, yes, perhaps ... but also beguiling. I liked the idea of the slow struggle – the prolonged meditation, the peaceful communion with a silent landscape. Besides which, I was competitive, tempted by the possibility of a 'first winter ascent', eager to find out how I would cope.

My 1976 debut was in fact not a true winter ascent, since we were climbing after 21 March. Nevertheless it had the feel of winter about it. Lindsay suggested a very steep ice runnel on the Aiguille du Chardonnet, first climbed by two Belgians in the 1940s and rising just opposite the hut named in honour of their king, Albert Premier, himself a keen alpinist who died rock-climbing in the Ardennes in 1934.

The approach to the Albert Premier hut takes about two hours in summer. In winter conditions it took nearly six and we arrived after dark in proper Griffin style. The next day it took several further hours to cross the glacier, double boots breaking repeatedly through the windcrust, plunging deep into fathomless powder. The climb started up brutal iron-hard ice. The runnel proper was much more enjoyable, until an afternoon snow flurry sent waves of spindrift – fine wind-blown snow – cascading over our heads, enveloping us with blinding, freezing, suffocating whiteness. I gasped miserably, hating this white hell, vowing never to return. Until the clouds suddenly blew over, the sun came out, and the snow-laden air sparkled with the kind of visionary ethereal beauty which induces instant amnesia.

It took two hours that night to hack out a ledge and we didn't get into our sleeping bags until eleven p.m. On Day Two, by the time we had sorted out ourselves and our monstrous rucksacks, we only made about eighty metres' vertical progress, before settling down for an even more miserable bivouac. All night long I shivered in my now-sodden sleeping bag, a wretched cur huddled at the feet of his master, who shivered in stoic silence. We finally reached the summit on Day Three, and on the descent Lindsay directed me down a series of abseils, avoiding the normal summer descent which was overlaid dangerously with avalanche-prone snow slabs. A final abseil, spinning free, took us over a huge overhanging ice cliff onto the glacier, which we crossed in the dark, finally reaching the hut at eleven-thirty p.m.

Waking up the following afternoon, secure under a heavy pile of blankets, listening to the wind shrieking in the hut roof, I felt immeasurably happy. It had taken us three full days to make the first quasi-winter ascent of a rather short route to a not-very-high summit, but the sense of achievement was exhilarating and I knew that I wanted to make more of those extraordinary winter journeys.

But first there was the summer – the hottest summer since 1959. Lindsay spent the great drought of 1976 in the Lake District, guzzling on an endless feast of rock climbs. I, with perfect timing, was committed to working a six-day week, indoors, in the south of England, and only managed one weekend's rock-climbing all summer. The work was repetitive and often banal, but the setting, Glyndebourne Festival Opera, was sublime.

We were a rum bunch – the seasonal extras hired for that summer's stage crew. Out of ten of us, one had to leave after a week with a nervous breakdown and another, a rather effete Parisian musician, realised that hefting scenery was not going to further his career. There was another man who was quite adequately butch, but had to leave halfway through the season to go to prison for a drugs offence. And one member of the crew later committed suicide.

The rest of us muddled on, learning to work efficiently alongside the regulars – Biff the head flyman; Rex and Frank the carpenters; Bert the technical director who bawled at us when we got things wrong; Ivor, the gentle giant of a stage foreman, whose father Arthur still worked in the garden and had, in the pioneering days back in the 1930s, been called in each afternoon from the vegetable patch to help the Opera's founder, John Christie, focus the lights for the evening show.

Our basic pay was just twenty-six pounds a week but it was better than that of the non-unionised assistants in Wigs or Wardrobe. We also benefited from the system of minimum four-hour calls when rehearsals or performances ran late, bumping up overtime rates. For the autumn tour a union representative came down from London to negotiate a pay rise, but was stymied by the statutory six-pounds-a-week increase limit imposed by the new prime minister, Jim Callaghan. Ever ingenious, the union man suggested that on Saturday night get-outs we, members of the National Association of Theatre Television and Kinematic Employees could help move props, normally the exclusive province of stage management, who belong to Equity. That ten-minute step across the demarcation line amounted to taking a different job, and could therefore be rewarded legally with a weekly bonus of fifteen pounds, way above Mr Callaghan's limit.

I hated all the nit-picking and the them-'n'-us resentment

of management; but I learned to keep my mouth shut, realising that for some of the regulars on the crew who were supporting families every penny counted. With my degree, other doors could always be opened; Glyndebourne was a temporary experiment and my future livelihood didn't depend on it.

Once I got into the rhythm of the work I began to enjoy being a part, albeit a tiny part, of this huge, complex, organic thing – this magical alchemy which turned the printed pages of a score into a live performance. After weeks of piano accompaniment, it was thrilling to hear the London Philharmonic Orchestra bursting headlong into the abrupt boozy opening of *Falstaff*, and to see the director-designer, Jean-Pierre Ponnelle, pulling together all the final details of the magical forest scene, dominated by the immense steel oak tree that we had to wheel on stage during the long interval.

Falstaff was a busy show with some very heavy scenery and five changes. *Figaro* was also quite hard work. The highlight backstage was curtain-down at the end of Act Two, when Ivor and his Prompt-Side boys ran the entire back wall of the Contessa's boudoir in a single running leap off the ramp stage and round to the scene dock, buxom-bodiced sopranos fleeing for their lives. It was always a virtuoso performance. The final minutes of Act Three were also fun, with most of the Props department standing in the wings mercilessly corpsing the two assistant stage managers dressed up as eighteenth-century footmen. And I always hung around in the theatre for the whole of Act Four, entranced by the magic of the final garden scene, convinced that I was in love with the pert young soprano, Lilianne Watson, who was playing Susanna that summer. After final curtain-down we would strike the scenery and then perhaps have to set up another opera for the next morning's rehearsal; or sometimes get away more quickly, with time for a drink in the staff bar before heading home through the garden, intoxicated by the honeysuckle-scented air under a sky which remained cloudless and starry for night after night of that endless summer.

The other three operas that season, all new to me, were

another Mozart work, *Così Fan Tutte*, Richard Strauss's *Capriccio* and Debussy's lugubrious *Pelléas et Mélisande*. In September we packed three of the shows, *Capriccio*, *Falstaff* and *Figaro*, into several articulated lorries and set off on tour. In Oxford and Bristol I stayed with friends; for the other three weeks – in Norwich, Manchester and Southampton – I slept in the mini-van that I had just bought, parked outside the stage door, saving every penny I could of my wages and of my forty-pound-a-week tax-free living allowance, determined to build a good reserve of cash to see me through a winter in the Alps once the tour ended in October.

It seemed that a summer and autumn of opera had not managed to cure me of the mountain habit. I had enjoyed my six months' employment. I had enjoyed being part of a big team. But at times I had also found it rather daunting – conscious of the immense gulf between my half-realised enthusiasms and the dedicated skills of some of the world's best technicians, designers, directors and musicians. One of the assistant stage managers (who eventually became a successful director) suggested that I should try and come back the next season on the stage-management team – a route into directing or, if you don't have the creative vision for that, at least into management. I was pretty sure that with persistence I could work my way up inside the organisation, or into similar organisations, making for myself some kind of career in the arts. And perhaps that is what I would have done if a letter had not arrived from Lindsay suggesting not just a prolonged campaign of winter alpine climbing but also, for the summer of 1977, something grander – an expedition to the distant ranges of Central Asia.

It felt strange pitching our tent in deserted, frosty Snell's Field in November. We set off immediately into the mountains, only to be hit by the first big storm of the winter, returning to find our tent crumpled under a pile of soggy snow. For a couple of days we wandered round Chamonix, at one point huddling round a rubbish fire like a couple of tramps, until we found

Madame Couttet who had a room to rent for a reasonable monthly rate. There we settled in for the winter, sharing a bathroom with a hippiesque truck driver, who would sometimes appear at our door with a newspaper package and ask whether 'Vous voulez fumer l'herbe?'

Madame Couttet seemed a little perplexed by the two Englishmen who lived, cooked and slept in the rented room upstairs, then suddenly disappeared, returning several days later looking very thin and very tired. After the initial abortive foray, our first big winter trip was to the remote Val Ferret on the Italian side of Mont Blanc. We made little impression on our proposed climb before the weather broke, but it was still a fantastic adventure to be utterly alone in that huge, wild, deserted winter landscape. From the end of the road it took twelve hours, trailbreaking with snowshoes, just to reach the tiny Rifugio Dalmazzi; nearly another full day to get from there to the foot of the climb; another two days to fail on the climb and return to the hut; and an exhausting fifth day to slog back to the car as the fat snowflakes of the next winter storm began to fall from a yellow-grey sky.

Disappointing. But also intensely exhilarating, feeding the appetite for more. Analysing our progress – or lack of progress – Lindsay suggested that our next objective should be something accessible, close to a cable car station. And something up which we could easily haul our heavy rucksacks – some suitably steep, smooth icy runnel. Then, mumbling in a whisper, as though all the alpinists of Chamonix were listening at Madame Couttet's door, he muttered, 'Well, my boy, we could have a look at . . . er, you know . . . that couloir.'

That couloir – the *Super Couloir* on Mont Blanc du Tacul – had been climbed by the local stars Patrick Gabarrou and Marc Boivin in May 1975. It had never had a winter ascent; in fact, it hadn't even had a second ascent at all. And it was reputed to be one of the hardest ice climbs in the Alps.

Lindsay studied the meteo by the hour, scheming, cogitating, procrastinating, until he was convinced that it was safe to commit ourselves. Mont Blanc du Tacul was the same mountain where four years earlier he had been caught out by the terrible storm on the summit and had had to fight for his life, deterred from one descent route by avalanche slopes, driven back from another route by ferocious winds, forced eventually to make his gruelling escape down the long, long ridge onto the Bossons Glacier. He didn't want to repeat that epic.

He finally gave the thumbs-up on 22 December and that afternoon we dragged our monster rucksacks onto the cable car, which whisked us up to the Aiguille du Midi. From there it was only a short trudge across the glacier and up a moderate slope to the foot of the *Super Couloir*, where we dug a comfortable ledge to spend our first night out.

Nowadays most parties approach the couloir obliquely. We chose to do the Direct Start. I was quite a slow climber; Lindsay was also quite ponderous and the terrain was steep and intricate. Many times we had to stop and blow furiously on numb fingers. It was only on the second day that we got into the couloir proper, stopping early to make a comfortable ledge below the first big ice pitch.

It might seem strange to spend the night of Christmas Eve cocooned in a sleeping bag, with just a centimetre of foam mattress between that and a bed of hard-packed snow; but I was intensely happy that evening, propped up in bed, sipping a mug of hot sweet tea laced with whisky, puffing occasionally on a Golden Virginia roll-up, watching the stars brighten and multiply, discussing the day's work, wondering excitedly what the next day would bring.

It turned out to be one of the best Christmas Days of my life. The *Super Couloir* was a blue ribbon set deep between pillars of red granite. Perched at belays, taking in or paying out the rope, looking out at the holiday skiers swishing down the Vallée Blanche, I felt quite happy to be where I was, in our sunless cleft. We were busy and we climbed eight pitches that day. The most memorable for me was the seventh, where the ice shrank to a thin transparent veneer. At one point, chipping away to reveal a tiny granite spike, draping a loop over the spike to clip the rope in, then reaching up to chip out a hold for my right foot, I was a craftsman at work, a cabinetmaker, utterly content, absorbed, oblivious of my rope-holder shivering at the belay below. By the time Lindsay was leading the eighth pitch all the skiers had left, the Vallée Blanche was deep blue and only the higher summits glowed orange. Then, one by one, they were swallowed up, as the shadow of Mont Blanc, highest summit in the Alps, marched eastward across the landscape, elongating, reaching out into the pink sky.

Forty metres above me, Lindsay was chipping away, traversing out left, searching for somewhere to spend the night. The sky faded to violet, then dulled to a prosaic grey. I began to shiver. I shouted up to Lindsay, 'Have you found anything?' An incoherent mumble wafted down, lost in a swish of spindrift. Then the scrape of steel on rock as he dug forlornly at what might prove to be a ledge. It was now pitch black in the couloir, broken only by the pool of light from Lindsay's head-torch.

In the end he had to abseil back down to me. There was nowhere to sleep above. Nor was there anywhere here, so we had to descend another twenty metres to one of the couloir's undulations, where a patch of snow lay banked up on a fifty-degree slope. Here, thrashing around in the dark, we tried to make ourselves comfortable. Lindsay huddled in a corner, under our bivouac sheet. I was further out, sitting in a snow bucket seat, right in the centre of the couloir, with Lindsay's nylon hammock draped over my head.

The temperature that night was about minus twenty-five degrees centigrade. Which would have been fine – if a north wind had not sprung up, grabbing all the powder snow on Mont Blanc du Tacul and hurling it down the funnel of the *Super Couloir*. All through the night it came, wave after wave, battering down on my head. From Lindsay I heard just the occasional soft moan or curse. Occasionally I shouted through parched lips, pleading for a drink, but even under his bivouac sack he was unable to light the stove and melt snow. At one point he did hand me a mini Mars bar, but it stuck in my dry mouth. I shivered in my bucket seat, feet braced against the slope, pressing through the sleeping-bag fabric, toes wriggling to keep circulation moving. I thought of the others at home, gathered round the dinner table in the warm glow of candlelight, the rich smell of roast meat and wine and brandy butter . . .

We were only four days past the winter solstice and the night was an interminable torture. At dawn the spindrift avalanches finally won, pushing me off my bucket seat. There was a little slack in the belay rope, so I slid a metre or two before dangling to halt. Then, on the most ridiculous Boxing Day morning of my life, I started front-pointing in my sleeping bag, kicking my way back up to the bucket seat, numb hands pulling on the icy rope.

It took hours to get ready, fighting inside sleeping bags to pull inner boots and outer boots onto numb feet, struggling with laces, stopping repeatedly to blow on wooden fingers, willing them back to life. Lindsay, terrified of aggravating the old frostbite injuries he had suffered on this very mountain, stayed buried under his sack. I was less patient, desperate for movement, so I volunteered to go up the ropes that we had left fixed the previous night.

Above Lindsay's highpoint the final vertical ice wall reared up. Above *that* we knew that the couloir eased off. In theory we had just to climb that final big pitch and then we could move more easily to the summit. But, mumbling through frozen lips, Lindsay reminded me that it was actually a long way to the summit. And then? He didn't want a repeat of his 1973 nightmare. Looking up at the spindrift deluge pouring over that ice wall, I realised that it just wasn't on.

It was hard enough just getting back to the highpoint, using prusik loops – thin loops gripping the rope with a special knot invented by one Alexander Prusik – and the hard labour barely reduced my shivering. By the time I reached the peg anchor that Lindsay had left the previous evening, I knew that we were not, this time, going to complete the *Super Couloir*. All that mattered now was survival.

We spent the rest of that short winter day abseiling, rope length by rope length, back to the foot of the mountain. I took a certain pride in going first, setting up all the abseil anchors. The repeated removal of woollen mittens resulted in a touch of frostbite and by the time the two of us were lying in our sodden sleeping bags that night, using the last of the gas to produce a cold orange-and-whisky on the rocks, the tip of the little finger on my left hand had turned to ivory.

The following day, trudging back up to the Aiguille du Midi cable-car station, the tiredness really began to take hold. From the terrace above I heard a caustic English commentary – 'They're moving again . . . ten steps . . . and . . . yes, another step . . . and . . . no, they've sat down again.' The voice turned out to belong to Bill Barker, on his way with the famous Mo Anthoine to attempt a route on Mont Blanc. They were turned back the next day as the north wind veered further west and developed into a full storm. Before setting off for their climb, Bill said, 'Show them your finger; they do a reduced fare for emergency descents.'

So at the cable-car ticket office I shoved my left hand onto the counter. The little-finger tip had now turned a pretty shade of mauve and had swollen into a large blister. The man grunted, 'Oui – dix francs pour vous; mais vingt pour le grand.' Lindsay had made a better job of looking after himself.

Thirty years on, I still suffer twinges of regret. The second ascent of the *Super Couloir* would have been a nice feather to stick in one's cap. If only we had completed that final ice head-wall before it got dark? Or if only we had set off a couple of days earlier, when Lindsay was still waiting for his unequivocal 'beau temps' forecast? Would we have got up and down successfully? Or would we simply have been caught on the summit in atrocious conditions, fighting for our lives?

While we were attempting the *Super Couloir*, over in the Bernese Oberland two other British climbers I would later get to know well, Dick Renshaw and Dave Wilkinson, succeeded on a brilliant new route up the Mönch. Nearer to us, Alex MacIntyre and Nick Colton triumphed on the North Face of the Droites. Hearing about their successes, I wished that we had been quicker, cannier, more efficient. A part of my regret was just banal egotism, but it was also a niggling sense of incompleteness – those Christmas days and nights had been so perfect (spindrift drowning notwithstanding), the climbing so beautiful, the whole experience so overpowering, that it needed that final rounding off of undiluted 'success' to make it perfect.

Our winter dreams ended there. My little finger took a few weeks to heal and was never quite the same again, the pad slightly wizened so that on the violin my fourth finger vibrato always sounded subsequently a little thin. As for Lindsay, old skin grafts on his toe stumps were damaged, putting him out of action for the rest of the winter, until a surgeon tidied up the mess and restored his digits to working condition. So we returned to England.

I did go back to the Alps in March to collect all our belongings and, while I was about it, made a winter ascent of the north face of Mont Blanc de Cheilon – a perfect line bisecting a perfect triangle above the Swiss hamlet of Arolla. My companion, Bill Stevenson, was the man who had been with me on the north face of the Badile in 1974 and who had struggled manfully up the Aiguille Verte the following year with glandular fever. Tough, blunt, scathing about my privileged background – his mother lived alone in a caravan in Hartlepool – and teetotal, he was an austere companion, but a dependable one. We left the hut below Mont Blanc de Cheilon by moonlight and climbed continuously through the night and the following day, returning twenty-two hours after setting out, exhausted but happy.

Back in England I did various jobs that summer, including working with my brother Mark for a London garden designer called Helen Dorian-Smith. The work was varied, and sometimes non-existent. As were the wages. Each Friday lunchtime we would all gather in a pub on the Fulham Road and wait for Helen to complete her calculations. One week, we got paid the then-gigantic sum of seventy pounds for a morning's grubbing-out of a few laurel bushes. Other weeks Helen would announce, with the unerring bravura of the English upper classes, 'Sorry, chaps, there just doesn't seem to be anything in the kitty. No pay this week.'

And so I lurched through another summer, interspersing odd jobs with climbing trips to Derbyshire and Wales and the urban rocks of the Avon Gorge, where my personal highlight was leading a route called *Krapp's Last Tape*, named after Beckett's bleakly comic radio play by the route's 1960s student pioneers – the brilliant climber Ed Drummond and his regular climbing partner, a future schools inspector called Chris Woodhead. The climb was compelling because it wove such an improbable tenuous line through an apparently holdless vertical wasteland. For me it was particularly memorable because I was climbing at my technical limit, triumphing over moments of doubt, even fear. And I couldn't help feeling a certain pride because I had coped competently in front of my partner that day, Roger Everett, who was a much better climber than me. And that seemed important because with him, and his girlfriend Julia Yeomans, and my old alpine partner David Lund, and Lindsay, I was about to set off on my first expedition – to the Afghan Hindu Kush.

Chapter Four

The Road to Badakhshan

The great Afghan adventure started on a patch of dirty grass beside London's North Circular Road. There, outside Totteridge tube station, on the afternoon of 1 August 1977, Lindsay and I boarded Budget Bus. We had each paid eighty-four pounds for a one-way ticket to Kabul. For an extra sixty pounds the company had agreed to carry six large sealed kitbags full of expedition food and equipment. Roger, Julia and David would fly out via Moscow, meeting us in Kabul in a month's time.

The bus was an old Bedford thirty-two-seater with the cramped prickly velour seats I remembered so well from school trips. Our driver, Ernie, had thinning curly blond hair and a truckie's T-shirt-straining paunch. At Dover he announced that we should stock up on essentials, warning that 'From now on you won't be able to find any bog paper.' The same paranoid xenophobia informed his choice of overnight stops, so that, as we journeyed through Europe and Asia, we were forced frequently to sleep either in crowded official campsites or steel-fenced industrial lorry parks.

By the time we reached Salzburg our busload of twenty-somethings had already begun to organise itself into a microcosm of society. There were the Australian travellers who had just done Europe. There were couples in search of adventure and single women angling for a bit of rough with Ernie. And there were the sycophantic good boys who sat up front, near the driver – Leaders of Men eager to organise all of us whenever the bus broke down and needed a push start.

Lindsay and I were referred to initially as 'one of the single-sex couples'. Even once we had established our hetero-sexuality Ernie still viewed us – and the sealed packages stowed in the luggage compartment – with deep suspicion, confiding to some of our fellow travellers that he was convinced we were spies, latter-day players of the Great Game bound for a top-secret mission on the Afghan-Soviet border. A more conspicuous spy than Lindsay's six-foot-seven frame, draped with a fluorescent green shirt and flapping flares, it would be hard to imagine; but we did nothing to disabuse Ernie of his fantasies. As we rolled slowly south through Yugoslavia, reversing the route I had hitch-hiked five years earlier, we realised that we belonged with the oddballs and misfits – the naughty children at the back of the school bus.

Amongst the rebels were two congenial graphic designers heading further east than us, to Kathmandu, hoping to trek to Everest Base Camp. One of them, Adrian from Stoke-on-Trent, had just split up with his wife. 'She got almost everything,' he muttered gloomily, 'but at least I managed to keep the tent.' Like all of us, he sometimes missed home comforts, and by the time we reached Istanbul he was bursting regularly into Keatsian rapture – 'Oh for a bowl of cornflakes, with fresh raspberries and Channel Island milk' – dwelling with Northern deliberation on the 'rasp' of raspberries. It was Adrian, too, who groaned the loudest whenever Ernie put on his favourite cassette tape of jazzed-up classics – a hideous travesty which he loved to blast through the bus's crackly speakers. I still shudder whenever I hear Mozart's Fortieth.

Twelve days after leaving Totteridge tube station we crossed the Bosporus. Three days after that farewell to Europe, lumbering eastward across the Anatolian plateau, the bus broke down and had to be towed by a friendly British lorry into Erzerum. There we hung around the bazaar while the Leaders of Men went in search of a new fuel injector. Four miles out of Erzerum the bus packed up again. But somehow that was sorted out and the following evening, trundling towards the Persian border, as shadows lengthened over the great golden plain below Mount Ararat where shepherds gathered their vast flocks of sheep and goats, I began at last to feel something of the magic of Asia.

Onward to Tabriz and Tehran. And then north through the Elburz mountains for a night swim in the Caspian before heading east again to the holy city of Meshed, where we infidels could only stand outside and gaze through the magnificent blue-tiled portal to the inner courtyard where thousands of pilgrims milled beneath a gold dome at the holy tomb of the imam Ali r-Rida who was buried here in 818. And then at last, the next day, continuing across a white-hot plain, sweltering inside our bus, bludgeoned by cod Mozart, we reached the Afghan border, flitted through Customs in a mere four hours, and arrived at the city of Herat. In the hotel that evening, sitting on carpets, we ate a vast pilau. Then Lindsay's eyes lit up as some local musicians came on to play. Then someone arrived with a large chunk of hashish and the music blended into a blur of mellow smoke.

I loved Herat. I enjoyed the brazen salesmanship of the turbaned men and boys in the bazaar; the horse-drawn carts clopping past the pale gleaming walls of the fort; the cluster of strange minarets, like ancient factory chimneys, at the ruined Musallah complex. But I was impatient now to get on with the task in hand – our expedition. Lindsay was ill with a combination of food poisoning and heat stroke, and the bus was waiting again for a spare part. So I went on ahead, on a fast, efficient public bus.

Ah – the freedom of the open road! It was wonderful to speed across the desert towards Kandahar, past beautifully domed adobe houses, while a full moon rose in the east just as the sun set on the opposite side of the sky. The last time I had seen that celestial coincidence had been beneath the Aiguille du Chardonnet three years earlier, with David Lund, who at this very moment was probably packing for the flight to Kabul. I reached the capital the next morning, found a hotel, changed into a clean shirt and trousers, and set off for the British Embassy. It was time to organise our permits for the mountains. Lindsay reached Kabul that evening and when Roger, Julia and David turned up the next morning, 31 August, I announced proudly that all our paperwork was ready for our departure for the mountains. How naively wrong I was.

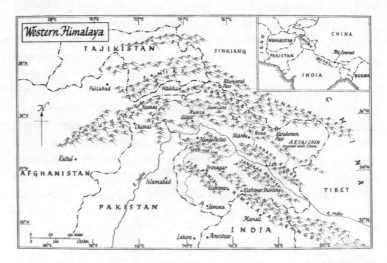

The Hindu Kush forms a mighty arc separating Afghanistan from its eastern neighbour Chitral. Since 1947 Chitral has been part of Pakistan, but it used to be the North-West Frontier of British India. It is a savage frontier, pierced only by tortuous high passes; in fact Hindu Kush means 'Hindu Killer', in reference to the Indian slaves who used to perish as they were dragged over the high cold passes by Arabian traders. The Greeks, who came this way with Alexander the Great, called the range Paropamisus from the Persian *uparisena*, meaning 'peaks over which the eagle cannot fly'. And yet the colonial officials of the more recent British Raj were convinced that Russian armies were poised to flood over these slave-killing, eagle-defying passes into India. Hence the treaty of 1895 which created the Wakhan Corridor, an anomalous appendix stuck onto the top right-hand corner of Afghanistan – a buffer zone separating the Russian and British empires, and, at its far north-eastern tip, brushing against Chinese Turkestan. The Wakhan Corridor was where we wanted to go in 1977.

We had chosen the area because – whatever the Greeks said about eagles – the mountains were not quite as dauntingly high as the greatest Asian peaks, the weather was generally good, and the bureaucratic obstacles with which Himalayan governments love to taunt their visitors were reputed to be easily surmountable. The first two assumptions were proved correct; the third was not.

It all started so well. The Gurkha officers at the gleaming stuccoed British Embassy, built by Lord Curzon to be the finest in Asia, were courteous and helpful; and the ambassador's staff provided the necessary papers for me to proceed to the Afghan authorities. I bumped into an American ex-pat from Leeds University, John Porter, who had just returned from a highly successful Anglo-Polish climbing expedition, and he showed me the bakery with the finest doughnuts in Chicken Street. Then I met our Afghan guide, a young man called Azim Amari, and he whisked me through various ministries, getting bits of paper signed. It was only three days later, after a long public holiday ended and the offices reopened, that we discovered they were the wrong bits of paper.

There followed an interminable game of snakes and ladders, trudging backwards and forwards between the Interior Ministry and the Foreign Ministry, sitting for hours in dingy waiting rooms beneath glowering portraits of President Daoud, the autocratic 'wolf' who had seized power and ended the Afghan monarchy in the coup of 1973. Although Daoud was opposed to the PDPA Marxist party, and the Afghan government was not yet controlled by Russia, the ministries seemed to be modelled on totalitarian lines, tormenting visitors with arcane regulations, including that most sinister blackmail – the 'Exit Visa': on the way back from the mountains, the whole complicated procedure would have to be repeated in reverse before we would be allowed to leave the country. At one ministry we saw a Swiss woman in tears, desperate to catch her plane, pleading to indifferent officials: 'I beg you, please, just let me go home!'

At one point we staged a sit-in, until some soldiers manhandled Lindsay – all six-foot-seven of him – out into the street. Walking gloomily back to the hotel in Chicken Street, he said, 'I think we're rapidly approaching fiasco point.' Roger had to get back in October to a new research post in Edinburgh; Julia, destined inexorably for a professorship, had to get on with her Physics doctorate; David had only finite leave from his employer, the software company Logica. President Daoud's apparatchiks were stealing our precious climbing time.

It took a full week to get clear of Kabul. But at last we were away, speeding north in the Toyota minibus we had hired, complete with driver Meherot and driver's boy Omar, whom, with great originality, we called Sharif. We passed the Panjshir Valley, scene of Eric Newby's seminal encounter with Wilfred Thesiger in *A Short Walk in the Hindu Kush*, and soon to be the stronghold of Afghan opposition to the Russian invaders who would drive their tanks down this same road in 1979.

At its highest point, 3,363 metres above sea level, the road passes through the Salang Tunnel, piercing the main mountain barrier between Kabul and Russia. Reversing the invaders' route, we descended the northern side of the pass into a hot desert land where camels stood tethered beside the black woollen tents of nomadic tribes; then through the major northern city of Kunduz; then on to a smaller settlement, where we stopped to camp on the town football pitch, feasting on huge succulent watermelons.

The next day we followed a dusty rutted track along the arid gorge of the Kochka River, to Faizabad, capital of Afghanistan's north-eastern province, Badakhshan. Leaving Faizabad on the third morning of our journey, we drove down an avenue of shimmering poplars, negotiating our way past a huge dusty flock of fat-tailed sheep. We continued up the Kochka River, to Baharak and Zebak, where we stopped to make tea and bearded turbaned men tried to persuade Lindsay to sell them our Primus stove, refusing to believe that we needed it ourselves to survive in the mountains. We were now deeper into those mountains. They could, perhaps, have passed for the Pyrenees, until you reached a village and saw the flat-topped adobe houses clustered beneath immense stately walnut trees, or drove over one of the cantilevered stone-and-timber bridges which are a such a quintessential feature of the Central Asian ranges all the way from Afghanistan to Bhutan.

We had a high-wheelbase minibus but there were still frequent clunkings on the tortuous road and we stopped repeatedly to wait while Meherot tinkered with the engine. Late that afternoon, crossing a final watershed, the road vanished completely and Omar had to guide Meherot through a river outwash, searching for faint marks amongst the boulders until the track became more pronounced again and we descended easily to Ishkashim, just in time to glimpse the River Oxus before darkness fell. We drove the last few miles into the western neck of the Wakhan Corridor and stopped outside the village of Qazi Deh. We had arrived.

Leaving Britain five weeks earlier, I had told myself that the journey would be a great adventure, whatever happened; if we actually climbed any mountains, that would be a bonus. And of course, it *was* a great adventure to drive into this remote corner of Central Asia. Thrilling to wake up to a double-humped Bactrian camel munching beside your sleeping bag outside a medieval village. Thrilling, also, to walk down to the stony bank of the Oxus River and look across to the Soviet Republic of Tajikistan where army trucks of the Cold War enemy sped along proper metalled roads. Thrilling to contemplate the valley rising eastward towards China. It *was* all very exciting, particularly after the weeks of incarceration on Budget Bus; but merely travelling – wandering, watching passively, all too aware of your ignorance in this land of Kirghiz, Tajik, Uzbek and Wakhi tribesmen, trying dimly to comprehend what was going on – that wasn't enough. I needed more of a purpose. So, after a day's haggling with ten local rogues determined to clean us out of our entire stock of dollar bills, it was a great relief to see them shoulder our expedition baggage and head up the Qazi Deh valley to Base Camp.

We didn't reach Base Camp. Or at least the men from Qazi Deh village had a different view about where Base Camp was. Never mind – they got us most of the way there and ferrying loads ourselves up the final stretch was a good way of getting fit. And while we humped luggage we were rewarded, at last, with the sight of our first big glaciated mountains, crystal sharp in the autumn sky.

Lower down the valley we had passed currant and rose bushes and, flitting beside the glacial torrent, the ubiquitous Himalayan river chat – a redstart with a dazzling white cap. Base Camp, four thousand metres above sea level, was a bleaker spot, with only a few wisps of grass and the occasional eagle flying overhead. But we found a flat terrace with space to pitch our tents beside a stone wall that we built to protect the kitchen from the evening wind.

Since the 1960s a steady stream of foreign expeditions had visited this valley and all the main summits had been climbed; but there was nothing to stop us climbing new routes to those summits and, in the process, discovering how we Himalayan novices would cope with the altitude. So far Roger and I seemed to be coping best, so Lindsay, ever generous, suggested that we had first stab at a mountain, while he and the others did the final ferries to Base Camp. Roger and I packed rucksacks and set off across the rubble-strewn Qazi Deh glacier, to unroll our sleeping bags beneath a mountain called Rakh-e-Kuchek. As we heated water on the gas stove for our evening meal, the temperature plummeted, daytime meltwater froze and expanded and the glacier beneath us came alive, creaking, groaning and firing loud pistol shots in the darkness.

By dawn we were on our way, clawing up the inviting tongue of white snow we had spotted the previous night, only to discover that it was just a flimsy sugary icing on tungsten-hard ice. Rope length by rope length, we laboured under a blazing sun, crampons and axes hammering wearily at unyielding concrete. Higher now than the summit of our familiar Mont Blanc, we panted in the thin air, stopping frequently to lean against the slope, foreheads pressed to the ice. It was a horrible joyless affair.

By nightfall we had reached a depression near the top of the north face, where we hacked a ledge of sorts out of the ice. My head was throbbing and I shivered all night. In the morning I just felt horribly lethargic and Roger had to galvanise me into action to complete the last two rope lengths to the top. Then, in this land of extremes, lagging far behind Roger on the easy descent, I stumbled under a blazing sun, dazed and enervated, slumped for frequent rests as I forced my pathetic body back down an eternity of strewn boulders. It was a sobering start to my Himalayan career and I just hoped that things would get better.

They did. After a couple of days' rest, Roger and I set off again, this time with Lindsay, bound for the enticing summit of Kohe Sakht. Kohe is a generic term for 'mountain'; Sakht approximates to 'hard'. During our torture on Rakh-e-Kuchek, Roger and I had looked across the valley of the Wakhan Gol and spotted a beautiful russet buttress leading to Kohe Sakht's summit – an irresistible siren singing 'Come and climb me.'

And so, three days later, the two of us and Lindsay made our way round to bivouac in the Wakhan Gol. That night, lying in my sleeping bag, watching the shooting stars streak across the sky, listening to the silence of Central Asia, I really felt at last that I had arrived – that this was what it was all about. At home it would be lunchtime. It was Saturday and it was my parents' silver wedding anniversary and the guests would all be arriving for the party – the last big family event before my parents moved to live near Bath. I thought of my last evening in Norwood Hill before I had set off to join Budget Bus – the last wander round the garden, looking out over the woods and fields to the North Downs. It was a quiet, unexceptional sort of landscape, but it was the landscape of my childhood and I felt a momentary twinge of nostalgia; but it *was* only a moment's pleasurable sadness, because this high Afghan valley was where I really wanted to be.

We continued up the Wakhan Gol at dawn, then turned right up a side valley leading to Kohe Sakht. The climb started with another slope of 'concrete' ice, this time mercifully short. Then, in the cool of evening, we were rewarded with the first real rock-climbing and the other two let me, the junior, have first lead up an enticing corner leading to a chimney where there was just room for the three of us to lie down for the night, wedged between walls of granite, looking out through a bright cleft to Chitral. Again, the same utter contentment. Nowhere else in the world I wanted to be. Again, a good night's sleep. And, again, the same eagerness to start the new day, wondering where our buttress would take us.

Lindsay led us out of the chimney and along a turreted ridge, climbing around pinnacles of gorgeously weathered granite. That afternoon we reached a big cliff cut by a single right-angled corner. I was lucky: it was my turn to lead, size twelve double boots bridged out across the corner, bare hands side-pulling and jamming up the crack, whole being immersed in the colour and texture and sculptural geometry of this magnificent cliff, thrilled for the first time in my life to be going where no one had ever been before.

Our south-east buttress emerged into a field of 'névé péni- tent'. These ice pinnacles, formed by the irregular melting of snow slopes, are typical of the Himalayan ranges, particularly the desert-hot Hindu Kush, and are named after the pointed hats worn by medieval penitential monks (a more precise, but nastier, description would be 'névé Ku Klux'). Roger thrashed up through the 'penitents', the rope snagging behind him as

Lindsay and I followed. At a final barrier he stopped and shouted 'Smile!' as I came up beneath him, sunburnt stubbled face framed cheerfully in a halo of glittering ice; then we did a sort of western roll over the final icy overhang onto the summit of Kohe Sakht, 5,780 metres above sea level, higher than any of us had been before.

Rather than descend boringly by the way we had come, we decided to traverse the long north-east ridge. That evening we just made a hundred metres or so before dropping down to a ledge on the south side to sleep. On Day Three we continued all day along the ridge, dancing the tightrope between south and north faces, light and shade, marvelling at the dizzy void on the north side. Sometimes we tiptoed on the crest; at other times we crab-crawled along the north flank; at one point on the south side we shuffled along an improbable ledge reminiscent of the famous *vire aux bicyclettes* in the Chamonix aiguilles.

Another bivouac. This time a perfect flat ledge, right on the crest of the ridge, complete with a large patch of snow for melting on our stove, to produce pan after pan of tea and fruit juice and soup as we watched the sun setting over the distant mass of a famous peak called Kohe Bandaka. On Day Four our ridge concluded with a final bonus summit – the pinnacle of KZ56 – and then all we had to do was fight our way down a lacerating gully of 'penitents' to the glacier, and on down to the Wakhan Gol and back to Base Camp, where Julia, David and Azim had returned from their trek to the Chitral frontier.

At our base camp Lindsay and I ruminated contentedly, reading, sleeping and eating, while Roger, fitter, stronger and devoted to Julia, accompanied her and David up a peak called Karposht-e-Yakhi. Then we decided the time had come to go seriously high.

At the head of the Qazi Deh valley, looming over the Chitral border, there is a huge massif called Noshaq, which means 'Nine Horns'. The highest point on its extended summit plateau is 7,492 metres above sea level. The normal route up the west ridge involves virtually no real technical climbing and during the 1970s it became very popular with climbers seeking an easy route up a 'seven-thousander'. Now that we were acclimatised we decided that the time had come to see how we would cope at that altitude.

We didn't cope very well. One reason, perhaps, was that Lindsay and I raced up two thousand full metres in the first day. This was the brave new world of 1977. Two years earlier the Tyrolean stars Reinhold Messner and Peter Habeler had stunned the world with their three-day dash up and down Hidden Peak in Pakistan – the first pure 'alpine-style' lightweight ascent of an eight-thousand-metre peak. If they could do it on an eight-thousander, surely we could do the same on a much easier route up a seven-and-a-half-thousander?

I felt like death after our first day's dash. Lindsay didn't feel much better, so the next day we sat tight, lying in our sleeping bags, trying to persuade ourselves that we were achieving genuine rest. Then we continued, plodding ever more slowly, to about 6,800 metres, where we erected our 'tent' for the second bivouac. Lindsay had taken the modern lightweight ethic to extremes, bringing just his single bag-shaped sheet of nylon, held up by a wooden pole he had found beside the Oxus, guyed with a piece of string. Inside this sloping hellhole we shivered in our sleeping bags and struggled to melt enough snow for rehydration on our pitifully weak butane stove. The following day we 'rested' again, slumped lethargically. A dead plover lay in the snow beside us, frozen in its improbable flight over the Hindu Kush.

Things cheered up a bit when David and Roger arrived, having set out a day later, leaving Julia at our base camp with Azim. They had a proper tent with real tent poles and seemed slightly less lethargic. In the morning all four of us continued towards the 'rockband' at seven thousand metres – the one real obstacle before Noshaq's summit plateau. I led the way, trying to force some kind of rhythm into my huge, clodhopping double-leather boots, trying to step with forceful deliberation up the snow-covered shale. But it was a pathetic performance and the dark clouds – the only really threatening weather on the whole expedition – didn't encourage. After an hour or two David – a man far too sensible ever to be a really ambitious climber – muttered simply, 'I'm going back down.' Without another word we all turned round and headed downhill.

It was a depressing high-altitude debut and, back at Base Camp, there was a feeling of things coming apart. Lindsay left to enjoy some solitude on a magnificent solo rock climb. The rest of us did one more climb, but I spoilt it by getting impatient with Julia, infuriating Roger in the process. As self-appointed fundraiser, quartermaster and cook to the expedition, I had spent far too much time bossing people around and airing personal prejudices, or arguing with the scientists, rising to the bait of remarks like 'Who are you to say that Saul Bellow's novels are in any way "better" than the James Bond books?', so perpetuating C. P. Snow's clash of the two British cultures. The petty stresses of expedition life were starting to show. Nevertheless, on the last day, as we walked back down the Qazi Deh valley, pausing at twilight to look back up at a summit where we had stood just two days earlier, I felt sad that it was all ending.

The long drive back to Kabul was entertaining. I remember late one night stopping far from any village at an isolated caravanserai where we were served tea from a samovar and a delicious pilau heaped on a cloth, from which we scooped handfuls of rice, feeling hopelessly uncouth trying to emulate the neat dexterity of our Afghan hosts. In Faizabad someone sold Azim an eagle owl to take home to his family aviary, and for the rest of the journey we took turns at having it on our laps, talons ripping our trousers to shreds, its huge amber eyes staring at us implacably.

The 'roads' of Badakhshan were destroying the Toyota and every few miles Meherot would stop, get out his knife, and scrape more loose rubber from disintegrating outer tyres. Near Zebak the radiator was holed by a stone, but because this was

Asia it was repaired in half an hour. Then, one by one, the steel leaves of the rear left suspension started snapping. When the last leaf had gone, Meherot lashed a poplar log in its place and every time we hit a bump Lindsay's head, never far from the ceiling at the best of times, crashed against the Toyota roof. So he lay down instead, and disappeared under a veil of fine dust blowing through the windows.

In Kabul there remained only the final purgatorial round of the ministries to extract our exit visas. The other three got to the airport just in time; Lindsay and I each paid fifty-eight pounds for an express bus ticket to Munich. With only ten pounds cash remaining, we took what was left of the expedition food – mainly porridge – to see us through to Germany, supplementing that with sugar cubes filched guiltily from roadside cafés. We made a sorry sight, two tramps huddled in the first winter snow on the Anatolian plateau, brewing breakfast on our Primus stove in the lee of the parked bus. On the eighth day we reached Munich, where everyone was searched by the police. One idiot tourist, having smuggled a kilo of hashish all the way from Afghanistan, was caught out by the sniffer dogs. He knew that if he had been caught in Iran he would have faced life imprisonment.

But it was not really drugs that the German police were after. We had returned to Europe at the height of the Baader-Meinhof – or Red Army Faction – crisis. One of the leaders, Ulrike Meinhof, had hanged herself – or had been murdered, according to some theories – in her prison cell the previous year. The rest of the gang on trial had been sentenced to life imprisonment in April 1977 for multiple terrorist offences. But there were others still on the loose. In September, while we had been driving up to Badakhshan, here in Germany they had kidnapped Hanns Martin Schleyer, President of the German Employers' Association. Then on 13 October Arab colleagues of the gang had hijacked a Lufthansa plane. On 16 October they had murdered the pilot. On the eighteenth of the month, while we were changing buses in Istanbul, German elite police had stormed the plane and killed all the hijackers, whereupon four of the imprisoned gang members, including Andreas Baader, had killed themselves (or, again, according to some theories, been murdered) in their cells. On 19 October, while we had been driving up through Yugoslavia, Schleyer's kidnappers had announced that he had been executed.

Lindsay and I had wandered straight into the biggest manhunt in German history. But, without enough cash for a train home, we were committed to hitch-hiking. We parted on Munich's northern edge, Lindsay still fighting his spilling luggage, trying to tame an old Polish tent he had salvaged from the West Ridge of Noshaq, as I waved goodbye and heaved my own two large rucksacks out to the autobahn. Later that night, waiting at an intersection near Düsseldorf, I was inter-rogated repeatedly by jittery policemen until a local man stopped and said, 'No one will give you a lift tonight, and if you stay here you will probably be arrested. I'll take you into town where I have a spare flat you can use for the night.' He left me at his flat, asking me to be sure to lock it up when I left in the morning, then adding, 'I do this because I am a Christian and it is a way of helping my neighbour.'

That simple gesture, amidst so much fear and hatred, close to the end of a gruelling five-thousand-mile journey, was heart-warming. As was the packet of biscuits that he told me to take with me in the morning, as I completed my odyssey. There was massive police activity at the Belgian border, with huge tailbacks stretching south on the autobahn, but eventually I got through to Zeebrugge and spent the last of my money on a ferry to Dover. The following morning, 22 October, having ascertained that my parents had not yet actually moved house, I turned up in Norwood Hill and sat down to what I had been dreaming about for three months – fresh brown toast, butter and marmalade.

On our last night at Base Camp, singing joyfully to himself after his magnificent solo rock climb, riding an ecstatic high, Lindsay had said to David, 'Oh, I'll be coming back to the

Himalaya, many, many times.' Although I hadn't ended on such a high, I think I also felt the same: I too would be coming back. But not to Afghanistan. Two years later, flying this time to India, I did touch down briefly in Kabul and the airport terminal was draped with a huge red banner welcoming us to 'The Land of the New Model Revolution'. In 1978 President Daoud and his family had been murdered by the Marxist PDPA party and replaced by a new revolutionary president, Nur Muhammad Taraki, who signed a treaty of friendship with the Soviet Union. Taraki in turn was murdered in September 1979 and replaced by Hafizullah Amin, who struggled to control Islamic opposition to the revolution, exasperating his masters in Moscow. On 27 December 1979 Soviet special forces, dressed in Afghan uniforms, took over all the main government buildings in Kabul and stormed the Kajbeh Palace, shooting Amin dead. The same day ground troops crossed the northern border and headed south across the Salang Pass while paratroopers were dropped onto Bagram airfield. In the years of war that followed – and which still continue – I often wondered what had happened to the people we met in Zebak, and Faizabad and Qazi Deh. I wondered what had become of our driver Meherot, and Omar. And, in particular, I wondered – and still wonder – what happened to Azim and his eagle owl.

Chapter Five

Fear and Loathing on the Matterhorn

Mark and I sat hunched over our bacon sandwiches in the steamy fug of an East End café, piebald in paint-splattered overalls, anonymous workers amongst the regulars from the Bermondsey Antiques Market. Just round the corner was the vicarage that we were decorating. Like a method actor sticking earnestly in character, I was reading the *Sun*. 'What's a sex pistol?' I asked my savvy younger brother.

'What are you talking about?'

'What is a sex pistol?' I repeated. 'It says here, "Sex Pistols banned in America".'

I *had* probably heard of punk rock, but I was hazy on the detail, out of tune with the *Zeitgeist*. In fact my whole life seemed out of tune, lacking direction. 1978 was a bad year for self-esteem. My father, desperate to help, suggested that I might think about applying for a trainee copywriter's job with an advertising agency. It could be fun to work with all those bright talented people. No chance at his firm, Ogilvy & Mather – that would be blatant nepotism – but he could make some calls to other agencies, ask them to talk to me at least. It was a generous offer but at the last minute I funked it, terrified of corporate life, unsure how I could ever make myself believe in the whole crazy business of persuading people to buy things they didn't really need.

Instead, I did a succession of casual decorating and carpentry jobs. But I did manage also to write two articles and send them off to a climbing magazine. The editor, Walt Unsworth, wrote back to say he would pay me fifteen pounds for each of them; better still, he used one of my shots as a cover image. And so Lindsay's magnificent home-made turquoise climbing suit appeared on the front cover of *Climber & Rambler*, resplendent against the amber granite of Kohe Sakht.

It was at least a start, but at fifteen pounds an article it wasn't going to get me very far and I needed some solid work. Having eschewed corporate stability, I applied for adventurous work overseas. I was turned down by the British Antarctic Survey. An outdoor adventure school in New England did offer me a summer job, but wrote at the last minute to say that there were legal problems and that I couldn't come after all.

So I worked instead as assistant to a photographer based near Bath. Some of the jobs, like photographing forty seemingly identical beds for a catalogue, were tedious; others were more amusing. One day we did an ad for a new motorbike tyre, which involved wheeling a gleaming Morini 500 into the studio and shooting hundreds of frames of a naked Page Three girl sitting astride the machine in a sea of dry-ice vapour. My job was to wind-blow the girl's hair with a long tube attached to the wrong end of a vacuum cleaner.

It all seemed quite surreal – photographer, assistant, art director and various other hangers-on, all men, gathered round this naked woman, trying to look nonchalant. Plucking up courage during the coffee break I went up to her – she now had on a dressing gown – and said, 'I hear you've just been doing a shoot in Crete.'

'Yeah,' she drawled unhelpfully.

I persevered, 'That must have been interesting.'

'Nah – it was really boring. Nothing there. Just a load of rocks.'

I wasn't sure where to take the conversation from there. The afternoon shoot was much easier – a sumptuous spread of food for a new fridge advertisement.

And what of the mountains? The trips? The projects which bookended the passing years, giving some kind of shape and focus? Lindsay and Roger were both away in the Himalaya that summer. I stayed mainly in Britain, but I did spend spring in the Alps with David Lund, fulfilling a long-term ambition – the high-level glacier ski route from Chamonix to Saas Fee. Since its first recorded winter traverse in 1911 the 'Haute Route' had become one of the great classics, probably the most famous ski tour in the world. I had done a little bit of touring, but most of my skiing so far had been on pisted downhill runs, using lifts. This would be different – using skis to go on a journey.

My mini had died, so David drove us out to Martigny, where we parked his car, shouldered rucksacks and skis, and took the train to our starting point, Argentière in the Chamonix valley. That afternoon we wobbled down from the Grands Montets cable-car station, dodging crevasses, trying to get used to skiing with twenty-kilo rucksacks as we trundled across the glacier to the Refuge d'Argentière. We were doing our tour on the cheap, paying for bunk places in the huts but eschewing expensive dinner menus in favour of minimal rations carried on our backs, handing over packets of soup and dehydrated meals to be heated up by disdainful hut wardens.

From the Argentière hut we skied over three passes to the Val Ferret. Then we approached the great terraced bulk of the Grand Combin. There is an easier version of the Haute Route which skirts the Combin to the north, via Verbier, but we were doing the classic route, traversing right up onto the southern flank of the mountain. First there was a gruelling 1,400-metre climb to the tiny Valsorey Hut, perched on a knoll redolent with memories of George Mallory, who came here on his first climbing season in 1904. And then the big day – the crux of the journey.

We left at six a.m. in high winds, zigzagging up an icy crust, cursing the artificial fur 'skins' strapped to our ski soles when they failed to grip, wishing we had additional 'couteaux' – down-pointing metal blades attached to the binding. Thirty years ago, ski-touring equipment was still quite primitive by today's standards. As for my own particular skis, the Australian temp at the Alpine Sports repair department in London had taken one look at them and announced, with the charming directness of his people, 'They're fucked, mate.' Determined not to be bamboozled into buying a new pair, I had taken the planks – an old pair of my mother's – back to the workshop at home and, with Araldite and home-made brass rivets, secured the metal edges quite satisfactorily. I skied several hundred miles on that pair before they finally disintegrated in 1982.

David and I followed the twenty or so other ski-tourers up the zigzags. Then removed skis and strapped crampons to our boots, to climb up and across a huge funnel-shaped ice face, kicking carefully to the final steeping. Using the skis as stakes, plunging them deep into the rim of a cornice we pulled ourselves over onto the crest of the Plateau du Couloir. It was eight a.m. and finger-numbing cold as we tightened bootlaces, clamped ski bindings into the downhill position and set off eastward over another col, then down into the cloud, groping through the murk and finally emerging at a wild, remote confluence of valleys where the Chanrion Hut was a welcome glowing sanctuary.

It snowed hard the next day. David, contented by nature, read in the hut. Restless, I strode out into the blizzard and climbed a little peak called the Pointe d'Ottema, enjoying my vigorous flounder up a ridge of snow-smothered pinnacles, returning elated to the hut for our dinner of freeze-dried mush, wishing that the budget could stretch to a bottle of wine.

The weather cleared that night and at dawn we were away first from the hut, breaking trail up the Brenay Glacier. I loved the steady rhythm of it – the fur-soled skis sliding alternately, cutting their twin grooves through the pristine surface, sinuous at first, then angular as we zigzagged more steeply through an icefall, skirting cavernous crevasses. Looking back to Dave I saw just a dark silhouette with a long, pencil-thin shadow stretched across a field of sparkling crystals. Later, as the sun climbed with us, the shadows flattened and the sparkle dulled, but for compensation we had the domed summit of the Pigne d'Arolla, which I had last visited with my brother Philip and our mother four years earlier, and from which I was now descending in an exhilarating whoosh to the Vignettes Hut with its incomparable lavatory cantilevered over an immense precipice.

We had ample opportunity to sample this long drop to beat all long drops, as bad weather kept us for a day at the Vignettes. Our reward for the delay was a generous skim of fresh fluffy powder for the Grand Finale – the crossing to Zermatt. We started before dawn, slithering over the dark glacier and then climbing into the light as we reached the Col de l'Evêque. From there a stunning descent, skis carving ecstatic S's, swishing down onto another glacier. Then the corollary of that – the inevitable pause to put on skins and start climbing again, steeply, to the Col du Mont Brulé. From there not much of a descent – more a sidling traverse, skirting round the back of the rocky turrets of the Bouquetins, the peak of the ibex – then climbing again, hot despite the clouds which were thickening around us, merging with the snow, white on white.

Soon we were in a total white-out, navigating by compass, checking altimeter readings to gauge our progress on the map, as the slope slowly eased off and levelled onto the featureless whiteness of the Col de Valpelline. It was a shame about the lack of a view, but we had the satisfaction of navigating success-fully through trackless snow, dodging the crevasses as we crossed the Gallic-Teutonic linguistic frontier and wove our tentative line down the icefalls of the Stöckli Glacier onto the Tiefmatten Glacier and on, down, down, down to Zermatt.

Three years later I did the Haute Route again, this time by the northern, Verbier, version, acting as guide to my parents. Again we were held up by bad weather at the Vignettes Hut, followed by fresh powder for the final day to Zermatt. But this time we had blue sky on the Col de Valpelline, allowing us to witness the visual glory of that climax to the Haute Route. As you trudge onto the crest of the pass – the third pass of the day – a white tooth appears in the sky. But then a second tooth, a sharper, darker fang, appears, further back. Then, as you glide down the Stöckli Glacier you begin to comprehend the sheer scale of the first peak – the Dent d'Hérens, with its immense ice terraces – and the even grander scale of the second, darker, more complex, intriguing structure – the Matterhorn – which stands completely alone, separate, unique.

It's like the Taj Mahal. It never disappoints. It remains endlessly fascinating, different from every angle, its mood changing constantly with the shifting light. Skiing the Haute Route from the west, its silhouette grows steadily more insistent, drawing you on, until that wonderful moment when you descend right beneath its private west face, then continue underneath the more familiar tilted planes of the north face, and finally reach Zermatt for the kitschy but irresistible view of a thousand chocolate boxes.

And then, if you are continuing to Saas Fee, as David and I did in 1978, you have a chance to look back at the slender triangle of the east face. And perhaps, as you stand on the terrace of the Monte Rosa hut at twilight, snug in your duvet jacket, you will see a great shaft of light angling leftward from the summit – like a searchlight aligned perfectly with the slope of the triangle – dividing the sky into two rhomboids, purple on the left, paler crimson and peach on the right. And, as you set off the next morning, continuing eastward towards the final Adler Pass – the pass of the eagles – there will be a moment when you look back and see the first rosy glow touching the tip of the spire, then creeping down the triangle, bright with the promise of another magical day.

So, with our crossing of the Adler Pass to Saas Fee, David and I completed our traverse of the Haute Route. David seemed totally fulfilled as he set off back to England. I stayed behind, less content. It had been a good journey but I had occasionally felt restless, hungry for something bigger. Now I was tense and anxious. Some American friends of my father were coming out in mid-May and I was going to act as assistant guide on their shortened east–west Haute Route. That would be fun, but in the meantime, with ten days to kill, I wanted to do something big. In Zermatt the biggest, most obvious, most mesmerising challenge was that dark tilted wall – the North Face of the Matterhorn. I had been pondering it for some time, wondering if I was up to it. Now I was certain: I wanted to climb it in winter conditions. And I wanted to climb it alone.

I brooded anxiously for several days, eking out my money in Paula Biner's Hotel Bahnhof – a self-catering bunkhouse for the young and impecunious. I envied the American students their carefree jollity on the ski slopes as I watched the clouds swirling around the Matterhorn and checked weather forecasts, half-hoping that they would remain bad, letting me off the hook. I visited the cemetery and found the grave of my father's cousin, James Ogilvie, who had died in 1948, falling off the Matterhorn roped to two fellow students. I imagined the battered young bodies . . . Aunt Mary's terrible grief . . . the sad questions about the lives that were never lived, cut short like the life of that other Oxford student, Paul Beney . . . and Dave Luscombe, who had been with me the last time I climbed the Matterhorn. For a moment I tried to imagine my own life similarly truncated, visualised guiltily the grief at home. I wondered whether I should abandon my idea, but then baulked at the thought of another evasion.

So, when the weather improved I left a note for Fraülein Biner and set off for the cable-car station, feeling like a condemned man. From the top station at Schwarzee I skied as far as I could, then lashed skis to my rucksack for the final trudge up to the Hörnli Hut, where a large red sign – 'Winter Eingang' – pointed the way through an upstairs window, clear of the snowdrifts. In summer the hut holds nearly two hundred people; in winter a small section is kept open, unguardianed. I was pleased to find some palatable leftovers, including some excellent freeze-dried chicken. The next day, 10 May, the wind was screaming, hurling banners of snow off the mountain, so I lay low, huddled under blankets, eking out the pages of a Hemingway book. That evening I went to sleep in a morbid mood.

But the midnight alarm brought a new mood of optimism. The sky was clear, the wind had vanished and by 12.45 I was away, alone under the stars, kicking steps through the deep powder, shuffling onto the great glacier shelf beneath the Matterhorn's north face, then climbing steeply up the big ice field which starts the route.

So far, so good. But then I found myself on thinning ice, with rock showing through. Tilting my head upwards, all I could pick out in the torchlight was more rock, awkward and threatening in the black night. So I stopped to shelter under my nylon bivouac sack, perched uncomfortably, waiting for the light.

At dawn I felt safe continuing. But why this precarious polished rock? Had the ice field really melted away? Only at 6.30, stepping round a corner, did I realise what had happened. The great ribbed sweep of snow was there, on my right, unmistakable: in the dark I had started up the wrong ice field. Now things improved, until the huge snowfield petered out on the shore of a featureless grey ocean of rock, dabbed unhelpfully with random blobs of snow and ice. The idea on this classic north face, first climbed in 1931 by the Bavarian brothers Franz and Toni Schmid, is to work diagonally rightwards into a 'couloir' which is really just a vague depression in a tilted spiral of rocky slabs.

So I edged rightwards, crampons shuffling on indeterminate holds, mittened hands seeking assurance. And the further I moved right, the more awesome was the exposure as I came above the huge overhangs which undercut the tilted spiral. At one point my feet shot off a ledge and suddenly I was dangling from my arms, heart stabbing, body juddering from an adrenalin overdose. Determined not to die, I took out my fifty-metre rope and began to protect myself on the harder sections, which meant descending after each pitch to retrieve the lower anchor. It was slow work and on one particularly delicate section I spent a long time removing crampons from my boots to get a better feel on the smooth rock.

Midday arrived and I had only managed about eight rope lengths from the top of the ice field. I still had at least eight hundred metres to climb to the summit. I had hoped that winter snow would blanket the difficulties, helping me to move fast, but the skim was too thin for that. With speed I had hoped to avoid bivouacking, or at least limit myself to just one night out. Now even the prospect of one bivouac was horrific. Over to the east, the familiar silhouettes of the Dom and Täschorn were looking murky under a veil of cloud. Here on the Matterhorn the wind had returned, blasting snow off the summit and even flinging lumps of ice through the air. I felt very small and very vulnerable and, to make matters even worse, the tip of one woollen Dachstein mitt was wearing through. If I continued up into the maelstrom I would probably die; at the very least I would get frostbite. It simply wasn't worth it.

What a relief to turn round.

I started down at 12.30 a.m., downclimbing where possible, abseiling on the harder sections. With only twenty-five metres of doubled rope for these diagonal abseils it was a laborious business. As for the anchors, I felt a pang of regret at leaving behind one of my home-made 'hexcentric' nuts. I had spent hours drilling, sawing and filing that lump of alloy donated by the Charlwood blacksmith, perfecting the asymmetric hexagon.

Only at 5.00 p.m. did I get back to the big ice/snowfield. Then I could speed up – half kicking, half sliding in a controlled glissade down tilted cushions of deep winter powder, down, down, down – racing the darkness.

Glancing down into the blue shadows, I jerked suddenly to a halt, panting in terror, slumped above a great emptiness.

The bergschrund! I had completely forgotten about the big crevasse which marks the break between ice field and glacier, because I had missed it when coming up a different way before dawn. Somehow, some dormant sixth sense had kicked in at the last minute. Thank God. And thank goodness He was the only person to witness my embarrassment. Trembling and chastened, I edged sideways above the void, finally finding a snow bridge where I could ease across and lower myself safely down onto the big glacier shelf.

The wind was now shrieking at me, battering me, flinging snow spume against my spectacles. My hands were numb and my whole body was shivering, trembling with nervous shock. Staggering wildly in the darkness, following the dim torch beam, I fought my way home through the tempest, a medieval peasant fleeing the shrieking demons that guarded the mountain. At nine o'clock I stumbled, white and frozen, through the window of the hut and collapsed, shivering, on the floor, only gradually finding the will to make my numb fingers undo frozen crampon straps and remove the steel spikes from my feet so that I could fall into bed and bury myself under a heap of blankets.

When I woke the next morning the demons were still howling. Walking back down from the hut to the point where I had left my skis three days earlier I was twice blown flat on my face. As I fiddled with the bindings, I realised that I dared not ski northward back to Zermatt as I had planned: the wind was too strong, so I would have to drop down the south-east flank of the ridge. I was just about to do that when I noticed that my fully loaded rucksack had disappeared, blown over the edge. Luckily it had gone the right way and, after climbing down with my skis, I found it lying in the snow. From there, more sheltered from the wind, I could ski safely back down to the cable-car station. And so back to Zermatt where at the Bahnhof Hotel Fräulein Biner lambasted me for taking irresponsible risks.

Perhaps my Matterhorn outing *was* irresponsible; I felt I had handled it quite well, knowing when to turn back, getting myself out of a fix. But it had frightened me. Never before had I felt quite so weak and vulnerable, so cowed by seemingly malevolent forces; never had dreams of glory been so resoundingly squashed.

The experience was so shocking that I almost succeeded in giving up climbing. Busy that summer with photography, I hardly touched a rock at all. In the autumn, dropping in to Oxford to see two stunning Mozart productions by my old colleagues on Glyndebourne Touring Opera, I longed to be immersed in the good things of civilisation, doing something creative. But what? One studio photographer looked at some of my earliest black and white prints and said, 'They're crap.' Then he suggested that I spend a few years working as an assistant, living on a pittance, driven by pure dedication. Did I have that kind of dedication? That single-minded conviction that this was the one thing I wanted to do?

In the end, like most people, I settled for a compromise. Ever since I'd been a teenager I had been tempted by the possibility of teaching. I liked the notion of sharing ideas and enthusiasms. And for all my abhorrence of team games, I rather liked the idea of being part of a community. And, of course, I was tempted by the prospect of holidays sufficiently long to pursue my own interests.

So I signed up for a return to university in October 1979 to do a Postgraduate Certificate in Education. In the meantime, thanks to an introduction from a mutual friend, I went to Oxford to be interviewed for a temporary teaching post at England's most prestigious prep school, The Dragon. One of the geography teachers was having a sabbatical. Would I like to fill in for the spring and summer term, and get a taste of teaching? And could I also do some English, and perhaps a few French lessons? The salary would be the basic teacher's starting rate; food and accommodation would be free. The fact that I had not seen a geography textbook since I was thirteen and had only just scraped through French O level didn't seem to matter. It was too good an offer to turn down. So, after spending New Year's Eve 1978 on a magical, glittering traverse of the Mamore mountains near Ben Nevis, I started my first, albeit temporary, salaried job, in Oxford.

The Dragon is a large school – probably the largest prep school in the country – with over five hundred children, who in 1979 were still almost exclusively boys. Although the school has probably produced more famous writers, academics, entrepreneurs and cabinet ministers than any other junior school in Britain, it caters for a wide range of abilities, and classes are streamed rigorously. My work was confined to the E Block, with the eight-to-nine-year-olds. Most of my time was with the lowest form but I taught Geography to all six forms in the year, starting with a project on islands around the world. Most scary was the top set of extremely bright, provocative eight-year-olds racing several steps ahead, with one precocious child asking me in my very first lesson to explain tectonic-plate theory.

After islands, I moved on to the Himalaya, and then Antarctica, which prompted one of those moments that make it all seem worthwhile. I was telling a class about Scott's ill-fated trek to the South Pole and had got to the doomed retreat over the Ross Ice Shelf when there was an interruption from a colleague collecting a book. Normally this would be an excuse for mayhem; but this time there was just quiet tension, with one boy putting up his hand and pleading, 'Sir, can we go on with the story?' We also spent some time on Shackleton's epic escape from the wreck of the *Endurance* and in a rare burst of dedication I stayed up for several nights preparing wall displays of Frank Hurley's legendary photos. Cutting and pasting into the early hours, I played one of Fats Waller's records over and over again; and for me those great empty white spaces of the far south are still associated indelibly with Fats Waller's masterful piano playing and funny, gravelly bass.

January 1979 was cold. While Jim Callaghan clung on in Downing Street, trying to survive his Winter of Discontent, at The Dragon the country's future power-brokers worked hard and played hard. One sub-zero night I took my turn rolling and hosing the school's whitened lawn on Bardwell Road, compacting snow to ice until my own hands froze and I was called in to drink a large tumbler of whisky with the two headmasters, Inky and Gov. The following day, at break time, hundreds of children took turns to skate on the transformed lawn. In their inimitably scruffy corduroy uniforms, dark on white, they looked like a scene from Breughel.

My own chance to play in the snow came during the Easter holidays, joining friends and family for a fortnight's indolent piste-skiing in Italy, then dashing up to the old Théodul Hut, on the frontier ridge between Cervinia and Zermatt, for six days' serious play.

First I soloed Pollux. Then, when he turned up from Britain, David Lund and I traversed the other heavenly twin, Castor, finishing with a stunning descent of the Zwillings Glacier, glad of others' tracks to navigate through a hummocky labyrinth of crevasses. Bad weather prompted David to bail out while I holed up at the Monte Rosa Hut, then skied back up to the Théodul to collect some gear and shoot down to Zermatt, meeting David, Roger Everett and my old sparring partner, Bill Stevenson, just as they were catching the Gornergrat train to come back up again. So I turned straight round and accompanied them back to the Monte Rosa Hut and the next day we all climbed Monte Rosa's highest summit, the Dufourspitze, the highest peak in the Alps after Mont Blanc. That seemed to satisfy the others, but I was greedy to fill the last day before driving home, so I stayed a final night at the hut and left before dawn to ski up the Grenz Glacier, dump planks at the top and continue on foot up the dramatic knife-edge of the Lyskamm. Once I had returned to my skis, all I had to do was enjoy three thousand metres of continuous descent to Zermatt.

Those six days of sun and snow, speed and movement, of pastel-pink dawns with the air cold and crisp in the nostrils, of hot white afternoons gliding down every consistency of snow from fluffy powder to sludgy porridge, of lingering melancholic sunsets, of living in and amongst some of the most famous mountains in the world, climbing four 4,000-metre summits in quick succession ... they suddenly brought back all the joy and tingling aliveness which had been bludgeoned by my Matterhorn fright eleven months earlier. Returning to a blossom-scented Oxford for the summer term I knew that I would not, after all, be giving up the mountains; there was too much to lose.

Several weekends that term I sneaked away to North Wales, or to the Avon Gorge, and all too often during the week, when I should have been marking exercise books, I sat in my room poring over maps, calculating, dreaming, imagining, planning that summer's trip to the Himalaya.

The plan was simple: fly to Delhi with just enough cash to survive for two months in the subcontinent. The first month we would spend in the arid mountains around Hunza, in north-west Pakistan; the second in the verdant Kishtwar region of Indian Kashmir. My youngest brother Philip had just graduated from Oxford with a Botany degree and his friend Jonathan Dawson was halfway through a medical degree in London. None of us had much money so it would be a shoestring venture. I still had the fibre-pile climbing suit that my grandmother Maudie had made me; Philip had an outfit put together by his fiancée Caroline; Jonathan, a keen needleman aiming for a career in gastroenterological surgery, made himself a pair of flamboyant drainpipe trousers and matching top in fluorescent lime-green faux fur, with 'Cartier' embroidered in gold thread across the left breast.

We flew to Delhi on the cheapest available flight – Afghan Airways. The plane left Heathrow a day late, then dumped us for a night in Istanbul while refuelling charges were negotiated; so we dashed into the city centre for a nostalgic return to the Blue Mosque, self-appointed tour guides to two girls from Bristol University. The next day we flew on to Kabul, to be welcomed briefly to that 'Land of the New Model Revolution' before continuing over Waziristan, Sind and the Rajasthan desert to Delhi.

It's a travellers' cliché, but that first blast of hot, wet, slightly sour-smelling air as you emerge from air-conditioned cool *does* take you completely by surprise. This vegetative mugginess was quite different from the sharp dry mineral heat of Iran and Afghanistan and it seemed extraordinary that life could exist in such an oppressive climate. Thank God for Omid, I thought, as we took a taxi to the apartment of Our Man In Delhi, otherwise known as Stewart Dutfield, a friend from New College days who was working for the Delhi office of IBM. His flat didn't have air-conditioning, but it was a peaceful haven where we could shower, and then stand wet and cool beneath ceiling fans. That night Stewart took us to the café in Greater Kailash Market for our first masala dosa – a golden crisp, wafer-thin pancake wrapped around spiced potatoes, accompanied by coconut chutney and washed down with mango milk shakes.

Heading west, we stuck perforce to the shoestring ethic, taking a night bus up the Great Trunk Road, assailed for eight hours by shrill Bollywood songs blasting from cracked speakers. Even at dawn, Amritsar was sweltering, but things cheered up as we continued on another bus through fertile farmland, crossing that cruelly arbitrary line of 1947 which partitioned the Punjab – the land of the five rivers – between India and Pakistan, Sikh and Muslim. Late that evening we reached Rawalpindi and the next day we found a bus into Pakistan's new capital, Islamabad, to book a flight to the northern outpost of Gilgit.

Twice we took off in the little Fokker Friendship. Twice we stared down at the dark line of the Indus, carved deep into empty brown mountains. And twice the pilot did a U-turn, sent by bad weather back to Islamabad, where we resumed stations camping out in the lobby of the Restaurant In The Sky. Stewart arrived from Delhi and, rather than wait longer for a plane which might never reach its destination, we all decided to head north by road instead.

The Karakoram Highway, blasted with Chinese aid right through the greatest mountain range on earth, had only just been opened to foreigners and it took four days to get the special permit before we could set off, four pale ragged foreigners crammed incongruously into a busload of Hunza, Balti, Wakhi and Chitrali tribesmen. But it was worth the wait, for this is one of the world's great road journeys.

First a long climb through a comparatively green landscape. Then a winding descent to start the long grind up the Indus River, passing through the bandit lands of Chilas, where even the Pakistan *army* makes itself scarce. Hour after hour, the road follows the twists of the river, overhung by immense mountain walls blocking out the sky. You get occasional glimpses of pine forest clinging to high side valleys, but the river is locked into a hot dry cleft, barely a thousand metres above sea level. At this point, hundreds of miles from its source on the Tibetan plateau near the holy Mount Kailash, the Indus is a rubbish sluice, thick with the sediment of the Karakoram glaciers – ice-ground rock in a saturated solution the colour and consistency of unfiltered milky coffee. Its roar fills the valley and beneath that surface din you hear the deep rumble of trundling boulders. On a fine day there comes a point where you glimpse the white snows of Nanga Parbat, nearly seven thousand metres above the road. Then, barely noticeable between dark umber walls of desert-varnished rock, the Indus valley takes a sharp turn right into Baltistan, while the main Karakoram Highway continues north up the Gilgit River.

It was around here that we stopped at nightfall and everyone got out for a roadside meal of chapattis and goat curry. Then we lay down on the tarmac, staring up at the star-filled velvet sky while Jonathan bemused the locals by singing 'Glory, Glory, Hallelujah'. At dawn we continued a few miles to the cause of the unscheduled overnight halt – a huge landslide piled a hundred metres high across the road, with already a well-trampled footpath crossing the slope of shifting rubble. Another bus was waiting on the far side to take us to Gilgit and later that morning we took a final bus to enter the province of Hunza.

It had taken nearly two weeks to get here from Delhi and it felt like the Promised Land. It reminded me superficially of Badakhshan two years earlier – the same green and gold patterns in a mountain desert – but in Hunza the whole scale and colour and luminosity of the landscape was magnified. And at over two thousand metres the air at last felt fresh, cooled by the constant rush of water, milky white, siphoned off from high glaciers through a brilliant network of irri-gation channels which nurture a tapestry of terraced fields and orchards spread beneath gleaming summits.

As we camped that evening behind the fort of Baltit, the 'capital' of Hunza, at just over two thousand metres, it was extraordinary to think that the summit of Ultar was 5,300 metres above us – a height rise of three and a half vertical miles in just seven miles of horizontal distance. I wanted to explore approaches to the mountain for a possible attempt in the future, so in the morning we walked up the gorge behind our camp, following some shepherds to high meadows. After about a thousand metres, trying to get onto the Ultar Glacier, we were driven back by a barrage of falling stones; but it had been thrilling at last to be moving, free in this stunning landscape. We spent a contented evening back at our camp, supplementing freeze-dried 'Chicken Supreme' with lemons, lentils, fresh mountain thyme and apricots.

Apricots are the most famous produce of Hunza's orchards and we had arrived in high season. Every flat rooftop was spread with drying fruit, orange against the silvery patina of beaten mica-rich earth. There were also still masses of ripe apricots on the trees, and the next day, as we walked through the village of Altit, people told us to fill bags with the sweet succulent fruit. And, because the people of Hunza are Ishmaelis, following a less austere form of Islam than their Shia neighbours in Nagar on the far side of the river, the women, unveiled, chatted with us. There was one particularly fine encounter over the garden wall between a garrulous white-haired grandmother and Philip, the latter looking for all the world like the vicar he would one day become, listening politely to one of his more bossy parishioners. Stewart looked more the cool traveller and was extremely fit; eight years later he would win the first punishing Everest Marathon in Nepal. Jonathan just looked completely at ease, with himself, with Hunza, with the world – the perfect travelling companion.

Everyone was happy to be here, excited by the adventure, as we headed east towards the next gorge that I wanted to explore, following a path which led up above the irrigated fields onto a parched hillside pungent with the scent of spiky desert plants. We continued under a blazing sun, dazzled by the glare of mica dust, followed by a lone goat which seemed to think we were its masters. Eventually we reached the gorge I was looking for. I ran ahead, down steep rubble slopes, then followed a faint track along the crest of an old moraine gouged out by the glacier which had long since retreated high amongst granite spires and minarets. I raced on down to a glacial river and at last, after four hours without a drink, scooped up handfuls of icy water.

How wonderful to be thirsty no longer. How wonderful to have arrived in this wild secret valley, with its complexities still waiting to be explored. But where were the others? Why hadn't they come? I had been waiting for fifteen minutes when Stewart finally arrived alone, shouting urgently above the river's din.

Jonathan had slipped off the crest of the moraine. Philip had found him at the foot of a ten-metre vertical cliff of crumbling conglomerate, just regaining consciousness and asking what country he was in. By the time Stewart took me to Jonathan his face was swollen and purple. His right elbow was gashed open to the bone. He instructed us, guiding us through bandaging the wound and putting the arm in a sling, then bandaging his jaw, which he suspected was broken, knowing that if it were left unsupported he could suffer permanent disfigurement. Tutorial complete, the consummate showman asked us to take a photo – 'I know, I know: I'm so vain' – before we set off down,

But down where? The river plummeted into a precipitous

gorge, walled with polished granite. Even without an injured man, we'd never get down there. As for climbing two thousand feet back up the rubble slopes, and traversing all the way back round to Altit, that was unthinkable. It was now evening and I was beginning to get just slightly worried. Then I noticed the irrigation ditch – a miniature canal chipped and blasted out of the cliff, contained by a beautifully constructed stone wall about a foot high. It would have to do. I went first, padding carefully along the crest of the wall, poised over a drop of about two hundred metres. Philip followed, guiding Jonathan, insisting that he walk with his feet in the icy water, safe behind the containing wall, just in case he passed out. It was a touching sight – Jonathan with one arm bundled under the bloodied lime-green Cartier jacket, the other around the shoulder of his friend tiptoeing along the precarious wall, Stewart following behind with a monstrous double rucksack load, and behind him the goat which had followed us all the way from Altit.

The irrigation channel got us out of the secret valley and onto an easy path into the isolated village of Amattabad, where a doctor from Islamabad happened to be taking his summer holiday. He looked after Jonathan while the rest of us camped in the orchard of a friendly neighbour. The goat was never seen again, so perhaps it was turned into curry. The next day poor Jonathan had to walk another five miles under a blazing sun before we could reach the road and hire a jeep. Stewart was due back at work soon and said he would escort Jonathan back to Delhi.

Philip and I felt rather forlorn that evening, left by the side of the road, thrown on each other's company, bereft of Jonathan's leavening wit. But rising at dawn the next day, loneliness was subsumed in transcendent beauty. Rakaposhi, the giant of a mountain which towers above the south side of the Hunza valley, was gleaming white in a sky of purest, darkest lapis lazuli, unearthly, ethereal. For the next six days this gigantic pyramid dominated our journey as we walked up the Sumayer valley leading south from the main Hunza–Nagar valley. There were moments of enchantment, like that first dawn, walking briskly through the cool dewy orchards of Sumayer; and camping that night, higher up, cooking on a fire of juniper twigs and dried cow dung, lazing in a meadow full of thyme, pinks, gentians and pale yellow potentilla reminding me of the garden at home. And there were grimmer experiences, like the breakfast we cooked higher up, using nearly all our sugar supply in a vain attempt to sweeten the wild rhubarb and the rice pudding which wouldn't soften because we didn't have a pressure cooker. But we continued, across the Silkiang Glacier to a high terrace where we rested a day before leaving the tent and travelling light, crunching up a slope of crisp frozen snow and continuing over crevasses and along a white knife-edge to a summit of about 5,500 metres.

We called our mountain Peak Dawson in honour of the friend who we wished could be sharing this glorious moment. Apart from the very easy traverse of the Pigne d'Arolla five years earlier, Philip had never done any climbing at all, and here he had been understandably nervous on the knife-edge ridge, following me on the rope, instructed to jump to the left if I fell to the right, and vice versa. But any fear was forgotten in the joy of arriving. The best summits are often not the highest ones. Here, at just 5,500 metres, level with a point only halfway up Rakaposhi, we got the full measure of that massive pyramid, first climbed in 1958 by Mike Banks and the Ullapool doctor, Tom Patey. Turning clockwise, to the north, we could now see the great barrier of the Batura peaks and Ultar, with the gorges that we had explored with Jonathan and Stewart. Continuing to turn eastward, the vista became more visionary, more luminous, more infinite – our first real grasping of the endless immensity of the Karakoram Range, peak after peak spiking the sapphire sky, dazzling with the promise of future adventures. Most exciting of all was to look up the huge gash of the Hispar Glacier to glimpse the distant turrets of the Ogre and, even beyond them, nearly a hundred miles from where we stood, the pale blue triangle of K2.

We must have stayed at least an hour on our snowy dome,

soaking up the beauty and contentment of it all. It was Philip's first – and probably last – ascent of a previously unclimbed peak. My first, too, but I hoped it would be the first of many. After the glory, came the bathos – the descent through drizzle, the eking out of the last desultory breakfast, the rapid reduction to the common animal denominator of hunger, the gluttonous feasting back in Gilgit, and, determined to avoid the bus journey, the long wait for a flight back to Rawalpindi.

From Pindi, rather than suffer public buses, we took the infinitely more civilised train back to Amritsar and Delhi. *This* was the way to travel – this gentle, dependable infrastructure, with its wide-gauge carriages trundling across the endless agricultural plain of the Punjab, its arcane rituals, its unvarying routine and its matchless fast food, in particular the platform stalls selling chickpea curry in banana-leaf bowls, accompanied by a stack of sizzling deep-fried puris. On the trains we began to relax and enjoy the subcontinent. We were also growing accustomed to the humid heat of the plains, realising that you can actually survive and be happy in those conditions.

Back in Delhi, chez Omid, we feasted on the creamy buffalo-milk yogurt which came in huge earthenware pots, and spent evenings on the verandah drinking neo-colonial whisky and soda, on one occasion going to dinner with the Mehtas, whom we had met on the plane, staying up late to play Noel Coward songs on their piano. It was good to see Jonathan again. Afghan Airways had still not managed to fly him home, and he was enduring a course of painful buttock-piercing penicillin injections. (He had also seen a dentist and declined the offer to have several apparently loose teeth yanked out – a sensible refusal, as his initial self-diagnosis had been correct: his jaw, as he later discovered, was actually broken in seven places.) Ever stoical, he accompanied us on a day trip to Agra, subsuming boredom and disappointment in the theatrical pearly translucence of the Taj Mahal. And then we parted again, Jonathan for home, Philip and I for Kashmir.

*   *   *

Ever since seeing some photos in a back copy of the *Alpine Journal* – and slides at one of Chris Bonington's lectures – I had dreamed of visiting a particular corner of Kashmir called Kishtwar. So, laden with provisions, we off set on the night sleeper to Jammu, capital of the troubled state of Jammu and Kashmir. From there it was a long hard day on the bus to the town of Kishtwar where, in 1979, Hindus and Muslims still lived peacefully side by side, then another bus to a collection of dusty hovels where the road petered out into a mule track.

In an ideal world Philip and I would have travelled with a luxurious bandobast of several well-loaded mules. But our budget was nearly used up, so we stuck to the shoestring principle, splashing out on just one human carrier to reduce slightly our rucksack loads, hoping that we would see him four days later when we reached a village called Machail.

After the austere desert beauty of the Karakoram, Kishtwar was a 'green thought in a green shade' – a sylvan balm to European sensibilities, an oriental version of our own Alps. For two days we followed the Chenab River – one of the five great tributaries of the Indus – the path undulating high above the water through a forest of deodar cedar and holm oak where the mules got high munching cannabis fodder. After two days the valley broadened into a green shelf at the village of Atholi. Staying at the house of a man called Surjeet Singh, we were taken to bathe in the hot spring of Tatopani, and were fed delicious dinners of home-cooked vegetables and made to drink the local potato wine while Surjeet asked earnestly, 'Are you feeling intoxication?' In these final years before the road was blasted through the valley to alter everything, goods could only arrive slowly by mule, so that our nicotine-hungry bodies had to wait a day for the arrival of the Gold Flake cigarettes. Life was lived simply, as Surjeet stressed: 'Here in Atholi, we have very good mantelpiece.'

'Mantelpiece?'

'Yes – mentalpeace . . . much mentalpeace, far from hue and cry of city.'

From Atholi we left the Chenab and followed a tributary

valley northward for two days. There was sporadic traffic of mule trains and families taking the chance to travel a route which in winter is closed because of avalanche danger. All along the path we found tattered remains of raffia sandals – the perfect biodegradable disposable footwear – but government officials were more pukkah, with their leather shoes and briefcases, striding briskly through the forest, doing their bit to maintain India's miraculous infrastructure which reaches out to every remotest corner of the subcontinent.

At the village of Machail we found and paid our porter, added his load to our rucksacks, and continued up another valley, stopping to camp just beyond the first Buddhist village, where the people suddenly looked completely different, with their Tibetan faces. The men wore close-fitting homespun tweed suits; the women long aprons and magnificently jewelled nose pendants. For a few rupees we bought a bowlful of freshly boiled new potatoes, accompanied by a lump of rock salt – the timeless currency of Himalayan trade between the Tibetan lands to the north and the predominantly Hindu/Muslim lands to the south of the mountain divide. The grandfather of the household was puffing contentedly on a hubble-bubble and offered me a drag. I suddenly felt deliriously light-headed and the whole world had a new, intense luminosity; it didn't taste like cannabis, so perhaps it was opium.

We continued further up the valley and were invited to take tea – a dark red milky brew – sitting beside a fire with two turbaned young Gujar men. The Gujars are nomads, whose origins are debated endlessly by scholars. One theory is that they came originally from the west, from Persia, to settle in the land now called Gujarat. Then they moved north and in the eleventh century they converted to Islam. They were subsequently shunned by Hindus and became nomadic, bringing huge flocks of sheep, goats, horses – and sometimes buffalo – up into the mountains each summer, returning to the cities for the winter.

Philip and I now climbed beyond the range of normal transhumance, trying to cross a pass called the Hagshu La. Thanks to my inability to read the lie of the land we missed the obvious pass and laboured wearily to a much higher ridge, only to be confronted with a hideous fifty-degree slope of grey ice snaking out of sight down the far side. Philip stated, not unreasonably, that he didn't fancy going down the slope, particularly as we had only one pair of crampons between us. We retraced our steps and then failed to find the better-known Umasi La.

Or, rather, we had lost the will to find it. We had now been in the subcontinent for seven weeks. Travelling on a very tight budget, with limited load-carrying capacity, we had simply got too hungry and too thin. Several doses of diarrhoea hadn't helped. And now all the mosquito bites on my ankles were turning septic. We were just falling to pieces.

So I had to abandon my cherished plan of crossing the main Himalayan divide to Zanskar and return instead to Kishtwar, the way we had come. Philip didn't seem to mind; in fact, he had probably had enough of my relentless slave-driving and was longing to get back to his fiancée Caroline. But I was disappointed and that disappointment was pricked on the journey back to Kishtwar.

We were sheltering from the rain in a smoke-blackened tea house in the forest, and, having run out of tobacco, were drying fresh cannabis leaves on a hot stone. Suddenly we groaned at the sight of a pink European face striding towards us through the rain. 'Oh no – some bloody Brit!' we groaned peevishly, resentful at this intrusion on our exclusive journey. Until I suddenly recognised the big wide smiling face, with the ginger sideburns and balding cranium: it must be Paul Nunn. His articles and stories had been one of my great inspirations – particularly his tales of prodigious Himalayan explorations. Now here he was, spending the evening with us, sharing our fast-dried spliffs – which seemed to have no narcotic effect whatsoever and went off like bangers every time one of the cannabis seeds caught light – telling us about his recent attempt on a mountain above Machail called Barnaj, reminiscing about other Himalayan adventures, dropping famous climbing names like Anthoine and Boysen, and dreaming plans for the future, before disappearing at dawn to walk forty-five miles in a day back to Kishtwar in order to get home in time for the first day of term at Sheffield Polytechnic where he lectured in history.

Paul's huge laughing energy was inspiring and put my pathetic little disappointment into perspective. There would be other journeys, other possibilities; one just had to keep working at it, and, above all, keep enjoying it. Of course it had been frustrating not to complete the big circuit – the crossing to Zanskar – but the line between 'success' and 'failure' is a blurred ambiguous thing, open to interpretation. By trying to cross the Hagshu La, Philip and I had enjoyed five days in a deserted hanging valley of exquisite beauty, walking through meadows brimming with flowers, camping beside crystal lakes. Coming back down the valley there had been a morning of autumnal enchantment – the kind of blue, frosty, glittery dawn which is more luminously intense than any opium vision could ever be – and, framed in the V of our valley, I had been entranced by the dazzling architecture of a mountain called Shivling – Kishtwar-Shivling. It was the very essence of mountain – the total perfection of everything a mountain should be. Unknown, untouched, aloof, but also alluring. A vision to take home and dream about.

One day, perhaps, I would come back. In the meantime, I had to get on with the business of training to become a full-time teacher.

Chapter Six

Sod's Law Peak

The old lady looked me up and down. Her scrutiny paused on my wire-rimmed spectacles. 'I'm not sure about the glasses: you look a bit of an intellectual. But are you practical? I do like brains; but I like brains *and* a screwdriver.' She peered closer. 'Do you know how to use a screwdriver?'

Lady Weare had an arrangement with the Oxford council to let condemned houses to students at a very low rent, with all the proceeds going to her pet charities. It was a brilliant idea, but open to abuse, and she was having trouble with a punk-rock group which was refusing to leave a crumbling Edwardian house at the far end of the Woodstock Road. 'The place is in a frightful mess and they owe three hundred pounds in electricity bills. I removed two of their electronic guitars and I have them here, under my bed – I said they can have them back when they've paid their bills. Anyway, if you think you can sort out the mess, you had better move in.'

Philip and I had already fallen in love with the ivy-clad pile we called Gormenghastly. We were both spending the year in Oxford doing post-graduate certificates of education; our second cousin James Ogilvie, nephew of the James who had died on the Matterhorn, was doing a BSc in Forestry and we were all looking for somewhere cheap to live. So, with Lady Weare's blessing, we moved in, repelling the punk rockers with our bourgeois mending, mopping and cleaning. Then a botanist friend of Philip's, Richard Henderson, decided that he wanted to come back and spend some more time in Oxford, so he took another of the large rooms. There was also a painter, whose name I have forgotten, and, in the attic, Jennifer who was doing an MA in French literature.

Philip returned from his first day at the Oxford University education department with the news that teaching was 'a highly motivating experiential phenomenon'; at Westminster College – the Methodist teacher-training establishment on the southern edge of Oxford – I had discovered the difference between phatic communion and ideation. Of course it was easy to scoff – in my case the lecturers were just trying to develop a greater awareness of language, explaining the gulf between the trite 'hello-chilly-for-the-time-of-year-isn't-it' conventions of 'phatic communion' and the genuinely meaningful exchange of concepts in 'ideation' – but there did seem to be an awful lot of psycho-sociological baggage attached to the course and I was not very good at hiding my contempt. I also struggled to accept the prevailing orthodoxy of mixed-ability teaching. And I refused – and still refuse – ever to call the children 'kids'.

I probably should have worked harder at the teacher training, but life had too many other attractions on offer, too many influences to absorb. At Gormenghastly Richard was busy making ebony and boxwood chessboards to supplement his income from biology coaching. He also taught me how to make fennel salads and mayonnaise and chocolate mousse and vine-leaf dolmades; and on the honky-tonk piano in the dining room he introduced us to the mesmerising harmonies of one of Bach's most extraordinary organ pieces, the Fantasia and Fugue in G minor. Philip and I were also rediscovering Wagner and I spent hours hammering out on the same twangy instrument a cacophonic travesty of the score which we are told changed the course of music in 1865 (the same year that the Matterhorn was first climbed) – *Tristan and Isolde*.

It was wonderful to have another year in Gerard Manley Hopkins's city, 'leafy amongst towers', but living this time on the margins, overlooking Port Meadow, where we could walk or run beside the Thames, heading for those Binsey poplars also celebrated by Hopkins. As an undergraduate five years earlier, I had missed so much. Now for the first time I saw Samuel Palmer's visionary jewelled landscapes at the Ashmolean; and in the intimate oval of the Hollywood Music Room heard the Allegri Quartet performing the Beethoven string quartets, never guessing that one day the cellist, Bruno Schrecker, would be a neighbour and friend.

Two relatives happened to live within five minutes' walk of Gormenghastly. Several times I visited Alan Richards, one of my mother's uncles, who in the 1920s used to 'motor' out to the Alps and do a bit of climbing, and who in Oxford had worked in the same medical practice as Graham Greene's brother Raymond, a mountaineer who had been on the 1933 Everest expedition.

Uncle Alan was quite diffident. Mary Ogilvie – my father's aunt, James's grandmother – was a tall extrovert woman who enjoyed being with the young. A passionate champion of women's education, her final job had been as head of the Oxford women's college St Anne's. As an undergraduate, she had been one of the callow young girls, fresh from school, who had entered Somerville College in 1919, angering the older Vera Brittain with their apparent lack of sympathy for the trauma that the Great War veterans had just suffered. If Mary *had* been ignorant she had soon made up for it, marrying a young don, Freddie Ogilvie, who had been wounded and gassed in the trenches and who as a result would die comparatively young after a life of indifferent health. Between 1938 and 1942 he was Director General of the BBC, handling the Corporation's treatment of momentous events such as the abdication crisis, Munich and the start of the Second World War. Aunt Mary talked about the times she had brought Churchill his cup of tea (surely champagne?) during his legendary broadcasts and about Freddie's reluctance to bury bad news: 'In the end he had to resign; Brendan Bracken, the Minister of Information, forced him out, you see – because

he wouldn't agree about the BBC being used for propaganda.'
She also talked fondly of her son James who had died on the
Matterhorn in 1948. She showed us the diary he had kept as
a young soldier travelling round the Indian subcontinent in
1946, visiting the Himalaya, soaking it all up, filled with youthful
wonder and idealism, adamant that India's imminent independ-
ence was long overdue.

Spring burst upon us in showers of white cherry blossom
and Richard began to unearth the buried glories of
Gormenghastly's overgrown garden. In a rare attempt to get
fit, I started running through the buttercups on Port Meadow,
lolloping alongside the masochistic oarsmen on the Thames,
or getting up early for dawn bicycle rides into the hillier country
to the east; I also continued to bicycle down the canal to Botley,
putting in statutory appearances at Westminster College, or to
the Iffley Road to do teaching practice in one of the big
comprehensive schools. I also managed to fit in a couple of
weekends in North Wales, rock-climbing with a phenomenally
talented student called Simon Richardson. And an evening in
the Lake District with an old friend, Phil Budden, on the back
of an interview in Keswick – one of several jobs I failed to
get.

Failed interviews notwithstanding, life was busy, bursting
with possibilities, and I seemed to be running on adrenalin,
generally sleeping only four or five hours a night, sometimes
less; and the sense of hungry urgency was intensified by final
preparations for that summer's expedition. My old mentor,
Lindsay Griffin, tempted by my 'reconnaissance' of the
previous summer, had suggested an attempt on Ultar – the
huge unclimbed peak in Pakistan's Hunza valley. Also keen was
Phil Bartlett. He shared Lindsay's laconic manner and had the
same passion for exploring esoteric corners of the world's
mountains. As an undergraduate I had hardly known him.
He had been one of the elite stars of the mountaineering
club – one of the in-crowd – and it was only recently we had
discovered that we seemed to get on quite well together.

We were all set for a three-man trip to Ultar when Lindsay

had an accident on the Anglesey sea cliffs which left him with serious injuries that would take many months to mend. It was a cruel shock, reducing Phil and me to a rather vulnerable two-man team, wondering about trying a slightly easier Hunza peak, hoping to sneak in unofficially, with no expensive permit or accompanying military liaison officer.

Then along came Dave Wilkinson. I remembered meeting him and his Edwardian beard in Chamonix four years earlier. He was older and more experienced than us. He also had an official permit to climb in Pakistan and a grant from the Mount Everest Foundation. And a newspaper deal in the pipeline. His only problem was that he was the sole member of his expedition. We went up to Birmingham, where he taught computer studies at the Polytechnic, and agreed to join forces.

It was very exciting and rather frightening. Dave's permit was for a peak called Kunyang Kish. At 7,850 metres, close to the magic eight-thousand mark, it was the twenty-second-highest mountain in the world. It had only been climbed once, in 1971, by a large Polish expedition led by a charming man called Andrej Zawada whom I had met in Kabul in 1977. One member of his team had died in a crevasse. Both previous attempts on the mountain had also resulted in fatalities. As for Dave's proposal – to attempt a completely new route up the north side of the mountain, based on a picture by the famous Blackpool photographer and Everest veteran Alf Gregory – this head-on view looked terrifying. And what about the altitude? On Noshaq, three years earlier, I had ground to a halt just short of seven thousand metres. Was I actually cut out for these Himalayan giants?

There was only one way to find out, and I threw myself into preparations, lured by visions of treading high in the sky where no one had been before. A fortnight before departure I went for an interview at a school in York and was offered a post teaching English and running the school orchestra. Bolstered by that promise of financial security, I rushed through a final whirl of parties at Gormenghastly, interspersed with sessions on Jennifer's sewing machine, making a new fibre-pile suit, adapting my father's old ski trousers and improving my rucksack. On the last Thursday, after sitting a final education exam, I took the train to Glyndebourne, where Anthony Butler, a friend in Props, had invited me to a new production of *Rosenkavalier* with a flamboyantly camp set by Erté. It was good to soak up all that lush gorgeousness; then dash back to London to see brother Mark – who drove me down to Bath to say goodbye to the rest of the family – before returning to Oxford where Dave arrived to pick me up on the Sunday afternoon and take me to Heathrow. England in July was very beguiling and it required a conscious act of resolve to say farewell and head again for those austere Karakoram mountains.

The journey was familiar from the previous summer's jaunt, but this was 'The 1980 British West Karakoram Expedition', complete with official permit and a charming liaison officer, Major Wali Khan, who came from Hunza and was pleased to be heading up the Karakoram Highway to his home territory. He was a handsome man with a fine moustache and twinkly eyes. He looked glossy beside the scrofulous foreigners entrusted to his care: Dave's beard was already getting unruly; I looked skinny before we had even reached the mountain, disreputable in my grubby shalwar kameez; Phil just looked puny.

'It's all in the mind,' I kept telling myself, 'all a matter of will.' And for all our lack of surface gloss, there was some good solid experience there. Dave, inured to bureaucracy by years of Polytechnic committee meetings, seemed actually to enjoy tussling with the various ministries in Islamabad, ploughing methodically through the paperwork. He also had a long track record of multi-day climbs: he was solid and reliable. Phil was more mercurial, driven by nervous energy, reliant on flashes of inspiration. Sometimes in the future he would suddenly drop out of an expedition, deciding that he would rather be at home with his violin, playing the Bach partitas or improvising Irish folk with his friends in the pub. But on this occasion he was focused totally on the mountain, always pushing ahead, always – infuriatingly – fitter and faster than Dave and me, indisputably a stronger climber. It was only later that I discovered he had been doing secret training all summer, running several times every evening up and down the only hill in Northwich, where he taught in a sixth-form college.

In my book that was tantamount to cheating. However, I too felt quite driven: I had made the decision that for seven weeks I would suspend disbelief, convincing myself that this mountain – this obscure object of our perverse desires – was to be the totality of my life.

After a week of shopping and packing, we set off from Islamabad, driving through dark muddy streets at two-thirty in the morning, shop shutters already being hauled up and tilley lamps burning, tailors sorting their bolts of cloth, ironmongers inventorying, grocers stacking shelves . . . and everywhere groups of men and boys – but no women – huddled round paraffin stoves eating their chapattis before cockcrow announces the start of the first fasting day of Ramadan.

We start up the long grinding Karakoram Highway, dicing with death on the crumbling edge of the Indus, resigned to the brinkmanship between bus drivers and manic truckies in their magnificent cabs decorated like illuminated medieval manuscripts. The wayside stalls are closed for Ramadan and we survive discreetly on banana-cream biscuits. Then we enjoy a brief interlude in the calm oasis of the Hunza Inn, recovering from final shopping in the Gilgit bazaar, where the temperature approaches one hundred degrees Fahrenheit. Then we continue to the Hunza valley, this time crossing by jeep to the other side, into the Shia province of Nagar, where Wali takes us to meet the Mir, who offers us exquisite almonds and apricots and is politely amazed by my ignorance of test cricket. As well as being an expert on cricket he speaks fluent English, Urdu, the Gilgit language Shina, and the Hunzakuts' Burushashki, which is not related to any other language in the world. Then we spend a day waiting amongst the rustling poplars while Wali does business with the Tessildar – the district administrator – signing on sixteen porters, each of whom presses a purple thumbprint onto his typed contract which we all know is meaningless in the real Karakoram marketplace. Then off we go, with a cheerful shout of 'Salaam Aleikum', each man lashing a hessian sack to his back with a skilful arrangement of plaited goat-hair straps.

To get to Kunyang Kish we had to walk up the gorge of the Hispar River. During the first night in the gorge it rained and the following morning some men coming the other way gesticulated excitedly, warning us of water-loosened rocks. Ten minutes later the trail disappeared beneath a steep slope of smooth scree. It looked innocuous enough and my only fear was of slipping down into the river: anyone falling into that maelstrom would almost certainly be drowned.

Halfway across Phil and I waited at some solid rocks just above the seething water. Looking up the huge slope, I shouted blithely, 'What a good scree run: imagine that on Scafell.' Then a couple of small stones came bouncing chirpily down the slope. 'Ah – the stonefall,' laughed Phil, but within seconds we both stopped laughing as more stones came clattering down, whirling and bouncing from a thousand metres above. Phil ran further along the river bank; I cowered behind the largest boulder I could find, rucksack held over my head. The clatter crescendoed to a violent barrage, whirring and crashing all around us, exploding, splintering and thudding into the river with percussive booms.

The bombardment lasted at least a minute. Several boulders flew straight over my head, one crashing into the river a few inches from my feet; one smaller rock landed on my protecting rucksack.

It was interesting to see how I reacted – there was no panicky terror, just a dull fear and curiosity about whether my legs would be smashed or whether a rock would eventually get my head – whether I would be killed outright, or just horribly injured. I felt terribly lonely and it was only after the barrage finished and I ran on towards Phil, fleeing the last trickle of pebbles, that I realised all sixteen porters had been caught out in the open.

Allah must have been feeling merciful that day. Apart from minor cuts and bruises to three of the men – and a very large dent in the tin kitchen box – there was no damage. But the rockfall did drive home the savagery of this Karakoram landscape where everything is in constant flux. For the fifteen hundred or so people who lived in Hispar, this unstable gorge was the only exit to the outside world.

After three days we reached the village, a cluster of adobe houses nestled amongst barley fields, with the huge black tongue of the Hispar Glacier lolling just beyond the fields, filling the bed of the valley with rubble. But once we had crossed the glacier and climbed up over the gouged conglomerate wall of the lateral moraine, we entered the utterly different world of the ablation valley – an enchanted sanctuary of clear babbling streams, grassy meadows and rose bushes. Moving in leisurely stages – the whole walk-in could at a pinch be done in two days, but the porters take six to maximise their pay – we ambled at last to Base Camp, paid the porters and settled into home. It was then that Wali announced that he had just got married and was hoping to see his bride in Gilgit. Would we mind if he left us to it? Of course we wouldn't mind; and while he was about it, we asked him if he would take home the useless cook he had hired for the expedition: it would be easier and cheaper to do our own cooking.

So we were left alone to see if we could make any impression on Kunyang Kish – three tiny humans, camped in a meadow nearly four thousand metres – thirteen thousand feet – below the summit. Just getting to what we grandly called Advance Base – a single tent pitched on the ice – was a four-hour slog up the Kunyang Glacier, traipsing repeatedly over a wasteland of rubble-strewn hummocks, carrying food, gas, stoves and climbing gear, stocking up for the climb ahead.

It was hard labour under the blazing Karakoram sun, but it was thrilling to be alone in that huge cirque, enclosed by gigantic 'seven-thousanders'. Trivor had been climbed just once, by Wilfrid Noyce – the man who had taught at my school. Distaghil Sar had been attempted by Alf Gregory, then climbed later by Wolfgang Stefan, a friend of the famous Austrian mountaineer Kurt Diemberger. Bularang Sar had never been climbed, but one day, walking alone to a high ablation valley, Dave met a twelve-man Japanese team attempting the mountain. They were extremely well organised and, ensconced for the whole summer, they had brought up chickens for fresh eggs and meat; they had even planted a vegetable garden.

In contrast to the methodical Japanese siege, four Poles had just made a lightning raid on the outlying summits of Distaghil Sar. One day they passed through our base camp on the way home.

They were enormous. The earth thundered beneath their boots, and immense rucksacks towered above their shaggy bearded faces, because they could not afford to hire porters for the return journey to Nagar. Stopping to chat, they crushed Phil's violin fingers with their devastating handshakes and cast disdainful glances over the three of us, wondering how on earth these puny weaklings thought they were going to climb a mountain. Later, I realised that they were amongst the elite of Poland's legendary Himalayan climbers, hardened by cold winters in the Tatra, determined to escape Communist oppression through Himalayan achievement. It was a tough, uncompromising school and one of the men we met, Tadeusz Piotrowski, would fall to his death six years later whilst descending from the summit of K2.

We might have looked weak and amateurish but we were actually very determined to succeed on Dave's dream project. I was enjoying the gradual familiarisation and naming of parts. The idea was to climb up a huge spur – the north-west spur – which swept up to a height of about seven thousand metres, where it abutted against the North Ridge. From there it would be another 850 metres to the summit of Kunyang Kish. After several days' exploration, all the while acclimatising gradually to the thin air, it was Dave who spotted a sneaky back passage which he called the *Garadh Gully*, because it was a gigantic version of a vaguely similar feature on Ben Nevis.

On 3 August, one month after leaving England, we set off for the first time up the *Garadh Gully*, leaving at 4.10 a.m., climbing by torchlight. The gully neatly bypassed a huge icefall and from its top we could traverse easily to the foot of *Broad Gully* – a huge ice slope leading onto the crest of our Northwest Spur. On this slope I succumbed to despair, slumped against my ice axe, lolling on the ice, staring up resentfully at Dave plodding ahead. And at Bartlett – why can't the bastard wait for a moment? Why isn't he feeling as terrible as I am?

I gave up a hundred metres short of the crest, unable to carry my load all the way, and descended gloomily, envious of Phil and Dave's excited chatter, unable to share the thrill of unlocking the mountain's secrets. But two days later everything was different. Setting off at 1.30 a.m. I felt at peace with the world, entranced by the starry sky. I added the previous load to my rucksack and by 6.30 a.m. was on the crest, taking photos of Phil forging ahead, a blue silhouette racing along a twisting white ribbon. At one point the crest narrowed to crumbly knife-edge, so we traversed on the steep flank, tiptoeing beneath a fantastic gargoyle festooned with icicles. We called this section the *Dance of the Sugar Plum Fairy* and just beyond it we stopped to dig a snow-cave which we called Camp One.

Why not pitch a tent? Answer: because tents are heavy and you have to carry them on your back and they get buried in storms. This was 1980 and we were emulating the new wave of Himalayan superstars – people like Messner, Habeler, Scott, Rouse, Béghin, Kurtyka, Boardman and Tasker, who were showing how even the biggest, hardest climbs could be done by very small teams, travelling fast and light.

It is a satisfying way to climb, but it is very hard work. At two a.m. the next morning the alarm rang for at least a minute before I agreed to rouse myself from contented sleep. We got away from the snow-hole at three-thirty and by nine o'clock had climbed right to the top of the spur, emerging onto the crest of the North Ridge into a dazzling vision of pristine peaks stretching north all the way to the distant giants of Kongur and Mustagh Ata, over a hundred miles away in Sinkiang.

There was only one snag. We had emerged on the left side of a small subsidiary peak, hoping to sneak round the back of it onto the start of the North Ridge of Kunyang Kish. That, we now realised, was impossible; so Dave, ever poetic, called the offending lump *Sod's Law Peak* – a sobriquet now immortalised on the official map of the Karakoram.

Never mind. Our brilliant reconnaissance had shown exactly where to go and, even though I had hated being Tail-end Charlie, I had nearly managed to keep up with the other two, reaching seven thousand metres without undue distress. After the Noshaq fiasco three years earlier in Afghanistan this was quite heartening: perhaps I *could* play this high-altitude game after all. Once we had rested at our base camp we should be able to climb the mountain in just a few days.

Back at base we ate huge lentil stews and debated tactics, Phil and I eager to get back up the mountain, Dave always more conservative, determined to rest fully before starting the next round of attrition. In the end Dave voted with his feet, arriving a day later than Phil and me at Camp One. While we waited, Phil and I talked inevitably of food and got round to the subject of the perfect Bircher Muesli, with bilberries and cream and grated apple, which started me on nostalgic reminiscences of Swiss holidays.

Returning to present reality, I was pleased to note that here at about 5,500 metres above sea level, my pulse rate was a respectable seventy. Ploughing onward the next morning, I took perverse pleasure in my own share of trail-breaking. Unable this time to go all the way to the crest of the North Ridge in a single push, we stopped to dig a snow-cave into the wall of a huge crevasse. Dinner that night was Chicken Cup-a-Soup, followed by 'Chicken & Mushroom Casserole', followed by coffee, two biscuits, one Aero bar and one mellow smouldering inch of a King Edward cigar.

The route we attempted on Kunyang Kish evaded neatly the 10,000ft high avalanche-raked North-West Face. The final section up the North Ridge was completed by another team in 1988.

We awoke to find ourselves buried alive. It had been snowing all night and, rather than risk continuing in dangerous conditions, we spent the day shovelling, trying to improve our temporary residence. Unfortunately we had dug the cave too shallow and that night, sleeping in the far corner, I had to fight claustrophobia as the roof sagged ever closer to my face.

A strange way to spend one's summer holidays. But we were committed, intoxicated by the very real possibility of completing this new route to one of the world's highest summits. So we continued, regaining the food cache we had left at seven thousand metres a week earlier, then traversing back down and up onto the summit of Sod's Law Peak, before continuing a short way along the North Ridge of Kunyang Kish proper to a convenient snow bulge where we excavated Camp Three. Later that afternoon, taking stock of food and gas supplies, we knew we had a real chance of the summit, even if we had to sit out a day or two of bad weather. Which was just as well, as it had started to snow, causing us to block the door with a plastic fertiliser bag. It was only when Phil suddenly keeled over semi-conscious that we realised our foolishness: we had cut off all air supply to the gas stove, which was now, instead of emitting harmless carbon dioxide, poisoning us with deadly monoxide.

The next day was to be Summit Ridge Day. Instead it snowed, as I noted in my diary: 'Saturday, 16 August. Marooned at Camp 3. 4.00 a.m. – Up for a crap. Vile wind and spindrift. 4.00–8.00 a.m. – Enlarge snow-hole. 8.30 a.m. – Weak tea with glucose, one cream cracker and sliver of cheese. Sleep. 12.30 a.m. – Clear doorway of spindrift. 1.00 p.m. – Lunch – cup-a-soup plus biscuit. 2.00–6.00 p.m. – Sleep. 5.00 p.m. – Phil clears avalanche snow from entrance. 5.30–7.30 p.m. – Supper – one portion of freeze-dried meal between three, followed by tea with two coconut biscuits and one Breakaway.'

Sunday was little different. 'Vile weather. Frequent blockages of doorway. Feeling lousy and sick with headache and feeling of claustrophobia. Conversation about Brahms's symphonies provided brief relief.'

'Monday. Hungry. Long conversation about meals we will have in Gilgit. Phil and Dave had a long and detailed discussion about all the transport cafés on the A74 between Carlisle and Glasgow.' I also noted rather gloomily that whereas Phil's pulse rate, even at seven thousand metres, was an impressively athletic sixty, mine was eighty; but at least it wasn't as bad as Dave's one hundred.

And so it went on, day after dreary day, the three of us lying side by side in our sleeping bags beneath the scooped dome of our cave, incarcerated in a silent blue twilit world, cut off seven thousand metres above sea level, strangely pleased that no one in the world knew where we were. For distraction, we had a copy of Thomas Mann's *The Magic Mountain* which Dave had borrowed from Birmingham Central Library and which he now ripped into three equal portions. I started right in the middle of one of the densest philosophical discussions in the Alpine sanatorium, reading several hundred pages before getting my turn to go back to the beginning. It was heavy going: as Philip Roth's Zuckerman put it, 'All that philosophy. All that snow. Reminds me of the University of Chicago.'

When no one could face any more Thomas Mann we talked, mainly about food. But one afternoon Dave spent several hours explaining the Irish electoral system of proportional representation. Another day he invented a new board game, cutting up pieces from a cereal packet. In the mornings he would rouse us with a pan of thin Dickensian gruel; at lunchtime he would distribute our three cream crackers, each spread with a sliver of cheese.

The only really hateful thing was clearing the cave entrance. On one occasion, needing to relieve myself, I had to do it in the middle of the night. It was hideous: getting out of my sleeping bag, struggling into anorak and overtrousers, double boots, overboots and mittens, then plunging head first into the suffocating bank of icy dry powder, burrowing and pushing through two metres of snow, to emerge spluttering into the blizzard, glimpsing hints of stars behind torn clouds, glancing down the three-thousand-metre precipice of the North Face, then fighting to pull down three layers of trousers and expose my bare arse to the biting wind. One night, waking to an urgent bout of diarrhoea, I was unable to burrow out in time. Powerless to resist the sphinctral imperative, I just had to scrape a hollow in the floor of the cave and defecate right there, apologising profusely to my bleary companions.

'Venables, you're repulsive,' rasped an irate Wilkinson.

'I'm sorry. I'll cover it up and it'll soon be frozen.'

'What kind of apology is that? You're disgusting.'

'Well, that's pretty rich, coming from you,' I retorted to a man never renowned for his personal hygiene.

I think that brief squabble was the only dent in our smooth unity. On the fourth evening the storm blew over and at 2.30 a.m. the next morning we emerged to a starlit sky, hoping to continue up the north ridge. Eager to discover what lay ahead, I took first turn.

It became apparent immediately just how much new snow had been dumped on the mountain, as I ploughed up to my waist in icy powder. After twenty minutes flailing, my vertical trench only extended about thirty metres. It was utterly point-less: we would just have to descend to Advance Base and wait a few days, regaining strength at reasonable altitude while the mountain got back into condition. Denied the summit, I longed to bail out immediately but Dave, ever shrewd, pointed out that we should wait for all the new snow to slough off the dangerous lower slopes. So we returned to the twilit grotto for twenty-four further stomach-rumbling hours, still rationing supplies, determined to leave as much food and gas as possible stocked at Camp Three for a second attempt.

When we did at last escape on the sixth morning I felt tense with foreboding. In the interest of lightweight speed we were climbing unroped and, as I led across one steep section of the ridge at dawn, traversing about ten metres below the smooth crest in case it was an overhanging cornice, facing horizon-tally into the white wall, there was a violent bang. Suddenly I was staring straight into the sky as a ton of collapsed snow poured down the precipice to the Yazghil Glacier. Where my ice axe was plunged into the slope there was now a jagged crest, level with my waist. Above it the entire section of ridge had disappeared.

Lower down, taking turns to lead down the North-west Spur, we tramped through a battlefield of avalanche debris and the following day, just beyond the *Dance of the Sugar Plum Fairy*, we had to step over fracture lines where snow slabs a metre thick, tensioned over convex slopes, had just snapped away, leaving hard old ice underneath. I thanked Dave for his wise insistence on waiting that final day at Camp Three.

By the time we returned safely to Advance Base we had been on the mountain continuously for twelve days. Dave and I decided to walk three hours further to the green comforts of Base Camp, where for a day we enjoyed the company of Tony Riley and Paul Nunn, who had been working for a big Royal Geographical Society project in the area and had dropped in to say hello. Phil, an ascetic hermit focused totally on the mountain, waited alone at Advance Base. Walking back up the glacier to rejoin him two days later, stopping for a rest and a cigarette, sitting on a boulder and gazing up at Trivor, immense and silent under a bright sky, I suddenly felt an overwhelming happiness – a total immersion in the moment, a conviction that right now there was nowhere else in the world I wanted to be. Despite the hunger and the hardship and the horrible experiences like the sagging snow-cave roof, this adventure had been so all-embracing, so intense, so positive that I wouldn't have swapped it for anything. And, best of all, I knew that we were so fit, so well acclimatised and so deserving of a lucky break that we were going to complete this route and tread that final white road, that curling ribbon in the sky, all the way to the top of this massive monument.

But we didn't get our lucky break. Instead, we just did a rerun of Act One. This time minus *The Magic Mountain*. And minus the hope, as another storm pinned us down at seven thousand metres and we wilted in the thin air, dreaming ever more urgently of food and, this time, dreaming also of home, so that when this second storm finally abated we knew that it was all over. We had tried our best and could do no more.

After another nerve-racking descent we reached Base Camp at dusk, climbing up the moraine from the glacier, leaving that sterile geological world and returning to the smell of flowers and the twittering of songbirds. As we tramped the final few hundred yards across the ablation valley to the little stone-walled Base-Camp kitchen, a figure came towards us, waving and shouting, then throwing his arms around our necks, tears of relief in his eyes. It was Wali, back from his honeymoon, relieved after several days' anxious vigil that we were alive. And *that* – not the summit of Kunyang Kish – was the only thing that really mattered.

The closing days of an expedition are like the end of term: the same eager, tremulous sense of well-earned rest and homecoming; but also, coming down from extreme altitude, a deliciously sensual returning to earth.

It started at Bitanmal, a bushy enclave beside the Hispar Glacier, where I suddenly heard music – the first music for many, many days – and spotted a young shepherd sitting on a rock, playing his flute. The arcadian idyll continued when we crested the moraine and saw the barley fields of Hispar, now golden ripe, luminous in the evening light. It was a shame when we got there that the first women we had set eyes on for seven weeks should flee from the fields. Never mind: what joy to hear the sound of children's voices and to be taken by two boys to the rest house, where we feasted on a giant omelette and fresh vegetables and fried slices of pigeon, all procured for us by Wali. The following afternoon, as I walked into the first orchard at Nagar, a man handed me a crisp fresh apple. Then there was the thrill of seeing all the lights of Hunza as a jeep drove us back through the valley and down to Gilgit, where Ghul Mohammed, owner of the Hunza Inn, was waiting at one o'clock in the morning with a three-course dinner.

We were very scrawny. Even barrel-chested Dave looked gaunt, worn down by the long siege. And when we arrived at Islamabad Airport four days later, we still looked so spaced-out that the British Airway reps murmured discreetly, 'The Drugs Squad is meeting this flight at the other end, so if you've got anything hidden in that luggage I should offload it now.' And, sure enough, at Heathrow Customs they took one look at the three mountaineers and called us over, dragging off poor Phil for a full body search.

The final storm at Camp Three had made me late for my new job and from Gilgit I had sent a not-strictly-truthful telegram to York: DELAYED INDUS FLOODS STOP SORRY LATE VENABLES. Now, arriving home at midnight to collect some belongings before heading north to York, I was met at Bath station by Mark who said, 'I suppose you heard that you failed the exam.'

'What – the PGCE? The bastards!' It seemed that my final essay – advocating complete autonomy for individual schools, greater parent power and increased pay for head teachers and department heads, financed by drastic pruning of local education authorities – had not gone down well. I was not an officially qualified teacher. However, my boss in York was very forgiving when I arrived a couple of days later, just telling me that I would have to do my first term on half pay, and make sure I passed the retake in November. In the meantime, I had better make up for arriving ten days late and put in some serious work.

The bell rang and I gathered my notes, heading to meet my first class. I had lost at least a stone in weight, I still felt very weak and my legs were jelly. Climbing the school stairs seemed infinitely harder than the long slog over Sod's Law Peak to seven thousand metres. It also felt a lot more frightening, as I continued along the passage then paused to gather courage and reach for the door handle behind which waited my class of twenty-eight eleven-year-olds.

Winter snow on the path to Everest as the author heads into the Kama valley. The mountain waits eighteen miles away on the right, with Lhotse on the left.

The author flying in Cornwall, 1961.

Zuoz, in the Engadine, 1965.

Relaxing with boots off after the Grande Casse, 1975. The appalling glasses finally went in 1977.

Budget Bus passes Mount Ararat during our month-
long journey to Afghanistan, 1977.

Lindsay Griffin during one of
several abortive winter forays, 1976.

Roger Everett and Lindsay Griffin on the
first ascent of Kohe Sahkt SW Buttress,
Afghanistan 1977.

Author on the ever popular Papillons
Arête above Chamonix, 1974.

My parents skiing past the Matterhorn, at the grand climax of the Haute Route, 1981.

Bill Stevenson on North Face of Mont Blanc de Cheilon, March 1977.

Gormenghastly – the condemned house in Oxford, a few months before demolition. Jennifer occupied the attic and a friend of hers kept the Packard in the garage.

Philip helping an injured Jonathan Dawson back down to the Hunza valley, 1979. As a medical student, Jonathan was well qualified to instruct us in bandaging his broken jaw.

Dick Renshaw on a fine Karakoram bridge, bound for Shimshal in 1984.

Kunyang Kish 1980. The author arrives puffed at the 7,000m summit of Sod's Law Peak, with Distaghil Sar behind. That night the weather broke and we were marooned in a snowcave for six days, sustained by Dave Wilkinson's copy of *The Magic Mountain*.

Carlos Buhler on the *Dance of the Sugar Plum Fairy* on a rare fine day, during the 1981 attempt on Kunyang Kish. The most distant pyramid is the summit of Rakaposhi, in Hunza.

Kunyang Kish 1980. Phil Bartlett descends windslab fractures during the fearful retreat after the first big storm.

Afternoon tea at Camp One, with Rakaposhi in the distance.

Earlier in the expedition, Dave returns from our first push to the upper ridge. Our tracks can just be made out to the left of Sod's Law Peak - the prominent summit on the skyline.

Peru 1982. Dave on summit ridge of Jatunhuma I. The previous day we had climbed the West Face, on the right. Now we had to find a way down the East Face, on the left.

Finsteraarhorn North-East Face, March 1983. Dick on Day Two (*left*) and leaving the bivouac on Day Three (*right*).

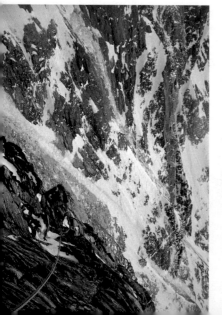

Chapter Seven

Chocolate City

They were kind to me, my Fulford School eleven-year-olds: they were keen and cheerful and mercifully cooperative. Other classes gave me a harder time. The girls were okay; but it was the boys who were most wearing – the fourteen- and fifteen-year-olds rampaging like frisky bullocks, flexing their newly broken voices, taunting the effete southerner with their broad Yorkshire accents. But when things went well I enjoyed my teaching, enjoyed the adrenalin rush and the challenge of trying to be aware of the 150 or so individuals I dealt with each week.

It must be one of the few jobs where on your first day you are simply thrown to the lions and left to fend for yourself, surviving by your wits. Or not. Trying now, a quarter of a century on, to recall *what* exactly I taught in my English classes, most of it is a blur, as it probably was at the time for my pupils. What does remain in sharp focus is the music. I remember my first nervous orchestra rehearsal, taking over from a hugely charismatic predecessor who had moved to London. I didn't really do charisma, but I did try at least to be efficient and we had fun with some rousing pieces, like the schools-orchestra arrangement of Berlioz's gloriously bonkers *March to the Scaffold*. Harking back nostalgically to Oxford days, I also found a score of the *Threepenny Opera Suite* for wind band, and had enormous fun accompanying my blowers and puffers on the piano, trying to capture something of Weill's sardonic Berlin lilt.

Arriving straight from Kunyang Kish, with no accommodation fixed, I lodged at first with friends in a village outside the city, bicycling to work each morning through golden September fields where peewits picked amongst the stubble and the crab apples were crimson in the hedgerows. I loved the wide space of the York plain, where the eye is always drawn in to the city and its pale Minster towering so serenely above the medieval clutter of the Shambles. Shopping in town, I often made a detour to wander round the building, entranced by the pale gleam of its Tadcaster stone and the eclectic mishmash of styles, from the restrained lancets of the north transept to the floral exuberance of the great west window, all of it somehow adding up organically, in the way that those great Gothic cathedrals do, to something huge and timeless and emotionally uplifting.

Three miles away, in the strictly functional 1960s block of Fulford School I was blessed with generous-spirited colleagues, particularly Ray Beecroft, head of my English department. He was kind, calm and avuncular, gently ironic, and dismissive of any administrative gobbledegook which might interfere with real teaching. Amongst my new-intake colleagues there was a modern-languages teacher called Karen who was also looking for somewhere to live, so we decided to rent a house together. Then a young French *assistante* turned up in the staffroom. She was called Béatrice and was doing her statutory year in Britain as part of an English course at Lyon university. She had lapis lazuli eyes and curly hair the colour of autumn bracken and, as we had four rooms to fill, I asked her if she would like to help pay the rent; she said 'yes' and then produced a fellow assistant called Philippe, a large rugby player from Haute-Savoie, with dark hair and crinkly eyes and charm by the bucketful. In November 1980 the four of us moved into Newton Terrace, just inside the old city wall.

Philippe liked to talk philosophy, deep into the night, his mellow French bass resonating through the house. When his audience tired of philosophy, he played the saxophone instead. Badly. I competed downstairs hammering out Elgar's piano version of the Enigma Variations. Also badly, confirming Philippe's dim Gallic view of English music. Béatrice contributed to the mayhem by baking impromptu quiches, usually at two o'clock in the morning, always making an atrocious mess of the kitchen. Karen, an organised, tidy sort of person, was very tolerant; perhaps she found the Bohemian atmosphere a cheering contrast to the hard grind of the classroom?

The CB radio geeks used to call York 'Chocolate City' and cocoa scents would often waft across Newton Terrace, either from the Terry's factory or from Rowntrees, depending on which way the wind was blowing. It was at the latter Quaker foundation that I was roped into a youth-theatre production of *Fiddler on the Roof*, trying to look like Isaac Stern – and trying not to shake too much – as I braced myself on the top rung of a very tall, very wobbly ladder, isolated in a single spotlight amongst the silhouette rooftops, bowing on the E string the transparent little tune which opens the show.

Once I had sorted out the nerves, it was huge fun and I particularly enjoyed doing my make-up each night, giving myself a long grey beard, furrowed brow and finely sculpted Jewish nose. I was on stage for several scenes and I loved the camaraderie of it all. It was like the best kind of expedition and I suppose the buzz was intensified by having to stay awake afterwards till three o'clock in the morning, ploughing through mock-GCSE exam scripts, sleeping briefly, then attempting not to bore a class full of twelve-year-olds when I went into school at nine o'clock.

Immersed in the new job, I had to push climbing into the background. Until one weekend in February when I hitch-hiked south for the annual gathering of the Oxford Alpine Club, which has just one function – to gather ex-university mountaineers in black tie or evening frocks, once a year, to eat a dinner. It would be nice to report that some of the men wear the frocks and the women the dinner jackets, but the OAC isn't yet quite ready for that. Nevertheless, it is a chance to see old friends and to rub shoulders with some fairly big names in the climbing world.

Anyway, at this dinner in February 1981 I enjoyed seeing Rick Bartlett, elder brother of Phil, with whom I had so recently been doing hard labour on Kunyang Kish. Towards midnight, as we were having a last drink, Rick suggested, 'How about a climb? I was talking just now to some old codger who made the first ascent of Tom Tower back in the 1940s; he says it's barely VS.'

Roof-climbing is one of Oxford's great traditions and perhaps its finest moment was Robin Hodgkin's solo first ascent of the Radcliffe Camera in the 1930s, using the lightning conductor to surmount Hawksmoor's magnificent Palladian cornice. (Rumour has it that Hodgkin's friend David Cox was offered his prestigious fellowship at All Souls' College partly in the mistaken belief that it was he who had made this historic first ascent.) Myself, forty years on, ever the late starter, I hadn't done much serious roof-climbing as an undergraduate, so I was keen to make up for lost time and Rick's suggestion of Tom Tower was irresistible. However, we were both unfit and slightly drunk, so we persuaded Simon Richardson – a younger, stronger, more sober climber than either of us – to boost the team.

I led the first pitch, chimneying up the V-shaped corner to the right of Christ Church College's grandiose main gate. It was well endowed with columns and corbels and windowsills, so I quickly passed the second floor, then climbed over the balustrade to belay below the final tower, bringing up the other two on separate ropes, arrow fashion. Then we handed over to the young star, Simon.

After a quick glance up and down St Aldate's street, Simon set off. The idea was to climb up to the clock face, then use the clock's minute and second hands to gain the slatted window of the belfry, and climb that to the final ribbed dome. It looked extremely precarious and a lot harder than the modest 'Very Severe' label given by the first ascentionists. For protection, Simon looped a large sling round one of the twin bollards which stand sentinel over Christ Church's main gateway. He clipped the rope into the sling, then stood on the bollard.

It wobbled. All two tons of it, emitting a deep geological groan. Simon looked down to his belayers: 'You know roof-climbing is now a sending-down offence? If the proctors hear about this I'll be thrown out, and that'll mean no degree.' On that degree hung Simon's lucrative future with the Royal Dutch Shell Company; but I was more worried about Sir Christopher Wren's bollard which, with its twin, mirrors so perfectly the ogee curve of the final domed spire. It would be a terrible act of vandalism to knock it off. And it would make an awful mess of the pavement.

Simon dithered for a moment, then scurried back down as a police siren wailed in the deserted streets: some mean-spirited busybody must have reported us. I grabbed the ropes, doubled them over the balustrade, flung them back down into the street and abseiled as fast as I could without sticking a rock shoe through any sleeping don's window. At the bottom I stage-whispered, 'Okay – you can come down,' then huddled in the shadow as a police car came nosing down St Aldate's.

'Pssst – keep still, Simon. Rick, get your head down.'

The police missed us in the shadow of the chimney and as they continued down the street the other two raced down to the pavement and whipped the ropes down, gathering them in record time. A minute later we were all sauntering innocently along the pavement, in our rock shoes, ropes coiled neatly over dinner jackets. By the time the police did finally see us they were powerless to do anything, but they did roll down the car window and make a sporting gesture. 'And what do you think you're doing with those ropes, gentlemen?'

'We're off to Bristol, to the Avon Gorge ... going climbing.'

'Are you, now? At two-thirty in the morning?'

'Ah well, we're very keen. It's an old tradition – the alpine start.'

The midnight skirmish on Tom Tower stirred dormant yearnings and back in York I joined the local mountaineering club and got to know Dave Garner from the local newspaper, Pete the inscrutable club president, 'Guido' who had big alpine ambitions and who worked at Rowntrees, and Dave Harper, whose 'shit-shifters' handled slurry for the rich North Yorkshire farmers. For a soft sappy southerner, Yorkshire chauvinism can be quite daunting but these Yorkshiremen – and they *were* all men: not a woman in sight – were quite forgiving. They *did* point out that real men drink Tetley's bitter, not Sam Smith's, but they did it gently and tactfully. And, when I got stuck halfway up a route at Almscliff, soloing beyond my abilities, they were kind enough to lower me a rope. Amused by my penchant for big white alpine peaks, they called me 'Bergsteiger' and as they gathered below the quavering rescuee spreadeagled on the warm summer rock there were gleeful shouts of 'Bergsteiger's stuck. Give 'im an ice axe, someone.'

Humiliation notwithstanding, I loved those summer evenings at Almscliff and Brimham and Ilkley, but especially Almscliff, a fantasy gritstone castle rising above the fields of West Yorkshire. To a southerner, gritstone epitomises everything harsh and blunt about the North – a vicious, brutal, unforgiving sort of rock and, compared to the golden oolites of, say, Bath or Oxford – or London's gleaming Portland stone – quite a dour building material. And yet on a summer's evening it can glow with real warmth; even Wuthering Heights can seem benign. As for the natural unquarried outcrops like Almscliff, the climbing is gorgeously tactile and varied, ranging from brutal flared cracks where hands and fingers have to be wedged painfully, to delicate-balanced moves up the rock ripples formed millions of years ago when the coarse grit was compressed and hardened in the beds of prehistoric rivers.

Evenings on the gritstone were restorative therapy after the turmoil of the classroom. I also escaped further afield during the summer half-term to climb on the sea cliffs of Pembrokeshire with Phil Bartlett, the heady delight of those samphire-scented cliffs intensified by the fact that we were accompanied by Béatrice, with whom I had fallen inevitably in love.

It had been a rather halting courtship, with understandable hesitancy on her part. My unintentionally crude Easter post-card from the Alps, written in bad French and confusing 'bises' and 'baises', probably hadn't helped. Nor had the competing Philippe factor, although the saxophone-wielding philosopher was now safely packed off out of the way with another assis-tante called Claire. Nor had my monumental sulk after one rebuff, when I had spent a whole week playing over and over again, with studied melodrama, the achingly sad slow move-ment of Beethoven's *Hammerklavier* Sonata. Nor had the general ambience of our outings together: we had spent the February half-term walking with monstrous loads through the frozen Scottish Highlands to a very remote bothy with no heating, no running water and precious little comfort of any kind. Now, having forgotten to bring a tent to Pembrokeshire, we were relying on the kindness of farmers allowing us to sleep in their outhouses, one night sharing our bed with a herd of prize breeding pigs.

It was romance of an acquired kind. Luckily Béatrice was young and adventurous and Anglophilic and she decided to give me the benefit of the doubt. So, after the years of miser-able unilateral affairs, the summer of 1981 turned out to be my summer of love. We went on long bicycle rides, west to the impossibly picturesque Yorkshire Dales, east to the rolling chalk of the Wolds. We went for midnight walks on York's old city wall, climbing over the locked gates, trespassing with that defiance of authority which is second nature to the French, delighting in the forbidden – young and carefree under a starry summer sky.

It had all the sweet intensity of a honeymoon; but a honeymoon without a future, because Béatrice was about to return to university in Lyon and I was about to return to Pakistan. Before leaving Islamabad the previous September, Dave Wilkinson had applied for a permit to come back in 1981. Phil and I had wavered at first, but our niggling regret at having unfinished business on Kunyang Kish couldn't be ignored: I couldn't forget that parting vision of a curling ribbon in the sky – an irresistible line dividing light from darkness, eastern dawn from the dark blue shadows of the North-West Face.

Phil had written an article on our first attempt which had been published in *Mountain* magazine. It had been billed as 'Himalaya 1980', alongside companion pieces by Alex MacIntyre and Joe Tasker. The former was the tousle-headed law student from Leeds whom I had once met at the foot of *Zero Gully*, on Ben Nevis; now he was the brightest, boldest, wittiest star in the Himalayan firmament. His article was about a brilliant lightning raid with Wojciech Kurtyka and René Ghilini on the east face of Dhaulagiri, one of Nepal's eight-thousand-metre peaks. Joe Tasker's piece was about an attempt with Doug Scott, Peter Boardman and Dick Renshaw on K2. While we had been sitting out our storms on Kunyang Kish, eighty miles to the east, Boardman, Tasker and Renshaw (Scott having left by this stage) had been battling even higher, getting close to the summit of the world's second-highest mountain, before escaping in an epic retreat down the notorious Abruzzi Spur.

These were big names. I had listened to Doug Scott lecturing at the Alpine Club, sat entranced when he described his historic 1975 bivouac close to the summit of Everest. Likewise Boardman. And Joe Tasker. His climbs were the stuff of legend; as a slightly younger alpinist aspiring to the same things, I had read and reread the accounts of his alpine seasons, envied his ability to realise dreams and marvelled at the apparent stoicism of his taciturn companion from the East Riding, Dick Renshaw.

Renshaw's name had often cropped up while we loitered in our snow-cave, chewing the cud of past experience, because he and Dave had climbed several times together. Dave had tried to persuade him to come on the 1980 Kunyang Kish trip, but he had already committed himself to K2 with Peter and Joe. This year, however, those two were booked to go with Chris Bonington to an unclimbed peak in Sinkiang called Kongur, and Dick was free. He agreed to join us.

We met for the first time at the Derbyshire house of Phil's parents, on the way back from Pembrokeshire. I made a poor impression, apparently far more interested in Béatrice than in discussing plans for Kunyang Kish. As for my first impression of Dick, he was, as Dave had said, quiet and unassuming, at times awkwardly shy. And he was surprisingly small. But for all his short stature, he had broad shoulders, purpose-built for carrying large rucksacks. He looked powerful. And when he did have something to say, it was invariably wise. He had once very nearly died on a Himalayan peak called Dunagiri; K2 had also been a fairly close call, leaving him exhausted – and, according to his wife Jan, completely spaced-out – when he got back just in time for the birth of his son. Now, with Daniel still not one year old, he didn't want to be taking any stupid risks on Kunyang Kish.

That meeting in Derbyshire finalised our plans. Back in York I did all the packing of the food and gear that we were taking out to Pakistan, and sorted out the final details of our British Airways sponsorship. My headmaster agreed kindly to let me leave a week before the end of term, as state-school holidays just weren't quite long enough for me to acclimatise for a peak of nearly eight thousand metres. It was a shame that I would miss all the French *assistantes'* incredulous reactions to the marriage of Diana Spencer to the Prince of Wales, but we needed seven weeks to have any hope of success. Once again I got caught up in the excitement of the project, the urgency of departure. But also, as the actual day came closer, the dread of parting.

It was a bright Saturday morning and Béatrice and I woke early to the birdsong in Newton Terrace. After a half-hearted breakfast we went for a last familiar walk along the river Ouse, trying to be cheerful. Then Béatrice said, 'All these people keep saying, "Good luck; get to the top" – but all I care is that you come back.' Until then she had always tended to hide behind flippancy, shying away from any admission of attachment, and the sudden emotional seriousness – and the reminder of the potential consequences of mountaineering – came as rather a shock. As did the tears, an hour later, when she ran red-eyed from the station and left me to go alone onto the platform and catch the train to London.

For the rest of that day – and the following days as we journeyed from Islamabad to Gilgit and Hunza and Nagar – I kept counting the hours that had passed, wondering what Béatrice was up to in York, wishing that I was there, not here. After all the bright brave talk to sponsors and supporters, I found it hard to be enthusiastic and it took a while to blend into the rhythm of the expedition.

Phil found it even harder. He talked about the dangers we had faced the previous year and one afternoon, after the first reconnaissance and load-carry to our old Advance Base, he suddenly announced that he was going home. Dave was furious, but Phil was adamant: 'It's not so much the risk: it's *knowing* in advance what the risks are. And it's not *just* the risks . . . there's no surprise, nothing new to discover. Because I know what's there I can't get excited about going back up again.'

He looked miserable and I sympathised completely. As did Carlos Buhler, an American climber who, along with Dick Renshaw, had swelled our team to five. Dick, too, seemed quite sympathetic, if a little surprised. Both he and Carlos had been extremely critical when they had heard about our climbing unroped to save speed and now, looking back on the previous year's tactic, I realised that although it was common practice to forgo the rope in the interests of speed and efficiency, in our case it had been more a kind of moral laziness.

So, determined to climb carefully and safely we stayed on, while Phil left to walk back down the Hispar Gorge. I prided myself, rather smugly, on having already accepted the dangers and the hardships – on having made the decision to put up with them, convinced that with a bit of luck we would have our chance at that final beguiling ridge.

But we never got that bit of luck. We repeated the old plod up *Garadh Gully* and *Broad Gully* to a much-changed *Dance of the Sugar Plum Fairy*. We spent a few days sitting around in bad weather at a new Camp One snow-cave, Dick and I in the smoking quarters, Dave and Carlos in the healthy wing next door. Above that we made just one foray, wading less than halfway to the old Camp Two before dumping a cache of food and gear which we never saw again.

It was a dismal wash-out and most of our time was spent at Base Camp, where the rain alternated with sleet and snow. Another summer holiday wasted. Or so it would seem, except that no experience is ever really wasted. I spent time reading *Middlemarch*, preparing notes for the sixth-form class that I would be returning to in September. George Eliot's *Silas Marner* had been read to me at school, when I was twelve, and I had enjoyed enormously its sentimental simplicities. But *this* was something on a totally different level – this richly layered monument of a book, which Virginia Woolf had called 'one of the few English novels written for grown-up people'. I also spent many hours with Charles Rosen's *Classical Style* – a dazzling commentary on the mature works of Haydn, Mozart and Beethoven – as background to the teaching I was going to be doing during the next year, taking an A-level music class. And, for light relief, I stayed up late one night reading *Alien*.

When we were not reading or sleeping in our tents, we gathered in the 'kitchen' – a drystone-walled enclosure with a polythene roof, which, with its sooty Primus stoves, hessian sacks and aroma of paraffin, stale grease and spices, became over the weeks increasingly redolent of the wayside cafés on the Karakoram Highway. Here our Hunza cook, Ali Murad, prepared immaculate chapattis, his deft fingers rolling and flicking the dough into perfect wafer-thin discs to accompany the national staple of curried lentils – 'dhal' – served with profligate quantities of tomato ketchup (or 'Catsup' as it said on the bottle, always putting me in mind of feline vomit) to satisfy the sugar cravings of our American representative.

Ali had worked for Dick the previous year on K2, guarding Base Camp while the three sahibs made their attempt on the Abruzzi Ridge. In their final camp, up in the infamous 'Bottleneck' above twenty-six thousand feet, the climbers had been caught by a big storm and then hit twice in one night by avalanches. They were almost buried alive and had been forced to cut their way out through the tent fabric with penknives. After that horror, all thought of the summit had vanished in the desperate struggle just to try and get down alive, descending through blinding wind and snow for many thousands of feet. When the men had finally returned to the safety of Base Camp, emaciated and exhausted, Ali and his companion had shown extraordinary compassion, symbolised one morning when Ali found a lone flower (perhaps a willowherb?) growing on the rubble overlaying the glacier, and had picked and presented it to Dick and his friends.

Now Ali was working for *us*, sustaining us with the same good-humoured concern for our safety. He talked a lot about his home in Hunza and, when we asked him how life had changed since the building of the Karakoram Highway, he was sceptical about the benefits of improved communications: 'Now everyone is wanting more things, more cigarettes ... and everyone is having to fight to get more money.' Although the traditional claims of extreme longevity for the Hunzakuts have probably been exaggerated, the high concentration of fruit and nuts – and limited quantities of meat and fat – in their diet was always probably quite healthy. But, as Ali pointed out, they also enjoyed their home-made alcohol: 'In the winter I am drinking every night Hunza water.'

'We'll report you to General Zia!' laughed Dave.

'General Zia is not touching me. I lock all the doors and windows.' Ali's contempt for the rigorous Islamic stance of Pakistan's current dictator was probably fairly typical of the Hunzakuts, who had only very recently had to give up their autonomy (under the British Raj they were never fully absorbed into the greater province of Kashmir) and whose real allegiance was to the Agha Khan, whose foundation funds all the seriously useful – and very specific – aid projects in the region.

The other Ali, our liaison officer Captain Ali, was by contrast a regular officer in the Pakistan army and was inscrutably loyal. He was also a devout Sunni and although he was very courteous towards the foreigners to whom he had been assigned, he did one evening give us a glimpse of his real feelings when he said, 'I sometimes have a dream, a vision . . . that one day the whole world will be Muslim.' Unlike Wali the previous year, this liaison officer stuck punctiliously to his post, enduring politely what must have been a very boring sojourn at Base Camp.

Carlos, the American friend whom Dick had met in Peru, was another new strand to the Kunyang Kish experience. He had the kind of easy, genial, long-haired blend of introspection and friendliness which would make you guess that he came from California, although he actually lived in Bellingham, in the North-West, when he was not travelling round the world on expeditions. I liked him very much and, not for the last time, found the American ability to open up rather refreshing. He was committed totally to the expedition life and two years later he would take part in the first ascent of Everest's Kangshung Face, reaching the world's highest summit with Kim Momb and Lou Reichardt.

I was captivated by Carlos's expedition stories and by his commitment to that semi-nomadic way of life. I was also inspired by Dick's commitment – outwardly more hesitant, but inwardly driven by extraordinary determination. These people clearly derived huge fulfilment from their adventures. They arranged their lives and their meagre earning activities around expeditions; whereas I was pretending to be committed to teaching, whilst actually focusing all my thoughts and energies on what happened in the holidays. Before leaving York I had already been thinking that perhaps I should give up school-teaching – once I had done a second year, just to prove that I had given it a chance. Now, sitting in this little meadow beside the Kunyang Glacier, that seemed increasingly to be the right path to take. The fact that I was coming to this conclusion whilst languishing in Pakistan, failing dismally to get up a mountain, seemed to validate the decision: this wasn't some instant gimmick inspired by flukey success. I knew exactly what I was letting myself in for.

The second homecoming from Kunyang Kish was bleak. I might have had grand long-term plans, but the immediate future seemed grim. At the Hunza Inn in Gilgit there was a letter from Béatrice, cheerfully wishing me luck for the future, inferring that our brief fling had been just that. I sat up late in the hotel garden, smoking cigarette after cigarette, brooding. Five days later, returning empty-handed to York, I slumped morosely through the first staff meeting, staring out of the window, seeking solace outside in the view of a bed of pink roses.

At the end of October I hitched out to Lyon to spend half-term in the Alps with Béatrice. The rosehips were bright scarlet against an early snowfall and at St Gingolph on the Swiss-French border, where Philippe was now teaching all the *douaniers'* children in the village school, we drank wine with him and listened to Mahler's *adagietto*, staring across Lac Léman to the twinkling lights of Vevey. Another day I helped Béatrice with her Keats, enjoying the suitably erotic subtext of 'The Eve of St Agnes'. But then Saturday arrived and I had to hitch back to York to sit out the rest of my year's teaching, marking time before embarking on a new life. Béatrice and I had different plans, different dreams and, as she waved goodbye and I was swallowed up by the autoroute, whisked northward to Paris, I wondered if I would ever see her again.

All the remaining holidays that academic year I devoted single-mindedly to mountaineering, determined to prove that I could follow this thing through. In the last summer term I even stopped playing in the local orchestra which I had enjoyed so much, because I wanted to get out for more rock-climbing: it was time to start doing something properly.

But dilettante habits die hard. Commitment is a fine idea in theory, but there is so much to lose, so much to sacrifice. York University has an excellent music department and I loved going to concerts in their Lyons Hall. One of the most memorable was an electrifying performance of Messiaen's *Oiseaux Exotiques* by the London Sinfonietta. The next day I took some pupils from Fulford to a workshop that the Sinfonietta was running, introducing children to Messiaen's birdsong techniques and getting them to compose their own mini-pieces, starting by combining just a few percussion elements. It was so inspiring that, back at school, I got a whole class of twelve-year-olds to try the same thing. They seemed to enjoy it, seemed pleased at having their own creativity sparked. This, I thought, was real education: this was what it could all be like if one put in enough effort. The highs could be ecstatic. But the lows – the grinding drudgery when you didn't give it everything – were awful. This job demanded selflessness, and I wasn't sure I had much of that: I wanted to pursue my *own* dreams.

So I played hard that summer of 1982. During the Whitsun half-term Phil Bartlett and I joined a friend of his called John Trythall on his thirty-three-foot cutter, sailing through the Hebrides. The sun shone and the cuckoo sang from the blue-bell haze on the wooded shore of Mull. Later that day we beat past the most westerly point of the British mainland, Ardnamurchan lighthouse, in a stiff breeze. Then the wind dropped and we idled through an oily sea, up the west coast of Rhum, where thousands of pale fulmars and dark Manx shearwaters swooped and glided around us in elegant display; and I remembered one winter, high on Askival and those other

Viking summits of Rhum, seeing the shearwaters' summer nests – earthy burrows, two thousand feet above sea level, with incongruous seashell middens scattered on the unnaturally colourful fertilised grass. Sky nomads, the shearwaters over-winter off the coast of Brazil. In summer, on Rhum, the parents take turns at the mountain nest, one guarding the young while the other disappears on fishing trips which may last several days and can take the bird as far away as the Bay of Biscay.

We advanced slowly, 'stately as a galleon' like Joyce Grenfell's ballroom dancer, reaching Barra Sound the following evening. Then we continued westward through the twilit northern night, taking turns at the helm, escorted by squadrons of gannets heading home from a night's fishing, all returning to the nesting colonies on St Kilda and its outlying stacks, which appeared guano-white out of the dawn ocean like some impressionist vision of snowy peaks.

A change in the wind forced us to leave St Kilda's precar-ious anchorage after just a few hours spent exploring the deserted gannet-hunters' settlement, and we sailed back east to North Uist for beer and Glenmorangie in the Loch Maddy pub, where an old man played the accordion brilliantly and Phil flirted with the barmaid. Then back south, down the Minch to Skye, motoring into Loch Scavaig on an evening of utter calm, with the sea liquid gold and the Black Cuillin not black at all, but glowing pearly pink. The Cuillin, they say, are Britain's nearest thing to the Alps – a great horseshoe of spiky summits worthy of Chamonix. I had never been to Skye before, so after supper, at ten p.m., we rowed ashore and crossed the narrow isthmus to the freshwater Loch Coruisk, wearing rock-shoes, hoping for a little bouldering on the immaculate gabbro rock.

In fact our bouldering turned out to be a thousand metres of pleasurable climbing all the way up the long 'Dubh Ridge', continuing torchless into the dark and arriving at one o'clock in the morning on the crest of the main Cuillin Ridge. At which point John and Phil announced that it was time to head back to the boat. But I had never done the main ridge, so I commandeered our two chocolate bars, promised to return to the boat by midday, and headed off into the night, running along the jagged crest.

A true purist would first have run back west to the proper start of the ridge at Gars-bheinn, but I decided to omit the first three summits rather than risk missing the midday rendezvous and my lift home.

Anyway, who cares if I only did nine-tenths of the ridge? It was a night of stolen pleasure, running from summit to summit, finding my way quite easily in the twilight which passes for darkness in the Scottish midsummer. It was thrilling to discover in the gloaming famous landmarks such as the Thearlaich Dubh Gap, where you have to climb down into a deep notch and up its far vertical side. Just below one of the biggest summits, Sgurr Alasdair, I gave myself a fright stumbling across a pod of bivouacking climbers snoring in their down cocoons. Then there was the steep V-groove of the King's Chimney, and the great gabbro blade of the Inaccessible Pinnacle, with its easy ascent but awkward *de*scent down a vertical wall. And later, at last, a little patch of old winter snow, so that I could wet parched lips as a great red globe rose high above the mist and hung in a pearly sky. Then more endless ups and downs, and some more rock-climbing on the magnificently chiselled Bhasteir Tooth, followed by the last major summit, Sgurr nan Gillean, and a couple of further peaks to complete the great horseshoe.

At seven-thirty I finished the ridge, then headed down into Harta Corrie, hot swollen feet throbbing in tight rock-shoes, my throat sticky-dry, reminding me of another endless hot descent from Rakh-e-Kuchek in Afghanistan. But here I came down to lush bog grass dotted with pink, yellow, white and blue flowers, the air balmy and buzzing with the sound of bees and twittering skylarks. At last a stream and long cool gulps of soft peaty water. Then another hot trudge through the warm heather, dive-bombed by a pair of strident sandpipers. A quick cooling swim in a lochan, and a brief interlude to enjoy hot sun on naked skin, before pulling clothes back on for the final trudge to the boat, which I reached at eleven a.m., thirteen hours after setting out. Then lunch and beer. And another swim – this time a salt-water dunking, diving off the boat into Loch Scavaig. Then on to Mull and the pub in Tobermory, leaving us all a bit jaded, but utterly content, for the final day's sail back to Loch Melfort.

It was a week of total enchantment and it made me wonder why we ever bother to travel abroad. But that contentment was shattered at breakfast on Sunday morning, back at John's flat in Newcastle, when we saw on the front page of the *Observer* the photos of Peter Boardman and Joe Tasker, both so young, strong and jaunty in their leather hats, bound for the great peaks of Central Asia. The two of them had just disappeared near the top of Everest's unclimbed north-east ridge. After several days' fruitless search the expedition doctor Charles Clarke and leader Chris Bonington had had to assume that the two men were dead. The fourth member of the climbing team, our friend Dick Renshaw, had already come home early, after suffering a mild stroke whilst climbing above eight thousand metres.

The disappearance of Boardman and Tasker made a deep impression on the public, echoing uncannily the similar disappearance of Mallory and Irvine in 1924. Although I never met Peter and Joe, I had followed their adventures closely, aspired to the kind of thing they did, and, through Dick, felt a tenuous connection. So it was almost like a real bereavement. And a warning. But a warning that I was not prepared to heed. I had made up my mind.

Fulford School's headmaster agreed to my request to leave a fortnight early on unpaid leave – 'you arrived here late, so you might as well leave early' – and, after one final riotous music lesson with a classroom of twelve-year-olds hammering out a raucous 'On Ilkley Moor Ba'tat', I left York. The reason for the early departure was that Dave Wilkinson and I were going climbing in Peru, and wanted to set off in early July for the best Andean conditions. On my last day at Fulford two of the girls in my A-level English class handed me a goodbye card. My lessons hadn't always been totally scintillating – at one stage the class had cruelly named me 'Casaubon' after the dreary pedant in *Middlemarch* – so I was touched by the card and its Paddingtonian message wishing me 'Good Luck in Darkest Peru'.

Chapter Eight

Land of the Incas

Peru welcomed me with a loud bang on the head.

After a twenty-four-hour flight we had landed at Lima in the early afternoon and made our way with four large rucksacks to a bus station in the suburbs, intent on continuing straight to Cuzco. Dave still had all his cash, traveller's cheques, return flight ticket and passport in the little leather attaché case which went on all his expeditions; he called it the diplomatic bag, and in the rush to leave the airport he hadn't yet transferred its contents to a money belt.

We were green gringos asking for trouble and the manager at the bus station shouted to us to bring all our luggage in off the street. So Dave ferried luggage into the station while I guarded the diminishing pile on the pavement. I had been warned about Peruvian thieves so when a couple of youths started pestering me, trying to interest me in a gold biro, I shooed them away. But they returned, fast and lithe, darting, grabbing, shouting – determined to confuse me. Then one of them ripped off my glasses and stamped them into the ground. Instinctively, foolishly, I dived for the pavement, whereupon the attacker started hitting me over the head with a stick. And as I fought back, flailing blindly, the other youth ducked in and grabbed the attaché case.

By the time I had got my mangled glasses back on to see

what was happening the thieves were running away through the evening traffic jam. A kind driver leapt out of his car and tried to stop them, but all he achieved for his trouble was a bloody nose. I just watched from the pavement, fists clenched, seething with impotent rage. After a long session of form-filling at the police station we found a cheap hotel – only to discover, when we checked in, that *my* passport had also been in the diplomatic bag.

We languished in our hotel through the weekend and on Monday morning went to the British Embassy who were extremely helpful, cashing a fifty-pound cheque to supplement our now limited funds and organising new documents; by Tuesday we were ready to return to the bus station, brand new passports stowed in money belts underneath our shirts.

We drove south along the Pan-American highway, following a coast of grey dunes falling into grey waves. We were at the northern fringe of the world's driest desert, the Atacama, but artificial irrigation nurtured fields of cotton, maize and oranges; out to our right pelicans patrolled the Pacific, feeding off one of the world's richest fishing grounds, sustained by the cold upwelling of the Humboldt Current, which also accounts for the fog that persists through most of the year over Lima. At dusk we turned east, inland, and began to climb. In the morning I woke with numb feet and saw frost on the ground outside.

Our fellow passengers, all Peruvian, were a cheerful crowd. Like almost everyone we met in South America – thieves excepted – they were friendly and polite. At one stage we had wondered whether to cancel the expedition, concerned that we might be treated hostilely so soon after the British war with Argentina; but apart from an occasional giggling refer-ence to 'Malvinas' the subject was hardly mentioned. I admired too the Peruvians' stoicism. During the fifty-three-hour journey to Cuzco there was never a murmur of complaint from the young children. How different from my class of fourteen-year-olds who had grumbled at the two-and-a-half-hour train ride from London to York. And how endearing, at the town of Ayacucho, to see such clean-scrubbed children walking to school in the bright Andean light, boys in shorts, girls in navy tunics, white shirts all immaculate. We stopped for breakfast in the inevitable Plaza de Armas that graces every Peruvian town, then continued through a sunny land-scape full of giant cacti and, everywhere, donkeys and horses. The next day we stopped at dawn in a town called Abancay, where we all descended into a subterranean meat market for bowls of soup with lumps of chicken floating in the oily juice. It was an unusual breakfast, slurped down to the accompani-ment of hacking butchers' knives and the tramp of feet on the skylights overhead. Revived by all that fat and protein, we continued through the Cordillera Vilcabamba, passing close to the famous ruins of Machu Picchu, and that afternoon arrived finally at the old Inca capital.

Most tourists fly straight from Lima to Cuzco, step out of the plane at 3,500 metres and feel like death. I preferred our gradual overland approach, which in 1982 was still safe, the Sendero Luminoso ('Shining Path') guerrillas having not yet established their fierce grip over that region of Peru. We arrived in Cuzco fully acclimatised and felt fine, fit to enjoy that first sight of the sloping plain filled with red roofs and cupolas. Beyond the city, on the southern horizon, we could just make out the white mass of Ausangate, highest peak in the Cordillera Vilcanota – our destination.

First, shopping. And in Peru that means potatoes. This is the global epicentre of *solanum tuberosum*, which comes in every imaginable shape, size and texture – long and thin, globular, oval, knobbly, smooth, waxy, flaky, fibrous, floury . . . and in every conceivable pattern and colour from yellow to pink to blue. Everywhere in Cuzco the multicoloured tubers were piled high on the pavement, tended by cheerful, stocky, pigtailed ladies in bowler hats, who laughed at our halting efforts to negotiate in Spanish. Of course, for many of them too 'Castigliano' is a second tongue – their first language is native Quechan. Everywhere in Cuzco there were reminders of an older civilisation: proud remnants of fine-jointed asymmetric

Inca masonry supporting the Spanish invaders' superstructure; although in the Plaza de Armas the cathedral – and the more floridly Baroque church of La Compañia de Jesus, completed in 1671 – have obliterated totally the Inca palaces and temples over which they were constructed.

Dave and I spent a day stocking up on potatoes – and onions and garlic and carrots and cabbage and bread and cheese and chocolate and tea and all the other stuff to supplement the dried rations we had brought from home. Then we dragged four now-gigantic rucksacks down to a square where someone said a truck would leave at nine a.m. before correcting that to three o'clock in the afternoon. At midday a bus appeared, so we boarded that instead.

It was a many-splendoured thing – a battered, snorting, long-snouted beast, which left Cuzco with much grinding of gears and backfiring, as laughing girls ran up and down the central aisle, selling fresh fruit juice. We drove for about six hours to a village called Ocungate, had some supper, then continued in the back of a truck, bumping along a rutted track, clutching piles of luggage, jolted against a confusion of bodies, looking up excitedly at an immense starry sky and seeing, on this my first trip across the Equator, the Southern Cross.

The road stopped in the village of Tinqui, where we slept in someone's yard and were greeted the next morning by a gaggle of tiny women laughing over the garden wall. They all wore the standard local costume of voluminously layered knee-length skirts, embroidered top and enormous yellow-fringed hat like a giant upside-down sunflower. While they chattered like exotic tropical birds, Dave did business with Gerrado, whose horse was going to carry our luggage to Base Camp. Price agreed, we set off – Dave and I, the horse, Gerrado and Gerrado's ten-year-old son Miguel.

The walk-in was a gorgeous contrast to the previous years' treks to Kunyang Kish. Here there were no oppressive gorge, no giant rubble-covered glaciers: just the undulating golden grass of the altiplano, rolling easily to the mountains, which rise with astonishing abruptness, encrusted and bejewelled with some of the most dazzling snow formations in the world. We camped that night beside a hot spring and got out the pressure cooker to make our first potato stew. The next day we continued to the foot of the five-thousand-metre-high Campa Pass, at which point Gerrado, who had been grumbling since breakfast, announced that the horse could go no further.

The horse didn't comment, but he seemed fine, so we grabbed his halter and carried on without Gerrado, plodding slowly over the pass and down the other side to camp beside Ticlacocha – a little lake at 4,750 metres. By the time we had pitched our tent Gerrado and Miguel arrived, looking mildy embarrassed, to collect their horse and their pay.

Our expedition was sponsored, as usual, by the British Mountaineering Council and the Mount Everest Foundation, but it was still a low-budget affair. 'Base Camp' consisted of one small tent that I had borrowed from my parents. So we were glad of the company of Fabrice, Danielle and Emmanuelle from Paris, who invited us to spend sub-zero evenings in their palatial kitchen tent.

Cordillera Vilcanota. Approaching the Campa Pass with Gerrado, Miguel and Gerrado's horse.

We enjoyed also the company of the llamas, which arrived each morning to do a ritual circumambulation of the lake. The only llama I had met before was The Um, which lived at the Snowdonia hill farm of Paul Work and Ruth Ruck, immortalised in Ruth's classic *Place of Stones*. On winter evenings at Ty Mawr, the llama used to join Ruth and Paul in their sitting room, wedged between sofa and fireplace, enjoying occasional sips of cherry brandy. Staying at the farm one time, I surprised The Um in a shed, stealing hen food; outraged at the interruption, she drove me into a corner, flattening her tufted banana-shaped ears and making retching noises. Before I could escape I was hit in the face by the inevitable jet of semi-masticated corn; the llama spits with prodigious accuracy.

The Andean Indians use llamas as pack animals and beside the fluffier alpacas, bred purely for wool, the former seem very elegant. With their disdainful stare they resemble the Asian camel; they also have quite similar feet – soft leather pads with two large clawlike toes on each foot. But even the llamas seem galumphing beside their elegant wild ancestor, the vicuña. I saw a herd one day on the big marshy plain just below our base camp, leaping through the snow like honey-coloured gazelles. There were also chinchillas scampering amongst the boulders and, down at the marsh, thousands of frogs and tadpoles, fizzing and popping in reedy pools, dodging the snipe and the huge black and white Andean geese.

It was a gorgeous spot to rest between climbs and Dave, ever methodical, was very insistent on those recuperative pauses. Between rest days we pushed our bodies steadily higher. First we climbed an easy little peak of 5,480 metres called Campa One. Then we did a more interesting route, winding up a glacier and a steep snow ridge to the 5,725-metres summit of Ccapana, named by the Harvard team who had made the first ascent in 1957 after a hacienda whose owner had helped them. Then we lay low for four days, while the weather prevaricated. Once the skies cleared again we were ready for our main objective.

I had spotted the photo of Jatunhuma I in an Italian book at the Alpine Club Library in Mayfair. The 6,094-metre mountain had first been climbed by a German team led by Gunther Hauser in 1954. Since then Jatunhuma I had had two or three further ascents, but no one had climbed its west face – a dazzling white sheet sweeping up to three extravagantly corniced summits. We decided on a direct line to the central summit.

Some basic climbing ability is always helpful when pioneering big new routes in the world's greater ranges, but what really counts is making yourself comfortable and having a good night's sleep. So, arriving at the foot of the face in the late afternoon, we were thrilled to find a five-star bivouac site where we could dig a spacious platform in mattress-soft snow beneath a protective rock roof. There was room to lie down at full stretch in our sleeping bags, ample snow for brews and a dry rock wall at the back of the ledge where we could hang up all the gear. What more could one ask for?

And the climb? That too had its own charm. At five a.m. I took first lead over the bergschrund – the big crevasse which usually marks the change of angle from glacier to actual mountain face. And then we were away, taking turns to lead out the fifty-metre ropes. On a big snow-ice face the actual movement can be very repetitive – just a steady kicking plod. The satisfaction is more aesthetic than gymnastic: a sense of shifting perspective as you climb steadily higher, ever more aware of the plunging geometry of white ribs and runnels. To anchor ourselves at the end of each pitch in the bottomless snow that is such a Peruvian speciality, we hammered in Dave's secret weapons – metre-long snowstakes made from high-strength L-cross-section alloy by a friend called Cho Brookes who worked, conveniently, at British Aerospace.

The big sweep of fifty-five-degrees snow was an extended hors d'oeuvre. Then, to refresh our climbing palates, we had two intricate pitches through a band of pink rock seamed with ice. And then we were into the real meat of the climb, as the face steepened dramatically and we entered a curving funnel, hemmed in by gravity-defying flutings of white sugar. The bed of the funnel was hard green ice, exhausting to calf muscles and axe-swinging forearms; the trick was to try and find the softer borderland between smooth ice and bottomless snow, on the edges of the funnel.

The geometry became ever more spectacular as the immense summit cornice – a huge bulbous balcony, striated with many years' accumulation of compressed snow – seemed to project ever more insistently over our heads, blocking out the sky. There was perhaps a tiny risk that the whole lot could crash down and obliterate us; but this was not some brittle, unstable 'serac': it was the solid summit structure – spectacular rather than dangerous. Of course we might have been wrong – this is not an exact science – but that kind of doubt had to be left behind at the foot of the face.

Evening drew in and I grew cold and tired, shivering forlornly at belays, hanging now from tubular screws hammered into hard ice. Dave, hugely experienced at these things, tied the two ropes together and led the final hundred metres in a single calf-wrenching pitch, climbing right up under the great balcony. I followed in the dark, grateful for the reassurance of a tight rope.

The icemaster was waiting in a little cave beneath the summit cornice and suggested that I have a look over the top. So I forced myself to wade up a final powdery slope, flopping out onto a dome of huge crystals glinting in the moonlight, with the yellower lights of a village twinkling far away in the black emptiness of the altiplano. There was a cold wind and no obvious bivouac site, so I rejoined Dave under the cornice. By eight o'clock we had excavated enough space to lie side by side, with just the feet of our sleeping bags sticking over the 700-metres face we had just climbed, and were sharing a pan of freeze-dried 'Mexican omelette' as our reward for a hard day's work.

In the morning we lazed over breakfast, staring out from our veranda at Ausangate, which was briefly orange, then white against the wrinkled pinky-grey altiplano. At eight-thirty we packed to leave, climbing up onto the central summit of Jatunhuma I. All we had to do now was get down again.

We had said all along that if we absolutely *had* to, we could at a pinch abseil and climb back down the west face; but the thought of reversing those precipitous runnels and flutings was extremely unappealing. So we looked around and discussed options. What about the far side of the mountain? Couldn't we get down onto that rock ridge and down onto that big glacier, then do a big trudge southward round Jatunhuma II and Jatunhuma III?

It looked feasible, so we set off along the summit ridge, burrowing through deep powder stuck at ludicrously steep angles on the side of the most fantastically baroque cornices I had ever seen, crossing the occasional crevasse which bisected the ridge, and sometimes looking through holes straight back down the west face. Then we sacrificed one of Cho's stakes as an anchor to abseil over an ice cliff, down onto the east face. There followed some easier snow-climbing. Then a long rock ridge, where Dave insisted with his usual good sense that we stop at dusk to bivouac luxuriously on a flat shelf of earthy rock, so much warmer than snow. Day Three started with a dizzy abseil from a steel blade peg that I had filched from the North Face of the Matterhorn four years earlier. One more abseil got us down onto the glacier, where we waded under a blazing sun, sustained by pineapple juice and our two remaining chocolate bars. It was a long hot plod back round to our own valley and we stopped three miles short for a final bivouac, returning to our base camp the next morning, five days after setting out, sad to discover that Fabrice had already whisked Emmanuelle and Danielle back to Cuzco, but pleased that he had left as consolation a congratulatory case of beer.

Jatunhuma quelled briefly the demons of ambition. At last an unqualified success on a big peak! A new route up a magnif- icent ice face. Best of all, though, a real *adventure*, where we had set off not knowing how exactly we were going to get back again, relying on experience, skill and a good dollop of luck to complete an ambitious traverse of the mountain. So I returned to Cuzco enchanted by the Cordillera Vilcanota, but also eager for Stage Two of the Andean adventure – the Cordillera Real, the royal mountains of Bolivia.

We took a bus across the border and arrived one evening at El Alto, the upper outskirts of Bolivia's capital which sprawl across a dusty plain at 3,600 metres. Then, suddenly, the plain fell away in front of us and we saw La Paz proper, filling a great scooped bowl dominated to the south by the gleaming swagged draperies of Illimani – Bolivia's highest mountain, floating in a purple sky beneath a full moon. It was ridiculously romantic and we were ridiculously hungry. We feasted on fish that night, and for breakfast the next morning blew our final seventy pesos on six bananas and a bag of salteñas – delicious fresh-baked pies a bit like Cornish pasties. Then we went to find Lindsay's relief expedition which had come out with funds to replace Dave's stolen cheques.

This was the same Lindsay Griffin with whom I had been to the Hindu Kush in 1977, accompanied now by his Welsh girlfriend Jan Solov, who would be coming with us to Base Camp. We were a bit concerned about how Lindsay, newly arrived at altitude, was going to keep up with two climbers who had already spent nearly a month on the altiplano, but acclimatisation was actually the least of our problems. Bolivia was going through one of its regular political crises and we had arrived bang in the middle of a national strike against the military government. All public transport had stopped and the streets were swarming with demonstrators. At least, while searching for a way out of La Paz, we could enjoy the fruits of an exchange rate that plummeted daily, dealing direct with the money changers who stood right outside the banks – brazen spivs brandishing suitcases full of banknotes. While most poor Bolivians struggled to make ends meet we gringos benefited from ever better rates, feasting on succulent steak and beer for well under a pound, on one occasion getting a perfectly respectable lunch for the equivalent of seven pence.

I spent contented afternoons in the Café Verona, writing my diary and reading, eating doughnuts or enjoying the frothy alcoholic tang of pisco sours, while a syrupy orchestration of the Moonlight Sonata played in the background. In a big covered market Jan and I shopped for provisions, discovering that bananas were sold in 'manos' – bunches of five – and taking a while to twig that the mysterious 'libra' which approximated to half a kilo was of course a good old-fashioned British pound – legacy, perhaps, of the British engineers like my Ogilvie great-grandfather who had built the Andean railways.

For the moment those railways were not operating and neither were the buses. In the end we found a man with a 'camionetta', who agreed to drive us to the mountains for $120. In the open back of the truck we rumbled northward along the turquoise shore of Lake Titicaca. We wanted to explore the Ancohuma massif, at the northern end of the Cordillera Real, from its far, eastern side, so we had to drive halfway round the massif, crossing a high pass to the old rubber town of Sorata. Here, down at 2,500 metres, the air felt damp and balmy, and mist drifted up from the unseen depths of the Amazon basin. But the next day we were climbing again, the truck laden with strike-breaking passengers, gears grinding alarmingly on the hairpins at 4,800 metres above sea level.

From the village of Ancoma we used three horses to carry our luggage over the high pass near Mina Candelaria – one of the thousands of mines which riddle the Bolivian Andes, this one employing just forty men to extract small veins of wolfram, the ore used to make tungsten. Condors circled overhead, fingered wings thrumming the air, but it was only when we descended to the village of Cooco and a pair of the birds flew low, skimming close like aeroplanes over the thatch roofs of the adobe houses, that I really appreciated the true scale of these giant raptors.

The horses had each carried about thirty kilos, but could

not do the next, steeper, stage, so in Cooco, camped on the village football pitch, we repacked the luggage into fifteen-kilo loads and hired six nimble llamas. I had a struggle to keep up the next day, and the llamas were already heading back down, unloaded, by the time I reached our base camp – a grassy shelf beside the little tarn of Chearcota.

We had identified the spot from a photocopied sketch map in an old *American Alpine Journal*. The map showed all the main peaks and we had a rough idea of what had and what had not been climbed. Again, that was the extent of our pre-planning. We were here to explore, not to follow a guidebook. So Lindsay and I wandered up a nice little peak to get a feel of the land and draw up plans for the next fortnight. Then, on the basis of that reconnaissance, we walked with Dave up to a glacier plateau and climbed a new route up a mountain called Llirini.

It wasn't a great ground-breaking first ascent, but it was a very charming climb for two reasons. First there was the dawn: Lindsay and Dave were dark silhouettes on the faintly gleaming ice, reflecting the first purple glimmer out to the east, which brightened quickly to orange and pink and yellow as the sun burst above an immense cloud sea stretching to infinity. Here, more than in the Cordillera Vilcanota, you were acutely aware of the greatest forest on earth: immediately to our east the mountains plunged direct into the steaming Amazon basin; to the west lay the dry brown altiplano and the turquoise expanse of Titicaca. The other great charm of our Llirini climb was the long summit ridge we followed, never very hard but always surprising us with new delights – delicate crests of pink granite, ice bosses, fields of penitentes (the same icy pinnacles we had seen in the Hindu Kush) and some wonderful tunnels where the ice had melted away from the rock, affording easy passage beneath huge cornices.

We climbed another peak on the way back to base, rested for a few days, washing clothes, reading, helping Jan to cook huge stews in the pressure cooker, and then returned to the glacier. Jan asked if she could come too, provoking Dave to one of his more angry outbursts. To her it probably seemed the typical rant of an intolerant misogynist; in fact, it wasn't her gender that precluded her coming, just the cruel fact that she was struggling with the altitude. So the three men went alone to bivouac that evening on a pile of rocks – rocks being warmer than snow – below the big granite pillar we hoped to climb on the highest peak in the massif, Ancohuma.

The granite on which we spread our sleeping bags was a pile of raw pale shards and, as we lay down on the rubble, I suggested that it might be there for a good reason, and that perhaps more would soon fall from where it had come. The other two were disinclined to move, insisting that the cold night would freeze solid any loose rocks above.

I couldn't help feeling a bit smug, as we lay staring at the stars a couple of hours later, when there was a loud clatter and a vicious whirring noise, followed by the thud of rocks landing in our bedroom. I grabbed my helmet, then held my rucksack over that for added protection and pulled up my legs to reduce my personal target zone. The bombardment increased. There was a softer thud and Dave shouted, 'Ouww – it got my arm!' Then came a scream as a shell landed on Lindsay's leg.

As soon as the bombardment let up, we grabbed all our equipment and dragged it out to a colder but safer bivouac site on the open glacier. Lindsay and Dave had got away with just cuts and bruises, but the injuries were bad enough to rule out a big technical climb. By way of consolation the next day Dave and I climbed a pleasant snow peak near the bivouac. Then we all headed down, Lindsay leaning on a walking stick made from two ice axes lashed together. Determined to salvage something from the wreckage of our Ancohuma plans, I left the other two at the foot of the glacier and returned to bivouac on a high pass, intent on at least getting *something* done on the highest peak. Before dawn I left all my bivouac gear and headed back across the glacier, this time passing the big rock pillars – out of the question on my own – and continuing to a steep ice couloir. As far as I know it had never been climbed before.

I felt strong and fit, and it was a good consolation prize, leading me onto a snow ridge, dazzling white against the turquoise glow of Titicaca.

At eleven o'clock that morning I sat on Ancohuma's summit, which the map told me was 6,427 metres above sea level. A few years later a satellite based aero-triangulation re-evaluated the altitude, and Ancohuma appeared in *The Times World Atlas* as 7,012 metres – higher than the hitherto highest mountain in South America, Aconcagua. By that stage bagging the world's seven highest continental summits had become a popular branch of the burgeoning 'adventure sports' industry. It would have been entertaining – and a much needed boost to Bolivia's economy – if all the Seven Summits conquistadores had had to come back and tick a different South American mountain to retain their places in the record book. Sadly that was never necessary: in 2002 an American-Bolivian team climbed to Ancohuma's summit with a global positioning device and came up with what seems to be a definitive height of 6,425 metres.

As for our own peak-bagging in 1982, Dave and I had climbed seven Andean summits and now I had this eighth. I also hoped to add a ninth – Illimani. After returning to La Paz, Dave had to leave for Lima to sort out a replacement for his lost plane ticket. Lindsay, Jan and I stayed for another week in Bolivia, taking a truck south from La Paz to a deserted road junction, where Lindsay, who had promised to take Jan up Illimani and whose leg had now recovered, continued to the regular western route, while I got out to hitch round to the east side of the mountain.

I had ambitions for a grand finale – the huge unclimbed, unknown east face, but when I got there the ambition crumbled. I spent two days sitting beneath the face, trying to make sense of its seven glacier icefalls and tortuous rock buttresses, trying to work out a safe line, trying to find the courage to set foot on the great wall, with only a large rucksack for company. The more I pondered the uncertainties – not least the complex topography of this huge rambling amphitheatre, which meant that I had no idea on which of Illimani's several summits I might emerge, let alone how to get down the west side to meet Lindsay and Jan – the more I realised how unrealistic I was being. But what really decided me was the thought of what I might lose. Sitting in that high valley, eking out my rations, feeling desperately lonely as I stared out at the Amazonian cloud sea, I remembered the first evening at Gormenghastly, in Oxford, three years earlier – my brother Philip, sister Cangy, her friend Tikki, James and Rachel, Jonathan up from London for the evening, funny and irreverent . . . all gathered in a warm glow of laughter and wine and cooking food. There was simply too much to lose: life was too good to throw away for the sake of a mountain. Better to leave the east face of Illimani for someone else.

So I returned to La Paz, size twelve double boots dragging on the long dusty road for one fifteen-mile stretch when no camions appeared. Lindsay and Jan, meanwhile, had climbed the regular route up Illimani, but had to wait several days for transport back to La Paz. I didn't see them until we all found ourselves on the same flight home from Lima.

After nine weeks in South America I was excited to be returning to Europe, but I was also apprehensive. Before finishing at Fulford School I had worked hard at trying to set up my future, firing off articles to magazines, sounding out travel companies, getting registered for a guide's qualification and, one Sunday evening in Gloucester, giving my first paid lecture, afterwards hitching back through the night to return to York in time for Monday lessons, determined not to blow the twenty-five-pound fee on a train.

My naive efforts had produced no real promise of employment and the future was an empty book. I had no idea what pictures and stories were going to fill those blank pages, but as we flew into Zurich airport the Alps rose sharp and bright above a cloud carpet. Their silhouettes were old friends, familiar and comforting, and it felt like a homecoming. But also a promise of new adventures, because there, to the left of the Jungfrau, set back a little, filling its own special place on the southern horizon, profiled against the pale autumn sky, was the eastern wall of a fine spire which had fascinated me for years, the Finsteraarhorn. That, I decided, would be the picture to fill the first blank page of this new chapter in my life.

Chapter Nine

Winter on the Finsteraarhorn

For years I thought, Anglocentrically, that it got its name from the shark-fin profile. The Finsteraarhorn *is*, like the Matterhorn, a magnificently proud, pointy peak; but 'finster' actually means 'dark': it is the Dark Peak of the Aar – the river which trickles down from the mountain's eastern glaciers and swells to a roaring tributary of the Rhine, flowing eventually into the North Sea. The mountain's southern snows melt into the Rhône – and ultimately the Mediterranean – and the people of the upper Rhône valley used to call it Schwarzhorn – black mountain.

Anyway, the Finsteraarhorn – to use its definitive northern title – is the highest peak in the Berner Oberland: higher than the Oberland's more famous Jungfrau, and to my mind more alluring – not because of those few extra metres' height, but because of its isolation: you have to make an effort to get to this mountain, and you have to make a particularly big effort to get to its remote, rarely climbed north-east face. And, in a game where history is everything, that mystique of isolation is intensified by the knowledge that this was the first of the great Alpine north walls to be climbed, and that the very first attempt in 1902 was made by an extraordinary traveller, diplomat, archaeologist and occasional mountaineer called Gertrude Bell. She and her guides were turned back by a fearsome storm and had to make a gruelling retreat from two-thirds of the way up the face. The route was completed in 1904 by Gustave Hasler and Fritz Amatter. Many years later, speaking about the climb at the Alpine Club in London, Hasler commented: 'Even after seventeen years I must say that I still consider the face a very serious proposition, not to be undertaken lightly.' More emphatic was the impression of the American climber Miriam O'Brien, who made the third ascent in 1930, guided by Adolph Rubi. In *Give Me the Hills*, she wrote: 'It is the only climb I have ever done which I cannot think about with pleasure. Not that it was the only occasion in the mountains when I have been frightened, but it was the occasion when I was most badly frightened, and for the longest period.'

That joyless terror was induced by the wall's notoriously shattered rock. But those early ascents were made in summer; climb the face in winter and most of the loose masonry is frozen securely in place. That was the reasoning which prompted Dave Wilkinson and Dick Renshaw to make the long approach on skis one midwinter in the late 1970s, only to be turned back when Dave sprained an ankle. Later, whiling away an afternoon in our Kunyang Kish snow-cave in 1980 Dave told us all about it. I was intrigued that others shared my own obsession with the Finsteraarhorn and the following year, having discovered that I seemed to get on quite well with Renshaw, I persuaded him to try the wall again, this time with me rather than with Dave. But the weather over Christmas 1981 was appalling. All we managed was an abortive attempt on the more accessible Fiescherwand, retreating the way we had come – through the window at the back of the Eiger – and walking all the way down the railway which winds through the inside of the mountain, hoping that no unscheduled train might be coming up the tunnel that night.

I returned three months later, in April 1982, with Phil Bartlett, this time paying to travel legally, in a train, all the way to the Jungfraujoch, then skiing several miles to the Finsteraarhorn Hut which is perched on the easy south-west side of the mountain.

Although the weather was fine that Easter the clarity was accompanied by a very cold east wind. Fearful of frostbite, Phil was nervous about climbing halfway up the mountain, then descending the far side to commit to the very remote north-east face. For consolation I climbed the normal route up the south-west side and from the summit gawped down the immense north-eastern precipice, which was even more awesome than I had expected. Phil and I then skied back to Concordia and up to the Hollandia Hut, where he sat and read while I soloed the north face of the Aletschorn, rounding off a glorious day by continuing along a great sweep of ridge, over the Klein Aletschorn and Sattelhorn, before returning to the hut and then skiing out to the Lötschental.

We hadn't set foot on our avowed objective but we had enjoyed a fantastic week's ski touring. I had also enjoyed the intensity of my skywalk on the Aletschorn, but the really memorable encounter that week took place on the veranda of the Finsteraarhorn Hut.

Skimping as usual, Phil and I were bivouacking in our sleeping bags outside, to avoid hut fees. The guardian was pretty disgruntled at having two tramps parked outside his hotel; his regular ski-touring clientele was also fairly disdainful as it stomped its way past us to the outdoor loo – one morning our inert forms were mistaken for frozen stiffs. But there was one young woman who stared, then smiled, then came over to say hello. Phil was always more gregarious than me – the kind of person who slips easily into conversation with strangers in pubs, particularly if they are women – and he chatted amiably while I hovered in the background. But after a while I came over and introduced myself. The girl had dark bright eyes and she was called Marianne. She had spent six months working as an au pair in Britain, loved speaking English and seemed charmed by our unusual sleeping arrangements. Half an hour an hour later she came back out of the hut and asked us to join her party: 'There is a rich man in our group, and he says he will pay for you to sleep in the hut.'

'We couldn't possibly do that,' answered Phil, 'but we'd love a quick drink.'

So we went into the cosy fug for half an hour, before returning to our sleeping bags. At dawn the next day, buried deep beneath frosty hoods, we were woken by Marianne kneeling on top of us and bearing a thermos flask full of hot coffee. Then she left with her group, but before leaving she wrote down her phone number.

A few days later, ski tour complete, Phil headed home with the friends who had driven him out from Britain. I stayed on, wondering whether to fit in one more lightning raid before hitching back to start my final term at Fulford. The weather was still fine and I looked up at the gleaming Lauterbrunnen Breithorn, pondering a solo attempt on its north face. But it looked so cold and aloof. Down here the buds were opening and the air was soft with the scent of flowers. After an hour of agonised schizophrenia I found a phone and dialled the number in Luzern.

'Hello. Meister.'

The surname was a bit intimidating, but it was worth a try. 'Is that Marianne? This is Stephen ... we met at the Finsteraarhorn Hut; I was the one with glasses. I was wondering if I could drop in at Luzern on the way home.'

She said yes, so I hitched over the Brünig Pass, found my way to the suburb of Emmenbrücke and knocked on the door of her flat. She had already cooked a meal and opened a bottle of burgundy. After dinner we walked into the centre and sat at one of the lakeside bars opposite the onion domes of the Jesuit Kirche. We talked all evening, wandering around Luzern, and eventually returned to her flat, arm in arm. In the morning she left early for the school where she taught. I got up a bit later, drew the curtains and looked out over cherry blossom to the serene outline of Mount Pilatus. I left reluctantly, walking out to the autobahn in a bitter-sweet glow which was only shattered after Basel, when I was picked up by three raucous American girls who drove me all the way across Germany in a rattling Citroën 2CV, singing repeatedly every single number from *A Chorus Line*, leaving me at the Belgian border with a final rousing rendition of 'Tits and Ass'.

Five months later, flying into Zurich on the way home from Peru, there it was again, the mountain which now seemed redolent with its own romantic subtext. After Christmas I nipped out to the Alps with Jonathan Dawson for a few days' skiing, then spent two days in Luzern with Marianne, who agreed hesitantly to the idea of my returning later that winter to live for a while in the flat that she shared with her sister, Therese. First I had to return to London for an exhibition of my photos, and to give a couple of lectures. Thanks entirely to the generosity of my parents, who were letting me use their house as a base with only nominal contributions towards household expenses, I was managing to survive on occasional lectures, decorating jobs and bits of carpentry. By the end of February I had saved enough to return to the Alps. The plan was to spend the spring in Luzern, but first to try again to reach the north-east face of the Finsteraarhorn with Dick Renshaw.

Dick and I stayed in the Naturfreundhaus at Stechelberg, a tiny hamlet at the head of the Lauterbrunnen valley. It is a beautiful spot, nestled deep beneath the Jungfrau on one side and on the other the cliffs over which James Bond hurled his evil pursuers whilst *On Her Majesty's Secret Service*; in winter it can feel very enclosed, especially during bad weather. The previous year that oppressiveness had been intensified by some fellow guests with a cassette tape of 'The Birdie Song', which they had played interminably in the communal dining room. This time our fellow inmates had less irksome musical tastes and Marianne came over for a couple of days to cheer us up.

Then the weather began to change. We took turns on a day-ski ticket at Wengen and I had the afternoon shift. Racing down the Lauberhorn run that evening of 3 March 1983, with the wind in my face and the Jungfrau glowing pink in a crystal-clear sky, I felt a great surge of joyful optimism. Surely, this time, we would be given a little luck?

*   *   *

Early the next morning we lugged our monstrous rucksacks onto the train and clunked up the rack railway to Kleine Scheidegg. For Dick it was a familiar journey, suffused with memories of his 1974 winter ascent of the Eiger North Face with Joe Tasker, who now lay dead on Everest. As if to reinforce those associations, we bumped into Guy Neidhardt, a colleague of the other friend who had died on Everest, Peter Boardman. Guy laughed about the time when Peter had nearly got lost on the Grünhornlücke while guiding ski clients through a white-out, then wished us luck as we changed to the Jungfraujoch train.

The descent to Concordia in deep fresh powder was a wobbly business with our top-heavy loads, so on the long climb to the Grünhornlücke we were delighted to find ourselves behind a guided party breaking trail. They were a hearty English group straight out of *The Sloane Ranger Handbook* and they were amused by our giant rucksacks, especially when we stopped to rest on the crest of the pass: 'Good God, look at that – they can *sit* on them, too'.

An hour later we let ourselves into the winter room of the Finsteraarhorn hut, unguardianed at this time of year, and made ourselves the first of many mugs of tea and soup. We put our fees in the box and signed the book, recording our destination: 'Finsteraarhorn Nordostwand, via Agassizjoch.' Louis Agassiz was one of the first scientists to carry out systematic investigations of Alpine glaciers in the nineteenth century. He virtually invented the science of glaciology and much of his work was on the glaciers beneath the Finsteraarhorn. He made the first serious attempt to climb the mountain and the saddle or 'joch' which is the lowest point on the north-west ridge is named after him. Our plan was to leave our skis there, then descend onto the Finsteraargletscher on the far side and traverse round on foot to the start of the north-east face. It seemed perverse to be climbing halfway up a mountain in order to descend to its far side but the alternative eastern approach from the Grimsel Pass, closed to road traffic all winter, would have been even longer and more difficult.

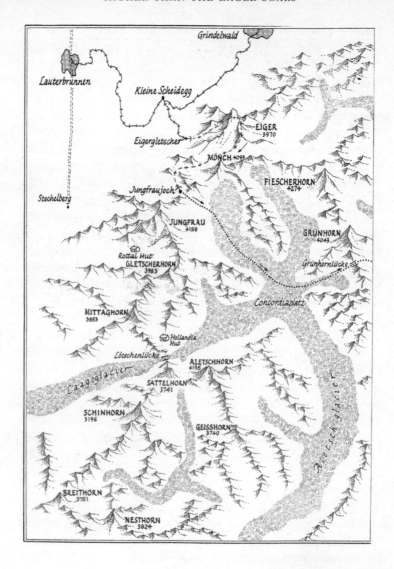

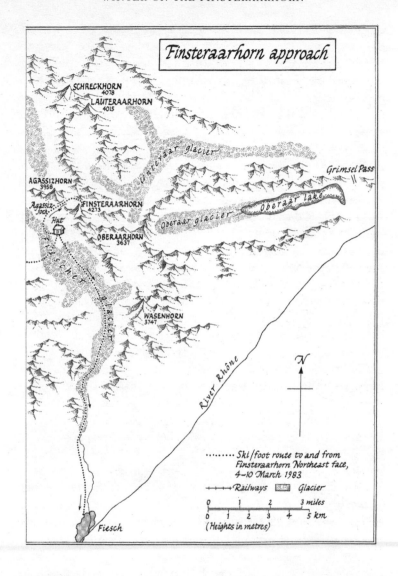

Finsteraarhorn approach

SCHRECKHORN
4078
LAUTERAARHORN
4015

Unteraar Glacier

Grimsel Pass

AGASSIZHORN
3958

Agassiz-
joch

FINSTERAARHORN
4273

Hut

Oberaar lake

Oberaar glacier

OBERAARHORN
3637

Fieschergletscher

WASENHORN
3747

River Rhône

N

.... Ski/foot route to and from
Finsteraarhorn Northeast face,
4–10 March 1983
++++ Railways ▨ Glacier

0   1   2   3 miles
0   1   2   3   4   5 km
(Heights in metres)

Fiesch

Anxious to make the most of the short winter day, we left the hut in the dark, using skins to zigzag up the western side of the Agassizjoch, roped together in case of concealed crevasses. I was in the lead just after dawn when I noticed parallel dimples ahead and took evasive action, turning sharply to zig back on the opposite tack. But as I turned up into the slope there was a sudden crumpling noise and my feet fell away beneath me.

At first Dick ignored the shouted oath, assuming that it was just Venables losing his temper again. But then I shouted louder and he turned round to see my head sinking beneath the surface. He whacked in his axe, braced his skis and whipped the rope tight. By which stage I was about two metres beneath the surface, hanging in an icy slot, skis dangling over what seemed in the light of my head-torch to be a bottomless chasm. The crevasse was only about two feet wide but at the very point of turning both my skis had been aligned perfectly with the slot, exerting maximum pressure on the fragile crust that concealed its maw.

I had never done a crevasse rescue before, but this was as good a place as any to learn. My prusik loops were already in place, one hitched between boot sole and ski, the other clipped into my waist harness. All I had to do now was work them – and my body – up the rope to the top of the crevasse. Which would have been easy if I had not been pulled backwards by my forty-five-pound rucksack. So, thrashing around in the narrow chasm, I had to wrestle off my burden and clip it into a spare length of rope lowered by Dick. That helped, but prusiking was still difficult with long planks swinging around on the end of my legs, catching on the chasm walls. The hardest part was the final exit; in the end I removed one of my skis, wedged it across the top of the crevasse and used it to heave out onto the surface where I flopped down next to Dick, completely exhausted.

All good character-building stuff, but it wasted at least an hour.

We continued in broad daylight to the Agassizjoch, swapped

skis for crampons, then abseiled and climbed 400 metres down the far side. The light was already beginning to fade as we waded across the glacier basin, taking turns to break trail through a minefield of crevasses, senses alert on one level to the slightest variation in the white surface but also, less pragmatically, alert to the thrill of being here, at last, in this remote cwm, with the great wall looming above, cold, grey and impassive.

That night's bivouac was *not* a five-star affair. We settled for a shallow scrape – a foxhole, not a proper dugout – and we paid for our idleness in the middle of the night when the wind began to strafe us with spindrift, forcing us to get out of bed and start digging again. So it was a rather curmudgeonly Venables who rose at dawn and eyed with Eeyorish gloom some purple clouds lurking on the eastern horizon. But they soon dispersed, the sun slid encouragingly down the great north-east wall and we set to work on the great central arête.

Describing her 1902 attempt, Gertrude Bell wrote to her brother: 'The arête . . . rises from the glacier in a great series of gendarmes and towers, set at such an angle on the steep face of the mountain that you wonder how they can stand at all and indeed they can scarcely be said to stand, for the great points of them are continually overbalancing and tumbling down into the couloirs . . . the game was beginning even when we crossed [the couloir] an hour after dawn.' Undaunted, Miss Bell and her guides, Ulrich and Heinrich Fuhrer, worked their way up the endless towers 'which multiplied like rabbits', getting progressively steeper until they were halted by 'a great tower leaning over to the right and made of slabs set like slates on top.'

We could see this Grey Tower 600 metres above, part of a huge pale streak daubed insolently across the wall by some indifferent geological artist. It looked repellent; but the couloir – the huge gully left of the arête – was white and silent, frozen into harmless immobility. So we sneaked past Miss Bell's fecund rabbits, sticking to the big snowy sweep of the couloir until late that afternoon when we followed a steepening tributary rightwards to the upper crest of the arête, well above most of the towers. Here, in the lee of a snow ridge, we dug a small cave, securing Dick's mini-bivouac tent over the entrance to keep out the wind.

Dick got in first to organise our sleeping quarters. Before joining him, I stuck my head over the crest of the snow ridge. I was hit by a cold northern blast and, staring down and across the great sweep of mountain wall, I felt intimidated by the raw grey rock and ice; it seemed not just indifferent but actually hostile, inimical to life.

I slid thankfully back down to the bivouac and joined Dick in the cave. As always, after a hard day's work, it was difficult to stay awake for the long ritual of melting snow for fruit juice, tea and soup. We usually added noodles to the latter. Biscuits, cheese and chocolate padded out the meal and we usually finished with a post-prandial Golden Virginia roll-up, the tobacco fumes adding a homely fug.

Then came sleep, fully clothed apart from boots, which in my case were leather so were kept in my sleeping bag, along with my camera, to stop them freezing. Then, far too soon, the hated purr of the gas stove announced that Dick had woken up and that soon I would have to get out of bed.

By dawn we were ready to leave. We pulled back the protecting bivouac sheet and looked out to purple fish-clouds nosing malevolently in a pale lemon sky. The weather man in Zurich, whom we used to phone regularly, had warned that there would be some cloud on Thursday morning, but that it would only be a brief blip in the anti-cyclone sitting over the Alps – nothing to worry about. But supposing the weather system had changed in the last few days? This looked like a proper storm brewing.

We dithered. Dick asked gloomily, 'What do you think?'

'I don't know. Why don't I go and have a look at the first pitch . . . just to see what it's like?' So, while Dick paid out the rope, I climbed back up onto the snow crest. I was hit immediately by a cruel blast. Clouds were now swirling round the face. I took a couple of steps along the ridge, then turned and shouted down to Dick: 'This is horrible. I'm coming back down.'

So that was it. End of dream. Another ignominious empty-handed retreat. Another failure.

I stared down the long complicated arête and the huge gully we had climbed. Thought about all those awkward belays on hard ice overlaid by powder snow. Pondered the grim effort of reversing at least six hundred metres. And then wading back across the glacier. And then? What if the storm was so bad that we had to retreat eastward to the little Aar bivouac hut? And then? An endless plod, up to our waists without skis, down the interminable trackless wastes leading to the Grimsel Pass. Or, if the storm blew over quickly, the alternative misery of climbing all the way back up to the Agassizjoch to ski down the west side of the Finsteraarhorn. I agonised over the grim seriousness of our position on this remote wall, miles from help. And the more I agonised, the more I came back to that meticulous voice in Zurich and his computerised weather forecast. Supposing he was right? Imagine the misery of turning back for nothing – wimping out unnecessarily. No, it would be ludicrous to give in so easily. Confusing my long-suffering companion waiting at the snow-cave, I shouted, 'No – I'm going *up*.'

It was bitterly cold and the swirling mist had coated the wall with hoar frost. But the heat of battle soon banished the cold and the fear and the doubts, so that by the end of the first pitch I realised I was actually enjoying myself. And as Dick came up to join me, looming out of the murk, he murmured, 'It's not too bad, is it?'

He took us round to the right. Then I took crampons off to lead two pitches up a sweep of pleasingly solid, granitic rock. And as I perched at the belay, bringing up Dick, I noticed that the clouds had gone and the wind had died and that I was having one of the best day's climbing of my life.

For the rest of that short winter day we were on the crest of the rib and as the light began to fade we found ourselves tiptoeing along a rock edge so fragile that it seemed to be swaying in the breeze. We were now on the band of pale grey rock streaked across the upper part of the wall. After one final tottering bollard we reached the foot of the Grey Tower. This was the point where Gertrude Bell had been turned back by the violent thunderstorm in 1902. Two years later Hasler had described the tower as 'perpendicular, monstrously smooth, [with] no question of frontal attack on that obstacle.' Seventy-nine years on, in the cold evening light, it still looked like concrete. As for Hasler's and Amatter's diversionary gully to the left, that didn't look much better either.

For the time being we took comfort in the immediacy of domestic arrangements, digging a large bucket seat in a steep snowbank where we could sit in our sleeping bags with the bivouac sack over our heads. And again, before joining Dick for supper, I had a last look out over the Alps – at the silent whiteness of it all, stretching far out to the east, mountain after mountain after mountain, all the way to those Bernina summits which I had first seen as a child, twenty years earlier. I turned to the left and smiled at the last pink glow on the Shreckhorn and Lauteraarhorn. Then I looked beyond to the lower shadowy northern outliers of the Alps. That one there, right on the northern edge, must be Pilatus. And just beyond it lay Luzern. And somewhere down there was Emmenbrücke, where Marianne would just be home from work.

Day Three dawned bright and cloudless, and the only sound was the crack of Swiss Army rifles somewhere out towards the Furka Pass. We packed up to leave and Dick, perhaps sensing my anxiety, took first lead of the day, descending leftward to the start of a very steep thin ice runnel, climbing that until it petered out, then tiptoeing left again onto a wall of stacked tiles. Describing his companion on this passage, Hasler wrote: 'Down that icy gully I lowered Amatter on the rope . . . then watched him work his way up the most impossible slabs I have ever seen, or wish to see. This particular place seemed to really extend him: he had for once in his life to climb all-out.' Three-quarters of a century later it still felt precarious but modern equipment gave us greater security so that, as I followed Dick up that first improbable pitch of the day, I realised again that I was enjoying myself enormously.

The detail of most climbs fades with time into a homogeneous blur but that third day on the North-East Face of the Finsteraarhorn remains in sharp focus. I remember vividly the fourth pitch, which I led. I remember the piton I found – the only sign of previous passage we found on the entire wall. I remember the bulging boss of transparent ice where I had to hook my axe pick delicately and step in a sling, because the ice was too thin to take crampon points. I remember the sixth pitch of stacked blocks, where I could only place one runner – a sling draped round a dubious spike – in fifty metres. And the next pitch, where you had to bridge wide with feet, balanced ever more steeply, relishing the thousand-metre plunge to the glacier because you felt in control, attuned to this precarious environment. And the final, eighth, pitch of the day, which Dick led, heaving past an overhang under which I cowered as he sent down a steady clatter of loose rubble, removing the rotten holds to find the good stuff underneath.

Some people prefer iron-hard solidity and so do I on the whole. But occasionally I enjoy the subtler challenge of more ephemeral rock. I like the textural variety. I like the delicacy of it – having to push rather than pull, spreading your weight more carefully. And here, on the fortieth pitch – knowing that it had taken two days just to get to the foot of this wall, and then another three days to climb it – the elation of following Dick in the dark and emerging beside him on the summit ridge was very sweet. It didn't matter that the gas finished that night, leaving us with just half a cup of lukewarm tea. It didn't matter that the down in our sleeping bags had become damp. I still slept blissfully. And woke equally happily the next morning, to continue breakfastless over the summit and down the northwest ridge, abseiling over the awkward sections, eventually regaining the skis we had left four days earlier and gliding back down to the hut, where a very generous Swiss guide shared with us the single bottle of wine that he had carried up for his two ski clients.

On the seventh and final day of our outing we skied south, down the Fiescher Glacier, glad of the guide's tracks through some complicated crevasse fields, then on, down snow-smothered scree slopes and meadows and forest tracks, until we had at last to take off our skis and walk, hobbling in our double boots, squelching through the newly uncovered earth, returning to the spring.

Dick left for home the next day, keen to get back to Jan and Daniel. I rushed over to Luzern and stayed there for the next few weeks, sustained by a lingering glow of satisfaction and by the pleasure of being in love. Marianne was affectionate and kind, while her sister Therese was astonishingly tolerant of the rather irascible Englishman invading the sisterly space. I argued too often with Marianne, playing devil's advocate to her feminist vegetarianism, was scornful about her music and sulked when she wouldn't share my rapture at a chance radio broadcast of Mirella Freni singing the heart-rending farewell in Verdi's *Don Carlos*. She coped with me humorously and generously, and when my cash was running low persuaded her father to take me on for a week's bricklaying on his new house extension.

It was a fretful spring in the Alps, with no return of the high pressure that had blessed our Finsteraarhorn climb. The warm föhn wind blew from Italy, sending the cows into bell-clanging frenzies and destabilising the high snows, with avalanche warnings on the radio nearly every day. But at the end of April, Marianne and I did manage to snatch a day's ski-touring in the Uri Alps, which in the nineteenth century had fascinated Turner and Ruskin, both of whom spent several months painting around Luzern. We used a tiny cable car to reach the snow level, then skinned for four hours up the Ruchstock, accompanied by a Czech émigré called Karel who was skiing on his own. From the summit he and Marianne descended in beautiful swishing S curves. I followed more jerkily and, it has to be said, a touch enviously. Marianne had to get back that evening as she was teaching the next day. I announced that I would stay up at a hut and climb the Wissigstock in the morning. So I left Marianne to ski off into the sunset with Karel. When I returned to Luzern the next day she told me what a courteous gentleman he was and how beautifully he skied and how he had bought her a drink. Three years later it came as no surprise when she wrote to say that she had met Karel again and that they were now living together. It was shortly after that, skiing again on the Ruchstock, that Karel broke his ankle. With spooky irony he later broke his leg a second time on the same fateful slope. I told him that I had cast a vengeful spell on the mountain.

Back in 1983, still ensconced happily at Marianne's flat, I met some local climbers and began to join them, bicycling out along Lake Luzern to climb on a beautiful limestone cliff on the side of Mount Pilatus. The rock was gorgeously pocketed, the movements fluid and gymnastic. The beech leaves were shimmering lime green, the whitebeams gleaming in their first fresh silveriness; and one evening two long-tailed tits gathered nesting material beside my belay on the clifftop. Racing home along the shore of the lake, glancing out at the crested grebes dancing their courtship rituals like comical water-skiers, I felt deliriously happy, seizing the moment because I knew that it had soon to end.

Marianne was leaving later that summer on a trip round the world with her friend Gabi. She would be gone for over a year. I needed to get back to Britain and do some work, earn some money and get ready for my next expedition. It was now four years since the morning with Philip when I had seen that beautiful mountain in Kishtwar and I had finally made the decision to go back and try to climb it. Marianne and I were going in different directions. It was time to say goodbye.

Chapter Ten

Painted Mountains

People often ask how you raise the huge amounts of money for a Himalayan expedition; but you don't necessarily need huge sums. The total cost of our 1983 Kishtwar-Shivling expedition was £2,423 (about £5,500 at today's prices). £1,200 came in grants from the Mount Everest Foundation and the British Mountaineering Council; the other half from Dick's and my pockets – just over six hundred pounds each. Still, those six hundred pounds had to be earned.

My fanciful notion of living off lectures and sponsorship had not yet materialised, so I spent the summer decorating houses near Bath. On free weekends I hitched occasionally to Wales to join Dick climbing on the Pembrokeshire sea cliffs. Then in July, shortly before departure for Kishtwar, I spent a week in the Lake District with Phil Bartlett, Jonathan Dawson and Béatrice, who was back in York, teaching at a girl's school. It was the perfect limbering-up for an expedition, but it was also perfect in its own right. I love the Lake District, even if it does sometimes look as though Mrs Tiggywinkle has been busy with her dustpan and brush: I *like* the picturesque artificiality of the man-made landscape. And, having always struggled with the unpronounceable nomenclature of the Welsh and Scottish hills, I like Cumberland's more accessible poetry.

Jonathan, Béatrice and I drove over Wrynose Pass, then

shouldered our rucksacks to walk up Mosedale to Throstle Garth, stopping for a swim in Lincove Beck. Then we continued across the springy summer peat to the Great Moss, where we sat beside our tent and drank a bottle of the vinho verde which seemed to be fashionable in the early 1980s. I soloed an easy route on Esk Buttress, recalling nostalgically my previous visit to this remote crag, eight years earlier, with Paul Beney. The next day we dropped over Broad Stand to the north face of Scafell. Neither of the other two was a very experienced climber, but they were happy to follow me up a dramatically narrow tilting plane of rock first climbed eighty years earlier by Frank Botterill.

Botterill's Slab was just one of the many classic routes I did that week, marvelling at the genius of the people who had the vision to discover these lines – and the boldness to climb them. When Phil arrived we did *Extol*, the line which Don Whillans forced through Dove Crag's beetling overhangs in 1960. Another day we ran up to Pavey Ark, stopping for a quick swim in Stickle Tarn before balancing up the slaty subtleties of Rob Matheson's *Cruel Sister*. For me this route brought the childish buzz of succeeding on my first E3 climb, teetering close to my personal limit, almost crying with relief when I completed the crux pitch and flopped onto a ledge bright with harebells.

We spent the last two days camping beside, and swimming in, England's deepest lake, Wastwater, Jonathan acting the butler, standing at the water's edge with a towel folded over his arm as a naked Béatrice rose Venus-like from the glittering water. That afternoon Phil and I climbed *Saxon*, perhaps the most beautiful route on Scafell's main crag. It was one of those rare moments when everything flows. Feet balance on the tiniest holds; fingers curl confidently over the most incipient rugosity; one's whole body moves with fluid ease. It's like a musician having the confidence to let go of the nervous tension and immerse himself totally in the music, unhindered by technical anxiety, mind and body perfectly synchronised.

By the time we were coiling the ropes at the top of *Saxon*

the whole crag was glowing orange. We raced back down for a couple of pints of Jennings bitter at the Wasdale Head, then the other two led us back to the lake and flung aside a camouflage screen of bracken to reveal glowing embers and a surprise celebratory spread of cubed meat and vegetables spiked to kebab sticks improvised from old fencing wire.

Three weeks later, sweating it out on the platform of Old Delhi railway station, waiting for the night train to Jammu, I longed to be back in Wasdale. Here the heat was muggy, the crowds relentless. Over the hubbub a loudspeaker asked us to be reasonable and not carry too much luggage, nor ride on the footplates, nor enter an air-conditioned carriage without an air-conditioned ticket, and please, while waiting for the train, not to sit on the platform but to use the seats provided. Which seemed unrealistic, when there were only four benches to cater for several hundred hopeful passengers packed onto the platform, not to mention the destitute families who just happened to live there.

The train arrived and we managed to get all eighteen pieces of luggage of the British Kishtwar-Shivling Expedition into the air-conditioned carriage, with the correct tickets. I slept blissfully but the following afternoon, ensconced in a cheap lodging room at Jammu bus station, I began again to yearn for Beatrix Potter Land. The frenetic din of scooters, buses, lorries, taxis and rickshaws; the smell of drains; the bandy-legged porters struggling with hundred-kilogram loads to our room; the disconsolate beggar's face attached to a shrivelled legless torso perched on the bus-station floor; the scrawny soft-eyed cows ambling nonchalantly amongst the crowds, nosing through piles of refuse ... it all seemed so ugly, so randomly cruel.

The pre-climb blues were not helped by a general lack of rapport. Patial, the Indian army officer assigned as 'liaison officer' to the expedition, seemed disappointed by the shoe-string parsimony the British Kishtwar-Shivling Expedition. He yearned for kitbags of shiny new gear and had difficulty following our English accents. We misunderstood his Indian accent, or got exasperated by his grandiloquent pronounce-ments: 'Communications is Must. Otherwise I don't know where you are going, and you will just be in hands of God.' But morale began to lift two days later when we reached Kishtwar and Patial arranged for mule transport to our base camp, announcing that: 'Tomorrow, after packing all the articles, we will proceed to our destination.'

After a four-day journey we reached the temple to the goddess Chandi, at Machail. I had a streaming cold, I was aching all over and I was splattered with mud; by contrast, the twenty pilgrim women and girls whose singing had enchanted us on the bus four days earlier all looked radiant in freshly laundered saris and glossy plaits, spotless after their sixty-mile trek through the forest. Not for the first nor for the last time, I felt acutely the uncouthness of the foreigner in India.

Dirt and illness notwithstanding, I was starting gradually to feel at home and I was delighted the next day, at 'Potato Village', to see the excited smiles of the family that Philip and I had visited as I handed them photos of their four-years-younger selves. And, later that day, after leading the mules across the river by a bridge of old compacted winter snow, it was delightful to make our base camp in a glade of gleaming birches, next to a babbling brook fringed by raspberry bushes.

Home-building was essential to morale. With birch poles and a large sheet of polythene we made a kitchen, lining the floor with hessian sacks. But before that, we started off the vital fermentation on a barrel of home-brew beer. Patial got to know the neighbours – an extended family of Gujars – and soon they came to visit, washing blankets in the hollow bole of a birch by the stream, or just sitting and watching us, intrigued by all our mountaineering paraphernalia. Other visi-tors passed by – traders heading over the Umasi La, bound for the high arid country of Zanskar. By way of acclimatisa-tion Dick and I spent a couple of days walking up to this high pass which had eluded Philip and me four years earlier, and on the way back down met a couple of monks in maroon robes who were accompanied by a retainer carrying a tree trunk over the Himalaya for roof repairs at their monastery.

Back in the valley some Indian soldiers turned up. 'Who *else* would have such a big tent?' I asked.

'Chris Bonington,' mocked Dick. But then he continued, 'Actually, I wouldn't mind . . .' as he recalled the well-appointed Everest base camp of the previous year. It was only sixteen months since he had led one of the hardest pitches ever climbed above eight thousand metres, only to experience that sudden momentary numbness down one side of his body. Only sixteen months since Charlie Clarke had warned him not to go to extreme altitude ever again. Only sixteen months since that cruel disappointment had been eclipsed, a few days later, by the tragedy of Boardman and Tasker disappearing on their last fatal climb.

Dick didn't talk much about his dead friends but he did occasionally describe how powerfully driven the whole team had been on Everest. He seemed to bring the same determination to this much lower climb. When we had arrived beneath Kishtwar-Shivling I had at first been daunted by what seemed an ugly travesty of the gleaming vision I had had four years earlier; whereas Dick had been calmly analytical, setting off on our second morning to recce a route to a suitable site for our advance base and spotting a possible line to the summit.

Whatever route we chose was going to commit us to hard, intricate climbing with no easy alternative; this untrodden peak was temptingly elusive. The main thing was to chose a *safe* line, and the broad ridge that Dick had spotted, butting up against the upper part of the north face, seemed to evade all the obvious dangers of the lower face which was threatened by unstable ice cliffs. On 29 August, nine days after reaching Base Camp, we both climbed up with heavy loads to establish Advance Base at a saddle on the ridge. Bad weather sent us back to base. We returned on 1 September, only to find ourselves stuck for two days, reading Galsworthy and Dickens as rain pelted the tent and, higher up, snow avalanches roared down the north face.

But at last, on 4 September, we were able to get above Advance

Base, climbing before dawn over steepening fields of rock and snow, then onto a winding ridge which led us to the first real obstacle – a vertical ice wall, which Dick led magnificently, red Gore-Tex suit bright against the turquoise ice as the sun slid down the mountain to meet us. We continued to a big snow terrace, then up a beautiful snow arête, arrow-straight, pointing the way to a crenellated rock crest where I was thrilled to stick my head round the corner and spy a convenient ledge bypassing the awkward battlements. Pleased with the recce, we left all the surplus climbing gear at our highpoint and set off back down, returning to Advance Base twelve hours after setting out.

Keen to dry out gear and rest thoroughly, we decided to wait one more day before starting the climb proper. I lounged contentedly in the sun while Dick nipped down to Base Camp to send off some letters, returning in the evening with a large tin of dhal cooked specially by Patial, along with a couple of eggs donated by the Gujar shepherdess to whom he had taken a shine.

The dhal was a kind gesture from the man who had adapted so generously to expedition life, but it gave me terrible indigestion and by the time midnight arrived – and I still hadn't managed to sleep – I was fretting to be away.

We left at two a.m., climbing in the dark up the fixed rope that we had left on the ice cliff. While I waited at the top for Dick to join me, 'the morn, in russet mantle clad' began to illuminate the peaks at the head of the valley. Remembering dimly that snatch of *Hamlet*, first heard fourteen years earlier, I marvelled at the improbability of it all, wondered whether as a schoolboy I could possibly have imagined myself here – perched on this ice cliff, witnessing this dawn, setting out on this extraordinary journey. All the doubts and the pathetic self-pity had gone; once again, I just felt profoundly happy to be where I was.

Laden with food and gas for possibly ten days on the mountain, we climbed slowly back up to our highpoint, then shuffled along the rock ledge to a convenient balcony where we stopped early to bivouac, sleeping so well on our rock bed that the sun had already risen by the time we got going the next morning.

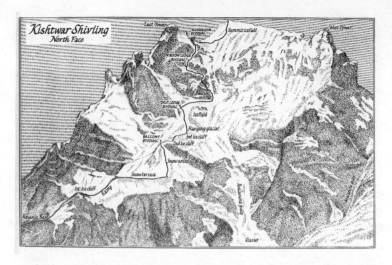

The first job was to get onto the huge glacial shelf stuck onto the middle of the North Face of Kishtwar-Shivling. To do this we had to climb two ice cliffs. Dick led the first, which was brittle and plum vertical. I led the second, which was slightly overhanging but generously endowed with a crevasse – a chimney into which I could squeeze and squirm up past the overhang. We stopped on the shelf above for a snack, then continued onto the upper wall, thrilled to find firm, hard, white ice, then even more thrilled to find a spot where we could excavate a ledge with enough room for the two of us to lie down at full stretch, tied securely to pitons and nuts wedged in the rock above.

The rock was a bit wet, so we called this second bivouac Drip Ledge; but by evening the drips had frozen to ice and we sat comfortably, drinking our soup, eating the smoked cheese that Dick had brought from Cardiff, watching the sun set behind Brammah – the peak about forty miles to the west which Chris Bonington and Nick Estcourt had climbed thirteen years earlier and which had been attempted before that by Charlie Clarke, whose photos had first alerted me to this gorgeous Kishtwar region.

On Day Three we managed to get away at first light, traversing

Kishtwar-Shivling, showing the four bivouac sites

rightwards to an almost vertical ice runnel that led directly to the summit. But when we got there we took fright. The white carapace lay thin and hollow over blank rock. How would we find anchors? And what about that summit cornice, looming so huge over our heads – did we want to labour for hours and hours, directly beneath it?

'I don't like the look of it,' Dick admitted. 'I think we should try out to the left, on the rock. Why don't you have a look at that chimney?' So I headed back left into a more comforting landscape where you could hook and grapple solid rock and make secure belays. And through this alternative landscape we meandered back and forth, following our noses – and what seemed to be the line of least resistance – until, late that afternoon, at the end of the ninth pitch of the day, Dick arrived at a pedestal beneath a very steep rock wall capped by an overhang. At which point we decided that we had had enough for one day.

On top of the pedestal was a large blob of snow. We hacked

hopefully at the blob, but the best we could produce was a sloping ledge sixty centimetres wide and thirty centimetres deep on which to sit though the night, upright in our sleeping bags, feet resting in a cat's cradle of suspended ropes, cooking stove balanced on the ledge between us.

Darkness fell and we lit our torches, answering Patial's flashes from our base camp, two thousand metres below. 'This is like sitting on a window ledge, on the fiftieth floor of a tower block,' observed Dick. 'Do you wish we had stayed in the runnel, on the direct line?'

'No,' I replied. 'At least here we have good protection and solid belays. I'm just not quite sure where we're going to go in the morning.'

The mood of a big climb is a finely tuned thing, always oscillating. For three days everything had gone so well; now I felt apprehensive, nervous about the overhang waiting above us in the darkness, resentful at being denied a good night's sleep. The discomfort was at least an incentive to get going early in the morning. And once we had completed the deli-cate business of packing up one at a time on our minuscule ledge, I was surprised to find that I was actually *enjoying* the new day, taking the first lead – removing crampons when I found myself on bare steep rock, climbing up into a deep chimney beneath the overhang, slotting in a camming device for protection, then reaching up over the huge suspended flake and discovering real holds. This was like being back on Scafell! On *Saxon*! Gorgeously wrinkled rock for fingers to curl over. Sharp edges where boot soles could poise confidently over the huge void.

That beautiful first overhang set the tone for the whole day. I led another pitch, then handed over to Dick to lead us up a stunningly geometric corner seamed with ice. Then I continued rightwards, balancing on snow smudges plastered to seemingly blank rock, then jamming boots up a crack, then balancing rightwards again, in the sun now, fingers loving the warm crys-talline roughness of the granite. While I brought up Dick I sucked boiled sweets and chunks of icicle, soothing my dry throat. Then he took us back into a whiter landscape where the rocks were islands in a vertical sea of snow and ice. Another pitch for me. Then Dick again, urging me to hurry as the sun sank in a sky now seething with clouds, handing me the gear and saying, 'You should be able to get us onto the ridge with this pitch.'

I kicked up near-vertical snow, to emerge on top of one of the huge bulbous mushrooms blobbed onto the crest of the north-east ridge. There, poised precariously between north and east faces, we rested, this time on a comfortable double bed with room to lie at full stretch. And everything would have been perfect if I had not, in a moment's carelessness, knocked the stove with my elbow.

There was a hiss of doused flame and I grabbed the stove, but the pan went over the edge, clattering down the east face. Dehydrated after a long day at altitude, Dick briefly lost his temper, pointing an accusing head-torch in my face and snapping, 'Bloody fool! We can't go to the summit now: without water we'll just have to go down.'

'But hang on,' I pleaded. 'I'm sure we can improvise.' I unscrewed the cartridge from the stove, tipped out the remaining gas and set to with my penknife, hacking the top off the cylinder to create a very inefficient but just functional mini-saucepan, in which I laboriously melted tiny cupfuls of snow, sitting up most of the night as punishment for my carelessness.

Day Five – Summit Day – dawned menacingly, with clouds lapping the feet of the mountain and evil lenticulars hovering high in the north-east. Determined to beat the storm, we travelled light, leaving all the bivouac gear on the Mushroom. We set off at five-thirty a.m., abseiling down the east side of the Mushroom, then climbing over a notch to get back onto the north face.

After the delights of the previous day, this was terrifying: no comforting tactile granite – just filigree snow flutings stuck precariously to brittle ice. Across this ephemeral, insubstantial snowscape we clawed and kicked our way, burrowing through a succession of flutings until at last, after four rope lengths, we found ourselves back in the main runnel – the line we had forsaken two days earlier – immediately beneath the summit. I led straight up for fifty metres, then stopped to cut a foot ledge and anchor myself to two ice screws driven to the hilt. The exposure was sensational and as Dick came up I stared down into the swirling void, imagining what would happen if the belay failed – the two of us catapulted from the face, flung down into the swirling white void.

It was starting to snow and the first spindrift avalanches were pouring down from the summit. Dick led another full rope length up to a notch, then I continued, panting heavily, groaning, 'Why do I get so tired?'

'Because you've hardly eaten for three days.'

The slope eased back, crusty ice gave way to soft powder and all I had to do was kick a few more steps out onto the flat white top of Kishtwar-Shivling.

For four years I had dreamed of climbing this mountain. Now we were here – the first people ever to tread on this elusive snow dome, protected on every side by plunging walls – this perfect dream summit. But there was no view, no joy – just the urgent worry of being out in a snowstorm, late in the day, a long way from our sleeping bags. Dreading the descent, unsure whether we could complete it before dark, I even suggested digging a snow-cave on the summit and descending in the morning. Dick was scathing: 'What, stop here!? Without sleeping bags? What happens if this develops into a proper storm? No – we're going down. You'll just have to pull out all the stops.'

So down we went, abseiling from our hard-won summit, sliding diagonally into the murk, fearful of the careless skid which could send us swinging back across the ice in a huge pendulum, grimacing at the cold smothering waves of spindrift, peering through iced sunglasses, trying to discern landmarks amongst the ghostly flutings as the light faded.

The last horizontal section could not be abseiled: we had

to climb – sideways. Dick led it in the dark, while I paid out the rope. The clouds had now lifted and I could see Patial's signal far below. Rashly optimistic, we had left our torches at the bivouac that morning, so I could give no answering flash.

I marvelled at Dick's courage when I followed with the security of a backrope threaded through the anchor I had left behind. When I joined him at the end of the terrifying traverse, determined to salvage some scraps of self-esteem, I insisted on leading the final pitch up vertical snow, in pitch darkness, to get us back to our bed on top of the Mushroom.

In the morning I woke to bright sunlight and the sight of Dick's sunburnt swollen-lipped face with the summit cone behind him, gleaming in a deep blue sky. We were tired – very tired – but this climb seemed blessed: the snowstorm had simply added spice to the summit struggle and now we were granted a lucky break for our descent. We did twelve abseils that day, getting all the way back down to Drip Ledge where spare food and gas were waiting. Then on Day Seven we continued down. I was tempted to linger. The bright autumn weather was unthreatening, the mountain – *our* mountain – luminously beautiful with its coat of fresh snow remaining from two days earlier. I wanted to absorb it, impress every detail of it on my memory, possess it completely. But Dick was determined to hurry down: 'I want to get the job finished. I don't see mountains as friendly things: they're hostile and dangerous, and the longer you hang around the more chance you have of being killed.'

I admitted reluctantly that he was right – that the enjoyment had to be savoured afterwards. We abseiled quickly, efficiently back down to The Balcony, where more food reserves were waiting, then kept up the hard concentration, descending the snow arête, rope length by rope length, then the first ice cliff, the lower ridge . . . and finally the last easy snowfield to Advance Base, where we packed everything into hideously bulging rucksacks and continued down, down, down, to the gentle green warmth of the birch glade where Patial was waiting, overjoyed that his eccentric charges had completed their crazy mission and that now he could go home.

The homecoming was blissful. Relaxing in the sun the next day with a mug of our home-made beer, whittling away at one of the wood carvings that would eventually lure him away from the mountains to a more settled life as a sculptor, Dick conceded, 'It was a hard climb.' That acknowledgement, coming from him, was hugely gratifying. It *was* a demanding climb. But it was also, apart from odd moments of discomfort, immensely enjoyable – both at the time and in retrospect. Back in Britain, reliving the climb through the photos, writing it up, preparing lectures, I felt that I had at last achieved something solid – something to quell, for a while at least, all those feelings of striving and yearning.

I even began to make a bit more money from my articles and lectures; but not enough to live off. So I returned to decorating and, more enjoyably, to carpentry – building bedroom cupboards, hi-fi cabinets and bookcases. My father, who had always been a very skilful cabinetmaker, had now retired from advertising and agreed generously to work with me on some of the more ambitious projects. I met the clients and did the drawings and quotations; he provided the expertise actually to make the stuff; we both worked for the same hourly rate.

I enjoyed the puzzling-out of technical problems, but also the sheer physical pleasure of working with wood – the smell of wood shavings, the fine edge on a Sheffield-steel chisel, the perfection of a good dovetail joint. There were obvious parallels with climbing, not least the tired fingers which would probably, as a result of all that strain, never be very lucid on the keyboard. Nevertheless, I did keep up the piano, my enthusiasm revitalised in the summer of 1984 by playing chamber music and falling in love with the trio's cellist, Kate.

Her family lived in a large gracious house with a beautiful garden and were very generous to me while I worked on several carpentry commissions. It was all very contented and domestic, far from the battles raging around the coal mines further north, and it was the same world – albeit a slightly grander form of it – in which I had grown up: a privileged, lucky world, but a world only maintained by periodic injections of talent and enterprise, or at least some determined hard graft. Inevitably, I questioned yet again my hand-to-mouth nomadic existence and wondered if it wasn't just the perpetuating of a bad habit. Returning that autumn to the Karakoram – with Dick again – was a wrench.

It was an open-ended wandering sort of expedition and, although we made first ascents of three peaks, there was a lacklustre feeling to the trip and I think it was only a dogged Protestant work ethic that kept us committed for several weeks, until I finally sent back a card announcing, 'The sedge has withered from the lake, it's bloody cold and I'm coming home.' Part of the gloom stemmed, I think, from the suspicion that when I did get home Kate wouldn't be there for me.

She wasn't. I got over the disappointment by immersing myself in an ambitious new bookcase job and by trying to learn Beethoven's *Les Adieux* sonata, sublimating dreams of what might have been in the joyful rippling arpeggios of the final movement, *Le Retour*. As for returning to *the mountains*, I wondered whether the time had come to pack in all that nonsense. And perhaps that would have happened if my temporarily jaded appetite had not been re-titillated by an invitation to the Alpine Club to send a team of climbers on a joint venture, with Indian climbers, to the Siachen Glacier in northern Ladakh.

Here was something to fire the imagination. A real adventure. I knew that the Siachen was the biggest glacier in the world outside the polar regions – an immense ice highway flowing eastward from the region of K2. The precise political status of this eastern part of the Karakoram range was never clearly stated when India was partitioned in 1947. Even after the second Indo-Pakistan war of 1965, when the Kashmir-ceasefire 'line of control' was ratified by international treaty, that line remained vague at its northern end where it reached the Karakoram, left ambiguously to 'following the line of the glaciers'.

The geopolitical question of the Eastern Karakoram was almost forgotten until in the late 1970s Pakistan began authorising foreign mountaineers, mainly Japanese, to cross high passes from their territory to attempt some of the peaks surrounding the Siachen Glacier – peaks that the Delhi government had always assumed were Indian. Sensitivity about this most northern point of India was intensified by the threat from India's much bigger neighbour, China – a threat which had been demonstrated graphically in the 1960s when Chinese troops occupied a Wales-sized chunk of Indian territory called the Aksai Chin.

The Siachen crisis came to a head in 1984 when the Indian army, supported by fleets of helicopters, occupied the glacier and established gun posts on key high passes overlooking Pakistan. This was the most ambitious mountain campaign since the Italian-Austrian Dolomite campaign of the First World War; but in addition to the dangers of cold and avalanche, these Indian soldiers – most of who had never even *seen* snow, let alone climbed it – had to face the physiological attrition of extreme altitude, living at heights greater than any Alpine summit.

Visiting the Siachen as guests of India a year later, our purpose was to validate that country's sovereignty over the area. I had no qualms about being a political pawn; in fact, I felt a slightly guilty thrill at the prospect of climbing in a war zone. And *what* a war zone – a wonderland of unclimbed peaks which only a handful of mountaineers had explored since the first pioneers – Francis Younghusband in 1889, Thomas Longstaff in 1909 and the formidable Fanny Bullock Workman, with her 'Votes for Women' banner in 1912 – had unlocked the secrets of Central Asia's greatest glacier.

The invitation had to be accepted, the opportunity seized, the adventure made to happen. Dave Wilkinson, my old companion from Kunyang Kish and Peru, was keen. The last time we had spent any time together had been the 1981 Christmas sojourn in the Stechelberg Naturfreundhaus, with Dick, assailed by the twittering 'Birdie Song'. The fourth person in that group had been a London architect called Victor Saunders, whom I had first met halfway up a rock climb in the Avon Gorge. He was short and lithe and climbed beautifully; his conversation was provocative, elliptical, insatiably curious; his appearance dark and foreign, belying the Anglo-Saxon public-school vocal delivery. His mother was Siberian, his father one of the Germans who had come to Scotland in the 1930s as educational fodder for Kurt Hahn's experimental new school, Gordonstoun. Victor followed in his father's footsteps in the 1960s and hated the school, but he did develop a passion for the mountains, first as a skier in the Alpine resort of Mürren – where he raced with the British junior team – and later as a very gifted natural climber.

Dave, Victor and I were all keen. As was Jim Fotheringham, a dentist from Westmorland whom we knew only by repute: two years earlier he had made the first ascent of another Shivling – Shivling West, in the Garhwal Himalaya – with Chris Bonington. As soon as we met Jim we all liked him and invited him to join the team. That made four from Britain. Then Meena Agrawal, a paediatric surgeon at Guy's Hospital, announced that she would like to come. Her Hindu family had fled Karachi in 1947 to settle in Bombay and, although she now lived in London, she knew the Bombay climbers who would be accompanying us.

The sixth member from Britain was sixty-three-year-old Henry Osmaston. He was born in the Himalaya, where his immediate ancestors included several distinguished leaders of the colonial survey and forestry services, and his first child-hood memory was of riding an elephant in the forests of Garhwal. Later he was sent to the inevitable boarding school in England. At Oxford he studied forestry and in the 1950s went to work for the Forestry Service of Uganda. His wife Anna taught him to climb and the two of them spent much of their leave in the Rwenzori – the Mountains of the Moon – on whose equatorial snows Henry founded the highly exclusive Ski Club of Uganda. By the time we met him in 1985 his four children had left home and he was well into his second career as a geography lecturer at Bristol University – a career he combined with running a dairy herd at the Jacobean farmhouse where he lived to the south of the city. Anna had the indulgent, long-suffering look of a woman who had spent much of her life waiting for her husband to return, late, from a dangerous encounter with a buffalo, or a near miss with a leopard, or yet another unplanned bivouac. He played perfectly the part of the absent-minded professor, consumed by his enthusiasms, charming to all his companions.

So now we were six from Britain, with Dave as nominal British leader. I was the fund-raiser, helped enormously by the President of the Alpine Club, Roger, the second Lord Chorley. He was senior partner in a big firm of accountants and used his clout to persuade various City colleagues to support us. He also tipped us off that Grindlays Bank in India might be able to help. Which they did, covering the entire costs of the expedition from Bombay onwards.

The advance party, Dave and I, flew at the end of May to Bombay and there we met our Gujarati leader Harish Kapadia, a chubby gastronome who made things happen through sheer force of personality. From the moment we met him at the airport we just knew that this expedition was going to be fun. The rest of the team were also hugely likeable. Dhiren Toolsidas was the youngest and quietest, a banker who was put inevitably in charge of bookkeeping. Zerksis Boga's slim aquiline looks were eloquent of his Persian ancestry: he was one of the many Bombay Parsees who love the Himalaya and he had already been on several expeditions with Harish. As had Muslim Contractor, whose thoughtful worried frown was always ready to break into a wry smile at the first hint of absurdity.

There was only one small intercultural problem to solve. Back at home I had produced a leaflet and expedition notepaper with the help of Adrian, the graphic designer whom we had met on Budget Bus eight years earlier. His design looked beautiful. No problem there. 'But,' said Harish, as he forced us to eat yet another succulent Alfonso mango, 'we cannot be called Anglo-Indian Expedition. This is considered very rude here.' In my ignorance I had labelled us a bunch of post-colonial half-castes; from here on, we would go by the pukkah title 'Siachen Indo-British Expedition 85'.

Yet again, the blundering uncouthness of the Englishman abroad. But our hosts were generously forgiving, impeccably courteous, determined to make this joint venture a success. A huge crowd of friends and helpers – men in crisply laundered shirtsleeves, women in saris – came to see us off from Bombay Central Station. Twenty-four hours and five states later, at Delhi, SIBE 85 was joined by Harsinh Senior, Harsinh Junior and Pratapsinh – hill farmers from Kumaon who worked for Harish each summer in return for financial support to their families.

From Jammu we continued by bus. But where two years earlier Dick and I had turned right up the Chenab, heading for Kishtwar, we now continued north over the mountains to Srinagar. Here, on the lawn of a comfortable hotel, I wrote letters, telling friends and family what a wonderful time we were having. In comparison to previous shoestring ventures, this expedition, with its more generous budget, had a feeling of expansiveness and big expectations. It was a treat to have local experts organising everything so smoothly, and gratifying to know that the commander-in-chief of all the forces in Kashmir was okaying our journey to the Siachen, in the meantime loaning a jeep and driver to ferry us between Srinagar's Mogul gardens.

The Shalimar is probably the most famous garden but my favourite was the Nishat. A series of geometric cascades and pools, framed by the solid mass of chinar trees – Kashmir's stately planes – draws the eye down to the Dal Lake, silver and ethereal, where a causeway of slender poplars and an arched bridge seem to float above the water; beyond the lake rises the hill of Hari Parbat with its massive fort, dark against the distant blue backdrop of the Pir Panjal mountains.

Later that day we took a shikara out to Char Chinar Island, besieged by children in other boats offering us lotus flowers. It all seemed so idyllic and it was hard to believe what resentment lay beneath the surface. This was the old heart of Kashmir, that state which the British had enlarged and extended right up to the Karakoram as a buffer zone against perceived threats from the north, never quite establishing the precise extent of its boundaries. In 1947 the Maharajah of this huge disparate state elected to join the new republic of India, whereupon the Muslim majorities in the western areas such as Gilgit, Hunza and Baltistan took up arms and sided with Pakistan. But after the ceasefire the bulk of Jammu & Kashmir state still remained in Indian hands. A large part of the state – Zanskar and Ladakh – was predominantly Buddhist. Other areas, such as Kishtwar, had mixed populations of Buddhists, Hindus and Muslims. Here in Srinagar, the vast majority were Muslims, and most of them felt more affinity with Pakistan than with India.

The war zone we were about to enter – right at the northern limit of Kashmir – was just the latest flashpoint in a situation that seemed as complex and intractable as Northern Ireland or Israel. The difference in this localised battlefield of 1985 was that the armies were fighting over mountains where no one actually lived. The battle was as much about symbolism as it was about real strategic or economic significance.

To get closer to that symbolic battleground we drove by bus for another two days, over the high passes of the Zoji La and Fotu La, crossing from a land of alpine greenery to the stark bright ochres of Ladakh and its capital, Leh, where Meena, Jim and Victor were waiting to meet us.

That night Harish ordered 160 momoes – Tibetan stuffed dumplings. Over the next few days we ate many more dumplings, visited monasteries and bathed in the icy waters of the Indus, while the army chiefs prevaricated over our permits to continue further north. Frequently we heard the roar of fighter jets taking off from the military runway and later we discovered that there had been fierce fighting around the Siachen Glacier that week, with several soldiers killed. It was one thing for the Indian government to invite the Alpine Club to climb its mountains; but they didn't want foreigners actually witnessing dead troops or – even more embarrassing – getting killed themselves in the crossfire.

After three false starts we continued at last, in a large truck, grinding for several hours up the endless hairpins to the Khardung La – at 5,486 metres the world's highest road pass – getting out to walk while the truck negotiated the precarious section across a permanent glacial snowfield on the far side of the pass.

The expedition was now complete, apart from Henry Osmaston, who was still marking exam papers in Bristol. He had hoped to come out independently and meet us at our base camp but the authorities in Leh were adamant that no one outside the main group could travel to the Siachen; so I had sent an apologetic telegram to Bristol, announcing: SORRY FINAL DECISION NO SIACHEN.

The rest of us and our ton of luggage now descended three thousand metres to the Shyok valley. Then we turned west, up the tributary Nubra valley, which we followed for a day and a half, passing the ancient zigzags of the Saser La – yet another pass, littered with the bones of dead mules, on the historic trade route from the subcontinent to Chinese Turkestan, or Sinkiang as it is now called.

The final, highest pass of all is the Karakoram Pass. Harish and his friends would visit it in future years, but for now we continued west up the Nubra valley, driving through villages where the Buddhist people were astounded to see Europeans. The truck lurched through a grand landscape of giant granite walls carved over the millennia by the glacier which had once filled the whole of this valley. When we eventually reached the present glacier tongue it was the usual drab Karakoram rubble tip with no hint of the glittering wonders beyond. We were instructed to camp a couple of miles away from the glacier, out of sight of the army base, and when the affable commander, a Colonel Gupta, drove over to visit us that evening he explained that we would only be allowed to walk up onto the glacier in the dark, to ensure that we witnessed no military secrets.

So, with local Ladakhi porters ferrying luggage, leaving before dawn, we set off in groups over the next three days. After much negotiation with the military chiefs, we had been given a permit to attempt a cluster of seven-thousand-metre peaks called Rimo, which lay at the head of the Terong Valley. The Scottish mountaineer Tom Longstaff had thrown down the gauntlet in 1909: 'When it is desired to survey this unknown corner, will the party please proceed five miles up the [Siachen] glacier and take the first turning on the right.' Which Jenny Visser 't Hooft, Dr 't Hooft, Khan Afraz Gul Khan and the famous Swiss guide Franz Lochmatter did twenty years later. Luckily for us the Indian-Dutch-Swiss team only published a cursory report of their brief visit and no photos of the Rimo peaks. So, fifty-six years later, we had the delicious pleasure of travelling almost into the unknown, heading for some of the highest unclimbed peaks in the world without knowing what they actually looked like. We could almost call ourselves explorers.

After following the well-worn army track, littered with marker posts and telegraph wires, up the first five miles of the Siachen, it was thrilling to reach that first right turning and see 'That Valley' (the literal translation of Terong) disappearing round a corner, knowing that a great massif of untouched peaks was waiting for us fifteen miles beyond that corner. We spent several days cajoling our reluctant Ladakhi porters, spoilt by inflated army wages, up the valley, ferrying loads between a succession of camps, with a knee-deep icy river crossing adding to the sense of adventure. Every morning we heard the boom of artillery fire further south near the Bilafond La – the main high pass leading to Pakistan – and one day I nearly exacerbated international tensions when I set off nobly, on my own, to help the porters by carrying a load myself. As I approached the load depot, the Ladakhis were all hiding behind a rock, watching warily. Then, recognising me, they all sprang out, shouting angrily, gesticulating, grabbing at my green jacket. I was perplexed by their hostility until Harish explained that evening. 'They thought you were a Pakistani spy.'

'*I* was a spy? I thought *they* were the ones playing hide-and-seek.'

'No – they said you followed them secretly. And when they saw your green trousers and jacket, they assumed you must be a soldier.'

I conceded that they might have had a point – the trousers *were* army surplus. 'But why all the fuss?' I continued, 'Now they know it was just me?'

'Ah, well, once they realised it was one of the sahibs they decided that you must have been sent by *me* to spy on them. Now they think I don't trust them.'

Norbu, self-appointed leader of the porters, raged for three hours, eyes blazing, fingers stabbing the air. Then, suddenly, he stopped. Everyone calmed down, and international entente was restored. Over the next few days we continued up the Terong Glacier, trudging first up the inevitable Karakoram rubble, then through an avenue of magnificent ice pinnacles – the 'névés penitentes' which Henry had hoped to come and study.

In Leh Harish had met an old man who had been here in 1929 with the Vissers and who said that there was a lake full of dead men's bones. So we called the glacial pond where we made our base camp the Lake of Bones. The man had described the main Rimo peak as a gorgeously striped 'Painted Mountain' and when the Rimo massif did appear one evening the poetry was vindicated by a magnificent display of granite pillars and soaring snow ridges incandescent in the pink alpenglow. Both Rimo I and the slightly lower Rimo III were beautiful, shapely structures – mountains to fire the imagination. (Rimo II was less striking – more a sub-summit of Rimo I.)

We were only equipped – and only had time – for lightning 'alpine-style' strikes. Given those constraints, Harish felt that his team didn't have the experience for tackling these formidable seven-thousanders. Instead, they roamed far and wide, plucking other fruit, while the four Britons hogged the biggest plums. The most dramatic success of the expedition was Dave and Jim's first ascent of 7,223-metres-high Rimo III in a six-day journey, crossing the high Ibex Col to another whole glacier system, then climbing on sight up the far side of the mountain. The irony is that their committing journey was consolation for having dropped out of an earlier attempt on the highest peak, Rimo I.

It had started from a high camp, watching and waiting immediately beneath the mountain during the last week of June. Victor was always fretting to be away, insisting that: 'You have to be opportunistic in the Himalaya.'

'A lot of people die in the Himalaya, Victor, and I don't want to be one of them,' Dave responded, a touch testily. It was like being back on Kunyang Kish – the old battle between young Turks and cautious elders. Except that this time Dave had added reason to be cautious, having broken his little finger tripping over a crevasse – the first time I had witnessed any injury on a Himalayan expedition.

On 2 July we all descended from our advance base to the Lake of Bones, for a convivial evening with Harish and the others. Harish reported a rise in the barometer and that night I stayed up late, photographing Rimo I gleaming in the light of a full moon, its south-west ridge surreally sharp-edged in the exaggerated luminosity. The weather looked set fine and two days later, exhausted after a punishing climb from Advance Base with heavy loads, the four of us reached the precarious crest of the ridge, hacked out ledges from a cornice and settled into two tiny dome tents.

It was the following morning, after continuing for just one rope length along the wild cornices and rotten rock of the ridge crest, that Dave muttered, 'This is crazy' and Jim replied, 'I've been waiting for someone to say that.'

We retreated to the ledges and repitched the tents for a day of agonised debate. In the end Jim and Dave decided to descend, leaving Victor and me to continue alone. I respected Dave's decision, but I didn't think the ridge was 'crazy'. Difficult, awkward, laborious – yes; but not unjustifiable. Moving as a twosome, Victor and I established a rhythm and purpose, taking turns to teeter carefully over towers of crumbling crockery. Even though he had really wanted to be climbing with Jim, not me, Victor showered me with paeans of praise: 'Well done, you're climbing really well.'

We only did five pitches that day; six the next, stopping early to bivouac, drying out boots in the hot afternoon sun as the stove purred, reducing shovel-loads of snow to precious hot drinks. A thousand metres or so below, we saw the tiny stick figures of Meena and Zerksis crawling across an immense snowfield towards the Ibex Col. To the south-west we could see the high saddle of the Bilafond La, where we heard the sound of artillery each morning. To the north-west, sixty miles away, we could see the highest giants of the Karakoram – Broad Peak, the Gasherbrums and K2, the world's second-highest mountain. What a privilege to see those familiar forms from this unique perspective, never witnessed before.

We continued our slow journey, now climbing steeply up a tower of rocky pinnacles encrusted with snow. It was intricate, delicate work, often on loose rock, reminding me of the Finsteraarhorn. The final, eighth, pitch on this third day since leaving Dave and Jim was led by Victor. It was a brilliant gravity-defying vertical swim up loose powder plastered on holdless rock. As I followed on a tight rope we were hit by an afternoon snow flurry, and as soon as I joined Victor we got digging, excavating a tent platform right on the crest of a gigantic cornice, tying the tent, ourselves and everything else into a rope lashed round the nearest solid lump of rock.

The wind battered our Gore-Tex dome that night, but Day Four dawned bright. So we continued up this magnificent ridge, inching ever higher and further from help, committed totally to the climb. The shadows were lengthening as I completed the seventh laborious rope length that day. I was going well, approaching yet again my personal altitude record of about seven thousand metres, enjoying the hard labour, enchanted by the ever-widening vista over the Karakoram – the greatest mountain range on earth. The weather was still miraculously fine, willing us to succeed. Another two days and we would be on that summit – one of the highest unclimbed summits in the world. I felt deliriously happy.

And then, in a moment, it was all destroyed. I was just starting to hack with my axe, cutting a ledge for the night, when I caught a movement in the corner of my eye and swung round to see my rucksack sliding away, accelerating, then bursting open as it tumbled out of sight down the West Face of Rimo I.

At first I just stared, calmly incredulous, remembering distinctly clipping the sack into the rope. All I could think was that, in a moment of tired double vision, I had not actually connected karabiner to rope. Then I started to retrace my steps, kicking fast back down the snow ridge towards Victor, shouting, 'We've got to go down!' The sack contained most of the remaining food, my duvet jacket and sleeping bag and the tent poles; most serious of all, it contained the stove – our only means of making water: continuing at this altitude without liquid would be suicidal.

I stormed on down, my vision blurred now by tears of rage. Victor took charge: 'Look, for God's sake pull yourself together. This is very serious, and I don't want to die. You have to concentrate on the job of getting down alive.'

The attempt and abseil descent on Rimo I, in 1985 one of the highest unclimbed peaks in the world.

He lowered me down pitch six, then climbed down himself, arriving at the bottom to find a howling madman. Later, at Base Camp, he treated the others to cruel re-enactments of my hysteria, but at the moment of crisis he was impeccably sympathetic: 'Don't *worry* – everyone drops things. At least it was the sack and not you. We've climbed the crux of the route; we've had six days of fantastic climbing . . . the summit isn't everything.'

'Yes, it bloody well is,' I raged. 'Why, why, why? Why did I have to fuck everything up, when it was all going so well?'

'Look – let's just concentrate on staying alive,' repeated Victor, as the sun began to set over K2. He set up an abseil to get us another fifty metres lower, to a point where we could scrape out an icy bivouac ledge. There we shivered under the claustrophobic pole-less tent fabric. Victor got into his sleeping bag and kindly gave me his duvet jacket. We sucked lumps of ice and boiled sweets to try and relieve our raging thirsts.

In the morning we were treated to yet another dazzling sunrise. It was a cruel mockery and the only possible therapy was action; so I took charge, going first on the abseils, taking responsibility for descending vertical and overhanging cliffs, bypassing the pinnacles which we had climbed so laboriously two days earlier. Eight abseils got us onto a huge snowfield, where we down-climbed for another 600 metres, step by step, kicking the white crust under a merciless sun, then traipsing wearily through the buzzing heat down to our old high camp, where we stopped to guzzle on tea and fruit juice before continuing down to the Lake of Bones.

At dusk I drew ahead of Victor and had almost reached Base Camp when I saw someone pottering around the glacier. I thought for a moment that it was Dave, out for one of his evening strolls. But the body language looked slightly older, the beard greyer. Then I suddenly realised: 'Henry!'

'Hello, how are you? You don't happen to have seen an ice axe lying around anywhere, do you? I seem to have mislaid mine.'

Following a few minutes later, Victor stumbled across the lost axe with *H. Osmaston* inscribed on its wooden shaft. Henry had ignored my telegram – charming, bluffing and cajoling his way through a succession of military checkposts, bribing officials with a supply of much-coveted NASA satellite photographs and making his way onto the Siachen, and on up the Terong valley, surviving off biscuits and a jar of Anna's marmalade, continuing up the North Terong Glacier, missing our base camp, but eventually bumping into Muslim and Dhiren and asking them if they were by any chance members of the Siachen Indo-British Expedition.

The weather stayed infuriatingly fine. I had to admit grudgingly that at least it gave Dave and Jim the chance to make their brilliant ascent of Rimo III; but the persistent blue sky nagged at my bruised ego, reminding me that we really could – and would – have reached the top of Rimo I. Victor accompanied me up into the untrodden cwm beneath the mountain to retrieve the post-lapsarian rucksack. It had burst open during its thousand-metre fall and many of the contents were lost, but we did find my sleeping bag, sprawled like a red corpse on the snow, reminding me again that it was better to drop a rucksack than oneself.

Henry's surprise arrival also brought a sense of perspective. Watching him pottering happily amongst the névés penitentes with his tape measure and notebook and – for some unfathomable scientific reason – dyeing selected ice phalluses fluorescent pink, untroubled by egotistical ambition, I tried to remember how lucky we were just to be here at all, summit or no summit.

And again I sought solace in action. Mahendra, our liaison officer, returned from the military base with the news that the Terong River we had waded through a month earlier was now swollen with summer meltwater, awash with mini-icebergs. He had almost drowned while crossing it and the level had now risen even further, cutting off our exit from the valley. So Victor and I walked down and enjoyed a day's rock-climbing, traversing smooth granite cliffs where the river swirled hard against the valley wall, fixing ropes to secure an alternative way out.

This ropeway was taken a few days later by Victor, Jim and Henry, all of whom had to return to their jobs in Britain. By the time they reached the Siachen Glacier it was dusk. They had been warned that any strangers approaching the army base after dark could be shot on sight, so as they ambled down the rubble hummocks of the glacier tongue they sang loud songs. On the final section, unsure whether this ruse was enough of a precaution, Henry turned to the other two and said, 'Look, I'm quite a bit older than you two and I've probably got less long to live. I'll go ahead.' And with that noble speech he set off down the final crepuscular slope holding aloft a white handkerchief on the tip of his ice axe.

The rest of us came down ten days later. In the interim Harish, Muslim and Dhiren made a huge trek to a high pass on the previously untrodden South Terong Glacier, while I spent six days alone, trekking up another glacier, the Shelkar Chorten, climbing a peak at its head, then crossing the South Terong glacier and climbing another, twin-summited peak which Harish named Ngabong Terong – the double-humped camel of Terong. The lonely journey felt like an expiation for my cock-up on Rimo, the modest virgin summits some consolation for the lost prize. It was also moving to be utterly alone in that immense ice wilderness and it was good to do some real exploration; but after six days of solitude I longed for human company and was overjoyed to catch up with the others as they started to ferry all the remaining expedition luggage over the river cliffs.

We didn't finish the ferrying that day, so we spent one final night camping in the Terong valley, sitting round a blazing juniper fire beside the river. English, Kumaoni, Hindi and Gujerati voices, the drone of the river and the crackle of burning wood all blended into a contented blur. Between us we had achieved an astonishing amount, climbing twelve new peaks and exploring an entire glacier basin in a region that few human beings had ever set eyes on. Even if my momentary blunder had cost us the summit of Rimo I, the journey as a whole had been a resounding international success, forging new friendships right in the heart of the world's highest battle-ground. As voices and embers died gradually away, I lay flat on my back, staring up at the immense starry sky until I could stare no longer. I rolled over and sank into a sleep of pure contentment.

Chapter Eleven

Mozart on the Eiger

Too much of my life seems to have been spent running away, evading opportunities. But just occasionally I do something genuinely brave. One of those occasions was at the end of July 1985, when we returned from Rimo to Bombay. I remained in India for a couple of weeks, and while I was staying with Muslim Contractor's family I forced myself to sit down at Muslim's desk and start the synopsis for a book.

Like most people, I had dreamed about writing a book for years without actually doing anything about it. Now, at last, I felt I had a good story. Despite the rucksack fiasco, our trip to the Siachen war zone had been a compelling adventure. Jim could write a chapter celebrating his and Dave's triumph on Rimo III; I could pad out the story by twinning Rimo with the earlier trip to Kishtwar-Shivling; Kashmir would be the thread linking the two expeditions.

Back in England I paid someone to type out my synopsis on a smart electric typewriter. Meanwhile I sat down with my old manual clunker and wrote a sample chapter. I had never met a publisher in my life, but I knew that Hodder and Stoughton had produced most of Chris Bonington's books, as well as Peter Boardman's inspirational *Sacred Summits*. So I phoned Hodder, and a girl with cut-glass vowels told me to send my proposal to Margaret Body. A couple of weeks later

I was invited to the Hodder offices that were then in Bedford Square and was taken to the top floor to meet Maggie, who I discovered had been editing books about mountain travel ever since she was asked to disentangle the garbled Patagonian maps of the great explorer Eric Shipton, back in the 1960s. In the world of mountain literature, she was the queen, and it was very gratifying when she said, 'I think we're going to have to make you an offer.'

The 'offer' was, needless to say, not huge, but the first dollop of the advance was just enough to keep me solvent until Christmas. I had three months.

What a treat to be able to immerse myself totally. My brother Philip and his wife Caroline kindly put me up at their quiet house in Oxford where Philip was now studying at theological college. I worked completely alone in the house most of the time, but one morning Philip and I shared the dining-room table. By lunchtime I had still failed to complete a single sentence of my chapter five and he had fared no better with his essay on Paul's letter to the Thessalonians. But most days the words flowed, or at least sputtered. In November I gave Philip and Caroline a break, moving to Newmarket where James and Rachel Ogilvie were renting a house at a stud farm. Here, surrounded by stableloads of equine investment, I enjoyed the more modest luxury of the Ogilvies' word processor to complete my manuscript.

Delivery, on the first working day of 1986, produced the inevitable anti-climax. After three months of monastic seclusion, the advance was spent, so it was back to the real world, making bookcases. I spent quite a bit of that winter working in London, dropping in occasionally to the Alpine Club for Tuesday-evening lectures. It was at one of these meetings that a man with very dark eyes and a large nose, dressed in a tweed suit, came up and asked rather deferentially, 'Are you Stephen Venables?'

'Yes,' I replied.

'My name's Luke Hughes. I know your cousin Lucius. I used to lodge with him in Bristol – you know, that house in

Totterdown – he said I could have the top room if I mended the leak in the roof. In fact, it was he who persuaded me to stop trying to be a lawyer and do something interesting. I run a little furniture—'

'Yes, of course – in Convent Garden.' Lucius Cary had often mentioned his woodworking friend who did some serious climbing on the side. I told Luke that I had just finished a book and mentioned Kishtwar-Shivling.

'You mean that peak above Sumcham? With the rock spike on the ridge – we called it the Yeti.'

'So you're the Hughes who wrote that piece in the *Himalayan Journal.*'

'Yes, we bumped into Harish Kapadia on the Umasi La and he bullied me into sending him an article.'

Connections established, we fixed to drive up to Scotland for a weekend's ice-climbing. Our first bivouac was halfway up the A74 when we ran out of petrol; our second, the following night, was at the foot of Ben Nevis's north face. We had walked up, blithely optimistic, without a tent, and as drizzle began to fall we dug a snow-cave, decorating its entrance with a rather fine Romanesque arch. The cave dripped and neither of us slept that night; the Ben was clearly out of condition and at dawn we fled back south, stopping in Glasgow to eat two 'full set' cooked breakfasts each.

As Luke put it back in London, it was a shame about the weather but the camaraderie had been good. At Easter we were luckier, driving up to Braemar with Phil Bartlett and a man called Adam Quarry, who had once been arrested for an alleged road offence in Afghanistan and had spent a month in Kabul jail; the tallest man in a large communal cell, he had been asked by his fellow prisoners to stand on tiptoe and unscrew the light bulb which the vindictive staff left switched on every night.

In our equally cramped tent, high in the Cairngorm snows, the four of us spent three convivial nights, with plentiful food and whisky, sleeping deeply after intense days on the remote cliffs of Bheinn a Bhuird. Luke was a steady partner, keen to try anything, happy to wait patiently while I led the harder pitches, laughing when I fell off in a harmless clatter of iron-mongery. We spent Easter Sunday on a classic route called *Mitre Ridge*, about which Jim Fotheringham had frequently waxed lyrical the previous summer on Rimo. With my unerring eye for the wrong line, I deviated inadvertently onto the harder *Cumming-Crofton* route up the side of the ridge. It was only later that I discovered the first winter ascent had been made by Dick Renshaw, and only much later that I got to know the Swabian mountaineer Nicho Mailänder whose Scottish uncle, Sir Ian Crofton, had made the original ascent in summer. More connections.

Luke was engagingly open about his ambitions. He wanted to climb the famous Nose on El Capitan, Everest and the north face of the Eiger. I couldn't help him with the first two, but I had longed for years myself to set foot on the Eiger. Perhaps we should give it a try? After seven successive summers in Asia and South America, why not return for a change to European roots?

So we made a date for the Alps, aiming for July, when I would be representing the Alpine Club at the celebrations marking the 200th anniversary of the first ascent of Mont Blanc; weather permitting, we could tag on a detour to the Eiger. In the meantime Luke was extremely busy in his Covent Garden workshop, but we did manage one Sunday in June to get down to the Swanage sea cliffs, abseiling fifty overhanging metres to the bottom of Boulder Ruckle.

Even on a fine summer morning, Boulder Ruckle is an intimidating place. The limestone has a soft sandy feel to it, the giant fossilised ammonites accentuate human insignificance and the unrelenting verticality saps weak arms. Luke had led about thirty metres up a route called *Lightning Wall* when he flashed off, a long way from his last piece of protection, his startled dark eyes wide as he flew back towards me in a wild pendulum swing. He slammed sideways into a pillar and as I lowered him the last few feet back to the bottom of the cliff, he was wincing with pain, one foot already ballooning inside its shoe. The moment he tried to stand on it, the foot collapsed.

We tried waving operatically to some passing sailing boats. They ignored us, but some other climbers arrived at the cliff edge and set up a very efficient pulley system, winching Luke to the top at high speed, spinning in the air while I tried to keep up. Then I drove him back to London and waited at St Thomas's while a doctor confirmed a broken metatarsal and told Luke not to weight the foot for several weeks.

End of Eiger dreams. Or at least, dreams postponed. Luke was adamant that he could get his foot serviceable by mid-August. I promised to keep that slot free for Switzerland. In the meantime I rearranged July plans for the Mont Blanc massif.

During one of the previous winter's flying visits to Scotland, I had spent a fantastic day on Ben Nevis, climbing the famous wall of *Orion Direct* with a man called Henry Todd. In an earlier incarnation as a city banker he had once employed guides to take him climbing. Then he had disappeared on an extended sabbatical, only returning recently to the mountains, on a smaller income and as a climber in his own right, rediscovering the thrill of alpine climbing. He agreed to come out to France in July.

Transport was provided by another Henry, Colonel Henry Day of the Royal Engineers, an urbane man whose c.v. included the second ascent of Annapurna in 1970; he was climbing with one of his ex-officers, Mark Upton, now a doctor.

We drove through the Mont Blanc tunnel to Italy and set up camp in the Val Veni, where Colonel Henry reclined on a camp chair, dressed as only an Englishman abroad could dress, in striped singlet, shorts, heavy-duty sandals and long black socks. We all warmed up on the south face of a peak called the Aiguille Croux and from its summit Henry Todd and I surveyed the infamous Frêney Glacier, down which the great Walter Bonatti had led his companions in 1961, retreating in a ferocious storm from the still unclimbed Central Pillar of

Frêney, wading through thigh-deep powder. Of the seven French and Italian men, only three had made it back alive. Bonatti's closest climbing partner, Andreas Oggioni, collapsed just one hour from the safety of the hut.

Two days after our Aiguille Croux climb, just before dawn on 16 July, Henry and I picked out with our torch beams the brass plaque commemorating the spot where Oggioni had died, so close to help, twenty-five years earlier to the day. We were crossing the Col de l'Innominata, and the grim coincidental anniversary accentuated the sense of commitment as we descended an oppressive gully and followed the line across the Frêney Glacier that we had spotted from the Croux two days earlier. We hurried through the labyrinth, racing past tottering towers. It was a relief to reach the far bank and step onto the solid granite of the South Pillar of the Gugliermina, first climbed in the 1930s by another legendary Italian master, Giusto Gervasutti.

Ever since skiing with my family at Courmayeur thirteen years earlier and gazing across the Val Veni, I had longed to climb on this wild southern side of Mont Blanc. Our grand plan was to do the Gugliermina, then continue along the mighty Peuterey Ridge and finish up with Mont Blanc's highest rock climb – the Central Pillar of Frêney, which Chris Bonington's party had first climbed in 1961, a few weeks after Bonatti's tragic retreat. But the weather began to turn and, after completing the Gugliermina, terrified of restaging Bonatti's epic, we decided not to risk entrapment on the highest summit in the Alps. Instead we retreated, to hitch-hike through the tunnel to Chamonix just as the storm broke, joining the other Henry at the Mont Blanc bicentennial celebrations.

Only the French could have put on such a magnificent party. Only the French could have had the nerve to proclaim, between two of the many sumptuous dinner courses, that 'la montagne est un lieu où on se trouve face à face avec La Vérité.' Only they could then produce a cadaverous man in evening tails to sit at a grand piano, looking like something out of an old horror movie as he performed a gloriously kitsch 'Hymne au

Mont Blanc' – at which point the President of the Alpine Club, Lady Evans, daughter of the renowned French climber Nea Morin, got the giggles.

It was all tremendous fun and it coincided nicely with an international meet of Femmes Alpinistes. Meena, our Rimo companion, was there, along with another Indian climber called Sharavati; and for the first time I met the hugely enthusiastic English mountaineer Alison Hargreaves.

The party ended and, with perfect timing, the weather improved. Denise Evans accompanied Henry and me in search of La Vérité, bivouacking with us beneath the Aiguille Charmoz, then waving goodbye as we left before dawn to bag first place in the queue for the beautiful but horribly popular Cordier Pillar. The following day, in one of my impatient misanthropic moods, I left Henry before dawn and went to solo the hanging glacier of the North Face of the Plan. No crowds there. And a few days later, finishing our campaign together with the stunning *North-east Spur Direct* on Les Droites, our only company was a cheerful pair of students from Leeds.

The Droites took two full days and it was the most beautiful Alpine climb I had ever done; but I was still hankering after the Eiger. First I had to hitch back to England and do some work on a book proposal, but by the middle of August Luke announced that, despite a lingering limp, he was game for some alpine climbing. Before we left for Dover we dropped in at Islington to have supper with my Rimo companion Victor Saunders, who wished us well and said that if we did get onto the Eiger we would be carrying two rucksacks – 'one full of gear and one full of history.'

That history is what makes the Eiger North Wall so special. At a purely geomorphological level it *is* mesmerising: the great concave limestone triangle which rises so brutally out of the meadows of Alpiglen – actually facing north-*west*, not north – is the biggest continuous mountain wall in Western Europe, nearly a mile wide at its base and over a mile high. But the real fascination is the accumulated sediment of human myth deposited on its ledges, ramps and infamous ice fields. Heinrich Harrer, one of the two Austrians who took part in the first ascent, wrote in his famous history of the wall, *The White Spider*, that the Eigerwand 'demands the uttermost of skill, stamina and courage.'

Modern techniques, equipment and rescue possibilities mean that those words are no longer necessarily true. But you still approach the Eiger with extreme respect, almost as a pilgrim, following in the steps of people who did undoubtedly have those qualities tested. Of the first ten climbers to attempt the wall between 1935 and 1938, only two returned alive; the others all froze or fell to their deaths. Small wonder that the Nordwand was called 'Mordwand' – Death Wall. But the fact that in 1937 the brilliant Matthias Rebitsch and his companion Wiggerl Vörg managed to retreat safely from halfway up the wall, after being turned back by bad weather, proved that an attempt did not have to be suicidal. Vörg returned to the Eiger in 1938 with another Bavarian, Anderl Heckmair. And this time, combining forces reluctantly with the rival Austrian team of Heinrich Harrer and Fritz Kasparek, they succeeded in unlocking the wall's secrets, following the line of least resistance, tracing an intricate zigzag for nearly ten thousand feet of actual climbing, ultimately battling through wave after wave of spindrift avalanches, as the storm broke and the four men knew that the only escape was up – over the summit of the Eiger, to complete one of the most heroic chapters in the history of exploration.

We approached the Eiger obliquely, light-heartedly, trying not to seem too keen, hoping it wouldn't notice that we were coming. Driving through France we stopped in the Vosges to see Le Corbusier's hilltop chapel, Notre Dame du Haut, Ronchamp, which seemed to tap the same numinous qualities as Himalayan shrines that we had both visited. We continued to Zurich, where Marianne was now living with her new man Karel, his leg still plastered from the mishap on the accursed Ruchstock. They warned us that the forecast was terrible, so we drove over the Gothard Pass, descending into Italy to enjoy scraps of sunshine on the picturesque limestone spires of the Grignetta, near Lecco.

My budget was as slender as usual, so Luke had stocked up with free rations from his Territorial Army unit in London, and we made a point of never paying for overnight accommodation. When it was dry we spread our sleeping bags outside. When it rained we had to improvise. Heading back north over the Susten Pass late one stormy night, we sneaked into a remote shed and found ourselves sleeping beside some Swiss retro-car-fancier's immaculately preserved Ford Anglia.

On to the Berner Oberland, where the mountains were still cloud-draped and sodden. So we continued to Solothurn and ate our supper on the steps of St Ursen Cathedral, Luke extemporising on the origins of Renaissance architecture, with – I think – a kernel of truth sustaining the cultural bullshit. The same bravura persisted over kirsch in a bar nearby, Luke valiantly chatting up the barmaid until she turfed us out. We wandered off to spread our sleeping bags in a peaceful court-yard, only to be woken at dawn by sniffing Alsatians and the voices of mystified officials; we had bivouacked in the forecourt of Solothurn police station.

They just asked us politely to move on. Which we did, later lunching beside a fountain in Moutiers. Suddenly an upstairs window was flung open and a woman pointed at our cheap Co-op *vin étranger*, shouting 'Vous ne pouvez pas boire cette horreur de vin. Tenez!' And without further ado she flung us a bottle of superior Rhône. And they say the Swiss are unfriendly.

In the Jura we unearthed a new climb up a beautiful lime-stone crag. Then we continued our encirclement of the Eiger, stopping at Leysin to climb a stunning classic up the great prow of the Sphinx, sleeping afterwards in someone's deserted garage. At last the clouds began to disperse and we homed in on the Berner Oberland, daring at last to approach the great Eiger–Mönch–Jungfrau triptych. Ten days' cragging had loosened us up, but before setting foot on the Eiger we needed to climb at least one proper mountain, so we walked for five hours up to the Rottal Hut, high amongst the Gothic towers of the Jungfrau, and the next day climbed the Inner Rottal Ridge to the summit of that lovely peak with its satellite Silberhorn gleaming above the deep green shadows of the Lauterbrunnen valley.

Two days later, with the first sharpness of autumn just tingeing a crystal dawn, we drove round to Grindelwald to check the weather forecast. The woman at the tourist office warned of heavy rain that evening, but promised the weather would set fine next morning. So we postponed the Eiger for another day and went to play on the granite slabs of Handegg where I took a fifteen-foot fall, cursing furiously as most of the skin was scraped from my back. We beat a retreat to Meiringen, where Marianne's sister Therese now lived. She bathed and bandaged my grazed torso, then gave us supper and offered us a dry floor for the night. As the rain thudded on the chalet roof, we thanked the weather forecasters for saving us a drenching on the Eiger.

The first challenge the next day was to *find* the Eigerwand. It was still mist-shrouded and when we got out of the train at Eigergletscher we dithered in the murk, watched by a carriage-load of curious Japanese tourists. In the end we just sat and waited amongst the eclectic debris that litters the slopes beneath the wall, Luke donning an abandoned pair of Micky Mouse sunglasses as he composed a variation on Masefield's sea poem: 'I must go down to the Eiger again; to the rock, the snow and the ice; and all I ask is a bomb-proof nut . . .' And so on, inter-spersed with snatches of the *Marriage of Figaro*, which we had been listening to almost non-stop during the last fortnight, both of us falling deeply in love with the Contessa's flirtatious maid, Suzanna. Then the mist evaporated and the wall revealed itself, hanging over our heads, bizarrely foreshortened, its legendary landmarks barely recognisable from this strange angle.

At four-thirty p.m. we crossed a tongue of hard old snow and stepped at last onto the Eigerwand. The idea was to climb the first two thousand feet or so that afternoon, moving quickly up the comparatively easy lower plinth. Easy, but still imposing, with vertical channels scoured smooth by the relentless pounding of water, ledges littered with rubble and occasional international human detritus. Classic accounts from the early years record Eiger candidates stumbling across actual body parts, but all we saw was a rusty lid labelled *Bulgarkonserv*.

A fortnight's stormy weather had left the wall plastered with snow and ice, which was now dripping in the afternoon sun, so we wore just anoraks and overtrousers, keeping dry inner clothes packed in polythene bags. After three hours we found an old fixed rope pointing straight up a smooth slab, so we followed it and arrived at a little cave. Above the niche, unmistakable from photos that I had pored over for fifteen years – ever since I was first captivated by Kurt Diemberger's account of the Eigerwand in his book *Summits and Secrets* – were the nail-smoothed edges of the Difficult Crack.

Determined to climb the crack while it was merely wet – rather than glazed with overnight ice – I did it that afternoon, fixing one of our ropes at the top and then abseiling back to join Luke in the golden evening glow. At 7.30 p.m. we crawled into the horizontal slot of the cave, pulled on all our warm clothes, lit the stove and made supper.

We slept well in our slot and were ready to leave before dawn the next day. All was sweetness and light until I got the ropes tangled while Luke was leading the first pitch above the Difficult Crack. Tugging at frozen hawsers, I cursed hysterically, my shrieks echoing around the great rock amphitheatre. Suddenly I heard an answering shout. It took a few moments to spot the little railway official in his peaked cap, hands in uniform pockets, standing nonchalantly on a snow ledge two thousand feet up the North Face of the Eiger. Alarmed by my shouts, he had wandered out of the railway window – the Stollenjoch – to see if someone needed rescuing.

Thoroughly embarrassed, I shouted down that we were fine, then shut up. It was bizarre, surreal . . . this doorway opening so casually onto the biggest wall in the Alps. And yet another reminder of the wall's morbid history, because it was from this same window that in 1936 an earlier railway guard had heard some very real, desperate cries for help as Toni Kurz dangled on his rope, swinging beneath huge overhangs, the only survivor out of four young men retreating down the face.

Two days earlier one of Kurz's companions, Anderl Hinterstoisser, had led the way across a smooth limestone slab, tensioning sideways on the rope. The other three followed with a backrope rope looped through a piton, but once they were all across they pulled the rope after them, focused totally on the summit as they were. Even when one man, Angerer, was injured by a falling rock they still pressed on, perhaps believing that, committed this high on the wall, their best chance lay up, not down. However, the following day they changed their minds and began to retreat laboriously down the face. By the time they got back to Hinterstoisser's tension traverse the weather had broken. First waterfalls, then snow avalanches poured down the wall and the barrage of falling stones intensified.

With no rope fixed in place, Hinterstoisser was unable to climb back across the slab, now even more slick with a fresh coating of verglas. The only alternative was to abseil direct, down over huge overhangs, into the great unknown spaces below.

We will never know exactly what happened next, as the only witness was Toni Kurz. But from Kurz's shocked, anguished cries, the railwayman gathered that there had been a fall, and Hinterstoisser had somehow become detached from the rope, tumbling all the way to the foot of the Eiger where his crumpled body was later recovered. The other three, roped together, were ripped from their holds. Angerer was yanked hard against a piton, where he froze to death. Rainer was strangled in the rope. Kurz survived, but was left hanging on the rope, held taut by the dead body at each end.

Grindelwald guides hurried up the railway that evening and climbed out onto the wall. They could do nothing that night, but shouted encouragement to Kurz, promising to return in the morning. With his gigantic will to live, the twenty-three-year-old survived the night. When his rescuers returned in the morning there were icicles hanging from the steel points of Kurz's crampons, and one of his arms had frozen into a stiff claw: yet still he found the strength to force himself down the rope and cut free Angerer's body, releasing a length of frozen hemp. But it wasn't long enough to escape, so Kurz had to unsplice it, laboriously, painfully, twist by twist with his one unfrozen hand and his teeth, until at last he could knot together the three separate strands to create a line long enough to lower to his rescuers and pull up two fresh climbing ropes.

Spurred on by shouts of encouragement, fumbling frozen-fingered, Kurz tied the two ropes together, threw an end down and began to abseil, spinning in space, controlling the rope with friction on a karabiner clipped to his waist. Slowly, agonisingly, he lowered himself through the air, forcing his frozen body to continue functioning. But then the knot joining the two ropes jammed on his karabiner. The guides shouted, pleaded with him to make one final effort. But the knot was implacable, his fingers were unable to function, the flame of life was finally flickering out. So close to safety, after so many hours of terrible struggle, Kurz just muttered, 'I'm finished' and slumped forward, hanging limp from the knot. The only way they could retrieve his body was by cutting it down with a knife on the end of a long pole.

Fifty years on the Eiger seemed, on this beautiful September morning, benign. But the knowledge of Kurz's agonised death throes was still hanging there in the air – along with all the other epic legends which give this climb such resonance. After sorting out our rope tangle and continuing for two further pitches, it was incredibly moving to reach Hinterstoisser's legendary traverse and start across the slab, which today was smeared with a thick veneer of white ice.

Beneath our feet the slab overhung space. Immediately above our heads old ropes were festooned from rusty pitons – pure mountain archaeology. Most impressive of all was the finish,

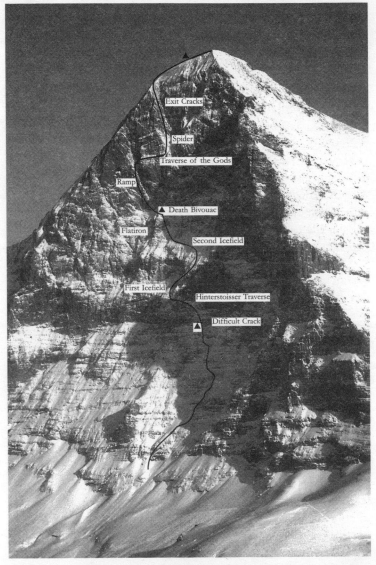

The original 1938 route up the North Face of the Eiger, with the Venables'
and Hughes' three bivouacs marked.

where you hunch right up under the roof and squeeze out through an awkward chimney, emerging into the little alcove called the Swallow's Nest. Here, in the blue morning light, we stopped to drink some fruit juice. Far below, just clear of the Eiger's shadow, one of the toy trains whistled its way up towards Kleine Scheidegg. Above us the wall loomed silent – encouragingly silent, without a single falling stone. Two weeks' bad weather followed by a hard freeze had immobilised the artillery.

How gratifying to step left onto the First Ice Field and find it coated generously with 'névé' – firm crusty thaw-freeze snow. Then, five pitches higher up, to find that, despite a gap between it and the underlying rock, the near-vertical Ice Hose was just substantial enough to take our weight. And then to find the Second Ice Field coated mercifully with snow, with only a faint peppering of limestone shards stuck to its white surface and, so far, no further stones falling from above.

Luke and I moved together across the Alps' most famous crab crawl, with the rope always clipped into at least two ice screws between us. Then, after several rope lengths, we left the Second Ice Field by an awkward knight's move – up, across and up again – scraping and hooking up steep ice-smeared rock onto the jutting prow of the Flatiron. And here, right at the heart of the wall, at the place often described as the point beyond which there is no return, we stopped to spend the night at Death Bivouac.

Luke was blithely vague about the Eiger's early history and didn't know about Sedlmayer and Mehringer, the two young Austrians – the first two people ever to attempt the face – who froze to death here in 1935, trapped by a ferocious storm, unable to go up or down. But he still looked pensive, sitting on the snow ledge, sharpening crampon points with the little file we had brought. We had stopped early deliberately, knowing that there were no comfortable ledges in the next section, the Ramp. Here we were content, but also anxious, just hoping that the good weather would hold, sparing us a fearful retreat back across all those acres of ice field. There was an occasional tinkle of ice, falling clear from a thousand feet above, but we were protected by an overhanging wall of yellow rock, from which we hung boots and socks to dry in the afternoon sun. Far, far below, at Kleine Scheidegg, the man in embroidered waistcoat and breeches repeated his mournful dirge on the alpenhorn. We responded with gruff snatches of Susanna's aria in the moonlit garden.

For our second night we enjoyed another immaculate sunset before lying down on foam mats, legs thrust inside rucksacks, and drifting into sleep under a sky full of stars. Some time after midnight I woke shivering, and it was a relief to get moving again at dawn, warming stiff limbs on the Third Ice Field, moving fast across this famously dangerous section where even at daybreak there was a brief spatter of stonefall.

Then we were into the great slanting gash of the Ramp, moving still further left, still following the line of least resistance. Bringing Luke up to one belay, glancing down at the immense sweep of the Second Ice Field and, beyond it, the huge overhanging cliffs at the far side of the wall – walls within walls – I recognised the view from the photo in Harrer's book and realised that this miserable sloping ledge was where the four men had bivouacked in 1938, higher than anyone had so far been on the wall. It was on the following morning that their undisputed master, Heckmair, had really begun to demonstrate his genius, battling with the hardest test so far – the Waterfall Chimney.

For us on the previous afternoon it would have been just that, drenching us to the skin. But now, in the morning, all we had to contend with was a glistening fringe of frozen globules; it was strenuous and dramatic, but mercifully dry. Above the overhang I recognised a steep edge from a photo of Dick climbing it in 1974, when he and Joe Tasker made the fourth winter ascent of the Eigerwand. The photo had shown Dick's fingerless mitts clutching dry cold rock, but today the stone was shrouded under a diaphanous layer of verglas, just thick enough to support ice-axe picks.

That endless unpredictable variety is yet another aspect of

Kishtwar Shivling – the vision in 1979.

Dick Renshaw on the 1983 first ascent,
Day Four – 'balancing on snow smudges
plastered to seemingly blank rock.'

The author following Dick across
the scary traverse on Summit Day.
The previous night had been spent
on the snow mushrooms behind.

Siachen Indo–
British
Expedition 1985.

Victor Saunders at the dizzy fourth bivouac on
Rimo I (*top left*) and at our high point (*right*),
with the North Terong Glacier descending
into a sea of unclimbed peaks.

Lonely tracks on the Shelkar Chorten Glacier
during the author's six day solo exploration at
the end of the expedition. The distant peak
above the ski sticks is K12.

Victor assisting Henry Osmaston's researches on the Terong Glacier penitentes, SIBE 85.

Dick Renshaw with the Gujars in Kishtwar, 1983.

Dave Wilkinson on the ropes, bypassing the flooded now uncrossable Terong river, SIBE 85.

January 1987. Isabelle, Willoughby and Bakonjo men at our last camp in the Mountains of the Moon.

July 1987. Worzel Gummidge Bartlett on Snow Lake and (*below left*) battling spindrift avalanches to the Khurdopin Pass with Duncan Tunstall.

Rosie at Ferntower Road.

October 1987. Camp Two on Shishapangma. Sixty miles to the east rise four more 8,000 metre peaks, including Everest.

Luke Hughes on the Eiger's Hinterstoisser Traverse in 1986 (*right*) and at the stormy highpoint on Shishapangma (*below*).

Everest 1988. Author's eye view of
Paul Teare waiting his turn on
Wesbter's Wall, with the huge basin of
Big Al Gully far below.

Ed Webster on his crevasse rope bridge.

Paul on the approach, camping at
Pethang Ringmo.

13th May 1988. Author returning with Robert Anderson to the South Col, after the night out in the open at 28,000 feet (✚). Robert and Ed had managed to shelter lower down in the abandoned Japanese tent (circled).

Safely down from Everest. The nose recovered, but Ed lost the end joints of seven fingers and one thumb.

Pasang, Kasang and Angchu celebrate our success with thongba - mulled chang.

(*Left to right*): Ed, Mimi, Stephen and Robert about to leave Advance Base for the last time.

the Eigerwand's fascination. As is the marvellous inevitability of the 1938 route, which follows such monumental natural features. The Ramp is the only logical path through bulging yellow-orange walls streaked black with the water-drip of millennia. But it is a wild path: come off here, unroped, and you would fall over four thousand feet before reaching the bottom of the face. And it actually feels as though you are hanging directly over Grindelwald, more like seven thousand feet below, where Luke could just spot the minute blob of his grey Volkswagen in the station car park.

From a distance the Ramp seems to lead almost directly to the top of the wall. In fact its upper reaches are blocked by huge overhangs and halfway up you have to take a crucial right turn onto the Brittle Ledges. Then there is a steep climb up the Brittle Crack before you emerge suddenly onto easy snow ledges leading rightwards, back into the heart of the wall. But, just to keep you alert, the ledges peter out at the last minute and you find yourself removing gloves to finger friable little holds, and looking down as you place your feet with infinite care, sidestepping delicately over the most awesome precipice imaginable.

They call it the *Götterquergang* – the Traverse of the Gods – and it does feel very Wagnerian; but Luke and I stuck to Mozart, still humming snatches of *Figaro*, comedy getting closer to the essence of life – and the joyful exuberance of our mountain pilgrimage – than bombastic melodrama. For we were now playing the final act on this most public mountain; and that sense of being in the arena, playing to the gallery, became most acute in the ice field called the Spider. As we laboured carefully up its fifty-degree tilt, its bottom lip obscured the entire lower four-fifths of the wall; there seemed to be nothing between us and the meadows and holidaymakers and the alpenhorn player nearly six thousand feet below.

Even the Spider, this mean little ice field set deep in the upper wall, took five full rope lengths. And then there were the Exit Cracks. The name suggests a perfunctory afterthought, but the 'cracks' are actually long and convoluted. Staring up at a vertical maze of ambiguous gullies and chimneys, I marvelled again at the genius of Heckmair, who fought his way up here in a storm, buffeted by avalanches. At one point he was knocked off and fell several metres, skewering Vörg's hand with his brand new twelve-point crampons. But once Vörg's injury was bandaged Heckmair just flung himself back into battle, leading his team to victory, somehow discovering the correct route through sheer intuition.

For us, on a clear afternoon, the famous yellowish Quartz Crack was easy to find; but that was followed by a long, unobvious traverse leftward, as we realised that this final section was yet another wall within a wall – a whole new facet, facing west into the afternoon sun. We passed the ledge where the woefully ill-prepared Claudio Corti languished in 1957, stranded out of his depth, waiting desperately for the rescue experts to lower a cable nearly a thousand feet from the summit and pluck him to safety. They were unable to return for Corti's companion Stefano Longhi, who was stuck with a broken leg on a lower ledge, crying, '*Fame. Fredo.*' – hungry, cold – into the swirling clouds until he eventually faded and died.

As if to remind us how things have changed since those grim days, a helicopter buzzed close to the face, perhaps checking on the two Englishmen. We knew that in fine weather it was now possible to lift people on a long line from most parts of the wall; but I don't think we had really considered consciously the possibility of rescue: the assumption was that this was still a very serious face and that we were on our own.

An old rope, frayed to the core, helped us across a tension traverse and then we were in the final chimney, which was like a staircase pushed to seventy degrees, with all the steps sloping downwards. There was only a trickle of water on the smooth treads and I was able to bridge up easily, enjoying the poise and balance of it all. But even this chimney went on for three rope lengths, with virtually no protection to clip the ropes in; plastered in ice, or pouring with spindrift, it could have been a desperate fight.

We emerged at last from the Exit Cracks, taking infinite care over rubble slopes and the final rope lengths up a sheet of glassy ice, until, at eight o'clock in the evening, fourteen hours and thirty pitches after leaving Death Bivouac, Luke posed for a photo on the summit ridge, silhouetted heroically against yet another chocolate-box sunset. Then we dug ledges just over the south side of the crest, to spend a final cold night in the open. On the upper ledge I dreamed a confused dream about being at a rather grand party with Kate, whose mother was also there, dressed very incongruously in a flouncy dirndl skirt, looking like one of the peasant chorus girls from *Figaro*. Shivering on the lower tier, Luke dreamed that an Irishman kept telling him to reach for the peg above his head – which he did repeatedly, only to find himself grabbing the inert form of his climbing partner. What fun the psychiatrists could have had with all that.

Dawn reality was less confused, but there was a moment of anxiety on the knife-edge summit ridge when Luke suddenly became terrified of falling six thousand feet all the way back down the North Face, as Gonda and Wyss had done after completing the twelfth ascent in 1953. Even romping back down the easy West Flank, we were still on edge, alert, and it was only when we reached Eigergletscher Station that Luke announced, 'I'll say it now. I didn't dare until we got down: "We Did It."' Half an hour later, at Kleine Scheidegg, he went up to the alpenhorn player and thanked him for serenading us in the Exit Cracks the previous afternoon. The young brass player beamed seraphically as he tipped spittle out of the horn bell, then looked crestfallen as Luke added, 'But tell me – don't you know any other tunes?'

The Eiger was a long-held dream fulfilled, but it didn't stifle the demon of ambition. While Luke, satiated, flew home to his workshop, I stayed on, roaming through the Bernese Oberland, researching a book I was hoping to write and in the process climbing several peaks. One radiant autumn day I walked up to a beautiful cluster of limestone spires called the Engelhörner. In the morning I romped round a comparatively

easy cirque of summits; after lunch I climbed the much harder
north-east face of the Kingspitze.

Free of dependants and responsibilities, I enjoyed the urgent
intensity of solo climbing. Earlier that year, at home, I had
spent occasional impromptu evenings in the Avon Gorge,
soloing classic rock climbs like *Malbogies*, *Great Central* and
Suspension Bridge Arête – the route up which I had struggled
so fearfully as a green nineteen-year-old. Now, aged thirty-
two, I was much more confident and even on this 500-metre-
high wall of the Kingspitze I felt quite light-hearted,
particularly as I carried a rope to protect myself on the two
hardest sections.

But the following afternoon there was nothing carefree
about my return to Kleine Scheidegg, a condemned man
labouring under a monstrous load of climbing gear, food and
gas, but even more burdened by the weight of misguided
ambition. Not content with the 1938 route up the Eigerwand,
I wanted now to climb the much harder Direct – the *Harlin
Route* – solo. Or at least, I *thought* I wanted to. But that morning,
buying last-minute provisions in Meiringen, I had watched
enviously as a group of Swiss pensioners set off for a day's
walk, chattering happily, content simply to *be* amongst the
mountains, untroubled by ambition. Now, settling down to
sleep on the scree beneath the face, I wondered again if I
was really ready for something so huge. In the morning I
woke late, half deliberately, relieved to see a hazy streak on
the horizon, pretending to myself that the weather was
breaking, but knowing that really, as on Illimani four years
earlier, weather was not the issue – the problem was that my
heart just wasn't in it. And, more to the point, I probably
wasn't good enough anyway.

I ran back down to Grindelwald and phoned Marianne,
telling her to ignore the letter I had just posted asking her to
alert the police if I hadn't returned from the Eiger in ten days.
She told me that I was crazy, and I agreed that perhaps I was,
but that even if I wasn't it was time to be thankful for my
blessings, wind up a wonderful Alpine summer and drive Luke's

car home. That night I stayed with friends in Basel. The following day I drove back to London and at eleven p.m. knocked on the door of Victor's house in Islington to ask if I could spend the night there. I ended up staying for three years.

Chapter Twelve

Bigo Bog and Snow Lake

Victor and Maggie Saunders ran their large terraced house along the lines of an Alpine climbing hut. Strangers would arrive for dinner, stay the night and often disappear before dawn. The more permanent resident who actually rented a room might come home to find a famous – and sometimes insalubrious – mountaineer in his bed. But the rent was so low – and the Bohemian atmosphere so generous – that it would have been churlish to gripe. And, in any case, it was good to be at the centre of things, living with new intensity.

The initial catalyst for staying in London, when I returned from the Alps in September 1986, was provided by Luke, who was short of a hand in his workshop. Each morning I bicycled down from Islington, past the Gothic splendour of St Pancras and on through stolid Bloomsbury to the little workshop on the edge of Drury Lane, returning at night with tannin-stained hands. Luke was an inspired designer with a clear sense of tradition – he's the only person I know who owns copies of the complete working drawings of Edwin Lutyens – and it was good briefly to be part of what would later become a design company employing over twenty people. I enjoyed the buzz of creativity in Covent Garden, but I was also keen to keep forging my own path, so it was very gratifying when I picked up the workshop phone one morning and my editor, Maggie Body, asked, 'Can you come to a ceremony at the Alpine Club on October the eighteenth? You've won the Boardman Tasker Prize.'

One year on from that first meeting at the Hodder and Stoughton offices in Bedford Square, *Painted Mountains* had just come out and this prize was a welcome boost. And an honour, for I admired immensely the books of the two mountaineer-writers whose lives it commemorated. Their friend Dick was one of the prize's trustees and he was at the award ceremony, skulking amongst the chattering crowd. When we got a chance to talk, he asked whether I fancied a trip to Africa. A friend of a friend had asked him to help guide a group of novices up the three highest peaks on the continent, but he didn't think it was really for him. Would I be interested?

And so, a few days before Christmas, dressed in a black dinner jacket and red beret, I boarded a plane for Nairobi. The beret was a present from Maggie Saunders, intended perhaps to keep me in touch with my feminine side. The dinner jacket was required dress for the inaugural expedition dinner at Nairobi's Muthaiga Club, which would also – in those days when South African wine was still banned in Kenya – be providing several cases of expensively imported French wine to take up Kilimanjaro, Mount Kenya and Mount Stanley. As well as agreeing to cover the extra porterage costs for wine, expedition members had also signed up to the principles of the I Will Not Complain club, whose founder, Anthony Willoughby had instigated the crazy project. Most of the takers were, like him, expatriates based in Tokyo; the rest came from London and Lyon. Apart from an uncomplaining sense of adventure and their tenuous connection with Willoughby, the only thing they had in common was a total lack of mountaineering experience. A local guiding company had been employed to run the show and I was enrolled as additional mountaineering expert, cook and general dogsbody. There was no pay, but all my expenses – wine included – were covered. I had never been to Africa and it seemed too good a chance to turn down.

The Muthaiga Club was chintzy, with leathery old ladies playing bridge and steely young blondes dancing through the night. How different, the following morning, to plunge into the clamour of the public bus station. What struck me most, in all that jostling noise, smell and poverty, was the resilient joyfulness of Africans – the singing and laughter, the garish clothes, the bright smiles of the children determined optimistically to sell us their bananas.

We crossed the border into Tanzania and continued after dark in pick-up trucks, sloshing along muddy tracks beneath the trees, Willoughby still in pinstripe suit and I Will Not Complain T-shirt, shouting 'Nothing like a bowler hat to keep the branches off your head.'

We camped in an invisible field and only the next morning did we see the great white dome of Kilimanjaro looming over the forest. Andrew Wielochowski, our chief guide, sorted loads with Camille, Melchior, Aloysius and all the other porters, then checked the team's luggage, trying to instil a bit of hardy mountain spirit with firm scoldings like 'No, Doune, you can't take your make-up.' Then we were off, ambling easily at first amongst tropical hardwoods underplanted luxuriously with ferns, begonias and orange fireball lilies.

Instead of the normal Kili approach from Marangu, Andrew was taking us up the wilder Umbwe route on the far side of the mountain. Soon we were climbing steeply up a narrow ridge entangled with mossy roots, heading for the only water – a murky little pond where we camped for the first night. Sharing the porters' fire under a rock overhang, I cooked potatoes, ratatouille and grilled steak. During supper we were startled by the burbling chuckle of tree hyraxes, unseen in the canopy above us; later we saw the more earthbound rock hyraxes, which look a bit like guinea pigs and are said to be related to the elephant. Over coffee and rum we stood amongst golden mossy tree trunks, awed silhouettes gazing out at a Caspar David Friedrich sunset, soft and misty on the plain far below.

On Day Two we continued up the narrow ridge, winding

now amongst giant tree heathers festooned with jade lichen. Then up into a higher zone of huge vegetative candelabra – the famous giant groundsels – extraterrestrial cabbages hanging over our heads as Willoughby recounted his Harrow schooldays. 'My housemaster told me I'd never be any good at anything. So I left, went to the American College, then hitch-hiked round South America, then took a one-way ticket on the Trans-Siberian railway to Japan, with two suitcases full of company addresses and the London *Yellow Pages*. The idea was to set up import agencies, but no one seemed to speak English, so that didn't work out.' He ended up as a leather-goods dealer, running a very successful company supplying commemorative key rings, photo frames and wallets. When pay day came on Kilimanjaro each of the porters was given his wages in a shiny wallet, complete with his own Polaroid portrait.

I was anxious about trying to climb a peak of nearly six thousand metres in barely a week from London. At least we were allowed an acclimatisation day beside the little tin barranco hut. We spent the day sitting in the mist, coaxing life into a fire of old heather stumps before cooking doughnuts and an early Christmas dinner. Only the next morning, 24 December, did the cloud lift to reveal the huge Breach Wall of Kilimanjaro, icicles dripping from rambling glaciers. Now the party split, with the porters escorting five of the team, including Willoughby's parents-in-law, round to the easier Barafu route. Willoughby, his wife Victoria, sister-in-law Alexandra, Doune, Megan and Guy continued up to the Western Breach with Andrew, Camille and I as guides. Everyone had to carry their own luggage.

That night we arrived in driving snow at the collapsed remains of the Arrow Hut, pitching tents amongst the debris. I had a thick cold and, at 4,800 metres above sea level, higher now than the summit of Mont Blanc, I felt terrible. Somehow I managed to rouse myself on Christmas morning, helping people on with crampons and leading up the frozen snow of the Arrow Glacier. But as we passed 5,500 metres, labouring over rocky steps dusted with snow, I just went to pieces. Doune, a radio journalist from Tokyo, eventually realised that I wasn't waiting politely for her. The final humiliation was when Andrew had to come down and relieve me of my rucksack so that I could drag my leaden body the last few feet onto the crater rim to collapse on flat gravel, snoozing for half an hour before finding the will to drag myself over to the tents. They looked like alien spaceships plonked beside the gleaming crystal columns of the Furtwängler Glacier.

'Stephen, is mountaineering always this miserable?' asked Doune at six o'clock on Boxing Day morning. 'No,' I insisted. But it had been a horrendous night: supper a nauseous struggle; water bottles tainted with greasy soup; sleep sketchy, interrupted by my bouts of feverish claustrophobia, at one point tearing off my sleeping bag and thrusting my head through the tent door, panicking for air. Now we woke to a grey dawn, grey frost, grey thoughts. Fetching snow to make tea was a terrible effort; packing rucksacks was a Herculean task. And what made it particularly galling was to see Victoria and Alexander so jaunty and bright, skipping round the crater rim, completely unaffected by the altitude.

The sun improved things slightly. With comic slowness we shuffled up to the encircling summit ridge where we met the stalwarts of the Barafu party, including Georgina Montagu, moving like a zombie, prodded gently forward by one of the porters murmuring kindly, 'Vomitty, vomitty – no problem.'

The summit was a joyless affair and on the halting retreat back round the crater rim I stopped frequently to doze, dreaming of cocktails beneath palm trees, only dimly aware of Willoughby shouting back, 'Is Stephen all right?' But then at last we reached the big scree slope, where we could run down the normal route, down, down, down, into the thick luscious air, returning to life.

Back in Nairobi some of the party left, to be replaced by Louisa and James from London, and Didier, Isabelle and their seventy-two-year-old father Maurice from Lyon. They all had now to suffer the purgatory of rapid ascent, while the rest of us were perfectly acclimatised for Mount Kenya. Again, the local experts had done us proud, laying on Land Rover transport to the road head near Chogoria, where we met our porters.

This eastern approach to Mount Kenya, alongside the deep Gorges Valley, is probably the most spectacular. And the mountain itself is an altogether more shapely object than Kilimanjaro. It too is a volcano, but the original dome has eroded away, leaving just a necklace of spiky remains around the central granitic 'plug' with its twin summits named after two Bantu chiefs, Nelion and Batian, by Sir Halford MacKinder, who made the first ascent in 1899 after a long hazardous bushwack all the way from the Indian Ocean. The name 'Kiinya' – which gives the country its name – means 'Hill of the Cock Ostrich' and refers to the piebald effect, now sadly diminished by climate change, of white snow on dark rock.

We spent New Year's Eve beside the gorgeous Hall Tarns, trying out potential rock-climbers on a small cliff nearby, and celebrating that night with a huge casserole and more bottles of wine than the high-altitude physicians would probably recommend. Two days later, half the party scrambled up the lower, easier summit of Lenana, while the Nairobi guide, Mark Savage, and I took the keener climbers up one of the two higher twins, Nelion. This was a proper rock climb, pioneered in 1929 by a district commissioner called Percy Wyn-Harris and a tea planter called Eric Shipton, who would both climb very close to the summit of Everest four years later.

After the shapeless rubble of Kilimanjaro it was good to be on architectural granite. Mark had three people on his rope, while I brought Mr and Mrs Willoughby up their first-ever rock climb, with much grunting, the occasional alarmed shriek and immense pride at reaching Nelion's 5,188-metre summit. We carried food and sleeping bags, and that night all seven of us squeezed into the tiny aluminium hut which Ian Howell had built on the summit in 1970, determined to enjoy the African sunset from a position of lofty security; it had taken him thirteen journeys up and down the Shipton Route to carry up all the prefabricated sections. Thick hoar frost the next morning precluded taking our party over the tricky Gate of the Mists to the slightly higher summit of Batian and we had to head back down, completing our traverse of the massif with a wonderful jungle-bash down the rarely travelled Old Moses Route.

Mount Kenya was fun, but the highlight of the Three Peaks Expedition was the final adventure in the Rwenzori – the Mountains of the Moon. The fifth-century Alexandrian geographer Ptolemy gave them their fantastical nickname, theorising correctly that in the heart of Africa there were high mountains whose snows fed the Nile. The first European actually to see the peaks was Romolo Gessi, but it was Henry Stanley who presumed to publicise them and gave his name to the highest massif. In 1906 the Duke of Abruzzi climbed the main Stanley peaks and named the highest point Margherita after his aunt, the Queen Mother of Italy.

To get to the Rwenzori we took a bus from Nairobi to Uganda's capital, Kampala, then continued south to Mbare and back north to Kasese, a market town close to the mountains, which straddle the Uganda-Congo border. Yoweri Museveni had only just taken control of Uganda after years of civil war surrounding the murderous regimes of Idi Amin and Milton Obote. It was sad to see what had been one of the best-run – and agriculturally most prosperous – countries in Africa in ruins. Shop shelves were bare of almost everything except Omo powder and chewing gum. Buildings lay half derelict, pocked by shellfire. The main road was cratered with potholes and patrolled by gangs of soldiers, many of them teenage youths. At one roadblock, the driver asked a thirteen-year-old if he'd mind putting down his rocket launcher before coming aboard to inspect our passports. We had one frightening encounter with a very drunk officer with a loaded automatic rifle, whom Willoughby handled with impressive tact; but generally the gun-toters were good-humoured, one of them laughing at my skinny frame and opining, '*He* won't get up any mountains.' As for the civilians, again there was that resilient African cheerfulness, unbowed despite two decades of intermittent slaughter.

At Kasese market Victoria and I stocked up with rations for the porters – glutinous kasava flour and the stinking dried fish which even the famously spartan explorer Bill Tilman had baulked at when he visited the Rwenzori with Eric Shipton in 1930. Then we drove up to Ibanda, where John Matte and his extended family ran the porters' cartel. I passed on best wishes from Henry and Anna Osmaston, who had spent so much time here in the 1950s when Henry was working for the Ugandan forestry service; and then we were off, climbing through the forest for three hours to the first hut at Nyabitaba.

In the morning the sun shone as we swam in the Bujuku River before continuing up the far bank, climbing steeply through man-eating brambles where progress would have been completely impossible without a well-slashed trail. And then came the rain, because Rwenzori means 'Rainmaker' and even in this January 'dry season' it is rare to go dry for a whole day. We shivered through lunch in a cramped cave, then continued through the giant heather forest. This is how Filippo de Filippi described it in the official account of the 1906 Abruzzi expedition:

Trunks and boughs are entirely smothered in a thick layer of mosses which hang like waving beards from every spray, cushion and englobe every knot, curl and swell around each twig, deform every outline and obliterate every feature, till the trees are a mere mass of grotesque contortions, monstrous tumefactions of the discoloured leprous growth . . . No forest can be grimmer and stranger than this.

But I loved the surreal splendour of these tree heathers growing fifty feet high. And I loved emerging onto the great hanging plain of Bigo Bog, jumping from tussock to wobbly tussock, then giving up and squelching regardless through the black ooze, with the huge spires of giant lobelias and leguminous groundsels looming out of the mist. It was an enchanted lost world and, provided you kept spare dry clothes wrapped in polythene bags, you could always be comfortable at night.

That evening, cooking on a fire of dead lobelia stumps, we heated a great cauldron of mulled wine, sloshing in plenty of Cointreau for good measure. The next day we trudged higher, through grey drizzle, to Bujuku Lake, which Tilman had described as 'a mournful, shallow mere, with its foetid, mud-lined shores ... in harmony with the desolate landscape surrounding it.' In a cave near here Anna Osmaston had once found an old Huntley and Palmer biscuit tin with a man's skull inside. She had immediately fallen ill and had had to be trussed up in a blanket suspended from a pole and carried down by the tough Bakonjo men.

Today, with temperatures dropping, even Bakonjo tough-ness was beginning to wilt; and Willoughby had to offer extra pay to persuade the men up the slimy sluice of Groundsel Gully, and on, barefoot, over lichenous rocks sprinkled with fresh snow, to establish the party at the Elena Huts. A pair of Henry Osmaston's skis was still nailed to one of the little trian-gular hovels perched beneath the Elena Glacier.

Five of us squeezed into the one usable hut; the others slept in tents. The next day they turned the ruined hut into a kitchen, preparing sunflower-seed bread, soup, tuna-and-avocado salad and pineapple-in-Armagnac, all brought to us by smiling room service. Meanwhile I tried to fit ten pairs of crampons to ten pairs of boots, hoping that the weather would improve the next day. It didn't, but we set off anyway, in the dark. I was the sole mountain guide for this third peak and feeling the responsibility, snapping irritably, 'No, Georgina, you've got your crampons on back to front,' then getting even more angry with Maurice, 'trying to establish his bloody geriatric altitude record.' He was impossibly slow, so Didier agreed to take his father on a separate rope, while I went ahead with the other seven people, zigzagging through the mist onto the Stanley Plateau where Shipton and Tilman had got completely disorientated in 1930.

I stopped the party and announced, 'I'm sorry but I really don't know where we are, and I'm worried that the snow is going to fill in our tracks. I think we should turn back.' But Willoughby would have none of it. Nor would the young bookselling heir James Blackwell, who persuaded me to have one more look at the sketch map in the Osmaston guidebook. So we took another compass bearing and continued into the pale murk, skirting some enormous crevasses, then contouring up onto a steep slope, winding amongst huge rime encrustations, frozen echoes of the 'monstrous tumefactions' fringing Bigo Bog.

On one traverse there was a shriek as Georgina shot over the edge, fielded adroitly by Louisa. We continued through great swirling frozen protuberances worthy of Gaudi onto the south-east ridge and fifteen minutes later we were all on a summit. I announced cautiously that 'It was a tremendous climb, but I'm not promising that this is actually the summit of Margherita.' It was only afterwards when Aloysius Matte confirmed that the two sticks we found had indeed been left by him on the highest summit of the Rwenzori that we were assured of victory.

Back at the Elena Huts we waited until Didier and Maurice returned from the summit at dusk, exhausted. Then we all raced down into the valley, glancing back at the now-clear horizon to glimpse the mountain we had just climbed, before thrashing on through giant vegetables to the hut beside the Kitandara Lakes. The curmudgeonly Tilman had described the lakes as 'two lifeless tarns which deepened the melancholy aspect of this grim defile.' But, flushed with success, I was in the Garden of Eden. And that enchantment lingered for the next two days as we completed the circuit back to Ibanda. I loved it all: the iridescent malachite sunbirds flitting amongst the giant lobelias; the vertical bog as we came over the Freshfield Pass, Isabelle somersaulting through the tussocks; the last night with all of us camped under the huge cave roof of Kabamba – porters with their fish-and-kasava gloop supplemented by a tree hyrax, foreign tourists cooking bread rolls on the fire – as a full moon rose above the shaggy black silhouettes of the giant-heather forest; and the final morning, dashing through the forest as the pearly dewed helichrysums

– the everlasting flowers – opened orange and crimson to greet the sun, and I stopped to swim in the Mubuku River, washing off layers of bog mud, afterwards lying on a smooth rock to feel the tropical warmth soak into my naked skin.

Five days later I returned to an icy London, where the star mountaineer Mick Fowler had just climbed a frozen column of ice up a leaking downpipe on St Pancras Station. It was a good winter in Britain, with fine freezing conditions on the distant Scottish Highlands, and I made the weekend trip north four times, inspired by the competitive, energetic *joie de vivre* of the metropolitan climbing set. I had three wonderful days on Ben Nevis with Alison Hargreaves and another effulgent day with my landlords Victor and Maggie. But the best flying visit of all was further north still, to the mountains of Torridon. On Friday night we were negotiating traffic jams on the Holloway Road; at dawn on Saturday we were walking into the wild empty cirque of Coire Mhic Fhearchair, on the northern flank of Beinn Eighe. For years I had gloated over photos of this thousand-foot-high triple buttress (yet another of those deferred ambitions) and now at last I was here, climbing the great central pillar – first on pink Torridonian sandstone, then on the upper tier of pale angular quartzite – with a bright young biologist called Noel Craine.

In the summer I returned with an equally bright but considerably older pathologist called Keith Cartwright to climb on the far eastern wall of the corrie, during a breathless four-day tour of Scottish crags. I had met Keith once or twice in Oxford, then hadn't seen him for years. Now it was good, belatedly, to get to know him, Pru and their children, Katherine, Vicky and Julian. I rather envied their family holidays – sailing, walking and climbing their way through Europe, unburdened by the harsher demands of actually making a living around the mountains. But, whatever the doubts, I was determined to follow that perverse course.

Living in London certainly fomented single-mindedness. It was exciting to be at the centre of things, in one of the world's most beautiful capitals. Cycling at night, or at dawn, over Waterloo Bridge always brought on a rush of optimism – a sense of limitless possibilities. Even in the microcosmic world of mountaineering, London climbers had an energy and resource-fulness which was stimulating. And, lodging with Victor and Maggie, at the epicentre of gossip, it was impossible not to be spurred on by a certain competitiveness. Luke, too, was an influence – less as a climber than as a designer and businessman who knew how to sell himself. I had now stopped working for him, to concentrate on setting up my own projects – a new book contract, more magazine articles, some proper headed letter paper, a professional-looking lecture brochure, mailshots to schools and clubs. With Victor's film-making friend Kees 't Hooft, we were discussing possible future film projects and more joint expeditions with our Bombay friend Harish Kapadia.

Lectures were the most enjoyable employment and brought me full circle, back to youthful dreams of the theatre. It was a chance to perform, to entertain, to hold an audience in the palm of your hand, as you wove a narrative around visual imagery. Unlike most television films of expeditions – which, with notable exceptions, tend to cobble dubious footage to a sensational commentary that bears little resemblance to the truth – in a lecture you could tell your own story, illustrated with your own pictures, about what actually happened. And, I was pleased to discover, I was quite good at it.

Deadlines pressed during that summer of 1987, as I had to have everything ready by 5 July when I would be setting off to spend four months in Central Asia. Henry Day had been scheming for two years to put together an expedition to the world's thirteenth-highest mountain, Shishapangma, in Tibet, and had asked me to be deputy leader. That would occupy September and October; but first I planned a return to old haunts in northern Pakistan, filling in some of the blanks on my own personal map of the Karakoram.

Inspiration came from Eric Shipton's much grander *Blank on the Map*, a classic narrative describing his 1937 explorations with Bill

Tilman and the poets' brothers Michael Spender and John Auden, one a surveyor, the other a geologist. Reading Shipton's account of that expansive journey, and its follow-up in 1939, poring over the beautiful, intricate plane table sheets of Shipton's Indian surveyor, Faizal Elahi, studying the resultant map in the Royal Geographical Society, we dreamed of a similar odyssey. It wouldn't be on Shipton's grand scale, but we hoped at least to get right to the heart of the Karakoram, to the glacial basin called Snow Lake, and from there to try crossing a high saddle called the Khurdopin Pass, a journey which had eluded Shipton in 1939.

Phil Bartlett, drawn increasingly to the bigger picture, more a wanderer than a climbing technician, was keen. So was one of the North London set – a young dealer from Shell called Duncan Tunstall, whose puppyish enthusiasm would be a good foil to Phil's more contemplative approach.

I knew they would be good companions; but it was still daunting to face a four-month absence. On the Sunday morning of departure, doing a spot of weeding in Maggie's garden, immersed in dewy greenery, I suffered the usual pangs of anxious regret at leaving gentle domesticity for one of the harshest landscapes on earth. It was like watching those carefree Swiss pensioners before setting off on my abortive Eiger solo. Why can't I be like them? Why can't I enjoy the gentle things of life? Why deprive myself of so many normal pleasures? Why not just potter contentedly?

And of course there was no simple answer. Just a hunch that yin and yang need both to flourish, that we thrive on contrast, that the shady garden sanctuary can only be enjoyed properly after we have first wandered thirsty in the desert. And, in any case, this wasn't just perverse masochism: I antic-ipated fun and adventure. And sure enough, three days later – after the old familiar night drive up the Karakoram Highway, waking up in our minibus to the bright silver light of the Indus valley, with Duncan enthusing about the spectacular scenery and the 'whacky ethnicity' – I felt glad to be back.

This time we took the right turn past Nanga Parbat, contin-uing into Baltistan. We spent a night at Skardu, then hired a jeep for the final jolting track to the village of Dassu, where seven pre-arranged porters were waiting for us. Five days after leaving Islington we were on the march.

Two of our porters, both called Ahmed, turned out to be from Ali Murad's village in Hunza. The rest were local Baltis. They were a joyful team, singing ebulliently with wild pink roses stuck in their ears. They were also exasperating, pocketing their equipment allowance instead of spending it on stoves, tents and boots. So roles were reversed, the sahibs donating their own flysheet to the porters and bringing them their bed tea.

On the second morning of the walk-in Duncan woke from a dream in which we chanced upon three beautiful women wandering up the Biafo Glacier. Duncan had ended up with the most demure of the trio, who proved to be the most passionate. Sex continued to dominate our conversation for the next few days, but later we descended inevitably to the basest denominator of all – food. Not that we were ill-provisioned. On the contrary, we had seven men to establish us right at the heart of the mountains with enough food, fuel and gear to be totally self-sufficient for the next three or four weeks.

One of our Balti porters, Gohar Ali, cooking for his companions at a camp beside the Biafo Glacier.

The walk-in took seven days. First we followed the Braldu Gorge, the pungent acid-drop scent of silvery artemisia bushes bringing back in a Proustian rush all those earlier Karakoram journeys. Then on the third day we turned left onto one of the great ice highways – the thirty-five-miles-long Biafo Glacier. Overnight camps were spent in the side aisles, in verdant abla-tion valleys full of birdsong, but by day we followed the central nave. This really was one of Ruskin's 'cathedrals of the earth', flanked by the most spectacular soaring pillars I had ever seen.

'Base Camp' was the grandiose name we gave to our single tent, pitched on a pile of rocks levelled with snow, at the junc-tion of the Biafo and Sim Gang glaciers. Here we counted out 1,000 rupees for each of our porters, who then set off home, leaving us utterly alone in the ice wilderness. After a day's rest we left at dawn to do a recce to Snow Lake, taking seven hours to walk the fourteen-mile return journey on snowshoes. The aim was to continue eventually to the far corner of this glacial basin and cross the Khurdopin Pass. But first, whilst dumping a cache of food and fuel at the entrance to the inner basin of Snow Lake, Duncan and I couldn't help drooling over a cluster of fairy-tale spires, all unclimbed, over on the western wall of the Biafo.

Phil wasn't interested in summits so, after doing a recce into the side glacier beneath our chosen peak, Duncan and I left him with Kierkegaard at Base Camp, and set off to bivouac beneath the most stunning tower, marked as 5,997 metres on the map. We didn't quite reach the summit, but we spent two and a half memorable days on what I called the Solu Tower, referring to the Solu Glacier on its far side. Descending late the second after-noon, tired and parched, to our little bivouac ledge halfway up the tower, Duncan dropped the stove into the abyss. Desperate for water, we caught a few drips from the wall above in a mug, but a few moments later the temperature dropped and the drips were frozen into immobility. I consoled myself with the smug thought that for once someone else had cocked up and smoked a contemplative cigarette as the sun set on some of the world's most spectacular summits: Masherbrum, the Ogre and, lingering last in the orange alpenglow, the distant pyramid of K2.

Back at base it snowed for three days. We stuffed socks in the tent's ventilation hole to keep out the driving spindrift and cooked as best we could in the porch. We made kedgeree, doughnuts and dhal samosas; then we enjoyed the coarser offerings of Greasy Dunc's Chip Shop.

When the weather improved we packed up Base Camp to start the big journey. The first afternoon we walked to the Snow Lake dump, to find that the ravens had ripped open a sack, stealing all the cream crackers and most of the tea bags. But we still had more food and fuel than we could manage and on the first full carry over Snow Lake we were each carrying thirty kilos, trying to believe Milan Kundera's assurance that 'the heavier the burden, the closer our lives come to the earth, the more real and truthful they become.'

Even with snowshoes on our feet, it was hard work breaking trail. Duncan looked debonair in the latest Patagonia anorak and jaunty panama; but Phil looked like a scarecrow – a high-altitude Worzel Gummidge draped in motley rags, with tatty home-made gaiters on his feet, an old floral sunhat of his mother's and a black kettle hanging from his ruck-sack. Instead of slick telescopic ski sticks, he carried two enormous wooden poles that he had picked up in the Skardu bazaar.

We felt that Shipton would have been proud. Yes, we were following in the steps of giants and, as always, the same heroic names cropped up. Martin Conway, who had attempted my Bolivian summit of Ancohuma, had also been here, in 1892, when he came up with the poetic 'Snow Lake', or Lukpe Lawa, as it translates in Balti. Next came the Bullock-Workmans. Their surveys were not always very accurate and tended to exaggerate; nevertheless, when Shipton's friend Tilman made the first proper survey in 1937 he did discover that the combined area of the Snow Lake and Sim Gang glaciers totalled a respectable 200 square miles. More recently, Canadian ice hydrologists had taken depth soundings and discovered a thickness of 600 metres. Further down at the Base Camp we had just left, where the Biafo was squeezed through narrow walls, the ice was over a kilometre deep. This landscape was on a colossal scale and as we approached the distinctive white pyramid of Snow Lake Peak, I remembered Mike Harber and his friends from Cardiff, who had disappeared here two years earlier. And I remembered chatting on the phone more recently to Ian Haigh, just before he set off in 1986 to cross the Khurdopin Pass from the north with two local porters. He had become terribly weak with dysentery. Then he had fallen into a crevasse. All the supplies had been lost and the two porters had made a desperate journey down the Biafo, surviving on wisps of 'grass' (possibly the leathery wild chives which grow here) and eventually summoning help. But by the time a search party had reached Snow Lake Ian had vanished.

Those sad tales reinforced our sense of remoteness. Bad weather also intensified the feeling of isolation as we carried half-loads to the pass on the third day, before returning to our tent on Snow Lake. It snowed all night and Phil, the sensible housekeeper, became very anxious about being separated from all the food on the pass. It was a close-run thing and in the morning we had to battle for several hours through spindrift avalanches to regain our supplies on the crest of the pass. Here, at 5,790 metres above sea level, we pitched the tent in a snowstorm and struggled to light the oxygen-starved Primus stove, warming it with a bonfire of *Don Quixote* pages soaked in paraffin.

Ah, 'the squalor of the high camps' as the Scottish writer Bill Murray put it. And the agony of the dawn start, with everything coated in icy dry powder. But then the reward: a sudden ethereal vision of the immense untouched north face of the Ogre, radiant pink over the Sim Gang, as the storm cleared. And the view of our northward descent onto the smooth white snowfields of the Khurdopin Glacier.

In 1939 Shipton had looked down this same glacier with the botanist Scott Russell. A few days earlier, returning to Snow Lake with messages from Gilgit, Russell had brought news that England was at war with Germany. The expedition, with all its hopes of continuing north and overwintering in the Shaksgam valley, was over. After our own return home in 1987 I met Scott Russell and his wife Anne, daughter of George Finch who had nearly climbed Everest in 1922. Scott gave me a copy of his book *Mountain Prospect*. In the final pages he describes looking north from the Khurdopin Pass in September 1939:

> Clear before us lay the route . . . which we had hoped but could not now follow . . . it seems that a gate was then closed – the gate that led to free planning of our lives, and the key to reopen it is still in an uncertain future.

He wrote those lines towards the end of the war, whilst incarcerated in Changi jail, in Singapore, not knowing whether he would starve – or be shot – before liberating troops arrived. Nearly fifty years later, enjoying a freedom we take so easily for granted, Duncan, Phil and I now started down the glacier which Scott had been denied. All the sketch map indicated was its rough orientation. Beyond that we knew nothing and it was that lack of knowledge which made the journey so alluring. All that day we laboured across what Duncan called The Cricket Pitch – an immense snowfield, where we took turns to break trail. Then, towards evening, we reached the brink of a great downfall and the smooth surface was riven by half-covered slots, into which we trod repeatedly, collapsing under the weight of our loads, floundering back and forth.

It became obvious that the icefall would be suicidally diffi-cult to descend, if not impossible, so we sneaked off to the side, overjoyed to discover a little valley with a stream – our first running water since leaving the trickle at Base Camp. Here we camped. And here, on a rock, I left my snowshoes for some future traveller. They were old-fashioned wooden 'raquettes'. Many years ago Lindsay had found one of them on the summit of the Aiguille du Fou, above Chamonix. In my father's work-shop, steaming ash lathes around a special hot iron, I had made a matching snowshoe frame. It was a sad moment now, leaving these old friends, but we were confident that they wouldn't be needed on the lower glacier.

Getting to that lower glacier the next morning was chal-lenging. First we had to climb down steep cliffs, Worzel Gummidge's kettle clanging on the rocks. Then a long snow gully. Then a hideous muddy scree chute, bombarded by stones. Then a maze of tottering blackened ice towers, through which we weaved and dodged, Phil muttering, 'You'd never do anything like this in the Alps.' But nor in the Alps could we have enjoyed this thrill of exploration – of problems solved, as we reached the main bed of the glacier and gloated back at the giant icefall we had circumvented, then stared ahead at an Amazon of ice flowing mile after mile down the valley.

The next day we tramped for nine hours through drizzle, Duncan joshing Phil about looking like 'an old bumbly from the Fell and Rock Club, out for a wet weekend in the Lake District.' We stopped three times for snacks. In the first break we each had a slice of salami; in the second a cup of soup with noodles and a third of a Mars bar; and then a final third of a Mars bar. Our loads were getting steadily lighter and we were getting steadily hungrier, watching jealously, checking that the knife sliced equal portions. But we were happy – absorbed by the constant surprises that the landscape sprang on us. On the fourth day after crossing the pass we finally reached the bottom of the Khurdopin Glacier and turned west into the main Shimshal valley. At one point we followed a false trail and had to abseil from a boulder down a cliff of mud-glued conglomerate to regain the river bank. Then we found ourselves on a Karakoram-Special scree slope, bombarded by artillery fire. So we escaped across the river, wading knee deep, climbing rope safeguarding us in the lethal icy current.

Another camp, this time in a shepherd's hut, where we cooked our last dehydrated meal. Then back across the river, using a wire cable that we had found, which led to another trail winding through white sand beneath black and orange varnished walls. And then suddenly, that afternoon, eight days after leaving our Biafo base, we stumbled on the green barley fields of Shimshal and a boy – the first other human we had seen for nearly three weeks – took us to the Distaghil Cottage Tourist Bungalow for green tea and a plateful of hot chapattis filled with oozing butter and goat's cheese.

Shimshal village had been established about three hundred years earlier as a dumping ground for the Mir of Hunza's more troublesome subjects, but we found them a hospitable crowd. Dr Farmanullah, who tended to the health of the 1,500 or so inhabitants, spoke perfect English. He had met Ian Haigh when he'd passed through the previous August, and he showed us the sad entry in the logbook. Then we found an earlier entry by a Canadian team which had crossed the pass from the other side, like us. And a more recent entry by a German team which had been defeated by the giant icefall. And some hippie-esque pages of rambling philosophy, concluding, 'Two days of mind emptiness and being waited on. Perhaps I'm ready to return to the world. Thuttock the Lonely Freak.'

We weren't necessarily ready to return, but Duncan and Phil had jobs waiting. We hired two local men and set off the next morning, running joyfully under minimal eight-kilogramme loads down the long Shimshal valley, descending into one of the most elemental gorges in the whole Karakoram. At dusk, as we raced down a zigzag path cut into desolate walls of black rock, hurrying to reach the freshwater spring at Ziarat before dark, I suddenly spotted, on the far side of the gorge, a thousand metres above the turbid river, sprouting miraculously in the desert, a lone tamarisk bush glowing pink in the sun's last rays.

That tamarisk in the Shimshal Gorge was a moment of perfection – a summation – a confirmation of happiness at the end of a perfect journey. Or almost perfect. There was just that niggling annoyance of the Solu Tower – the peak that Duncan and I had not quite climbed. The unfinished business rankled, but I still had four weeks spare before I was due on the Shishapangma expedition and I was hoping secretly that I might find someone to accompany me back to the tower. So, when we reached the Karakoram Highway and boarded the Gilgit bus I was delighted to bump into a London acquaintance called Steve Razzetti.

Razzetti wasn't a climber but he loved trekking, and spent at least five months of each year in the mountains, his enthusiasm for the great ranges of Central Asia as gleeful as his passion for Jamaican music. (His nomadic lifestyle was supported by seasonal work at the Alpine Sports store in Kensington.) He was irrepressible and in 1987 he had still not visited the great glacial junction from which we had just come. So I suggested that he accompany me back to that crossroads, but this time by a different route – the Hispar Glacier. I didn't mention the Solu Tower.

We spent two busy days in the Gilgit bazaar stocking up with food, then hired a jeep to take us to Nagar, where we found two men to help with the luggage, allowing us to walk with reasonably light sacks. The weather was perfect. The Hispar Gorge was mercilessly free of rockfall and, after the old Kunyang Kish turn-off, we continued into new territory, for the most part following the enchanting ablation valley along the north bank of the Hispar Glacier, camping in flowery meadows and watching magical sunsets as I yearned for Mahler and Steve dreamed of Burning Spear gigs in Brixton. On the seventh night we camped in the last tiny pocket of greenery and at dawn the next morning we took to the ice – and then the snow – zigzagging up the glacier's final rise to the Hispar Pass. Hamid Ali had brought sunglasses for use against the dazzling glare but his companion had none, so we made some goggles out of a biscuit packet and string, with pinholes piercing the cardboard.

By ten o'clock that morning we were on the pass. We thanked and paid the men, and they set off home, leaving us alone with the immensity of the Karakoram, incredulous that the Ogre, towering so huge over the Sim Gang Glacier, was actually fourteen miles away. In the morning we roped up to descend to the Sim Gang, laden now with thirty-kilo rucksacks. Everything sparkled and, as we passed the entrance to Snow Lake, Razzetti was ecstatic.

He was also ecstatic when I told him that Phil, Duncan and I had left a stache of surplus food at the old Base Camp that we were now approaching. But I was tense, envious of Razzetti's carefree pleasure, because we were now walking beneath the fiercely tilted wall of the Solu Tower. I cursed the immaculate weather and wished there were some way of evading my self-imposed destiny – the terrible need to achieve. For a moment I was tempted to scrap the plan, as I had scrapped the ill-conceived Eiger Direct solo eleven months earlier. But this was different: it was feasible, justifiable. Or at least worth a try. Fear of future regret outweighed fear of the risks. So, as we reached the old camp and Razzetti unearthed our stache, confirming joyfully, 'Yes – tuna, dhal, *Quaker* oats, real *Italian* tomato purée', I asked whether he would like to have a rest day while I went to do a little climb. He did like the idea, so I began apprehensively to get ready – washing, eating, sorting what little climbing gear I had and filling tin cans with four litres of water to carry up the climb, because Razzetti was keeping our only stove for some serious gastronomy.

That evening I walked back into the cwm beneath the Solu Tower. Despite all the July snowfall, the overall level of the glacier had sunk and our month-old tracks, where the snow had been compressed, now stood proud of the surrounding ablated surface. The huge crevasse which Duncan and I had stepped across so easily was now a gaping chasm three metres wide, so I had to detour down into it and climb up a wall of vertical snow on the far side. Then I got out my sleeping bag, to lie in the dark watching the shooting stars, wondering morbidly whether this might be my last night on Earth.

Solu Tower first ascent 1987.
Left-hand route to south summit: Tunstall and Venables 23–25 July
Right-hand route to main summit: Venables 24 August

At 11.15 p.m. I left the bivouac and started up the Solu
Tower, climbing the same initial snow ramp that Duncan and
I had followed a month earlier. But this time, instead of turning
left, I continued right to the top of the ramp, arriving at
2.30 a.m. at the foot of a steep granite wall. I waited two
hours, shivering in the dark, then at first light roped up for
three pitches of beautiful rock-climbing. I stopped on a ledge
for a mug of cold Ovaltine and as I sat in the warm sunshine
a kite flew past, glancing briefly at the intruder. The sudden
flash of fellow animal life – like that brief encounter with the
kestrel on the summit of Rhinog Fach twenty-one years earlier
– seemed a good omen, banishing the dark fears of the night;
so I continued up a line of ledges, slanting diagonally across
smooth granite walls – the perfect Eiger-Rampish line of
weakness – with just one vertical ice-choked chimney providing
fifteen minutes of exquisite tension, before I arrived at midday
on a projecting boulder, where I stopped for a second rest.

Then I was on the summit snowfield, hoping with shocking vanity that Razzetti was watching from five miles away, recording on telephoto this tiny ant crawling so doggedly towards the sky.

The snow was hollow and flaky and I almost stopped twenty metres short of the top. But hubris triumphed over doubt, and I persevered, kicking with infinite care, fashioning solid steps, laboriously, all the way to the final crest where I could at last stand up straight, arms held high in gratitude for being allowed to complete my self-imposed task – for the privilege of being the first human ever to reach this beautiful summit.

Now everything seemed perfect, complete. Untainted by regrets, the world shone with a new intensity the next morning as I walked back to base, to be cosseted by Razzetti, plied with buckets of tea and platefuls of fried cheese-potato cakes. Shouldering a twenty-seven-kilo rucksack a day later, to start the final stage of our journey, felt almost effortless. Even the purgatorial sun-seared climb to the Sokha La – Razzetti's first ice climb – couldn't erode that serene contentment. On the contrary, I just felt thrilled to be here, on this wild gap in the Biafo wall, making the first crossing since Scott Russell's in 1939, descending into yet another glacial basin in this endlessly alluring wilderness. It didn't matter that the Primus stove packed up that night, forcing us to cook on a bonfire of paraffin-soaked paper (Tolkien this time), because a day later we were down off the glacier, camping in a glade of birches with plentiful firewood and fresh sorrel to flavour our supper. It didn't matter when we reached the village of Bisil that there was no jeep: we just kept on walking. And when there was still no jeep at Doqo the next day – the fifth day after leaving the Biafo – we just walked again, hour after hour under the sun, feeling as though we could walk for ever; but actually delighted that evening when we finally crossed a wobbly suspension bridge and reached the main road near Dasu, where I had started this odyssey with Duncan and Phil two months earlier, and where we now finally found a jeep to drive us back to Skardu.

Two days later I said goodbye to Razzetti in Gilgit and took the public bus back down the Karakoram Highway, dozing on the front seat, crammed up against the engine for the long hot drive through the night. Then from Rawalpindi I continued south by train, for another thousand miles, crossing the huge Punjab rivers, then the empty sands of the Sind Desert, all the way to Karachi, where I spent two days in a cheap hotel, eking out my last rupees and keeping just enough for the taxi ride to the airport on 7 September.

The Karakoram journey was over, but as I boarded the plane for Kathmandu I heard Luke's familiar fruity tones and knew that I had connected successfully with the Shishapangma team. The next expedition had already started.

Chapter Thirteen

With the Colonels to Shishapangma

It was all was dreamed up by two colonels in the Royal Engineers. During twenty years of professional soldiering, Henry Day had managed his seamless progress to high rank whilst simultaneously disappearing for weeks at a time on Himalayan expeditions, successfully working a service which in those days still valued 'adventure training'. Now, with Tibet recently opened for the first time to foreigners, he was keen to try the untouched east face of the world's thirteenth-highest mountain, Shishapangma. But how to find the £50,000 or so which the avaricious Chinese Mountaineering Association demanded for providing the necessary 'services'?

Enter Colonel John Blashford-Snell, pith-helmeted hero of the Blue Nile and the Darien Gap, founder of Operation Drake and Operation Raleigh, an orotund raconteur whose showbiz skills could magic money into the whackiest project. A deal was struck. Colonel John would find the money, provided that Colonel Henry's expedition came under the umbrella of his Scientific Exploration Society and included a team of geographical scientists. Because all things military must have a code name – and because the official Chinese spelling of Xixabangma was an unpronounceable turn-off to any potential western sponsor – the colonels agreed to call the expedition Jade Venture.

And so, after two years of planning and negotiating, a disparate collection of thirty or so soldiers, climbers, administrators and embryonic scientists assembled in Kathmandu on 7 September 1987. After two months' isolation in Pakistan, I was new to all the last-minute preparations: Kate Phillips, the youngest, prettiest member of the team, posing in an inflatable boat beside the Embankment with Colonel John, the latter telling the television reporters how he planned to establish the world's boating altitude record; my old friend Lindsay Griffin being interviewed by Radio Four whilst engaged in 'intensive training', which was actually emergency physiotherapy for his latest injuries, courtesy of the RAF rehabilitation unit; Henry Osmaston (yes, we had rounded up all the usual suspects) demonstrating the ICI-sponsored steam lance with which he hoped to probe Tibet's glaciers and discover interesting facts; Colonel Henry jetting to Hong Kong to meet our other main sponsor, Eric Hotung, on his floating-junk gin palace.

Like the Siachen expedition with Harish two years earlier, this venture was gregarious, bursting with pleasurable anticipation. And for me, after the Islamic strictures of Pakistan, it was refreshing to visit Kathmandu for the first time and be in a land where women weren't hidden away. It was good, too, to acclimatise by trekking for a week in the green Nepalese hills, following a ridge to the holy lake of Bharib Khund, high in the Jugal Himal.

An ex-Gurkha officer called Mike Cheney organised the trek beautifully, with teams of local porters to carry luggage and Sherpas running the mobile kitchen. I had never done this kind of trekking, with servants bringing tea and hot water to your tent each morning, and cooking three-course meals each evening. The only hardship, during this tail-end of the monsoon season, was the leeches lurking on every branch and frond. The recommended alkaline deterrent was washing-up liquid on the shoes, so we squelched through the forest, foaming at the lace holes; but the leeches still got through. One of Henry Osmaston's geography students, Claire, was studying the day's botanical collection one evening, bent over Oleg Polunin's classic *Flowers of the Himalaya*, when a blood-gorged leech fell from her scalp and flopped like a large bloated slug on the open page.

The following day Blashford-Snell said a temporary goodbye. The butane-propane gas cylinders for cooking at high altitude had been impounded by Indian Customs and he was going back to wield his clout, and try to liberate the vital supplies. It was typical of the man: beneath the clowning rumbustious self-caricature, kitted out in full battledress for the Siege of Mafeking, there lurked a very generous spirit.

So Colonel John went down and we continued to our holy lake for a spot of acclimatisation. Later we all met again at the Tibetan frontier, where two squaddies commandeered by Colonel Henry supervised the transport of hundreds of porter loads over Friendship Bridge to waiting trucks on the far side. Back in Kathmandu we had been supplied with T-shirts embroidered 'Jade Venture: The Empire Strikes Back', and it did feel as if we were re-staging Colonel Younghusband's ill-conceived 1904 'Diplomatic Mission' to Tibet. The only problem with this 1987 bandobast was that once we reached the road head at the village of Nyalam the supply chain ground to a halt. From the village it was a walk of about thirty miles to Base Camp and all the food and gear had to be carried up by yaks. Unfortunately we had arrived in the middle of the potato harvest and nearly all the potential yak herders were busy. So we ended up with very extended lines of communication, with just three yaks hauling a slow dribble of supplies up the valley. At one point a Shropshire forestry consultant called Julian Freeman-Atwood – our token rustic – was sent to scour the mountainside round Nyalam and try to round up more of the truculent beasts, but all he could catch were some tiny donkeys which arrived at Base Camp three days later, labouring under pathetically small loads.

We supplemented yak power with our own limited load-carrying abilities. Brian Davison, a research chemist who had given up two years' holiday entitlement to join the expedition, muttered, 'Let's face it – we're not going to do any climbing. The object of the exercise is to get all the boxes to Base Camp and then take them all back down again.' Most of the boxes were high-altitude compo rations, full of tins and tubes and packets of 'biscuits, brown – four for the use of' complete with foolproof instructions. I explained to Kate, 'Soldiers aren't supposed to think for themselves', at which Captain John Vlasto struck a camp pose and minced, 'Well, if you think you can do better, why don't *you* go and fight the Russians?'

John, with his First in Philosophy and nonchalant manner, was the most unlikely soldier and was about to leave the army to make lots of money as an investment banker. Nigel Williams was more obvious officer material, a delightful Leader of Men who later became director of Scotland's national mountaineering centre, Glenmore Lodge. Jerry Gore was an ex-Royal Marine with a keen sense of tribal loyalties; he loved baiting Johnny Garrett, our one guardsman, who complained about the crippling cost of bearskins and was as English as clotted cream. Sharing a tent with Johnny one night I was disturbed by shouts of 'Emma! Emma!' as he thrashed out what seemed to be some nightmare of unrequited love. 'Who's Emma?' I asked the next morning.

'Emma? Oh, she's the family golden retriever.' He had dreamed that he was being pursued down the icefall by an avalanche and had found himself in the field at home in Devon, running to his room and hiding under his bed, chased by the dog.

The icefall in question was the right-hand one of two great cataracts falling from the eastern cirque of Shishapangma. Several of us in the advance party, influenced by the wariness of my old mentor Lindsay Griffin, had staged a mini-rebellion, telling Colonel Henry that we didn't like the look of his hypothetical route up the unclimbed east face. It just looked too dangerous. Or at least too threatened by potential avalanches for the kind of old-fashioned siege approach we were employing, with several Himalayan novices expecting to be strung out on repeated journeys through the danger zone. Henry accepted graciously our proposed Plan B – to climb the left-hand icefall, then the unclimbed east face of a satellite peak called Pungpa Ri, then the three miles of connecting ridge to the summit of Shishapangma itself. It was a perversely indirect approach but it looked reasonably safe and it would still qualify as a new route up a prestigious eight-thousand-metre peak. Honour would be satisfied.

*   *   *

The eastern side of the Shishapangma massif, rising from the Phola Glacier. As far as we know, no one had set foot on this glacier before 1987.

On 29 September Jerry Gore, Brian Davison and I set off from Advance Base to recce the left-hand icefall. After some improbable weavings through crevasse mazes and vertical ice cliffs we arrived the next day at a suitable site for Camp One. Jerry and I continued to have a look at a gangway heading towards Pungpa Ri. It was wonderful to be up high, looking down on the lower glacier and its huge melt-lake dammed by an ancient terminal moraine. Then to see beyond to a bigger lake, the Kung Tso, dark cobalt amongst pink and grey hills. Most exciting was the view east to a cluster of giant pyramids, sixty miles distant – Cho Oyu, Makalu, Lhotse and . . . my first sight of Everest.

We returned to Advance Base, pleased to report a feasible route. On 1 October Luke announced on the radio from down the valley, 'We're sending up the last yak caravan – eight oxygen cylinders and Jerry Gore's parachute.' By 5 October the whole climbing team was finally at Base Camp and above. While the military, led by Nigel Williams, took over the lead, I spent a few days on yak duty, shunting luggage, fretting and fussing, convinced bossily that the soldiery was not pulling its weight up above. On 12 October I finally did my first carry to Camp Two, to find Brian Davison there, at 6,200 metres, dressed in sterile white overalls, digging a six-foot-deep grave. An expert on analysing air pollution through glacial sampling, he was interested in possible after-effects of the recent explosion at Chernobyl, four thousand miles to the west.

Above Brian's grave a line of fixed ropes now led part of the way up the icy 'Headwall' leading to Pungpa Ri. I was keen to push the line higher but we were short of nuts and pegs for anchors. Over the radio that evening there was a lot of macho huffing and puffing, with everyone expecting someone else to bring up the vital supplies and no one actually volunteering to do anything about it. Then at dusk we saw a lone figure plodding up the huge empty snow basin with a rucksack full of gear. It was Kate, the only woman on the climbing team.

Armed with these supplies, Luke and I pushed the route out another 250 metres the next day. Then, tired by his first blast to altitude – and keen to see his girlfriend Annabel who had just arrived at Base Camp with the scientific team – Luke went down for some R & R. Jerry Gore took Luke's place and at 5.15 a.m. on 15 October we set off with loaded rucksacks up the headwall. Jerry struggled in the thin air and I cursed him unsympathetically, leaving him to follow while I pushed ahead, running out further ropes. Near the top I had to climb a near-vertical bulge of ice between rock walls, rushing as best I could between malevolent blasts of spindrift that funnelled down the bulge, revelling in the fight.

We emerged onto the ridge of Pungpa Ri at 6,900 metres and immediately started digging a snow-cave to escape the wind. Three hours' delving produced enough room to lie down and on the radio that night Colonel Henry said 'Bloody well done!' Our job was to establish a large secure cave – Camp Three – from which the Gang of Four, led by Nigel Williams, would then attempt the long traverse over Pungpa Ri's summit and on to Shishapangma itself.

So the next morning we banished high-altitude headaches with hard labour, hacking and shovelling to extend our icy grotto. Stopping for a coffee break, Jerry gasped, 'I'm really pissed off – doing all this work so that someone else can go to the summit.'

'But, Jerry, I thought that's what it's all about for you soldiers – team work.' But Jerry was a thoroughly modern, Thatcherite, entrepreneurial, school-of-free-enterprise sort of man: big siege expeditions were just not his style. Later that morning he suddenly suggested that we should make a lightning commando raid on the summit ourselves, right now. I just snapped, 'Keep digging, Jerry.' By evening we had completed a palatial four-man cave and the following morning, 17 October, our task complete, we set off back down the fixed ropes.

For several days now there had been worrying streaks of dawn cloud. This morning the wind was fierce, there was an ominous luminosity over Nepal, and Everest's summit, sixty miles away, was clipped by grey lenticulars. We stopped at Camp Two to chat to Lindsay Griffin and Chung, our Hong Kong climber. Lindsay was concerned about the weather signs, but down at Camp One the Gang of Four was preparing optimistically to move up for its summit attempt. We carried on down the labyrinthine icefall to Advance Base, now run by the two squaddies Jim and John. Julian the forester was also there with the doctor, Mark Upton, whom I hadn't seen for a month. Later that afternoon we left the glacier and walked down the gentle grassy valley to Base Camp. Colonel John was now in residence with his daughter Emma and most of the scientific team; but climber-scientist Brian Davison was away on a distant glacier, trying to help Henry Osmaston and two of his Bristol University students operate the steam lance.

Jade Venture was spread far and wide across the wilds of Tibet and cloud had now veiled the whole sky. On the seven o'clock radio schedule that evening, Nigel announced from Camp Two, 'It's been snowing for two hours here.' Then Lindsay came in from Camp One, 'It's been snowing for forty-five minutes here.' At eight o'clock it began to fall at Base Camp.

*　　*　　*

Colonel Henry woke me at nine the next morning. 'Stephen, can you come and talk to Lindsay? He left Camp One at ten o'clock last night. He's halfway down the icefall with John House and he's lost.' Alone amongst the climbers, Lindsay had acknowledged the seriousness of a huge Himalayan snowfall and was trying to escape with one of the non-climber squaddies. At one point, navigating in the dark through driving snow, he had slipped into a crevasse. Mountain novice John had managed to check his fall and had shouted desperately, 'What do I do now, Lindsay?' Ever laconic, the master had said very calmly, 'Just hold on to that rope, my boy.'

I tried to give some useful directions, and they eventually reached Advance Base at three o'clock that afternoon. Down at Base Camp the snow abated for a while. Colonel John set off in full battledress to look for Tibetan mice. Later we joined him and the scientists in their kitchen tent, where John regaled us with jungle stories until Emma said, 'Give it a break, Dad.' Back in the mountaineers' kitchen our Sherpa cook, the wonderful Ajamba, found some compo tins labelled 'pudding' and proudly presented us with bowls of steak and kidney pudding coated liberally with custard.

At five o'clock that afternoon the snow started to fall again. It continued all night, drifting in high winds. At nine o'clock the next morning, Monday, 19 October, 1987, news came through that Lindsay and three others were heading back from Advance Base, leaving just Jim and John, the two loyal squaddies, at their post. The latter came through on the radio that afternoon, announcing, 'We're only just keeping our heads above the snow.' Far above them, at Camp Two, Nigel Williams was fighting for survival with guardsman Johnny Garrett, paratrooper Duncan Francis and Al Wells, a young civilian who had only recently left school. The main food and gear depot had disappeared under an avalanche, but the tents – moved earlier to a safer site by Lindsay – hadn't been hit. Nevertheless, they were digging round the clock just to clear the snow falling out of the sky.

Even at Base Camp the snow was drifting waist high. Colonel John, who had a short-wave radio, told us that evening that there had been a hurricane in the south of England, blowing down thousands of trees, and that the stock market had crashed. It all seemed strangely irrelevant.

The snow continued relentlessly through the night and at four on Tuesday morning I was woken from deep sleep by Jerry shouting outside. His and Chung's tent had collapsed and

The ever-cheerful assistant cookboy, Dil, off to fetch water in snowshoes and bin liner.

he was now intent on rescuing the rest of us. My feet were trapped under one collapsed end of my tent, but my head end was still clear so I asked him ungratefully to bugger off and let me get back to sleep.

Then at last the snow stopped and we emerged at breakfast to a transformed landscape, glittering under an ice-blue sky. Later that morning Brian Davison staggered into camp. He had spent the previous day wading through snowdrifts, trying to persuade Henry Osmaston to abandon gear. Brian had gone on ahead, bivouacked on the glacier moraine and woken at daybreak to find himself in the dark, buried under several feet of drift; he had managed to dig himself out with a stone. Henry and his two students came in later, helped by Luke, who had gone to meet them with snowshoes. Henry plodded like a zombie, dazed and hypothermic on his sixty-fifth birthday. Lindsay's team, meanwhile, had spent the night huddled beside a boulder on the glacier and they only came in at six in the evening.

Only later did we discover that many people in Tibet and Nepal died in that storm – climbers, tourists and locals. Perhaps the most tragic was a young Sherpa cookboy, Nima, working for Doug Scott on the north side of Everest, who was buried by an avalanche on the normally innocuous path above the Base Camp. At the Rongbuk monastery nearby the head lama said that he had never seen such heavy snowfall in sixty years. We, thank God, were spared, but most of our supplies and gear were buried under tons of compacted powder. Nevertheless, Colonel Henry announced that evening that we would try to salvage what we could from the devastation. Luke and I, comparatively rested after three days at Base Camp, would make an attempt on the summit. Kate Philips and John Vlasto would accompany us in support. We would leave the next morning, 21 October.

The sun shone ineffectually out of a frigid sky and it took an age to warm our numb toes before we set off, snowshoes padding on the glittering wind crust. At Advance Base we found Jim and John barricaded in their tent, now two metres below the surface with just the tip of the radio mast protruding. Later that afternoon the Gang of Four arrived from Camp Two. Nigel told us how he had kept looking at the photo of his baby son while the avalanches crashed down from Pungpa Ri, wondering if he would ever see him again.

The next day it took us seven and a half hours to wade back up the icefall to pitch our lightweight bivouac tents on top of the buried remains of Camp One. Then, on 23 October, we continued into the upper cirque of the glacier, Luke, John, Kate and I taking turns to break trail, a hundred steps at a time. Again I was impressed by Kate's quiet stoicism, but she was feeling the altitude so we agreed that she and John would wait at Camp Two while Luke and I continued to Camp Three on the 24th.

We left at five a.m., relieved to find the fixed ropes still intact on the 400-metres-high Headwall. Photographing Luke as he came up to one of the anchors, looking down past him at the tiny ant furrow curving down the plunging perspective of the icefall, I felt proud of our expedition – this bizarre collection of individuals, working to create this improbable route where no human beings had ever been before, still plugging away at it, determined to carry on despite the storm havoc.

We emerged several hours later onto the ridge crest, to look over a Tibetan landscape transformed from pinky-grey to white; but up here, scoured by the wind, there was actually less snow than when Jerry and I had left a week earlier.

In the snow-cave that evening, at 6,900 metres, we began again to feel the altitude. I had been frustrated during the day by what I saw as Luke's slowness. Now he told me how tired and irritable I was getting, at which I snapped petulantly, 'Talk about the pot calling the kettle black.' But then Colonel Henry came in on the radio – urbane, imperturbable, generous – wishing us the best of luck for the long journey ahead, and I tried to follow his example.

On 25 October we finally broke onto new terrain. We started anxiously at sunrise, traversing steep snow, then hard ice, into a chimney. Luke seemed tense and I was impatient, but the mood relaxed when we emerged onto a twisting snow ridge and Luke commented, 'It's just like the Biancograt – you know, on Piz Bernina'. And like that other twisting snow ribbon on Kunyang Kish which had eluded me six years earlier. But this time the weather was smiling on us, willing on the old Eiger partnership. It was fantastic to be up here, now following the route of Alex MacIntyre, Roger Baxter-Jones and Doug Scott, who had made the first ascent of Pungpa Ri, from the south-west, in 1982. After six hours' climbing we reached a little notch at 7,370 metres and dumped our rucksacks before continuing up a final slope, zigzagging wearily for another hour to the summit of Pungpa Ri, 7,450 metres above sea level. Then we got out the T-shirts that Luke's brother had given us – 'Bloomsbury Joiners On Top' – held them up over bulging duvet jackets and posed for a summit photo.

At last I had broken the seven-thousand-metre barrier. And reached a respectable summit! I felt strong and confident, longing to get to grips with the ridge ahead – the continuation to Shishapangma. But Luke was more circumspect. And we were both slightly worried by a band of cloud on the horizon, so we compromised, stopping early to camp at the notch, rather than committing ourselves to the far side of Pungpa Ri.

That night on the radio we heard Henry and the others, several miles away, wondering anxiously where we were, but the battery was fading and we were unable to respond. Camping higher than either of us had ever been before, we passed a restless night. We woke on the 26 October to thick hoar frost coating the tent fabric. It took hours to melt snow for breakfast and we didn't get away until nine o'clock in the morning. We planned to traverse the huge south-west face of Pungpa Ri to a saddle at its far end, from where the final ridge of Shishapangma, tantalisingly foreshortened, twisted up towards the ultimate objective. Our only hope was to travel light, leaving tent and sleeping bags, but as a precaution we took some food, the stove and a shovel.

It was a glorious day. In the sharp blue light we could stare for hundreds of miles west over the Langtang peaks to famous giants like Manaslu, Dhaulagiri and Annapurna. In the other direction rose Cho Oyu, Everest, Lhotse, Makalu and Kangchenjunga: including the one we were standing on, we could see nine of the world's eight-thousanders. We were spacewalking, cut off totally from the expedition. It was intoxicating. But also frightening. Luke seemed increasingly subdued and several times I gasped impatiently, 'Are you all right? . . . You want to carry on? . . . You realise we'll probably have to bivouac?'

After three and a half hours we reached the saddle on the far side of Pungpa Ri. We stopped and lit the stove to make a brew of tepid water, and while the snow melted we took off boots to warm numb feet. The sun shone out of an indigo sky and our little thermometer gave an air-temperature reading of minus twenty degrees centigrade. At 1.30 p.m. we continued, Luke telling me to set a nice steady pace. So we plodded ever more slowly upward, eventually reaching a snow knife-edge where we belayed each other carefully, shuffling 'à cheval' astride the ridge, glancing nervously down the gigantic precipice of the south-west face falling away to our left. Looking back to yesterday's Pungpa Ri summit, I could see that we were now well above it, approaching 7,700 metres above sea level. I could *do it*! My lungs were coping: I could play this high-altitude game! But it was an awesome game. We really were walking in space, cut off from all help. And what about all that cloud smudging the darkening horizon?

At four p.m. Luke cautioned, 'The one thing I don't want is an epic. Let's stop and dig a cave.' So we got out the shovel and took turns, panting furiously, knees going numb as we knelt in the cold crust, excavating a hovel for the night. After two hours' labour there was room for the two of us to crawl inside. We sat on the rope and our neoprene-foam overboots and lit the stove. As the sky darkened outside, we took turns to sip tepid soup. Then Luke was sick into the pan, so we had to clean it out and start again.

By now the wind was blustering outside, flinging ice crystals at the cave entrance. We sat and shivered miserably, refusing to believe the thermometer's claim that the air temperature in the cave was no lower than minus fourteen degrees centigrade. We tried lying in a half-crouch and I think we even dozed a bit, until at five a.m. I had to go outside to relieve myself, whereupon my bum-flap zip broke and I had to reverse bare-arsed back into the cave to have it mended by a long-suffering Luke.

Then we began to get ready for the summit, removing our boots and warming feet in each other's armpits. Ah, the intimacy of the high camps! There were long delays to blow on fingers, between fumbling attempts to lace boots and sort out the icy rope. But at last we emerged stiffly from our cave into a lurid dawn, with purple cloud boiling over Langtang and a vicious wind whipping our numb faces.

It was evil, but I had three layers of clothing on my legs and five on my torso, plus gloves, fleece mitts, down mitts and Gore-Tex mitts on my hands. I still believed that I could function and as I put my head into the wind I felt the heat of battle. It was going to be a long hard day, but I was sure we could do it.

Until, after just a few minutes there was a tug on the rope and Luke shouted through the wind, 'I'm not doing four hundred metres in this.' He looked miserable and his nose and lips were swollen and blue. I knew that he needed to go down but, clutching at straws, I shouted, 'Why don't you wait in the snow-cave while I go on my own?'

'What – wait here? All day? With no sleeping bag and no food? And precious little gas? Are you serious?!'

At that moment I hated Luke for being right. For being so bloody sensible. For showing up my selfishness. Reluctantly, angrily, I turned round and we headed straight back down the mountain. I hardly spoke, and when I did it was to snap resentfully, furious at being denied our summit. Without the glow of success, it was a weary struggle and as the wind subsided to leave the sky clear for another perfect day I became even more bitter. At midday we got back to the tent on the far side of Pungpa Ri. There we rested, feeding joylessly on sugarless

We had made the first ever route up the eastern side of the Shishapangma massif, but the highest summit eluded us.

tea and the last packet of noodles; several of Luke's fingertips were discoloured with frostbite and I had to admit grudgingly that it would have been mad to have stayed longer in the snow-cave. The next morning – our eighth day out from the Base Camp – we packed up the tent and started down.

We had only been gone a few minutes when, like phantoms from another forgotten world, John Vlasto and Nigel Williams suddenly appeared beside us. Although we had been spotted on the summit ridge two days earlier, nothing had been seen or heard of us since then, so Henry had asked these two to look for us. We assured them that we were fine and encouraged them to carry on and make the third ascent of Pungpa Ri, while we descended nervously down the long snow ridge to the Camp Three cave, then on down the fixed ropes to Camp Two, where Johnny Garrett welcomed us with hot chocolate, cigarettes and a tin of steak-and-onion casserole.

Three days later everyone was back at Base Camp. It was now the last day of October and oppressively cold, even at Base Camp, but the sun still shone out of a clear sky. We had left three tents at Camp Two, 'just in case', and there were still some rations at Advance Base. With Al Wells – the youngest, keenest member of the team – I plotted one final attempt, all the way back to Pungpa Ri and beyond, desperate to see the thing through. Colonel Henry, who had been plagued by throat infections and was unable to go high himself, stood loyally by us and said he would wait while we tried.

We might just have made that final attempt on Shishapangma if we had not received an urgent radio message from the Chinese Mountaineering Association on 1 November, ordering the expedition to leave the mountain immediately. A month earlier we had heard the first rumours about demonstrations in Lhasa that had been punished by beatings and shootings. Eleven years might have passed since Chairman Mao's insane murderous rule had ended, but his legacy still lived on, particularly in Tibet, where any dissent was stamped on ruthlessly. Like every totalitarian regime, the Chinese government feared foreign witnesses. They wanted us out of the way. And, just in case we had not got the hint, they sent up eighteen hired Tibetans as a 'rescue party' for which we would be billed 300 yuan per 'rescuer'.

The 'rescuers' were loath to carry anything so, staggering under thirty-five-kilo loads, salvaging what we could of the expedition's gear, turning our backs on the mountain, we plodded back through the snow, in the most exhausting day's walk of my life, thirty miles back to Nyalam. From there most of the team made their way home via Nepal, but Luke, Henry Osmaston and I were asked to accompany the management on the longer route through Lhasa, Beijing and Hong Kong, paying at least five times the market rate for transport and accommodation, in order to bolster the coffers of the CMA. At Lhasa airport Henry Osmaston was jostled by surly officials who confiscated his geological samples. Brian's laboriously collected snow samples were 'lost'. In Beijing our passports were held and only returned to us once the final expedition bill had been settled. We were almost free at the airport when the hateful Chinese Red Army officials noticed an irregularity on my visa and threatened to detain me. I lost my cool and only escaped thanks to the diplomatic intervention of one of our Hong Kong expedition members. An hour later, as I sunk into my seat on the Cathay Pacific jet and a gentle, beautiful air hostess smothered me in loving kindness and brought me my gin and tonic, I murmured blissfully, 'Thank God for capitalism.'

Our brief brush with Maoist intransigence left a sour taste in the mouth. As did my overreaction to Luke's caution. I left Shishapangma angry and resentful, but also rather ashamed by my own lack of compassion towards Luke, whose frost-bitten fingers were being treated with painful penicillin injections, saved for cabinetmaking posterity. However, the bitterness wore off as I began to remember the fun and the beauty and camaraderie of those autumn days in Tibet. Even as we left on the long drive to Lhasa, glancing back at our high point on that impossibly remote ridge, I was beginning to shed the regrets and concentrate on the pleasures. My four-months-long odyssey through the mountains of Central Asia was coming to an end, and of course I was looking forward to returning to London, but I wasn't satiated. It was *good* – this mountain life – and I wanted more of these adventures.

It was a beautiful evening with a full moon rising over the endless mountains which extend northward, beyond the Himalaya. Hares raced across the frozen snow. Groups of Tibetans rode on ponies past the crumbling remains of old fortifications. Then we rounded a corner and there it was – the mountain which they call Chomolungma and we call Everest – towering crimson above the blue shadows. Henry, Luke, Nigel and Johnny would be coming back to try and climb it with a big Joint Services Expedition in four months' time. I had other plans, other mountains, other dreams; but perhaps one day I too might attempt that highest peak of all.

Chapter Fourteen

Neverest

The chance to attempt that highest peak came much sooner than expected. On my first evening back in London I phoned my parents to tell them that Luke and I had not – contrary to reports in all the national newspapers, spawned by Colonel John's over-zealous publicity machine – reached the summit of Shishapangma. By way of consolation my mother said, 'Some American called Anderson has been calling from New Zealand, trying to get hold of you. I should phone him as soon as you can, as it's an invitation – a very nice invitation. He wants you to go to Everest.'

I should have been thrilled, but my first reaction was wary. Knowing nothing of this Anderson person, I assumed that he must be leading some large unwieldy team up the well-trodden normal route, with Sherpas humping loads of oxygen for the summit bids. All of which had been very fine in 1953, when John Hunt and his team were pushing out the boundaries of the known world, but would hardly be a ground-breaking adventure today. Of course it would be wonderful to climb Everest, but what really mattered now was *how* you climbed Everest.

Cynical doubts were quickly quashed when I got through to Robert Anderson a few days later and he told me that he had a permit for the biggest, arguably most dangerous, facet of Everest's three-sided pyramid – the Kangshung Face. Frightening images flashed through my mind – *National Geographic* pictures of my old friend Carlos Buhler and his American companions making the first and only ascent of that giant wall in 1983: puppets dangling on immense towers of striated rock capped by giant ice meringues; tiers of ice stacked up in the sky; avalanches crashing down the three-miles-high face and filling the valley below. Trying to quell heart palpitations, I said weakly that I would be very interested. After all, I could always say 'no' later: it's not every day that you get asked to go to the Kangshung Face. The stranger at the other end of the line remained laconic. Said he was talking to several people and not to cancel any plans I might have. 'I want to keep the team small,' he added. 'Maybe six climbers. And we're not taking oxygen.'

What he didn't say was that just about every well-known Himalayan climber in North America had turned down the invitation to join his lightweight attempt to scale the biggest face on the world's highest mountain. As had the New Zealander, Peter Hillary, son of Sir Edmund. And a well-known British climber called Adrian Burgess. But Robert Anderson was a master of presentation, undaunted by the scorn of a few experts. He ran his own advertising agency in Auckland and he was a born entrepreneur. When the Chinese Mountaineering Association had told him in 1986 that Everest's North Face was booked up for at least ten years (Nepal was booked even further ahead), he had simply taken their alternative offer of the esoteric east side – the Kangshung Face – and paid a deposit for 1988. Then he'd hired Wendy Davis in Manhattan to help with fund-raising. One of her marketing initiatives was to call the 1988 expedition the '35th-Anniversary Ascent'. Hence the invitation to Peter Hillary. And to Norbu Tenzing, son of the other 1953 summiteer, to join the support team. And to Lord Hunt, leader in 1953, to be 'honorary leader' of this sketchy new venture. And so, in this serendipitous game of chance, thanks to having once met the famous Welsh life peer in a pub, and having got to know him a little,

I found myself recommended as a suitably pushy mountaineer to represent Britain on a team commemorating 'what was after all,' as John Hunt reminded Robert, 'a British expedition.'

At Robert's request I sent a c.v. to Auckland, then plunged headlong into a busy round of lectures while he made discreet enquiries about the British climber he had never met. The first hint that he was serious was a letter from Rolex, one of the expedition's main sponsors, asking for my wrist measurement. Then, a few days later, returning at midnight from a school lecture, I found beside the telephone a note in my landlord Victor's spidery handwriting announcing that, 'Robert Anderson wants you for Everest.'

I couldn't join the team for their Christmas meeting in Colorado; instead I flew to New York in January for the official expedition launch at the Explorers' Club. Robert made a point of coming to meet me at the airport. He was tall and lithe, with dark hair and blue eyes, friendly, upbeat and effusive about my 'hyooge amount of Himalayan experience'. That warm welcome set the tone for the whole expedition. We discussed plans, checked kit lists and raced through a series of photo opportunities with the official expedition photographer Joe Blackburn, dragooned by press officer Wendy. I met Mimi Zieman, our gorgeous Brooklyn-bred expedition medical officer and – it later transpired – Robert's temporary girlfriend; Miklos Pinther, the Hungarian émigré UN cartographer who was hoping to send us to the summit with special measuring devices; and Norbu Tenzing, the American-educated eldest son of Tenzing Norgay, who was making all the travel plans. Along with food organiser Robert Dorival and expedition treasurer Sandy Wylie, they all hoped to come with us as far as Base Camp; our doctor Mimi and photographer Joe would remain there for the duration of the expedition, while the others returned home.

As for the actual climbing team, it now stood at four: Robert, me, Paul Teare and Ed Webster. Paul, a Canadian carpenter based in Lake Tahoe, was, like me, a stranger recommended by a friend of a friend. He had a couple of Himalayan expeditions under his belt and was by all accounts a very strong ice-climber. Ed Webster, a New Englander now living in Colorado, was one of America's great rock-climbing pioneers. He had also been twice to Everest, first on the West Ridge with Robert – and just about every other Colorado climber – in 1985. As he put it to me when I eventually met him: 'I spent two months slogging up fixed ropes, carrying oxygen cylinders for other people.' His second Everest expedition, photographing on the North Face in 1986, had been more rewarding and had included a memorable solo ascent of Everest's neighbour, Changtse. On the way home through Beijing he had bumped into Robert clutching his new Kangshung Face permit. Ed had agreed to join the 1988 team on the condition that his Sherpa friend Pasang Norbu came as cook. Once enrolled, Ed had studied what photos he could find of the Kangshung Face and come up with the idea of a new route up an unclimbed buttress on the left side of the face, leading to the South Col.

And that was the plan: four climbers, three of whom had still not met, supported by an ad hoc base-camp team, sponsored to the tune of about $200,000 to attempt a new route up the world's highest mountain which might well, on close inspection, prove impossibly dangerous. The only other option from our eastern approach – the original 1983 route up the Kangshung Face – had occupied fourteen climbers over two expeditions, using several miles of fixed rope, an aerial cableway, five camps, and bottled oxygen for all the summiteers. Small wonder that most of the experts thought we stood little chance of success. And a good chance of not coming back.

Myself, I hoped very much that I *would* come back. But I also intended to try and make this thing work, for once in my life to be totally committed. So, after the initial fears and nightmares had passed, I became increasingly excited by the project. And in a curious way, friends and family were also excited. For once I was heading for a mountain that people had heard of: brand recognition brought with it a kind of approval. Only one person seemed doubtful, and that was Rosie.

We had met, very conventionally, at a wedding. At the time

she had been married unsatisfactorily to someone else but now she was single, living in a small flat in Wandsworth and, against all her better instincts, making frequent trips across London to visit me in Islington. She was beautiful and intelligent, with a fiery temper, frequently driving off in the middle of the night after lambasting me for my latest selfish gaffe, then returning five minutes later to knock angrily on the door and tell me to come round to the next street and push-start her temperamental car. She had spirit and I admired her for giving up her advertising career to take a degree at Goldsmiths College and become an extremely competent deputy head of a large inner-city nursery school.

On New Year's Day 1988 I drew up a chart for the six weeks remaining before departure for Everest. Between lecture bookings, meetings and article deadlines, I blocked out all the remaining spaces, assigning them optimistically to writing an overdue book. Seeing the chart pinned up above my desk, Rosie said, 'And what about *me*? Where are *my* times?'

'Er—'

'You've just been away for four months and now you're about go away for another four months. What's in it for me?'

'But,' I grovelled, 'I have to be single-minded . . . this is my living . . . I've dithered for too long.'

'So is spending time with me "dithering"? Am I that unimportant?'

At the time I didn't realise that we would eventually marry and have children – I assumed that my rather haphazard career precluded that kind of thing – but I still didn't want to lose her yet; so the book waited (in the end I managed just two draft chapters) while Rosie and I snatched precious moments between ever more frantic preparations for departure – first to Bombay, where I was due to give four lectures, then Delhi, and then Kathmandu, where I would meet Paul Teare and Ed Webster for the first time, before heading north with them to Tibet.

Time contracted horribly and the last night came far too quickly. It was 11 February, Rosie's birthday, and we went out to dinner – the two of us alone together, clutching at dwindling moments. At dawn we crammed all my luggage into her 2CV and she drove me to Heathrow. After checking in all the kitbags, we had a cup of coffee, talking desultorily until she said as brightly as she could manage, 'Well, I'd better get back to work.' A quick hug and kiss and then it was time for me to walk through passport control, smiling bravely and waving goodbye. It was only several months later that Rosie told me that when I disappeared through that barrier she wasn't expecting me ever to come back.

Our Everest adventure seemed blessed with enormous goodwill. In Bombay I spent a contented week with the Kapadias, simultaneously unwinding from the London rush and building up strength for the adventure ahead. It was good to see the Rimo team again, and to climb with them on the sea cliffs and coconut palms nearby. Geeta fed me sumptuous meals and performed a special 'pujah' in the family temple, giving me a protective silver Ganesh to hang round my neck. The two boys, Nawang and Sonam, each gave me a little envelope of flower petals from Sri Auribindo's ashram in Pondicheri.

Then I flew to Kathmandu, where it took a whole day to track down three of the people who would be my constant companions for the next three months – Paul Teare, Ed Webster and Pasang Norbu. Paul, the Canadian from Tahoe, had an easy, loose-limbed charm. Ed's wide-open blue-eyed stare was more intense, his anxieties about the dangers ahead more transparent. Both welcomed the British intruder with touching generosity. As did Pasang Norbu, a Sherpa who had lived all his life at Namche Bazaar, on the south side of Everest, and had himself climbed to the South Col in 1969. He was short and tubby, with a gold tooth adding lustre to his dazzling smile. As expedition cook he was busy amassing pots, pans, stoves, gas cylinders, vegetables, rice, ghee, potatoes, eggs, spices and everything else we had to take up to Tibet to supplement the American supplies which had been shipped out to Beijing several weeks earlier.

The Everest climbing team. Left to right: Ed Webster, Stephen Venables, Robert Anderson, Paul Teare (photo © Ed Webster).

After ten years of Himalayan wandering, I had come late to Kathmandu – I'd only visited Nepal for the first time the previous autumn. So it was good to have some time amongst the pagoda-shaped temples and the huge domed stupa at Bodrinath where we were each blessed by the resident Ringpoche and given protective red threads to wear around our necks.

Again, that sense of goodwill. And a burgeoning confidence as the four of us drove north up Friendship Highway, repeating my journey of five months earlier, climbing right through the great Himalayan barrier, past Shishapangma, and over the Lalung La where, at 5,500 metres, I was pleased to find myself only slightly breathless.

Then down to the ruins of the old 'crystal fort' of Shegar Dzong, familiar from all the photos of the pre-war British expeditions, to meet Robert and the support team. Then onward, all of us together, jostled amongst a ton of luggage, jolted and dust-drenched as our truck laboured up to the even higher Pang La and our first full-on view of Everest – the classic northern vista of the great detached pyramid, its sedimentary layers redolent with heroic names from another era

– Bruce, Mallory, Irvine, Finch, Odell, Shipton, Smythe, Tilman, Somervell and Teddy Norton – the man who in 1924 almost reached the top of the world without oxygen.

Nowadays trucks can drive all the way to the old pre-war base camp beneath the North Face. But there is another gravel track which forks left, skirting round the mountain to a cluster of villages known collectively as Kharta. Here the road stops and here we started walking. The plan seemed simple enough. Fifty or so yaks, hired at specially inflated rates through the Chinese Mountaineering Association, would carry all our luggage thirty miles to our base camp. The walk could be done comfortably in five days.

We set off from Kharta on 7 March, twenty-three days after I had left London; but it actually took another twenty-three – not five – days to reach Base Camp. For fourteen of those days we sat and waited at what we called 'Pre-Base Camp'. Winter snow still lay deep on the high pass that we had to cross, and more kept falling. The Kharta villagers refused to lead the yaks – their most precious possessions – through the drifts. They agreed to work as porters instead – a hundred men and women carrying loads on their backs. But each time we thought we were about to set off, bad weather intervened.

All the supporters like Wendy and Norbu, who had done so much to make this expedition happen, had to leave for home, wading back down to Kharta. Reduced to the hardcore nucleus, sitting out the siege, our team suddenly felt very small. On 16 March we managed a recce, breaking trail to the 5,500-metre pass – the Langma La – for the most mesmerising mountain vista I had ever seen. Makalu, the world's fifth-highest mountain, was almost eclipsed by the soaring pillars of its lower sister peak, Chomolonzo. Eighteen miles away, at the head of the Kama Valley, Everest's summit was shrouded, but Robert had his telescope trained on the lower, visible, part of the Kangshung Face, already gauging, wondering, daring to imagine possibilities, as Paul chipped in, 'Look at those ice mushrooms' and someone else said, 'More like cauliflowers – the Cauliflower Towers!'

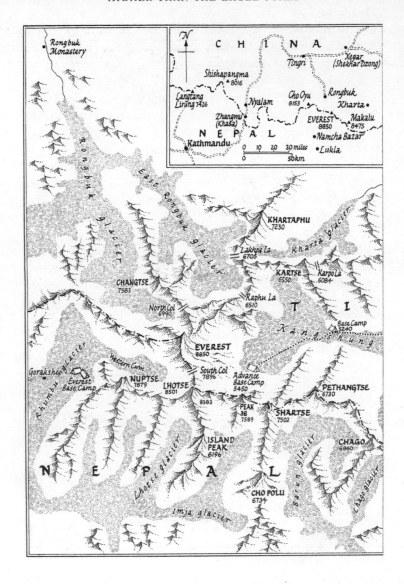

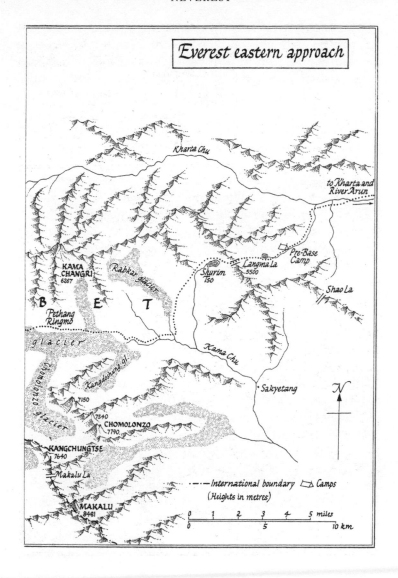

Everest eastern approach

Kharta Chu

to Kharta and
River Arun

Pre-Base
Camp

KAMA
CHANGRI
6267

Rabkar glacier

Langma La
5500

Shurim
750

Shao La

B E T

Pethang
Ringmo

glacier

Kama Chu

Chomolonzo glacier

Kangdoshung gl.

Sakyetang

N

7150

7540

CHOMOLONZO
7790

KANGCHUNGTSE
7640

Makalu La

International boundary   Camps
(Heights in metres)

MAKALU
8481

0   1   2   3   4   5 miles
0   5   10 km

A week later we were back, re-stamping the trail. And again, the following morning, up before dawn to race up to the pass for sunrise photos, then running back down to our pre-base camp for breakfast, noting in my diary that, even after a large meal, my pulse at this altitude was a reasonable seventy-two. For all the frustration, the delays were making us stronger, fitter, better acclimatised. And also better bonded as a team. I liked its bold, New World enthusiasm and even if at times I succumbed to all the old cultural resentments – against the new global masters, the tramplers on the British Empire, the Hollywood bullies who typecast all Brits as dastardly villains or effete wimps – even if I sometimes railed ungraciously against my hosts, these North Americans were a kind lot, tolerant of the cuckoo in their midst, never chafed by my rough edges. About a year later, commenting on a team photo taken at Pre-Base, the journalist Ed Douglas summed it up nicely: 'The Americans and Canadian loll idly, cross-legged in their chairs, with studied cool. Our Man in Tibet, however, sits stiffly to attention, toes pointing inwards, looking for something enthusiastic to say.'

Cultural differences notwithstanding, we became quite a close family: Robert, Paul, Ed and I. And Mimi and Joe. And gentle Pasang, who at forty-eight was a kind of father figure. Whilst waiting for the big kitchen frame tent to arrive from Beijing he had hired a moth-eaten old canvas pyramid from a woman in Kharta. She had quoted Pasang a price of one dollar a day. Then she had added, 'And you can take my son, too.' So Kasang Tsering, a pigtailed young man of about twenty, became cookboy and the eighth member of our family.

On 23 March a weather window finally allowed this Sherpa-Tibetan-Anglo-American-Canadian family to cross the Langma La with about a hundred local men and women carrying all the supplies which would keep us self-sufficient for the next two months. As we crested the pass, each Tibetan stopped to tie a scribbled prayer, or an illegal picture of the Dalai Lama, or a feather, or just a scrap of cloth to the shrine of bamboo wands sprouting from a tall stone cairn. Like so many mountain people, these Lamaistic Buddhists had a deep sense of the numinous quality of landscape. And of this landscape in particular, because we were now descending into the Kama valley, which is one of Tibet's most sacred 'beyuls', centres of sacred power.

For us this landscape was an arena for the gratification of vain ambitions: everything was focused on that vast wall of unclimbed rock and ice waiting for us at the head of the valley. Except that it wasn't as simple as that. However driven I was to make this climb happen I knew that the odds on getting up were slim, the summit only a remote possibility. It was essential not to make happiness contingent on 'success'; brash desire had to be tempered with a little humility. It was an extraordinary privilege just to be here, striding down on a dazzling morning into the Beyul Khembalung, Pasang pointing out the ruined remains of the Kangle monastery, and the valley beyond where Norbu's father, Tenzing Norgay, had probably been born, beside a holy lake where his mother was making a pilgrimage.

Another massive snowfall pinned us all down in the bottom of the Kama valley for two days, our porters suffering miserably in caves and primitive tents. Only the promise of increased quantities of Chinese banknotes persuaded them to continue to the camping ground called Pethang Ringmo where I wrote in my diary:

Monday, 28 March. Evening camp. Scent of juniper and yak dung fires. Tents perched on dry hillocks of grass and figures with firewood bundles silhouetted against lambent mountains. Clouds swirling round crazy pinnacles of Lhotse's summits with Scottish grass-and-snow streaks in valley foreground. Magical moment as sun disappears – a huge white globe sinking behind South Col, half obscured by swirling diaphanous clouds.

The next day we walked right up into the heart of that great cirque and arrived finally at the grassy meadow on the north bank of the Kangshung Glacier which would be our home for the next two months. Twenty porters stayed on for a couple of days to carry supplies a further five miles up the glacier to

Advance Base, then our family of eight was left entirely alone, cut off from the rest of the world. Pasang performed the traditional pujah, hanging up the prayer flags and tossing grains of rice into a juniper fire; and in the evening Mimi took us through the Passover ceremony, substituting dull tea for the traditional four glasses of wine. The next day she and Joe accompanied Ed, Robert, Paul and me up to Advance Base. It was time to find out whether our proposed route to the South Col really was actually climbable.

Ever since that first frightening glimpse of the 'Cauliflower Towers' from the Langma La, we had been naming parts, trying to personalise this huge, inanimate mass of geological and glaciological features. Robert liked the look of the 'Scottish Gully', sneaking up the side of our proposed buttress, because it reminded him of Ben Nevis. To its right, between our buttress and the towering cliffs of the original 1983 route, was a much bigger gully – a huge funnel overhung by the monstrous ice snout of Paul's 'Big Al'. A mile or so further right, beyond the 1983 buttress, were the huge 'Trinity Gullies'. We were eating our breakfast porridge on 3 April when a wave of snow and pulverised ice poured down one of these gullies, billowing out over the glacier to our right. Two minutes later there was a blast to the left of our buttress as an ice cliff broke away and fell two vertical miles down the face of Lhotse, then exploded onto the glacier, ballooning a thousand feet into the air as it raced towards us. 'That's the "Witches' Cauldron",' observed Paul. 'Just as well we're camped well back.'

This was my first day's climbing on Everest and already my Kangshung nightmares were being realised. It was cataclysmic. Apocalyptic. And yet here we were, Robert and I, rushing to finish coffee, pull on harness and crampons, and set off regardless.

And now, at 6.30 a.m. here we were, in the dazzling morning sunshine, walking the remaining mile up the glacier, getting right up underneath those millions of tons of snow and ice. What presumption. What hubris. What insanity.

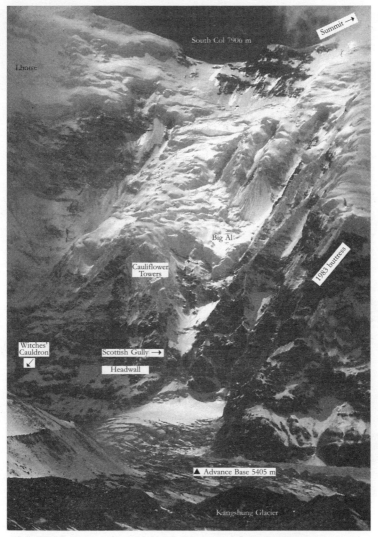

The Kangshung Face from five miles away at Base Camp.

Or so it might have seemed to the casual observer. But we had been watching and waiting, weighing up risks. Between the death traps of the Witches' Cauldron and Big Al Gully, our buttress seemed to offer a haven of sanity. Not a hundred per cent safe. No – that would have been asking too much: those Cauliflower Towers looked a bit dodgy; and there were other stumps of old glacial ice, loose teeth protruding gawkily from the lip of the Buttress. Eventually they would all succumb to gravity. But, by and large, they looked set to fall down the left side of the Buttress, and our route – the hypothetical line that we had been discussing for the last few days – sneaked up the right side, hunched in close beneath protecting rock walls.

That was the theory, anyway. And, despite the breakfast *son et lumière* show, I was feeling bold and confident, thrilled to be here, in this dazzling cirque, roped to Robert, climbing now up a final snow gully, right onto the toe of the Buttress and taking my first steps onto the Kangshung Face.

Robert was a generous leader and, after we had zigzagged for several hundred feet over a series of ledges and little cliffs to the foot of the first real obstacle, he said, 'Why don't you lead this bit? I haven't been doing much technical climbing recently.' So I had the treat of leading the 'Headwall' of beautiful layered granite and quartzite and being first to pull over its ice-glazed rim into the Scottish Gully.

Paul and Ed followed, checking anchors, tightening ropes and making shipshape the rigging which would be our lifeline up and down the mountain for the next few weeks. Apart from a few fixed ropes on Shishapangma the previous autumn, I had no experience of this 'siege' climbing: working away at a route, section by section. But I was enjoying it. What a treat it was to zip down the ropes and return to the comparative comfort of Advance Base for afternoon tea with Mimi and Joe. And Pasang and Kasang, who had walked up from Base Camp with a load of food and gas. Before they headed back down, Pasang came specially over to my tent and said, 'Stephen, we are going now. In two days we come back and bring you what you want. Goodbye. Be careful.'

The author, terribly enthusiastic at three o'clock in the morning.

What kind people, I thought. What a treat to be here, part of this bizarrely convened family, creating this thing – this improbable line up the mountain – all of us working so hard to make it succeed.

From Day Two I bullied the Yanks into getting up very early, in the dark, determined to be up and on the buttress before the sun came to soften snow, loosen rocks and wither our frail bodies. I detested the shrill alarm, rousing me from the warm goose-down nest of my sleeping bag; and I hated the reluctant torchlit breakfast. And it was eerie setting off in the dark, particularly one morning when Ed had to stop and relieve himself, and had just pulled down his trousers when we heard a roar and sensed a freezing cloud blasting towards us, showering us with ice shards. But the reward was to be up high, already at work on the Buttress, as the sun rose over the distant forked summit of Ama Drime, far out beyond the Kama Valley.

On Day Two, Robert and Ed pushed the route to the top of the Scottish Gully and beyond, traversing rightwards along the flank of the Buttress. On Day Three, Ed and I took the route further, but the next morning we idled at Advance Base, breakfasting late with Mimi, chatting, drinking coffee, watching the other two through the telescope. For three hours Paul was hidden from sight, somewhere up close to the Cauliflower Towers, forging his way up an immense ice sheet. In the evening he returned ecstatic. 'I was gripped, man. It was awesome – eighty degrees, sometimes vertical. Mainly good ice, but it was plating in places – dinner plates, not banquet plates, but still scary. And there were big rocks – "television sets" – just stuck in the ice.'

Ed and I moved up the line on Day Four. It was now quite a long journey to the front, using camming ascenders to climb three thousand feet of rope to Paul's highpoint. And his ice sheet really *was* awesome. As for the 'television sets', they – and all the other rubbish threatening to crash down without warning – scotched our plan to sneak out right past the Cauliflower Towers. The only option was for Ed, now on his first big lead, to take us right to the top of the ice sheet, onto the crest of the towers themselves. He put on a fine performance. Then, after a lunch of chocolate, raisins and nuts, he treated me to an even more dazzling show, climbing straight up the overhanging ice wall of the third Cauliflower Tower, hammering in long aluminium stakes to make progress. Following up his rope, spinning in space as I tried to remove the stakes and ice screws, staring down past my feet at the Kangshung Glacier three thousand feet below, I whimpered and jibbered, for the first time acknowledging Ed's superior skill.

Back at camp that evening Paul was ecstatic, embellishing the vegetable theme. 'You were amazing on that 'shroom, Ed. Kasang was here, watching through the scope. He was jabbering, man. He couldn't believe it . . . Webster's Wall.' Then he threw in a sidelong reference to Ed's current girlfriend: 'You did it for Randa, hunh? Randa's Shroom'.

Our Leader was also ecstatic. 'You know – soon we're going to be at the top of the Buttress. It took those other people in '83 twenty-eight days to climb *their* buttress, and we're going to crack ours in a week. I brought you guys to lead all the hard stuff, but once we're up the Buttress all we have to do is wallow. And I'm an expert wallower. I'll wallow for five thousand feet and you can wallow behind on a three-millimetre rope, all the way to the South Col—'

'And then we just clip into the television wires,' interjected Paul, keen to gatecrash the Asian Friendship Expedition's tele-vised summit traverse which was already at work on the north and south sides of the mountain. 'But – hey, man, these wires don't fit my ascender!'

In just five days we had almost cracked our route and at this rate we would be on the summit before the end of April. We were riding a high, all puffed up with our success, scorning the sceptics. Kangshung Face, four climbers, no oxygen: no problem.

On Day Six we were knocked firmly back to earth. The previous day I had been with Ed on the mountain for four-teen hours but after five hours' sleep, despite leaden legs and a dry cough, I forced myself to go back up with Robert and Paul, determined not to miss the fun. At sunrise, as we started the long haul up the ropes, Paul joked morbidly, 'Look at the beautiful pink alpenglow on the ice cliffs hanging over our heads.' Four hours later we reached the highpoint and I started up the fourth Cauliflower Tower. The weather was now breaking, cloud swirling around the face. We were swimming in a storm-tossed sea, flotsam on the grey-green waves poised to crash into the depths. Calf muscles screamed for relief, teetering on eighty-degree ice. I ran out a hundred metres of rope and Paul brought up more, urging me on with generous shouts: 'Look at him go – like a machine. You're awesome, Venables!'

I was stabbing manically, panting, clawing, rushing to crest the wave, all buoyed up by Paul's generous praise, but as I teetered up one final glassy wall I found myself clinging, arms wrapped over an ice edge, staring down into a green chasm. A huge crevasse, at least a hundred feet deep, had peeled open, right across the top of the Cauliflower Towers. The far wall was a clean slice through the layered years of glacial deposit, smooth and overhanging, its upper lip towering above me, about forty feet away, far too far to jump. Our route to the upper Kangshung Face was blocked.

Three rather deflated climbers made the long series of abseils back down to Advance Base to tell Ed that we had not, after all, cracked the Buttress. This climb, which had started so promisingly, was not going to be a pushover after all.

But the timing was good. After six days of fantastically intense work, the weather had now turned, giving us the excuse to walk back across the glacier to Base Camp. Down in the comparatively balmy air at 5,240 metres it was blissful to wake late to the smell of coffee, pancakes and omelettes, to walk out of your tent onto gentle flat grass, to bathe in a huge cauldron of water heated on a yak-dung fire, to while away the day eating more meals and reading. On a big high-altitude climb, pace is everything and this gentle recharging of batteries was essential. But we were also planning the next move, wondering, debating, chewing the cud of possibility. Having gawped into what Ed had christened the Jaws of Doom, I was convinced that we could tackle the big crevasse head-on, rather than waste time on dubious evasions. It just required someone to abseil down into the Jaws, climb up the far wall to its upper lip, and string a rope across to create the world's highest Tyrolean Traverse.

The others came round to the rope-bridge idea. Having sown that conceptual seed, I rather fancied bringing it to flower myself: it would require some spectacular athleticism, at about 6,500 metres above sea level.

And this was where Robert issued one of his very rare Leader's Directives, announcing quite firmly that something this technical was clearly a job for our veteran of the canyon walls of Colorado. 'I think I'll go up,' he announced, 'with *Ed*. He's best at that kind of thing. If we put our first camp just below Webster's Wall, Ed and I can work from there, while you and Paul ferry up gear.'

So, after our base-camp interlude, Paul and I spent three days on yak duty, beasts of burden humping luggage up the ropes to the little yellow tent now perched on the crest of the Cauliflower Towers. On the second morning we arrived in murky weather to find Ed and Robert still in bed. In my diary that night I scribbled self-righteously:

Arrived at 10 a.m. to find Robert and Ed still in bed, lethargic and negative. Paul also angry. I spent the descent envisaging total failure due to American apathy and inability to do anything except in perfect Colorado/ California weather.

What I neglected to mention was (a) that both men were feeling the altitude after their first night sleeping high; (b) that, for all my deriding of Colorado, Ed's pioneering in the Black Canyon of the Gunnison had, over the years, involved difficulties far beyond my own experience; and (c) that a little caution was not such a bad thing anyway. Having learned my mountaineering in the stormy European Alps I was probably more blasé about the weather. And about risk in general. The next morning, as I was photographing Paul on the fixed ropes, catching his dwarfed profile against the huge spaces of the Kama Valley, he suddenly flattened himself against the wall, hunched beneath his helmet, as a rock whistled past. 'Hold it there,' I shouted. 'That looks fantastic.'

'You're crazy, Venables!' he barked. 'It missed me by inches – a cantaloupe.'

'What's a cantaloupe? Don't move – it's a lovely pic—'

'Melon, Dumbo. Put that fucking camera away. It could have knocked my head off.'

'Just hold it—'

'It could have *killed* me!'

'Well, it didn't, so you're okay. See you at Camp One.'

This time when we arrived to dump supplies Robert and Ed had left for work. From back down at Advance Base that afternoon we saw them emerge from the maw, two insects crawling three thousand feet above our heads. Only when they returned the next day did we hear how Ed had tried to follow the snow-choked bed of the chasm, hoping for some sneaky escape ramp round the corner; how he had just missed being crushed when a huge leaning pillar of ice crashed down beside him; how he had then abandoned any attempt at evasive action and had just tackled the back wall of the crevasse direct, engineering his way up overhanging ice, dangling in his stirrups from tubular screws, hoping they wouldn't all unzip, and after about sixty feet shouting down anxiously, 'How am I doing, Robert?' To which our laconic leader had replied, 'Just fine. Keep on going. That's what I brought you here for.'

Three days later, on 21 April, Paul and I had our first trip across Ed's Tyrolean rope bridge. I went first, hanging in my harness from the tensioned rope, wondering what Ed had fixed it to on the far side as I stared down at the jumbled ice debris in the bottom of the crevasse, then learning to relax, trusting Ed's skill, shouting to Paul to fix the moment on celluloid as I dangled, clowning, over the void.

We pushed on, the headstrong Briton dragging the Canadian in his wake, determined to crest the Buttress, wading up over a great snow hump, then scampering through a jumble of groaning blocks jammed in the mouth of another huge crevasse, then panting round a final corner to arrive on the shore of a billowing ocean of snowy hummocks. As far as we could see, there were no further obstacles; thanks to Ed's brilliance, we had cracked the Neverest Buttress.

Back at Camp One, sitting in our yellow dome, Paul urged me to drink: 'Five litres a day you're meant to have.' Then he mused, 'That was awesome up there . . . isn't it weird – you and me, such different people, sitting here on Everest . . . alone on these crazy towers?' It *was* weird – this improbable collection of disparate individuals, thrown together, growing steadily more fond of each other, complementing each others' strengths and weaknesses. The next morning, after more snow had fallen, when I was fretting to be away, anxious to push the route further, it was Paul who insisted, 'These slopes are getting loaded. We shouldn't be on them.'

'Well, let's wait here a day and see what happens.'

'That's dumb,' he replied. 'If we sit here we're just burning fuel, eating food. All that stuff has to be carried up. And we'll burn out at this altitude. Better to go down and wait at Base.'

And of course he was right. So we raced down the ropes, collected Robert and Ed, and continued all the way back to Base Camp, arriving in time for lunch.

This time we were grounded for a whole week, as the wind whipped clouds over the world's highest summits. But often it would clear in the evening to reveal a turquoise gleam of ice, high on Chomolonzo. Or the jagged ridge of Makalu. Or Everest itself – the mountain which Pasang and Kasang called Chomolungma, filling the head of our valley, laden with legend and memory and expectation.

Just above our little tented village, on the crest of the moraine which bounded our enclave, Pasang had built two tall cairns. Walking round the meadow one evening, I noticed that the cairns were lined up directly with the 'Pinnacles' three miles above us on the long, long North-East Ridge of Everest. It was there that Dick had suffered his stroke in 1982. There that Peter Boardman and Joe Tasker had subsequently disappeared on their brave summit attempt. In the twilight our cairns seemed like memorial chortens to the two men who lay somewhere up there. And to all the other people who had not returned. Consumed by melancholy, I returned to the warm glow of the kitchen-dining tent, grateful for companionship. Despite the obvious doubts and fears, we were becoming convinced, after three weeks on the Neverest Buttress, that we really could complete our route to the South Col. And above that? Boardman and Tasker had died attempting the summit without oxygen; but they had faced their hardest climbing well above eight thousand metres. We had already cracked the hardest part of our climb. And we knew that the final part of the 1953 route, which we would join at the South Col, was easier than anything on the north-east ridge.

Riding this optimistic wave, we prepared a mail package for the South Col. Pasang had Sherpa friends who would probably be there, working for the Asian Friendship Expedition and the Australian Bicentennial Expedition from Nepal. They could take the package down and have it sent on from Namche Bazaar. Our South Col exchange would be the highest mail collection in history.

I sat down one morning to write two long letters – one to my parents and one to Rosie – telling them all about our extraordinary adventure on the Neverest Buttress. In the end the letters were never delivered, so I cannot check exactly what I wrote; but I suspect that I underplayed the dangers and concentrated on the beauty of the Beyul Khembalung – this enchanted sanctuary which had become our home – and the closeness of our isolated expedition family, and the pleasure of our extraordinary climb, and the growing belief that we might just, if were very, very lucky, pull this thing off.

Phase Three started anxiously for Ed and me, both of us feeling weak, our insides rumbling with indigestion after a week of overeating and inactivity. But Paul and Robert, ever relaxed, waited a day at Advance Base. Then we all climbed to Camp One. The other two slept there while Ed and I descended, returning the next morning with a second ferry of food, gas and other supplies.

We idled pleasurably at Camp One, eating, drinking, photographing and chatting; and at dusk Paul and Robert returned from above, reporting reasonable progress on the upper slopes. The next morning, 1 May, all four of us left Camp One at dawn. We put in eleven hours' hard labour with heavy loads, first following Robert and Paul's tracks, then breaking a new trail. I led for several hours, dragging Ed behind me; until I burned out and the tortoise took over, wading in front, now forcing *me* to follow, insisting that we reach Paul's Flying Wing – a huge ice roof, where we could leave supplies for Camp Two, secure from avalanches, at about 7,400 metres above sea level. And then all we had to do was race down, tobogganing the easier sections, all the way back to Camp One, to melt snow for restorative drinks and supper before collapsing into exhausted sleep.

At dawn on 2 May, my thirty-fourth birthday, desultory debate drifted between the two tents. Robert and I were keen to press home our advantage, pack personal gear such as sleeping bags, and head straight back up to our Camp Two cache. If the weather held, we could be on the South Col by 4 May, and try for the summit on the next day – the one scheduled for the Asian Friendship Expedition's summit spectacular: we could realise Paul's dream of gatecrashing their telly show.

But Ed was adamant that we needed a rest after our May Day exertions. So we skulked at Camp One, Ed presenting me with a birthday mini Mars bar, with a cigarette lighter for a candle. And that evening it began to snow.

It snowed all night and on 3 May we had to abandon summit hopes and abseil, rope length by rope length, anchor by anchor, all the way back down to Advance Base. We seemed to be fighting a phoney war, never properly getting to grips with the enemy – playing an interminable game of Snakes and Ladders where the snakes always won, sending us repeatedly back to Go. The weather improved tantalisingly on 5 May. An aeroplane flew over the summit and, through the telescope, we saw tiny ants crawling onto the final white dome of Everest, three miles above us. Sustained by an army of 250 workers, with plentiful supplies of oxygen at their high camps, the Nepalese, Japanese and Chinese elite squads of the Asian Friendship Exhibition had stuck to their computerised timetable.

That afternoon our shoestring team set off again up the ropes, but at dusk it started to snow again. Ed and Paul turned back. Robert and I continued doggedly. Hauling up two hundred metres of rope in the Scottish Gully, we heard a huge roar to our right as an avalanche thundered down Big Al Gully. Luckily it wasn't big enough to spill over the retaining wall into our smaller gulch. We continued by torchlight, all the way to Camp One, where both the tents were buried. By the time we had dug them out and got to bed it was midnight. It snowed most of the night, but cleared later the next morning, so we continued, wading through blustery wind to the Tyrolean Traverse before admitting that we were wasting our time and heading thankfully back down, bumping into Ed and Paul – the 'South Col Support Team' which had come up to see what was going on.

Back at Advance Base, Mimi and Joe were getting increasingly exasperated by the climbers who seemed incapable of climbing the mountain. Joe was missing his wife and daughter. Mimi, after two months of unrelieved male company, was longing to talk to another woman; but the only other female present was The Lady of the Lake – a naked snowwoman carved by Joe on the frozen glacial pond next to the tents. At sunrise the next morning Joe's busty sculpture provided a surreal foreground as Ed snapped a monster avalanche thundering down Big Al Gully, clouds of snow billowing up for hundreds of feet, almost onto the crest of the Cauliflower Towers. By the time the fallout reached us at Advance Base the avalanche's power was spent, but if we had been up on the ropes that morning it would have been very frightening indeed and we might well have suffered serious injuries.

Once the avalanche had subsided, the silence was palpable. All day long the mountains shone under an ultramarine sky and not a breath of wind disturbed the token cloud plumes fluttering benignly from Lhotse's and Everest's summits. The only weather forecasts we had were the sketchy nightly bulletins on the Nepal national news, crackling on the transistor radio back at Base Camp, which invariably promised 'Fine weather in the kingdom, with possibility of snow on the mountains.' So we just had to guess it, seizing opportunities whenever the sky was clear, hoping that we were in for a sustained spell of high pressure.

The signs looked good that evening. Five weeks after taking our first steps onto the toe of the Neverest Buttress, with Camp One well stocked – and supplies for Camp Two waiting under the Flying Wing, ready for the final push up the east face – we had done everything we could to prepare. We weren't going to get any fitter or any better acclimatised. It was time to see this thing through.

At two-thirty the next morning, 8 May, I slid reluctantly out of my sleeping bag and shuffled over to the kitchen shelter to make coffee. Paul and Robert said they'd be coming up later. Ed agreed on the alpine start, but took ages to get ready, so I returned to my tent for half an hour, got out my Walkman and put on a tape of Liszt's Piano Sonata. It was a present from my sister Cangy and I had been listening to the sonata nearly every day in Tibet, mesmerised by its passion, its grand architecture and its outrageous virtuosity. But also by the lyricism of its luminous second subject, where the right hand decorates with an ethereal filigree of tinkling bells at the upper limit of the keyboard. Lying there that morning, in the dark, under the huge jewelled Himalayan sky, the music seemed a fitting send-off – a precious memory of earthly beauty before we took off into the stratosphere.

There was time to listen to the whole sonata, all the way to the final fading bass note which brings the journey full circle. Then Ed called from his tent to say that he was ready. It was time to start our own journey. At about four o'clock we set off into the darkness, shouting 'Goodbye, Mimi; goodbye, Joe. We'll try and do it this time. See you in a few days.'

Chapter Fifteen

The Longest Journey

It was my tenth trip up the ropes to the Cauliflower Towers and I was pleased to do it in my fastest time yet – four and a half hours, door to door, Advance Base to Camp One. That simple proof of growing fitness was pleasing. But so too was the sheer physicality of moving up the mountain. And the growing intimacy with the vertical landscape that we had made our own: the edelweiss nestled on that first outcrop at eighteen thousand feet; the rock headwall that Robert and I had first climbed five weeks earlier; the ice daggers framing the Scottish Gully, glinting in the eastern sunrise; the little cave above where we would stop to have a drink and reapply sun cream; then the huge traverse towards Big Al, with the meticulous double-check at each anchor as you transferred from one rope to the next; then that higher traverse I fixed with Ed, around those dark shattered breeze-blocks; then another upward heave to the next anchor; then the final two-hundred-metre sweep of ice, stopping halfway up for a rest, feet slotted into Paul's 'letter box' before the glassy wall bulged to vertical and you stabbed with one cramponed foot against the ice to stop yourself spinning on the rope as you stared down past your feet at the next person starting the rope below – a tiny helmet-blob dwarfed by the immensity of Big Al.

At Camp One we rested all day. I loved this white balcony perched so improbably on the Cauliflower Towers. I loved the view across Big Al Gully to the Rococo snow flutings flanking the 1983 Buttress. And I loved the bigger view down the valley, with our Kangshung Glacier snaking eastward past Chomolonzo's triple summit. It was a good place to relax. But also to make a kind of meditation, trying to visualise Summit Day, daring to hope that it really might happen.

When I had left London three months earlier, I had given myself a ten per cent chance of climbing Everest. Now I had raised those odds to about fifty per cent. I really believed that we might just do it. Chatting in the sun, Ed and I focused on all the little details which could make a difference above eight thousand metres, when we would have to run on autopilot. We filed our crampon points razor-sharp. We trimmed harnesses and slings to reduce weight. And, while it was still easy, we melted pan after pan of snow, consuming two meals and several litres of fluid.

Robert and Paul arrived later in the morning, light-hearted, optimistic. The air was calm and only a fluffy wisp of cloud hung from the summit, still nearly three thousand metres above us. After an early supper, we settled down in our sleeping bags at five p.m. But I was far too excited to sleep and, after seven hours of restlessness, I roused everyone at midnight, telling them that we might as well have breakfast. In our tent I made porridge and hot chocolate and filled up water bottles. Then I got dressed and packed my rucksack, checking every little vital detail – sun cream, sunglasses, sunhat, cameras, film, sleeping bag, warm clothes. Then swung my legs out of the tent to clamp crampons to boots. Then, before climbing up into the black night, I checked with Ed: 'Are you bringing the two spare cigarette lighters? And the mail package for the South Col?'

I left at three a.m. and it was still dark as I swung across the Jaws of Doom. It was three weeks since Ed had fixed his traversing line; the aperture was gaping wider and the fiddle string was now tauter, tuned a couple of tones higher. One day the whole lower jaw would collapse, taking the line with it.

Robert joined me at the top of the fixed ropes as the sun burst luridly over a cloud sea. Then we noticed higher clouds – menacing lenticulars snooping round the back of Makalu. I looked the other way, at the endless billows of soft new snow draped above us – with no trace, save the marker wands, remaining of the path that we had created so laboriously a week earlier – and muttered, 'I *suppose* we might as well continue?'

'Of course,' Robert replied cheerfully. 'Of course we're going up.'

So the two of us started the big wallow, taking turns to wade, mouths becoming desiccated in the thin air. By the time Ed and Paul had caught us up it was snowing, and we were reduced to checking one of Joe's large-format photos to try and work out where we were in a blur of white shapes. Hour after hour we trudged through the cloud. At one point we had to traverse left to avoid a splintered jumble of ice towers. There was a deep vibration as a car-sized section sagged forward and collapsed at Ed's feet. Then there was a louder rumble as a large 'delivery van' rolled forward and slid silently down the slope, disappearing into the depths of Big Al Gully.

'Why does this always happen to *me*?' shouted Ed.

'Stop being so fucking melodramatic, Ed,' I mumbled under my breath, while Paul shouted more charitably, 'Just your luck, I guess.'

We moved swiftly out of the danger zone. Or as swiftly as our oxygen-starved muscles could manage, taking turns out front on the treadmill. At one point Paul said, 'This is stupid – going *up* in this weather; if this snow continues we'll be trapped.' Robert and I reasoned more optimistically that we had enough supplies at the Flying Wing to hold out for several days if necessary. As it was, our gamble paid off. After fourteen hours of continuous labour, just as we reached the Flying Wing the snowfall stopped. By the time we had the two tents pitched under the ice roof the clouds were melting away. And when I stuck my head out of the frost-fringed doorway at five o'clock the next morning I was greeted by an immaculate blue sky. This was it! Our chance to complete our new route up the East Face of Everest.

Ed later called it our Great Day. The whole world glittered with expectation as we set off at 7.45 a.m., dressed just in thermal underwear, with four layers of clothing stowed in gargantuan

The complete route to the South Col – the first ascent from Tibet.

rucksacks, along with tents, sleeping bags, stoves, gas and food. All we left behind at the Flying Wing were some scraps of food and three gas cylinders to safeguard our retreat. Our rucksacks each weighed at least fifteen kilos. Even if oxygen had been available, without high-altitude porters we could never have managed that additional payload as we headed into the upper atmosphere.

The Great Day started gleefully, Ed and I vying with each other (and Ed almost invariably winning) for the best photos, as the four of us emerged from a corner of the Flying Wing onto a great snow terrace with huge new vistas opening around us. What a treat, I thought again – what a fantastic privilege to be here, completing this new route up Everest.

My first turn in the lead coincided with a firm windcrust. Then Paul took over and laughed, 'Typical!' as the crust gave way to the usual deep powder. Back to wallowing.

We wallowed ever more slowly, taking ever shorter turns in the lead as the slope steepened again. Morning drifted into afternoon and I realised that I was now higher than Luke and I had been on Shishapangma, higher than I had ever been before. Paul slumped on his ice axe and said he felt slightly dizzy. Then he gasped, 'Whatever happens, at least we're going to make the South Col; we're going to finish our route up the Kangshung Face' – as if setting out a fall-back position.

A scrap of paper danced in the wind above our heads, blown off the South Col – the first sign of other people since we had started our climb. Then a pair of black choughs – those consummate high-altitude scavengers – appeared, dancing in the westerly gusts. We stopped to balance one-legged and don another layer of clothing. And then another. And then another, preparing to do battle with the wind. I set my sights on a tiny rock outcrop in the white desert, but failed to reach it. So Robert took a turn, until he too ground to a halt. It was Ed, the stoical tortoise, who finally broke through the cornice, haloed in a flurry of snow crystals dancing in the westering sun as he climbed out onto the huge wind-scoured plateau of the South Col – the first human being ever to reach this place from Tibet.

*　　*　　*

We were expecting cheery Australians shouting, 'Good on yer, mate' and Sherpas ladling out steaming mugs of tea as we handed over the mail package; but all we found was an empty monochrome wasteland. The South Col is slightly convex and although we later discovered there *were* other climbers there that day, they were hidden from us, several hundred metres to the west. So we had to fend for ourselves, Ed leading the way, head into the wind, ropes whipped horizontally. Shouting and gesticulating through the screaming maelstrom, we settled on a patch of hard snow amongst black boulders. Then we battled for survival, clinging to flapping tent fabric, terrified of seeing our homes flung back over the great precipice that we had just climbed.

'Hand me some rocks,' I shouted to Ed as I lay inside our tent, fighting to pin it down. 'Thanks . . . good . . . and another . . . now the poles.' The icy metal burned through my thin gloves, and I had to keep stopping to blow on my fingers before fumbling another section of pole into place. By the time the tent was secure, lashed to a boulder with our climbing rope, the sun was setting in Nepal, shafts of light slanting up through the clouds blasting round Everest's invisible summit pyramid.

'Where does the route go?' shouted Ed.

'Not sure. Up a gully, somewhere – doesn't it?' I shrugged, vague on the correct line of the 1953 route, and, right now, not really caring very much: we could deal with that later; right now all that mattered was domestic survival.

We filled a bag with ice chippings, shouted goodnight to the other two, and crawled into our cramped dome, taking turns to fight our way into sleeping bags, pausing repeatedly to gather breath, trying to resist panicky claustrophobia by relaxing, allowing diaphragms to draw deep and fill every space in our lungs. And we forced ourselves to eat and drink, laboriously melting pan after pan of ice on the hanging stove.

We had hoped to do the last stretch to the South Col in four or five hours. According to Ed it actually took eight. I thought it was more like nine or ten. Time was becoming increasingly elastic, perceptions ever more subjective. Whatever the precise timing, it had been a long exhausting day, and our plan to continue straight on for the summit, after an afternoon of restorative brews, was now abandoned. We were in no fit state to climb Everest that night. Instead we slept. Or rather, we dozed intermittently. I lay on my back, with just my nose and mouth protruding from the sleeping-bag hood, forcing myself to breathe deeply, concentrating on slow exhalation, thankful for the yoga classes that Rosie had dragged me to in that other world, eight thousand metres lower down, where people were designed to live. Here, at perhaps minus twenty-five degrees centigrade, the single skin of Gore-Tex fabric stretched over heads thickened with freezing condensation, showering us with hoar frost every time it flapped in the wind.

So this was what it was like – life at eight thousand metres (or 7,906 metres, to give the precise altitude of the South Col). After all the excitement and beauty and laughter of the lower climb, this seemed a grim, joyless business. And yet there was a kind of satisfaction in coping – in sticking it out, seeing the thing through, surviving.

The tent shook all night and at dawn on 11 May the wind was still too strong for us even to think about the summit. In any case, there were other more urgent concerns. At about six a.m. Robert appeared outside our tent and said, 'Paul threw up twice during the night and he's got a bad headache. I think he's getting cerebral oedema. Someone's got to go down with him.'

We mumbled blearily through the tent fabric, then roused ourselves to make some breakfast. While the ice melted I glanced at Ed, cocooned beside me in his sleeping bag. He looked terrible and I rather hoped that he would offer to go down. We had often discussed this possibility, reasoning that, with four of us, it would always be possible to escort someone down, and still leave two people with a chance at the summit. If Paul really was showing the first signs of cerebral oedema – a potentially disastrous seeping of fluid into the brain cavity – he undoubtedly *did* have to go down: if he stayed up here he would die.

Over breakfast we talked desultorily. 'Do you think you'd be able to climb all the way back up here again, if we went down?' Ed asked me.

'*Maybe*. I suppose so ... but we'd probably need a week's rest at base, before coming up again.' I wasn't sure that I would actually have the patience and strength to repeat that long haul. Or the luck with the weather. According to Ed, I actually voiced my naked hopes, saying, 'I definitely want a go at the top.' That was certainly how I felt: Robert and I – I thought – were probably the most driven, the most prepared to stick our necks out; and I was rather hoping that Ed would volunteer to go down with Paul, even though I felt that, really, it should be me. Ed had been part of this project from the start and had put in all the hard work, packing supplies in Colorado; he deserved the summit far more than I did.

After three hours of sluggish pondering I had convinced myself that *I* ought to do the decent thing and volunteer, when Paul appeared outside our tent. 'I got sick,' he said, 'so I'm going down. I'm going alone.'

'But shouldn't we—'

'No, I'll be fine on my own,' he insisted. I mumbled guilty thanks. Ed said, 'I love you, Paul.' Robert wished him good luck. And then he was gone, a lone figure striding across the windswept high-altitude desert, shouting back, 'Get up the fucker. Do it for me.' And then he disappeared, over the brink, descending back into the great basin of the Kangshung Face.

We knew he almost certainly *would* be fine. The rapid descent would immediately cure his incipient oedema – if it *was* oedema. The trail through the upper slopes was clearly marked; and on the lower Buttress we were always alone on the fixed ropes anyway. Nevertheless, there was an uneasy feeling that we had evaded moral responsibility, accepting too easily Paul's generous gesture. Just supposing something went wrong and no one was there to help? How would we ever live with that? I felt awkward and guilty. But also enormously grateful at being given a chance at the summit. Renunciation is the hardest thing and in choosing to go down, rather than wait there and risk everyone's safety, Paul had made the only genuinely courageous decision on the whole expedition.

* * *

Later that morning I had to go out, uncover myself to the evil wind and deposit a dry hard turd on the South Col. While I was outside I took a couple of photos, one of them showing Robert's tent, hard-edged in the bright light; beside its door a yellowish splash of vomit and urine – another human stain on the sterile whiteness; behind it the summit ridge with cloud banners tossed into a cobalt sky so dark that it was almost black. Ed came out, and asked me to take a shot of him sitting beside the tent. His face was ashen and puffy, but there was still a palpable spark of will. Everyone had worked so hard for this new route that we had to hang on, at least for one day, hoping that the wind would drop and give us a chance at the summit.

Back in the tent we dozed. I found that I was coping better now, managing to breathe, learning to relax. Contrary to received wisdom, I seemed to be recuperating at almost eight thousand metres, so I dared to believe that I might have the strength to go still higher.

At about five o'clock that afternoon Robert came over and commented that the wind seemed to be dropping slightly. 'What do you think?' he asked.

'If it clears up, we should go tonight,' said Ed. 'If not, we'll have to go down in the morning.' Even if we did seem to be coping, we knew that another day's waiting could be disastrous: at this altitude the human body is effectively dying. Very fast. But if the wind really did drop? 'I think we should set off at midnight,' suggested Robert.

'No, earlier,' I insisted. 'Ten o'clock.'

'Make it eleven,' said Robert. Ten years before, on the first oxygenless ascent of Everest, it had taken Peter Habeler and Reinhold Messner ten hours to get from here to the summit. But to some extent they had been helped to the South Col by the infrastructure of a large expedition operating from Nepal: they had probably arrived here in a fresher state. In any case they were phenomenal athletes, Habeler in particular. At the time, in 1978, when I was floundering around on the Matterhorn, I had never dreamed that *I* might be capable of emulating them. Even now it seemed presumptuous and I was sure that, even if we could drag our bodies to the summit, those 950 metres of ascent – almost an equivalent height interval to climbing Snowdon from sea level, but starting at nearly 7,900 metres – would take at least twelve hours. And then we had to get all the way back down to our tents. We knew that we would be operating at the very limit of human physiology and we knew that of the twenty people who had so far reached the summit without oxygen, four had not returned.

At about seven o'clock Ed and I began to prepare hopefully. First we cooked some noodles. Then at about eight the wind died right away. There was a shout from the other tent, 'Well, team – it's a go!' Even through the hypoxic fog of altitude, I felt a surge of excitement. Three months on from that distant birthday supper with Rosie, I really was setting off on the last stage of this fantastic journey.

Ed and I talked little, saving precious breath, each of us busy with the kind of mundane detail that can make the difference between living and dying – a litre of fruit juice laced with concentrated carbohydrate powder, stowed in an inner pocket; spare gloves and mittens; spare torch bulb for those long hours of darkness; socks and inner boots pre-warmed inside a sleeping bag, laced as loosely as possible, trying not to constrict the circulation already sluggish from dehydration and the thickening of extra haemoglobin in the blood; hands insulated by thin liner gloves, then down mittens, then fleece mittens and then a final protecting layer of Gore-Tex. I wore four layers of clothing under a protective windsuit – the same arrangement as on Shishapangma – and, although our plan was to return to our tents the next day, perhaps subconsciously I was preparing myself for the hideous possibility of an unplanned bivouac in the open.

At about ten-thirty I crawled out to collect additional rocks, handing them in to Ed to secure the tent. Then I fought unsuccessfully with my crampons, trying to get numb fingers to clamp the icy steel to unwieldy foam overboots. In the end Ed – kind, considerate Ed – helped me. Robert was still slumped in the doorway of his tent, trying to find the energy to put on his own crampons.

At last we were ready. Ed handed me his compact camera and I photographed him and Robert, eyes staring manically through slitted hoods, headtorches barely penetrating the black moonless night. And Ed photographed me, looking rather intense, teeth bared in a frozen attempt at jollity. Then he uncoiled the short length of seven-millimetre rope we had brought to the South Col. We had talked a lot about this, Robert and I both feeling it would be better to climb unroped on Summit Day; but Ed wanted to sustain that symbolic bond, so we tied on, Robert first, then Ed, then me. And at exactly eleven o'clock we set off into the darkness.

The rope jerked falteringly across the black plateau and after about ten minutes I asked if I could take over the lead. Rhythm was our only hope, and for a while I managed a soothing pattern of twenty paces followed by a short rest. But as the slope steepened the rope jerked me back, breaking the rhythm.

'We've got to move faster than this,' I insisted. 'Do you mind if we unrope?'

'I agree,' gasped Robert. Ed was silent. I knew he wanted that psychological bond; but I also knew that at our current stumbling pace we had little chance of reaching the summit today – this new day of 12 May. 'I'll trail the rope,' I offered as apology, 'in case we need it higher up.' And then I ploughed ahead, leaving the other two to follow more slowly.

It seemed a callous denial of the camaraderie that had sustained us over the last two months; but down in the comfort of the valley Robert had stated repeatedly that each of us should be responsible for himself up here, each person deciding how far he wanted to push himself into what is often called, with justification, the Death Zone. And I knew that I wanted to push myself right to the limit. After all the years of ambivalence and retreats and lingering regrets, I wanted to seize this wonderful opportunity; and I was determined, ruthlessly, that this time no one was going to hold me back.

So I pushed on alone, still not quite believing that I was here, on this summit slope of the world's highest mountain, my whole world reduced to a flickering pool of torchlight. I was climbing a broad snow couloir. At that stage I didn't realise that when Everest was first attempted from the south, in 1952, the Genevan climber Raymond Lambert, with Norbu's father Tenzing Norgay, climbed further right – up a shorter gully, leading quite quickly onto Everest's south-east ridge. That was the same route which the British expedition took a year later, when Tenzing fulfilled his summit dream with Edmund Hillary. But nowadays people followed this longer, broader snow tongue. I passed an abandoned oxygen bottle, a tatter of rope, crampon scrapes on the crusty surface. Later we discovered that two members of the Asian Friendship Expedition, Padma Bahadur Tamang and the famous Sherpa, Sungdare, had been here two days earlier.

The tracks seemed to lead left, so I followed them. But they petered out and I found myself on steeper ground, sensing a big drop to my left. So I headed back right, the trailing rope snagging on piles of loose rock. Below me there was a confusion of shouts and arcing torch beams – impotent searchlights trying to pierce the darkness. It was only years later that I discovered that Ed had been following some way behind Robert, crossing precarious tilted rocks, asking him which way we had gone.

I continued rightward and found a section of fixed rope, which I followed upward to a yellowish boulder. When I got there, the boulder metamorphosed into a tent with a name stencilled on its domed fabric – Dunlop, one of the sponsors of the Asian Friendship Expedition.

So this must have been their top camp. From here, a week earlier, they had set off to meet the northern party on the summit. Our tiny oxygenless team could never have carried a camp this high. I wasn't sure how high, but I was fairly certain I must now be above 27,000 feet. Two years later, when the great Bostonian geographer Bradford Washburn produced his definitive Everest map, I worked out that the tent, pitched beneath the prominent Black Tower, was at just above 8,300 metres – about 27,260 feet above sea level.

Ed and Robert were still a long way behind in the dark. I left the rope coiled by the tent – a token gesture of encouragement

– and continued upward, still feeling my way uncertainly in the dark, unaware that from here most parties followed a rightward gangway to reach the South-East Ridge at a point called the Balcony. I just ploughed on up what seemed the most obvious direct gully, zigzagging to make the steepness bearable, trying to kick firm steps in the white powder, pausing sometimes for several minutes to lean on my ice axe and gasp.

At the end of one zigzag, turning to look behind me, I became aware of a pale glimmer. Then of shapes remembered from books: the rocky swirl of the Yellow Band, snaking round the Western Cwm – that extraordinary hanging basin which the Swiss called the Valley of Silence; the jagged ridge of Lhotse and Nuptse; beyond it other famous Nepalese summits, like Ama Dablam, its face now smiling encouragement in the golden sunrise, banishing the doubts and confusions of the night. Over in the east that great pyramid of Makalu again. And beyond it, sixty miles away, Kangchenjunga. I took a couple of shots on my Nikon, then put it quickly away as the cold metal began to burn through my inner gloves. I caught the Western Cwm on the warmer plastic compact camera, swapped clear spectacles for sunglasses, then quickly pulled my mittens back on.

Six o'clock in the morning. Seven hours since leaving the Col and still no ridge. I ploughed on. The gully steepened and my zigzags tightened. Twenty paces was now impossible: three or four seemed to be my limit, and the pauses were getting longer. Robert and Ed were still out of sight, hidden by the curve of the gully. But they had almost ceased to exist. The whole world had shrunk to this one human organism – to this lung sucking at nothingness, trying to will life into leaden legs.

I grew impatient with the interminable zigzags and switched to climbing direct, facing in to the white wall, trying to rush three steps at a time, then collapsing, slumped against the slope, mouth gaping like a fish out of water. But the wall was shortening, the gully ending. I managed one final flourish – six, seven, maybe eight continuous, lung-wrenching steps – and I was over the rim, floundering ecstatically on the broad gentle crest of the South-East Ridge.

Now, nearly twenty years later, scrutinising Washburn's beautiful Swiss-drawn map, I can place that snowy ledge at 8,530 metres above sea level – a whisker under 28,000 feet. Precision with timing is less easy, but I think I reached it at about nine a.m. What I do remember is the warm glow – both real and metaphorical. The world from up there was dazzlingly beautiful. I gazed fondly down into our home – far, far below on the Kangshung Glacier – and wondered if Paul and Joe and Mimi were watching. Wondered if perhaps Pasang and Kasang could see me from Base Camp, silhouetted on this immense white ridge. I rested for perhaps an hour, legs stretched out horizontally, allowing the blood to flow, feeling the warmth return to numb toes. I forced myself to eat a few squares of chocolate. And I drank some of my precious fruit juice, hoping that some of the calories in the carbohydrate solution might seep through. But I couldn't make the effort to take a photo. I was sleepy. Desperately sleepy. Since leaving Advance Base four days earlier, none of us had had more than seven or eight hours' sleep, maybe ten. So now it seemed sensible to doze and dally, hoping that Ed and Robert might catch up and join me on that final plod to the South Summit, which now looked so close, so easy, so attainable.

But they didn't appear; so, reluctantly, I stood up and returned to work. The snow here was wind-whipped into big flaky whorls, catching at my clodhopping boots. I stumbled lazily, ploughing my field, somewhere in Spain – a peasant farmer despairing of his poor soil. What a state this land was in! Typical. Lazy Latin types, I thought. Then jolted back to reality, appalled that my North European subconscious should harbour such prejudice.

I continued, wandering slowly across my crumbling field, despairing at its steepening slope, stopping ever more frequently to daydream. An hour passed – maybe two – before I could reach the first of some prominent ribs of yellowish rock. That would be much better, I reasoned. Rocks are solid, reliable, traditional – the kind of thing the Old Man likes. He can't be doing with this ephemeral flaky whiteness.

So I took this older man up onto the rocks. But he became anxious. And then I realised that he didn't exist. It was *I* – no one else – who was climbing these rocks, the same rocks which Tom Bourdillon and Charles Evans had climbed thirty-five years earlier when they became the first people to reach the South Summit of Mount Everest. The rocks were a little less soul-destroying than the shifting snow, but the holds were small and I felt vulnerable. I grabbed an old bleached rope, but tried not to pull too hard – forced myself to be self-reliant, like a proper climber. Then tiptoed sideways, back onto the white powder where I could dig a seat to slump and doze without fear of tipping over.

Afternoon cloud was starting to gather, but the sun still dazzled. I stared down the white slope and spotted a dark body sitting in the snow. It must be Hannelore Schmatz, I thought, recalling Chris Bonington's account of passing her corpse near here three years earlier. She had died in 1979 after failing to return from the summit to the South Col – a sad tale of oxygen running out, willpower waning, Sherpas trying heroically to revive the woman as she drifted into an irreversible coma . . .

I stared harder and the corpse turned into a rock. So it wasn't Frau Schmatz after all. Her body must have got buried. Or perhaps it fell down the South-West Face. But here was a *real* person. Robert? No – Ed, following my wavering tracks, climbing up to join me. I'll wait here and we'll go together to the summit, I thought.

I dozed off. When I next looked down Ed was quite close and I shouted to him, asking if he could come and break trail. But he mumbled, 'I don't think . . . I can't stay awake . . . my brain . . .' Ed's hallucinations, unlike mine, had become fully visual: when he looked up he saw me sitting amongst Tibetan monks in their maroon robes, with prayer flags fluttering around the South Summit. But at the time I didn't realise how far gone he was, and in my idealised version of events I said something innocuous like, 'Oh well, never mind.' Ed reminded me later that I actually shouted, 'You mean I've wasted a whole hour waiting for you?'

I don't recall the anger – just a desperate realisation that Ed couldn't help me, that either I was going to have to admit defeat or I was going to have to do this thing on my own. Mimi had given us some caffeine pills, so I swigged a couple down with a trickle of half-frozen juice. The caffeine seemed to help, because I stood up with a new determination not to be beaten by the flaky snow. Instead of being a passive observer merely watching my body, I took control again, forcing it up the steepening snow face, relishing the challenge of a tiny crevasse – a mini-bergschrund – mundane at sea level, but here requiring a gigantic effort to reach high and pull over.

I was cruising now, managing three steps at a time, sometimes even four, with minimal rests. And then I emerged onto a narrow crest and saw the South Summit just ahead. I shouted down to Ed, 'Almost there!' and continued along the precarious crest to the South Summit, glancing back with satisfaction at the clouds swirling around Lhotse, the world's fourth-highest mountain, now well below me.

Time for a pause. Time to take stock. Time to scrutinise the ridge ahead – the ridge imagined so often, seen in so many photographs, starting with that first classic image taken by Hillary thirty-five years ago. Time to ponder that final bridge still to be crossed. Time to weigh up the risks.

I was 8,751 metres above sea level – higher than any other summit on Earth, apart from the main summit of Everest, ninety-nine metres higher and about a quarter of a mile distant. But between me and that still invisible prize there was this narrow causeway leading to an abrupt cliff called the Hillary Step. It was now 1.30 p.m. We had been on the move for over fourteen hours and in another five hours it would be dark. I looked again across the bridge, wondering if I would ever get this chance again. I decided that I would continue at least as far as the foot of the Hillary Step and see how I coped. And I decided that, whatever happened, I would turn around by four o'clock.

It hurt to lose precious height, descending from the South Summit into the gap, passing a shallow cave where I noticed old scraps of gear and empty oxygen cylinders. I stopped to take a photo – the first picture since sunrise – then continued across the bridge, traversing carefully, well down on the west side, fearful of cornices overhanging the East Face, but also terrified of the alternative eight-thousand-foot plunge down the South-West Face. There was a moment of panic when I saw red and green spots dancing in my eyes, and I thought for an awful moment that oedema had struck, but the spots vanished quickly. Everything seemed to be okay. This body was functioning. It was even enjoying itself up here, at almost 29,000 feet above sea level, edging across these rocks, doing real climbing.

Clouds were now swirling around me. It felt like a misty November afternoon and for a moment I drifted into a Dublin pub, where I sat beside a fire, sipping the creamy foam on a pint of Guinness, smiling at a woman with long blonde hair who must have been Rosie. And then I was back on Everest, proud to be coping, clipping myself into one of the fixed ropes on the Hillary Step. Just in case.

What a treat! What a privilege to be here – mittened left hand feeling for holds on that same rock first touched by Hillary and Tenzing all those years ago, right hand plunging my axe into the snow where Hillary had squirmed up a narrow chimney, hoping that the whole blob of snow, stuck almost vertically on the side of the mountain, wouldn't collapse and catapult him out over the three-thousand-metre precipice of the Kangshung Face. What a joy to discover that I could do it – that everything was working.

I glanced back towards the South Summit, still hoping that Ed and Robert might appear, wondering vainly if Ed might get a photo of me on the Step. What a shot that would be! But they still hadn't appeared. With a flailing gasp I squeezed past a rock pinnacle and I was over the Step. I unclipped from the rope and continued across an easier slope. Glancing back, I tried to take it all in – tried to memorise the urgent intensity of the clouds swirling round Lhotse, the immense gulf of the Western Cwm, that huge traverse across the South-West Face where Scott and Haston had come thirteen years earlier, and the long, plunging line of the West Ridge, descending towards that domed summit far, far below, which must be Pumori – the peak that Mallory named for his eldest daughter.

On the final ridge I was thrilled to find a firm crust where I could walk on the surface. Now nothing could stop me, and for the very first time since leaving London exactly three months earlier, I knew, with total certainty, that I was going to reach the summit. It was just a case of taking it slowly, carefully, patiently, not allowing legs to outstrip lungs and bring on a fit of coughing, being sure to stick well to the left, clear of the fragile cornices overhanging the Kangshung void.

I plodded on across my great white roof, driven by euphoria, overjoyed by my good fortune. I crossed two or three hummocks until it became clear that the West Ridge was rising to meet me from the left, culminating in a final white hummock where three people sat silently in the snow, their hats stirring in the first breeze of the late afternoon. What a glorious coincidence! What a textbook finish! They must be some of the boys from the British Joint Services Expedition, successfully up the West Ridge. Perhaps one of them was Luke? Or Nigel? Or Henry? I shouted 'Hello,' then collapsed in a coughing fit, chiding myself for not having completely given up smoking. The soldiers remained impassive; so I shouted again, 'Well, are you going to bloody talk to me or not?'

They continued to ignore me, so I plodded closer. Next time I looked up, I saw that my 'soldiers' were actually small lifeless objects, closer than I had thought. And a moment later I was kicking up that final slope, one step at a time, drawing three breaths to every step, emerging onto the last few feet of the West Ridge, and tramping, deliriously happy, onto a white dome in the sky decorated with three empty oxygen cylinders.

I have very few regrets about our Everest climb, but I do feel sad that my summit self-portrait never came out. At the time I was so proud of making the effort, gagging on empty air as I bent over to position my heavy Nikon in the snow, contorting my neck to squint through the viewfinder and frame the shot, then hurrying back up to sit on the highest mound and stare at the camera as its self-timer whirred and the shutter clunked. How professional, I thought. It was only a month later that

Wendy phoned from New York to say that they hadn't found the roll with my dawn shots and summit photo. Perhaps the roll was lost on the journey home; or perhaps I never loaded it properly and was shooting blanks.

But I did manage a back-up record on the little compact camera – a distorted image of my head and shoulders reflected in one of the yellow oxygen cylinders marked CNJ for China-Nepal-Japan. Prayer flags hung from the cylinders and beneath them, amongst the abandoned battery packs where fresh snowflakes were already settling, I scattered my own offering – the flower petals from Pondicherry given to me nearly three months earlier by Sonam and Nawang. I left the two envelopes, with their pictures of Sri Auribindo and The Mother of the ashram, in the snow, and made a point of including them in several frames I shot.

The other and bigger regret was that the others were not here with me. At one stage we had dreamed that all four of us might make it to the summit. But it was now 3.40 p.m., the weather was deteriorating and it seemed very unlikely that even Ed or Robert would make it. So I just had to make the most of my lonely meditation, trying to soak up the experience. Once the rituals were complete I lingered for a few more minutes, savouring the exquisite physical pleasure of sitting still, breathing almost normally. The glittering view we would have had in the morning was now smothered in cloud, leaving just a pallid glimpse of the North-East Ridge dropping towards the Rongbuk Glacier. Without knowledge of all those pre-war attempts – of Norton and Mallory and Smythe and all the rest of them – it could just have been any old ridge, the summit just another blob of snow in the sky. Even the knowledge that the limestone beneath me was laid down in an ocean two hundred and fifty million years ago and was eventually pushed higher than any other point on Earth was only the result of others' calculations. The importance of this place was a purely human construct. And yet it felt incredibly moving to be here, alone in the cloud, listening to the deafening silence, still not quite believing that I *was* here. I felt enormous pride for our team which had worked so hard – and, until the last day or two, so pleasurably – to reach this improbable goal. *That* was the real meaning of it – that long journey, so full of doubts and fears and laughter and wonder and beauty and growing belief in what we were doing; without all those days and weeks of Neverest, this blob in the sky, for all its geographical supremacy, would have held little appeal.

I felt as though I could sit there for ever but I knew that every minute I lingered would reduce my chances of survival. Having reached the summit at 3.40 p.m., at 3.50 I picked up my ice axe and began the long journey home. I had believed all along that I might be capable of getting *up* Everest without oxygen; what had always terrified me was the possibility of not being able to get *down* again. Now, as I started to grope through the cloud, trying to reverse my own tracks through the enveloping whiteness, mouth gasping, legs wobbly, I realised just how weak I was. Robert and Ed must by now have turned back. Neither they, nor anyone else, could help me. I was utterly alone on top of the world and in two and a half hours' time it would be dark.

Chapter Sixteen

Night on a Bare Mountain

Summit euphoria sustained me long enough to stop and collect a few pebbles from the bald patch of shattered limestone just below the top – the last of my summit rituals. But then the fear began to intrude and I rushed headlong back to earth, determined to live.

The wind was stronger now, stinging my exposed face, flinging snow against my sunglasses. My body was weakening and several times I stopped to kneel on one knee, resisting the urge to sit down, because that would make getting up again so much harder. At one point I found myself straying too far to the right, down a steepening curve, towards the swirling abyss of the South-West Face. So I turned left, scanning through frozen sunglasses, trying to find my upward tracks, terrified of going too far the other way and straying onto the huge snow cornices, camouflaged white on white, hanging over the even bigger precipice of the Kangshung Face. But then I found it – the dark rock spike marking the top of the Hillary Step.

Thank God for that fixed rope. I clipped it to my waist kara-biner and started down, legs splayed, leaning out over the cliff. To save weight I had left my sit-harness down near Camp One and had just a knotted loop of tape round my waist, which pulled up against my diaphragm, squeezing the precious air out of my lungs. At the bottom of the step I collapsed, mouth gaping, hyperventilating. For a moment nothing seemed to be going in: my lungs were completely empty. But then the breath came back, in anguished sobs of relief.

But I was so weak. And, for the first time since leaving the South Col over seventeen hours earlier, cold. And blind, because my sunglasses were now iced over. I had to do something about them. That meant taking off mittens and exposing thin inner gloves to the snowstorm. I pulled off the sunglasses and left them hanging round my neck, but as I fumbled in a pocket for the regular clear prescription glasses I had worn every day of my life since the age of ten, my fingers began to go numb. It was too late. I'd have to manage without glasses – just make do with blurred vision.

Quick – get those mittens back on. Quick! Now – before your fingers freeze. First one, easy. Now the second. Come on – pull. Use your teeth. Don't give up. Pull! That's it. Now have that rest, just for a moment, lying here, sprawled on this knife-edge. Nepal one side, Tibet the other. Perhaps I should stay here, draped over this edge? Lie here and go quietly to sleep. We did our best.

No – that's not good enough. How pathetic to climb Everest and then lie down and die. We have to go on. Come on. We'll just take it slowly, carefully. So we stood up, the Old Man and I, and I led him, clumsy and stiff, back over that bridge, crouched, maintaining a low centre of gravity, always keeping three points of contact, staying well down on the west side, away from the edge.

But then we had to climb closer to the crest and his leg suddenly plunged through the snow and the shock brought on a fit of coughing and hyperventilating, chest heaving, desperate for air, terrified of suffocation. Poor old man, he was finding it all a bit too much. Perhaps I should let him stop here, in this hollow beneath the big South Summit rock. We could lie on that dry gravel, amongst those old oxygen cylinders. This must be where Boardman and Pertemba waited in 1975, while Mick Burke filmed his solo summit bid. They sat here for over an hour, waiting forlornly until it was nearly dark and Boardman told Pertemba that they would have to go down: Mick Burke wasn't coming back.

Boardman made the right decision, ensuring that only one person – not three – died that afternoon. Nearly thirteen years on, after toying briefly with the idea of bivouacking in the dry hollow, I too forced myself to carry on, collapsing again, in another fit of spluttering, as I had to climb back *up* onto the South Summit.

And then we continued, the two of us, stomping half blind, back along the little knife-edge ridge, but this time heading slightly further onto the west side, confused by faint tracks in the snow. Didn't see them on the way up. Where have they come from?

At about one-fifteen that afternoon Ed had taken his last photo of me – a small blurred shape disappearing over the crest of the South Summit.

Ed then forced himself to continue, pushing himself very, very slowly, all the way to the South Summit. But by that time the cloud was thickening and there was no sign of me. He checked his watch and saw that it was already 3.30 p.m. He looked across to the dim outline of the Hillary Step, half obscured by cloud. And, like me, he remembered Mick Burke disappearing on that huge summit roof, possibly straying onto one of the crumbling cornices overhanging the Kangshung Face. And Ed realised that if he continued to the summit he would probably die: even if he didn't fall off the mountain, he would end up stuck there all night, freezing to death.

Almost with relief, knowing that he had made the right decision, Ed turned round. He had descended perhaps fifty metres when he met Robert – dogged, stoical Robert – still moving up. Robert said he thought he could still do it. Ed wished him luck and carried on down. He knew that if he hurried he might just get back to our South Col camp before dark. But he didn't do that; he stopped on the ridge shoulder where we had emerged from the gully, cut a ledge in the snow, and waited for Robert.

He stood and shivered in the gathering gloom. Then at last, after perhaps an hour, he saw Robert and me. But we were below him. Perhaps he was waiting at the wrong place? He shouted to us, but we ignored him. He shouted again, but we disappeared into the clouds. A few minutes later the clouds shifted, but the slope was empty, with no sign of the two descending figures.

Ed grew more and more worried, wondering again whether he was waiting in the wrong place. Then he looked back up towards the South Summit and there they were! Thank God for that. But the two figures ignored him, plodding very slowly – silent zombies descending into the abyss and disappearing a second time.

Desperate to reconnect with reality, Ed looked again at his watch. It was coming up to six o'clock. In less than an hour it would be dark. He decided that he would have to bivouac right here, lying out in the open, and was just starting to enlarge the ledge with his ice axe when a single figure appeared just above him, stumbling half blind. This time it was the real Robert, his face haggard and encrusted with ice. He muttered weakly, 'I reached the South Summit.'

'Did you see Stephen?' asked Ed.

'No,' replied Robert. In the murky half-light he had barely seen anything. He had found himself following some puzzling tracks, only to realise that they were his own: he was walking round in circles. It was at that point that he, like Ed, had made the bravest decision of all – to turn back. Now the two of them rushed on down the steep gully, hurrying to find their way in the last minutes of daylight. There was nothing they could do for me.

It was probably just as Ed and Robert disappeared back down the gully that I came over the South Summit with the Old Man, fleeing the mountain, desperate to lose height, frantic for air, driven by pure intuition. The South Summit passed in a blur and soon we were descending steeply, first kicking steps, then sitting to slide, because sliding is faster.

This is better. Whoosh! Faster, faster! The Old Man is a composer riding his cello. What a great sledge, this hollow polished shell – sliding faster and faster, riding the crest of the wave. But this is almost an avalanche. We're going too far left. Heading for the Kangshung Face. Too fast. Much too fast. Stop. Stop!

I dug in my heels and leaned frantically on my ice axe and came to a shuddering halt, collapsing in another fit of coughing, sobbing for air. Then I realised that the Old Man needed a pee so I told him to do it in his pants, because that would keep him warm. And then, as the warm wetness seeped through deep layers of clothing, I thought furiously, 'What nonsense. What are you talking about? And what was all that stuff about the composer?'

I had to get a grip, had to pause and rest. I dug out a bucket seat and leaned back against the steep snow slope. But the cold soon seeped through all my layers of insulation, so I decided to try and continue the descent, kicking my way side-ways, onto the more secure crest of the ridge. It was now dark, so I pulled my head-torch out of a pocket. And, at last, managed to get my glasses on, bringing vague crepuscular shapes into focus. But even with my torch beam it was hard to grasp scale – to distinguish a small boulder from a deadly cliff. I zigzagged back and forth, searching for the correct exit into the gully, trying to make sense of rocks in the snow. But I was terrified of making a mistake and getting lost, straying onto the South Pillar and tumbling through the darkness. So in the end I decided that I would just have to wait for daybreak. The wind had died down and stars were showing between clearing clouds. I ought to be able to survive the night.

We'll put the Old Man on a rock, I thought – that'll keep him warmer than snow. So I sat him on a sloping slab. But he didn't like it. It felt insecure. And it was tiring, having to brace himself with his feet. He needed to lie down flat. Reluctantly, I got up and traversed back onto the snow slope and started digging with my axe.

If only I had been stronger I could have dug a proper cave, as Luke and I had done on Shishapangma; but all I could manage was a rather short ledge, with just enough room to lie down on my left side, facing out, legs slightly bent, right foot balanced on top of the left. For extra insulation I used one spare mitten to pad my hip and the other for my head. My ice axe was thrust into the slope in front of me – a fence post to guard against slipping over the edge. And there, on that cramped frigid bed, I lay, hour after hour, waiting patiently for the dawn.

Now that Everest has been so comprehensively mapped, measured, quantified, I can identify my bivouac site, quite a way above the Balcony, above even the point where our direct gully emerged onto the South-East Ridge. It was 8,560 metres – 28,083 feet – above sea level. The temperature, in May, was probably about minus thirty degrees centigrade, perhaps a few degrees colder. At sea level, with my five layers of clothing, that temperature would have been quite tolerable; but at this altitude, without supplementary oxygen to boost a chronically weakened metabolism, it was potentially fatal. Nevertheless, I was fairly confident of surviving the night. Not through arrogance – just from the knowledge that others had been here before. In 1963 Tom Hornbein and Willi Unsoeld had been caught out by dark somewhere near here, after their historic traverse of the summit, with fellow Americans Barry Bishop and Lute Jerstad. All four men survived, albeit with a reduced tally of fingers and toes. Doug Scott and Dougal Haston, after making the first ascent of the South-West Face in 1975, bivouacked even higher, right up at the South Summit, and didn't even have the decency to get frostbitten. And Scott didn't even have on a down suit because he claimed he hadn't managed to find one that fitted him properly.

Of course there were others who were less fortunate. Like Hannelore Schmatz. And the Bulgarian climber, Hristo Ivanov Prodanov, who perished in 1984, descending the West Ridge. Like us he had been climbing without oxygen. I remembered Meena Agrawal telling us how she had been at Base Camp at the time, talking to Prodanov on the radio, trying to encourage him, trying to will him to survive the night.

Perhaps, if we had had radios, it might have helped me to talk to someone; but I think I would have been too exhausted, too drawn into my animal shell. In any case, I'd had lots of company on my ledge. The Old Man – that gentle alter ego who seemed both a burden and a comfort – had disappeared, but others came and went during the night. At one point the great Everest pioneer Eric Shipton helped warm my hands. At the other end of the ledge various people seemed to be crowding round my numb feet, trying to stave off frostbite. One of them was Doug Scott's son Mike, whom, like Shipton, I had never met.

I had tried so hard *not* to get frostbite, monitoring feeling in my toes throughout the long summit day. And I had made a point, on this ledge, of lying horizontal to maintain circulation to those remote outposts of the vascular system, even getting up at one stage to enlarge the ledge. But I dared not remove my boots and try to rewarm my toes manually, for fear of dropping a boot, which would have meant almost certain death. In any case, it seemed better to concentrate on keeping my hands warm, leaving toes to the phantoms. And if the toes should be lost . . . well, worse things had happened to people.

So I lay and shivered, willing the hours to pass, drifting in and out of reality. Once or twice I swung my legs round, and sat up for a change of position. I made the effort to remove mittens and reach inside my windsuit to pull out the remains of my Hershey almond chocolate bar. It tasted like cardboard. No offence to American confectionery: even Godiva would have tasted foul at that altitude. I forced down a couple of squares with a half-frozen trickle of juice remaining in my bottle. I had consumed nearly a litre since leaving the South Col the previous night; the recommended daily intake at altitude is a minimum of five litres a day.

Perhaps if my brain had been clearer I would have suffered more, but the hypoxia seemed to dull sensation. This bivouac, so very close to the limit of human physiology, didn't actually feel as bad as my Christmas night in the *Super Couloir*, all those years earlier, on Mont Blanc du Tacul, or that more recent Christmas night on Kilimanjaro. Here, higher than every other human being on Earth, I didn't even feel particularly sorry for myself. Until I drifted off again into semi-consciousness and some of the people crowding the ledge told me that they were going to walk over to see some Tibetan yak herders nearby. They left me in peace, and I may even have slept for a short while. But then they returned and told me how they had sat round the yak herders' fire, sharing a meal. Then someone said they had been offered hot baths.

Hot baths! In Tibet! Here, at twenty-eight thousand feet! I jolted back to reality, desperate for warmth and human company, bored of my mind's surreal ramblings. Then I think I dozed again, because at some point I became aware, quite suddenly, that it was no longer dark. Everything was suffused with pastel light and far, far below only soft pillows of cloud remained in the valley where Mimi, Joe, Paul, Pasang and Kasang would be asleep in their tents. Then the sun rose over Ama Drime – that forked summit far out beyond our valley, which had been like a talisman right through our expedition, ever since we first saw it from Pre-Base Camp all those weeks ago – and the world shone and sparkled once again.

I stood up stiffly and wobbled down the slope. In the daylight it was all so simple and clear, and I quickly reached the levelling where I had to turn right into the gully. Then I was hurrying down, sliding wherever possible, rushing back to the South Col. I suddenly noticed two people and for a moment I thought that I was back with the phantoms. Until I realised. They were Ed and Robert, standing beside the Japanese tent which we had passed on the way up, over twenty-four hours earlier.

They too had failed to get back to the South Col and had huddled through the night in the empty tent. Robert had found an oxygen cylinder with some gas still inside and had opened the valve, giving the tent a quick blast of life-support before the hissing died away. Then they had shivered, like me, without sleeping bags, hour after hour, Robert suggesting repeatedly that they should go down to the South Col, Ed insisting that they should wait for the dawn.

Ed reckons that they emerged from the tent at five o'clock in the morning; I think it may have been more like six. They barely spoke, saving their strength for the descent to the South Col. My fate wasn't even discussed, because there was nothing they could do about it: climbing back up would have been physically impossible. They were just about to leave when Robert nudged Ed and gestured up the gully at a dishevelled drunk staggering down towards them.

I wanted to laugh and cry. I wanted to hug my friends. But all I could manage was to slump down beside them as Ed handed me his water bottle, offering the last dribble of half-frozen sludge to wet my blue lips. Then he photographed me trying to force sluggish facial muscles into a smile. Ice driblets hung from my beard. My nose, exposed all night, had turned dull grey. Frosted spectacles obscured my right eye, but the left eye was just visible, staring grimly, with no hint at all of the inner joy.

We had done it: we had climbed Everest without oxygen and survived. And now we were going home, the three of us together. I was very, very happy.

In a touching token of friendship, Robert took out the short rope I had left here over twenty-four hours earlier and the three of us descended linked, Robert guiding me over awkward rocky steps while Ed followed behind. Down at the South Col Ed took out his camera again, snapping Robert with a protective arm over my hunched shoulders. Then I managed to rise to the occasion, holding my ice axe aloft for an official victory shot. Then I followed the other two, stopping every few metres to kneel in the snow as we trudged back to the tents. By the time Ed and I arrived Robert was already ensconced in his tent. In ours we sank blissfully into our goose-down nest, luxuriating in the glow of sunshine percolating through yellow fabric, savouring the long-awaited purr of the gas stove melting the first panful of snow.

Then we inspected the damage. Both my heels were numb and the toes of my left foot had already turned a pale shade of purple. Ed also had frost-bitten toes. More seriously, one thumb and seven fingertips had changed colour. 'It must have been those shots I took at dawn,' he confessed. 'Wasn't that sunrise amazing? My fingers got a bit numb. That often happens, but this time they didn't come back again. What do you think?'

'Well, they don't look much worse than Luke's did on Shishers. Or that fingertip I froze in the Alps. I think they may be all right.' What brave, blithe talk; what naive optimism. And how stupid to warm them – first Ed's fingers and toes, and then my toes – in the pan of tepid water, before we added a tea bag and drank it. I had read somewhere that slow warming was the best hope of saving frozen tissue. What I neglected to remember was that this had to be done somewhere safe and sterile, once frozen digits could be immobilised and hospitalised; we still had to descend the whole of the east face of Everest and walk several miles back to our base camp. And then, somehow, travel the thirty miles back over the Langma La to the road head.

So, blissfully unconcerned about frostbite, we concentrated on immediate pleasures. It was wonderful to drink – even this unsweetened, dirty, tepid tea. And to lie back on a soft down bed, letting the warmth soak deep into our limbs. And to know that, for the moment, we didn't have to go anywhere, do anything. Somewhere, deep in our collective subconscious, there was the knowledge that this was dangerous – that we had now spent nearly three days above 7,900 metres and that every hour we lingered would weaken us further.

But, hey, you have to be flexible. It was a shame – a great shame – that we hadn't managed to stick to the blitzkrieg plan: arrive at the South Col at midday, go for the summit that night, back the next afternoon and get the hell out of there, back down the Kangshung Face before our bodies knew what had hit them. That would have been wonderful; but after the slow wallowing attrition on the way up, it had proved impossible. Never mind, we had still done it. Now we just *had* to rest, to lie down, to get our first sleep in two days, to recover enough strength for the descent.

I had one frightening moment in the tent when my throat suddenly blocked and I dragged myself to the door, unzipping frantically, desperate for air. But there was no more air outside than in. So I heaved and pushed, remembering the gentle missionary doctor, Howard Somervell, descending the north ridge in 1924, alone, some way behind Norton after they had both turned back at above twenty-eight thousand feet, suddenly unable to breathe, saying to himself with impeccable British reserve, 'Oh, well, cheerio' as he prepared to die of suffocation, but then managing in a last-ditch effort to give himself a Heimlich manoeuvre and cough up the mucous lining of his larynx, allowing the air to rush back into his lungs. Sixty-four years later, in our tiny dome tent, I too managed to cough up a great gob of green phlegm and experience the same joyful reprieve as the air flowed once more.

But *what* air? Here it definitely felt more substantial than it had done at the summit; but the pressure was still barely a third of what we were used to at sea level, inadequate to sustain life for long, seducing us into false relaxation by dulling our brains. We did manage to have a drink or two, but felt no inclination to eat the remaining scraps of solid food. Some time in the afternoon our final gas cylinder hissed to a halt and we had our last sip of liquid. Then I realised that it was dark. I slept intermittently, drifting in and out of confused dreams, eventually sensing the bleak light of a new day, 14 May. The cold was now seeping through my thin inflated mattress. My mouth was dry and I longed for a drink. 'Robert,' I shouted, 'are you going to melt some snow?'

There was a muffled shout from the other tent, but at least an hour seemed to pass before we heard him light the remaining gas in his stove. Ed and I lay inert, content to doze, abdicating all responsibility until Robert brought breakfast. Two or three hours passed. Occasionally I croaked hoarsely, 'Robert – where's that tea?' but it was only much later that morning that he handed in a pan of tepid water. Even after that I procrastinated, too lazy to move. It was Ed, in the end, who forced me to sit up and start the exhausting job of packing my sleeping bag into my rucksack. Even more daunting was pulling on my boots. Realising how weak I was, I decided to save weight by ditching the windsuit which had saved my life on Shishapangma and here on Everest. I also left behind my spare mittens and ski stick. Ed didn't even bother taking his down salopettes, leaving them with the mail package, hoping someone might find it and deliver our letters. As for the tents – not a chance: this was the Retreat from Moscow.

The last photo Ed took before leaving the South Col. Stephen is trying to find the energy to stand up and follow Ed down the East Face. Robert is still sitting in his tent. The rope, for some inexplicable reason, was left behind.

Ed got away first. I watched him disappear over the brink of the South Col as I lay on my rucksack outside the tent. I had managed proudly to complete the Herculean task of putting on crampons and felt I had earned one final little nap before setting off. Robert was hunched in the doorway of his tent, still melting snow. He handed me half a pan of tepid water, then he too set off. By the time I reached the edge of the Col and stared down into the white depths of the Kangshung Face he was already about two hundred metres below.

Speed, I knew, was vital: we had to get down as quickly and effortlessly as possible – down, down into that rich nurturing air. So I shouted, 'Okay to glissade?' and assumed that the muffled reply was 'Yes.' Then I leapt off the Col and slid down into Tibet, accelerating, surprised that the slope was steeper than I remembered, alarmed now, braking hard, leaning on my ice axe, trying to stop, failing, then shooting faster, then – crack

– a blow on the hip as I hit a rock and was flung in a rag-doll somersault through the air, sensing the ice-axe loop being ripped from my wrist as I landed in the snow and slid again, in a confused choking flurry of white powder.

I came eventually to a halt, blind and gasping, terrified of dying. Pulling off my right mitten to clear my glasses, I dropped it, so now I had to split the left mitten – wearing down on one hand, pile and Gore-Tex on the other. Desperate for human contact, I shouted down to Robert, 'My axe has gone. The Rolex nearly went too.'

'Well, that's a relief,' he shouted. 'Don't want to lose that. I tried to stop you glissading, but you didn't hear. I got avalanched.'

Still joking after being swept down in an avalanche! What a gentleman. What a star. 'Please wait,' I pleaded, as I waded down to join him. I asked if he could lend me an ice axe, but both his tools had also been lost in the fall. Ed had gone ahead with the only remaining ice axe, giving Robert his ski pole. I looked at the pole and Robert shrugged, 'I suppose I could break it in half?' And then he ploughed on after Ed.

I followed last, dragging on the big slope above the Flying Wing, stopping far too often to sit in the snow. It was now dusk and snow was falling. Shivering in the gloaming, I drifted back to the Mountains of the Moon – to that evening beside Bigo Bog, heating glühwein on the fire. I smelt the intensity of sweet wine, Cointreau and spices. Then I drifted further back, to that winter evening in the Val Ferret in 1976 – the end of a twelve-hour trudge on snowshoes, waiting for Lindsay at that bar, sitting on a tall stool and feeling the warm sweetness of a large Cinzano Rosso percolate through my body. I longed for that sweet intoxicating rush of warmth to the blood, that cosy interior, that human comfort, and wished that I could catch up with Ed and Robert. Later, as it got dark, I shouted to them, hoping unreasonably that they might help me change my glasses and get out my head-torch; but I had to manage on my own, forcing numb fingers to their task. Then I ploughed on, still calling, 'Ed . . . Robert' as I followed their furrow, back to the bamboo wand we had left on that Great Day so long ago, marking the crevasse crossing at the northern end of the Flying Wing. Somewhere dimly I registered a guilty admission of laziness – of our foolishness in leaving that length of rope up at the South Col.

I followed the tracks carefully, stepping wide over a dark hole. And then all I had to do was shuffle back south along the underside of the great ice roof to a welcoming glow of torchlight. The other two were already in their sleeping bags. Robert had brought his burner down from the Col and screwed it to one of the gas cylinders we had cached here. By the time I had settled into my sleeping bag he had produced a drink, using one of the paper tubes of instant coffee that he had found in the Japanese tent two nights earlier. But we had no sugar to relieve the bitterness. Everything now seemed to taste foul, distorted by the metallic tang of ketones, the carbonyl compounds released as our bodies, desperate for fuel, consumed their own reserves of fat and muscle.

Thirst and a croaking cough woke me the next morning, 15 May. I coughed up more phlegm, then pleaded with the other two to light the stove. There was no response; so I forced myself to lean up on one elbow, spooning snow into the pan and lighting the stove. About half an hour later, as the first panful of liquid was nearly ready, the stove fell over. It took another hour or so to produce a second panful, which also fell over. By the time I finally produced our first drink the sun was burning cruelly through a thin cloud haze, forcing us out of our sleeping bags. But still we dallied, too lazy to move. Robert suggested some food, so I rummaged amongst the last scraps and said, 'What about the clam chowder?'

'Not the chowder, *please*!' croaked Ed. We settled instead on plain instant mashed potato, made by me because I was the only one without frost-bitten fingers. Even this bland offering tasted foul. Ed wouldn't touch it, but I forced down a few spoonfuls; Robert ate comparatively heartily. Then we slumped back on our sleeping bags.

I felt angry that we had allowed ourselves to get into this

state, ashamed at our profligacy with time, appalled by our apathy. And yet it seemed so hard to act on that rational under-standing – so difficult to do the right thing.

It was only at 3.45 that afternoon that we finally set off down from the Flying Wing, as clouds closed around the Kangshung Face and it began to snow again. Ed led the way down, steadying himself with our one remaining ice axe, but he still shot over a small ice cliff hidden under powder snow. We didn't see his second slip, lower down. We only heard his anguished shouts: 'This is crazy. I only just missed falling into a crevasse. It's a complete maze down here and it's going to be dark in two hours' time. We're never going to make it to Camp One.'

Wearily, reluctantly, we agreed that we would have to climb back *up* to the Flying Wing and spend another night there. Ed and I went first. When we got to the bare ice bulge that he had fallen over, we had to climb side by side, crampon points balancing on a fifty-degree wall. Ed whacked in the axe as high as he could, then I teetered up beside him, clutching his sleeve for balance. We repeated the manoeuvre several times to surmount the bulge, then Ed reached back down as far as he could and left the axe stuck in the ice for Robert. 'Thanks,' said Our Leader, with just a hint of reproach, 'And how am I supposed to reach it?'

'Jump?'

He must have sorted something out because he rejoined us later, after dark, just as we were settling into our sleeping bags. I managed to produce one small pan of unflavoured water and promised to follow with some more calorific mashed potato, but never got round to the main course before falling asleep.

It was Ed who took this expedition – this pathetic, disinte-grating rump of an expedition – and shook it by the scruff of the neck.

As we woke blearily to another harsh sunrise on 16 May, he croaked urgently, 'If we don't get down today, we're going to die.' He looked like an old man, lean and haggard. His hair hung lankly and he stared in horror at his swollen blistered fingers. He was only voicing what we all knew, but it took that one person to provide the initiative, to grasp the leadership. That was one of the great things about this team: everyone worked phenomenally hard, but each of us knew that, should we flag, one of the others would step in and take charge. And when it came to the most important thing of all – getting back down – it was Ed who provided that leadership.

I only discovered several months later that on Everest Ed was still grieving for a girl called Lauren Husted, who had died in his arms four years earlier after slipping off a ledge, unroped by her own choice, in the Black Canyon of the Gunnison. Only much later did I hear about the route that Ed had subsequently climbed, solo, as a kind of expiation, up the great rock wall of the Diamond, naming it after Lauren's favourite Keats poem, 'Bright Star'. But during our intense days of Neverest he never mentioned any of this, nor the dreams in which he still saw her so vividly. Or at least not to me. He was happy to confide in Paul, but I was a harsher companion, less patient, more focused on the dangerous job we had come to do, suspicious of any hint of self-indulgent melodrama. For me that kind of tragedy – the irreplaceable loss of loved ones – was still an unknown world, waiting in the future. Perhaps if I had realised what Ed had suffered, I might have been more patient and sympathetic, appreciated more readily his inner strength.

And his generosity. As he set off at ten a.m., he croaked, 'Don't wait long, Stephen. You've got to get up and move. If you don't get down alive you won't be able to enjoy being famous.'

I managed to swallow two remaining granola bars in a token effort to generate some energy, washing them down with dirty water. Then I forced myself to strap on crampons. Robert left without a word, but I still lingered, indulging myself with a final rest, perched on my rucksack, elbows on my knees, my head cupped in my hands, swaying slightly, almost drifting off to sleep as I dreamed of life after Everest, luxuriating in the end-of-term euphoria.

It was nearly eleven o'clock when I finally roused myself. Already the clouds were closing in again, exaggerating the crippling greenhouse effect of our white suntrap. I tried to stand up, but nothing happened. Come on – try harder. But again, the body refused to obey. I began to worry. Suppose I really was too weak? Or suppose I did manage to stand up, but then collapsed, face down in the snow, like those two Austrians on K2, two years ago? Or the Polish woman, Mrufka, who got halfway down the fixed ropes, but then collapsed and was found hanging on the ropes a year later. At least I hadn't died in my tent, like poor Julie Tullis. Or Alan Rouse, unable to get out of his sleeping bag, dry lips parted to plead, 'Water, water.'

Their predicament on K2, pinned down by a storm at the top of a much harder descent route, had been far worse than ours. I had no excuse to fail: it was simply a matter of fighting this pathetic laziness. Let's try once more – third time lucky.

I knelt forward in the snow, reached behind me and pulled my rucksack onto my back. I was ditching my sleeping bag, so the rucksack now weighed virtually nothing. But I still had the hardest task to face. First I raised one knee. Then pressed with one mittened hand on the knee. Then willed the other leg to rise and brought both legs into a wobbly standing position. Then, arms held out for balance, I took two or three shaky penguin steps to the edge of the shelf under the Flying Wing and looked down the Kangshung Face. For a moment I was tempted to sink down again and have another rest, but I knew that might be fatal, so I directed every particle of my ravaged brain onto those two withered legs, willing them to keep moving, six steps down the slope. Only then did I allow myself to sit down briefly, before getting up to take another six steps. And then another six steps. It was going to be a hard, hard struggle, but I was going to make it.

Ed led us down the mountain. Paul's descent tracks from five days earlier had been obliterated by successive snowfalls, and only a few key points were marked with bamboo wands. Near-white-out conditions didn't help. By the time I caught up with

Ed and Robert, they were having to traverse back up the slope, having missed a left turn to avoid a huge crevasse. Ed was ploughing ahead like a man possessed, dredging up the deepest reserves of will-power, burning the very last calories in his withered body, determined to force it all the way down the mountain.

He led us on – down the big ice ramp I had led on the way up and which later featured in the Rolex ad, past the collapsing ice cliff, down the long winding slope below that, with all those complicated zigzags. All the time he was listening intently, waiting for the horrible crump of a slab giving way. This had always been our terror – descending at a time when these lazy-angled slopes were laden with new snow waiting to avalanche. But I was slightly less worried than Ed, fairly sure that the complex undulations of our slope – with frequent little troughs underpinning the steeper slopes – reduced surface tension, helping to keep the whole fragile structure in place. But perhaps that was just blithe self-delusion. Or a refusal to contemplate disaster when we were so close to journey's end. In any case, there was little we could do about it: we just had to keep moving down the snowy spur.

There was *one* small avalanche. Determined to stop being a mere passenger, following in Ed's wake, I took a turn in front, trailbreaking. Descending one steep section, I suddenly felt the surface crack with a horrible, breathy 'hrumpph' and I was away, riding the wave, all arms and legs, tossed over an icy bulge and down into a hollow where I came to a halt, buried up to my thighs. I dug myself out and waded on, emerging now from the clouds, recognising blue-remembered features, negotiating the last few zigzags, then arriving triumphantly at a marker wand.

Ed arrived to find me scrabbling in the snow. 'What are you doing?' he asked.

'We need our harnesses and descenders.'

'But we're not at the ropes yet.'

'Yes, we are. Look – down there – where that bit's sticking out of the snow.' And when he saw it, Ed was overjoyed. Nothing was going to stop him now. I watched feebly, too lazy to stop him scrabbling with his frozen fingers in the snow, pulling out equipment, buckling up his harness with numb claws and setting off immediately down the first rope.

I was anxious about Robert, but he appeared a moment later, wading down our trench. 'See you at Camp One,' he shouted. But Ed replied, 'No – we're going all the way. To Advance Base.'

I followed in his wake, fearful of what we might find at the Jaws of Doom. But no, it was all right – everything was still in place. For the last time I whizzed across the Tyrolean Traverse, then transferred to the next rope, half sliding, half rolling down the fourth Cauliflower Tower. But, on the terrace below, the rope was buried so deep that we had to unclip, wading unprotected to the very brink of Webster's Wall, groping over the lip of the overhang for the next rope. Ed rushed on past Camp One, but I stopped briefly to grab my helmet, barely registering the fact that a big chunk of ice had fallen from the Jaws of Doom and collapsed one of the tents.

I caught up with Ed at an anchor fifty metres below Camp One, trying to clip into the next heavily frozen section of rope. 'Look, this is crazy,' I insisted. 'I'll go first and clear the ropes'.

So, as another night closed around the mountain, I took the ice axe and went ahead, sliding down into the immense basin of Big Al Gully, pausing frequently to scrape ice off the rope. When I reached the anchor by Paul's letter box, the rope below was frozen into the slope. I tugged desperately but couldn't free enough slack to feed into my figure-of-eight descender. So I just had to wrap the icy nylon round my wrist and descend that way, until at last I could get leverage and pull the whole fifty metres of line clear. It took nearly an hour to dig out the next anchor and by the time Ed slid down to join me it was pitch dark. Then we discovered that Ed's torch bulb was dead and in the numb-fingered confusion of trying to get out my spare I somehow dropped both the remaining viable bulbs. So, on a moonless night, we had to continue in pitch darkness, relying on feel and memory. To make matters worse, one of Ed's crampons had come loose and was hanging loose from his ankle. He couldn't fix it with his frozen hands and now I was terrified of freezing my own fingers; so, lazily, selfishly, I left it dangling.

I will never know how he managed to negotiate the long, long descending traverse across the flank of Big Al Gully. All I could hear was the acknowledging shout, each time I reached an anchor and told him that he could start the next section of rope. Once upon a time – in that other life when we had started this great adventure, so full of bold hopes – we had planned to remove every trace of our camps and of these disfiguring ropes. Now we were barely removing ourselves.

All my life I had wondered what it would be like: how it would feel to be faced with the great epic escape? Reading Herman Buhl's account of his solo first ascent of Nanga Parbat, bivouacking alone, in shirtsleeves, at nearly eight thousand metres, retreating hour after hour down that long winding ridge, I had often wondered: how would I cope, if it were me? Or if I was with Bonatti, fighting through the storm on the Central Pillar of Frêney? Or David Lewis, dismasted, alone in his stricken yacht amongst the mountainous rollers of the Southern Ocean? You didn't go deliberately seeking those situations. You tried, with what skill and experience you had, to avoid going that close to the edge. But, on this Everest climb, we had, through a compounding series of events, reached that edge; and it was happening, right now: this was the big moment. And we *were* coping. Four days after crossing those apparently impossible hurdles near the summit, we were still dredging up new reserves, crossing new barriers. And for all the weary, desperate longing for it all to be over, there was also a kind of sadness. As I pulled up in the dark to yet another anchor – recognising by feel the particular combination of alloy and steel, fingering for the last time those knots which Ed had tensioned so carefully, each detail so redolent with memories of those wonderful days, seven weeks earlier, when we had first discovered this passage up the Neverest Buttress – I felt a kind of regret that it was all coming to an end and that, probably, no adventure – on mountains, at least – would ever again be quite so intense.

But there was also a mounting euphoria. Soon, very soon, we would be down. We would be safe. We would be free to enjoy our success. Dragging myself down the Scottish Gully, wrenching the ropes clear, heaving my legs out of soggy snow, I bellowed hoarsely over the silent glacier, 'Mimi, Joe, Paul! Put on the tea.' All day long I had been fantasising about great buckets of tea and fruit juice, dreaming of a life without thirst.

At last I got to the bottom of the Scottish Gully and lowered myself carefully onto the vertical Headwall, only to find the rope encased in a two-inch-thick column of frozen meltwater. All I could do was wrap the steel hawser round my arm and slide down as carefully as possible, until the rope was clear again to feed into my descender. God knows how Ed managed with his frozen hands.

Below that there were just series of snowfields and rocky steps. And again a moment of lump-in-throat nostalgia as I remembered that brilliant morning when Robert and I had taken the first steps onto the Neverest Buttress. And then, at last, the end of the 1,600 metres of fixed rope, where my spare ice axe was waiting as I had left it nine days earlier, and, a short way below that, the little cave where I had left a length of rope to safeguard our return across the crevassed glacier.

Ed arrived about half an hour later, tied onto the other end of the rope, and we started the final stage of the long journey home. Normally this trudge across the glacier took barely half an hour. But in the dark we got lost, wandering into a maze of crevasses before finding our way back to the usual route. Even then our trials were not over. With the warm monsoon approaching fast, the snow was imperfectly frozen. We would tiptoe anxiously on the surface for a few steps, then plunge up to our thighs in fathomless sugar, then heave ourselves back to the surface, dreading the next plunge. Frantic to get back to Advance Base, blinded by my craving for comfort and security, exhausted to the point of despair, I still failed to sort out Ed's crampon with my perfectly healthy fingers. So he floundered behind, loose spikes catching in the heffalump traps while I tugged impatiently on the rope. Robert was nowhere to be seen and we assumed, correctly, that he had stayed up near Camp One for the night.

By starlight we could just discern the landscape. On our right the remembered shapes of Peak 38 drew tantalisingly closer until we were opposite a familiar slanting buttress near Advance Base. For about the tenth time, I shouted 'Mimi, Joe, Paul! TEA!' But there was no response, no hint of life in the glacial wasteland. Ed sank yet again into a pit of mushy sugar. At which point – almost nine days after setting out on our journey, having travelled through whole new realms of experience, fighting together to cross previously unimaginable barriers – I finally cracked, shouting cruelly, 'What *are* you doing, Ed – scratching around like a bloody chicken?' Ed said nothing. Desperate to find Advance Base, desperate for someone else to help us, I just untied from the rope and carried on walking through the darkness.

When Paul left the South Col on 11 May he was determined to lose height as quickly and efficiently as possible. It took him just seven hours to retrace the whole of our route down the Kangshung Face and walk back across the glacier to Advance Base. There he recovered immediately from his incipient oedema. Then he sat down with Mimi and Joe to wait for our return.

They never saw us on the summit ridge the next day. On 13 May, although Sungdare Sherpa saw three mystery figures descending towards the South Col where he was still encamped, we were hidden from the Kama Valley and our friends saw nothing. By the time we dragged our lethargic bodies back down onto the Kangshung Face the following afternoon the mountain was hidden in the clouds. That night none of us could make the effort to stand up and signal with a torch from the Flying Wing. On the 15 May we again set off so late that we were obscured by cloud. Our tracks above, from the South Col, had already been filled in by fresh snow.

By now the others had assumed the worst. Mimi was in tears, convinced that she was not going to see Robert again. Bracing herself for bereavement, she was wearing an abseiling device of his – a token memory – on a string round her neck. In the faint hope that we might have descended by another route, Paul sent Joe to our base camp with a message for Angchu – a local man who had been helping the expedition – to take to Kharta, asking our Chinese liaison officer to alert the authorities and request a search of the other two Everest base camps – Rongbuk beneath the North Face, and the Nepalese base camp at the foot of the Khumbu Icefall.

The following day, 16 May, Mimi and Paul were on the verge of abandoning Advance Base, but decided to wait one more night. Just in case.

Exhausted by the long fretful vigil, they dosed themselves up with sleeping pills to get through the night. Paul was fast asleep at three-thirty on the morning of 17 May when hoarse cries nearby began to penetrate his consciousness. As he fumbled in the dark, searching for his torch, there was another shout and Mimi woke up, asking blearily, 'What is it?' And then they heard that English accent, hoarse with despair: 'Where are the bloody tents?'

Paul leapt out of the tent and rushed towards me, his torch beam dazzling my eyes. And in a pathetic joke, recalling all those alpine starts in that other life when we first set foot on the Kangshung Face, I croaked cheerily, 'Three-thirty in the morning, Paul. Time to go up the ropes.'

He moved closer and put a hand on my shoulder, staring from behind his head-torch. 'Venables! What happened to your nose? Black snout!'

'It got a bit cold. But we did it. Please will you get Ed? He's just a short way back – down on that flat bit. I think Robert's at Camp One.'

First Paul helped me over to the tent and pulled off the three layers of boot which I had last removed on the South Col, four days earlier. He was chattering excitedly, brimming with energy, hyper-alert. 'Look at those toes ... we thought you were dead ... no tracks. Nothing. Mimi was just crying and crying.' Then he set off to bring in Ed, while Mimi took over, melting ice to produce the bowl of fruit juice I had been dreaming about for so long. 'I think Robert's still up on the ropes,' I said. 'But he should be down soon.'

'I'm just so happy you guys are alive.'

Soon Ed arrived and he too was enveloped in tenderness as Mimi began a twenty-two-hour stint of non-stop nursing. As the new day brightened and she bathed our frostbite injuries in sterilising solution, I finally registered the extent of Ed's suffering. His damaged toes, like mine, were simply black. But his hands were a different story. The long night on the icy ropes had wrecked the protective blisters so that the skin hung loose from claws of putrefying flesh. And where my face, black snout notwithstanding, was just a little wizened, Ed looked like a war painting by Goya, bloodshot eyes staring in traumatised horror.

For the first time Ed now realised that he was going to lose the ends of his fingers. It was a terrible price to pay for a climb, but as Mimi clamped a mask over his face and turned up the valve on our one bottle of medicinal oxygen – a token gesture at regeneration – he became calm and, like me, dozed off to sleep.

I woke a little later to the sound of voices outside. Paul had returned from the glacier, annoyed at twisting his knee while trying to go and meet Robert, whom Mimi had spotted making his way down the ropes a mile away on the face. Then there was more commotion and Kasang rushed into camp and thrust his head through the door, amazed, relieved and horrified. Pasang arrived and knelt down beside Ed, full of compassion. And finally Joe, explaining excitedly, 'We were looking up this morning from Base Camp and I suddenly spotted these tracks on the face. We couldn't believe it. We just had to get over here as quick as we could to check.'

Robert finally arrived that evening and stayed awake for several hours as Mimi listened to his wild ramblings. But already the next day, when I managed – just – to walk ten yards over to his tent, the old, coolly amused, self-deprecatory Robert was back on form, joking about his tenth night out on the mountain. 'I just couldn't find the pink rope over Webster's Wall. I didn't dare go any closer to the edge, so in the end I decided to cut down the rope above and use that to belay myself. I couldn't find my knife, but I had this hyoogely brilliant idea to cut the rope with a crampon. So I took one off and there I was – at midnight, holding this blunt crampon in my frost-bitten hand, trying to saw through the rope. In the end I gave up and just lay down, curled in the snow. I wasn't too worried: after getting down that far, I kind of knew I wasn't going to die now.'

Whereas Ed had damaged whole joints, Robert's frostbite was limited mercifully to just the very tips of a few fingers. The blisters had remained intact and were already hardening to ebony carapaces, secure against infection. His toes had suffered less damage than either mine or Ed's, but he looked just as scrawny and haggard.

The next day, when we were strong enough to hobble back across the glacier to Base Camp, the journey which I had done in two hours when fit now took six and a half. It was a hard struggle, but a wonderful homecoming – like that return from Kunyang Kish eight years earlier, but this time with the emotions tuned to a higher intensity – leaving the sterile world of the glacier, dragging wearily up one final slope and emerging into an utterly different world where a fine afternoon drizzle was releasing the sweet soft smell of damp earth.

That was just the first of countless sensory treats easing us slowly back to normality: the two cans of beer that Robert had saved secretly for our celebration; the American trekkers who appeared the next day – the first outside people we had seen for over two months; the laughing Tibetan women, men and boys who arrived to help us back to the road head, sixteen of them running shifts on the two stretchers that Paul had made to try and limit the damage to Ed's and my toes; the primulas at our first camp on the way out; the pale yellow rhododendron blooms the next morning; the turquoise shimmer of the Shurima Tso – the holy lake which had been a frozen white sheet when we last saw it; the first cuckoo, heard just outside Kharta as we waited for two Land Cruisers to come and drive us home.

Kasang left us at Kharta. The rest of us parted company at Shegar on 30 May, eighteen days after I had reached the summit.

Before dawn Mimi, Joe, Robert and Ed loaded their vehicle for the long drive to Lhasa. I held Mimi in a long hug, wishing that we were all going home together; but Paul and I were bound for Kathmandu with Pasang, hoping to sell all the remaining gear there to settle some unpaid bills and pay for my flight back to Bombay.

By the time we reached Kathmandu, Robert would have had a chance to contact Wendy and tell the outside world about our climb. Already he was talking about maximising publicity for the benefit of sponsors, proud that his crazy project had succeeded, generously unfazed by the fact that he hadn't been the lucky one to get to the summit. Ed was equally generous – and has always remained so – despite the trauma of losing the end joints of seven fingers and one thumb, as well as toes: never once criticising me for pushing on alone, so ruthlessly, to the summit.

But of all of them, Paul was the real hero: the one who was brave enough to turn back, and who then picked up the pieces, joking, cajoling, nursing and cosseting the rest of us on the weary journey home, sustaining us through three interminable days in Kharta as we waited for transport – Ed crying, 'For God's sake get me out of here' – then helping me back across the frontier to Nepal, commandeering a bus and a crate of beer when we had no money and then charging other tourists to come on board and pay for them, and finally staying with me for five days in Kathmandu, always cheerful, never once resentful of the praise and congratulations which were focused inevitably, unfairly, on my solo push to the summit.

And what about *my* return to earth? I think that first morning back at Advance Base, knowing that at last we were safely down, was one of the happiest moments of my life. For all the delays and mistakes, it was immensely gratifying to have experienced that raw, brute, animal struggle for survival – to have fought and won. But also to have created such an improbable route through those ephemeral ice towers. To have lived and worked for so long on the mountain, unlocking the secrets of its vertical landscape. To have enjoyed that growing intimacy with one of the most beautiful valleys on earth. To have witnessed our little team grow in strength and confidence. To know that, for all my occasional irascibility and selfishness, I had worked as hard as anyone, totally committed to making our project a success.

We had been away from home for nearly four months and it would be disingenuous to pretend that I wasn't looking forward to returning to Western comforts. Of course I was. I couldn't wait! And I was also looking forward to telling people about our adventure. For all its arcane introspection, a great climb seems pretty meaningless to me unless you can share at least some of the beauty and intensity with other people. But in the end it is your own deep satisfaction that is the ultimate reward. As Paul and I drove across the Tibetan plateau after saying goodbye to the others, we stopped briefly near the village of Tingri for a last look at the great pyramid of Chomolungma. It was a luminous morning and the mountain glowed pale in a blue sky above a plain softening with the first green haze of summer. The frostbite on my nose was already hardening to a brittle scab which would soon peel off to reveal fresh pink skin. The toes on my left foot were faring less well – they were starting to smell like a dead rat – and I was fairly sure that I was going to lose them; but that loss was a small price to pay – a mere nuisance. I was still pitifully thin and weak, but I would soon get strong again.

I had no idea what I would do next. I assumed that there would be more mountains, because climbing mountains was what I did. But that didn't seem very important, because there would also be other adventures, other challenges, other still-unknown paths to follow. And even if life in the real world would always be more difficult and more complex than the beautiful simplicity of our microcosmic existence on Everest, there would always be the sustaining memory of that climb. For me those precious weeks in the Beyul Khembalung had seemed a blessing – an extraordinary coincidence of good fortune, a culmination of all the climbs that had gone before. By pure chance I had found myself sharing a perfect adventure with a perfect team. Together we had staged a great performance. We had created something special. And whatever harder journeys we had to face in the future, no one could ever take that away from us.

Postscript

Rhinog Fach

One fine summer morning twelve years later I rose early and tiptoed downstairs, careful not to wake my wife Rosie and our two sons, Ollie and Edmond. We were on a rare holiday, in the Rhinog mountains, and Rosie had given me a pass – a temporary visa – to slip off for a quick climb, provided that I returned at breakfast time to help with the children.

I laced up my boots and hurried away from the house, down the same springy turf where I had once run barefoot as a boy. Then I continued up the old cattle-drovers' road until I reached a stile in a wall and headed right, up a fainter path. Then I left that, to wade through untracked heather, panting as the slope steepened, impatient to reach the foot of a rock buttress.

Rock-climbing had become a rare treat. These days I could usually only justify going out climbing if someone was paying, and the only other mountain excursion that year had been a working trip to South Georgia, taking part in a film. I had also been to that Antarctic island ten years earlier, in 1990, with Julian Freeman-Attwood – the forester I had got to know on Shishapangma – and Lindsay, and Brian Davison, and Victor's film-making friend Kees 't Hooft. Since Everest I had also been back to the Himalaya five times, but three of those trips were just brief trek-leading jobs, earning money to pay the mortgage on our house in Bath. Most of the time

I was at home, writing articles and books, or on the road, lecturing.

Domesticity appealed. It was good finally to have my own house, shared with someone I loved. Good to have a garden to nurture, even if it wasn't nearly big enough to realise our grand ambitions. Good to have time to play the piano, kidding myself that it was still not too late to improve. But it hadn't all been easy. Bringing up children demanded that selflessness that I had always found elusive and our elder son, Ollie, needed a lot of care. He had been autistic since the age of two-and-a-half and leukaemia at four had exacerbated his difficulties. He was over the leukaemia now, at least for the moment, but it had been a long struggle – both the cancer and the more enigmatic condition called autism. Now, after several years of exhausting home-education experiments, we had sent him to a special boarding school and the wrench, for Rosie in particular, had been agonising. As for Ollie, his resilience made a complete mockery of any notion of mountaineers being courageous. With him, the courage was real.

Edmond was bright and cheerful, with a fierce temper and a fiercer love for his quirky, enigmatic, non-talking elder brother. He liked it here in the hills and it was gratifying to see him respond to the aesthetic lure of the mountains. Ollie too, as far as one could tell, seemed to find a kind of solace in this wild landscape. It was good to share it with the boys; but just occasionally I yearned for that old freedom of movement, so I was making the most of this early morning romp onto the flanks of Rhinog Fach, the mountain I had first climbed thirty-four years earlier.

I stopped to change into rock-shoes. A cobbler at the factory had specially adapted one shoe to fit closely round my truncated left foot, following the contour of the amputated toe stumps frost-bitten during my night on the bare mountain. Narrow cracks and pockets were out of the question but, with its reduced leverage, the stumpy foot worked brilliantly on small protruding holds – far better than the longer, more bendy right foot with all its superfluous toes.

Fat moss cushions oozed green slime over the rock, heather clumps obscured vital holds and the cliff, like all cliffs, turned out to be steeper than I had expected. After twenty feet I realised that continuing could be disastrous. So I had to reverse the moves and, like all reversed moves, they were harder on the way down than they had been on the way up. I was unfit, unsure of my strength, unable to commit to a long reach down with outstretched foot. How many hundreds of times had I been in this situation before? Trembling and dithering, wishing I had a rope, or at least a sling to use as a temporary hand-hold? Terrified of the backward plunge and the broken bones and the wrath of a wife suddenly lumbered with a crippled husband? Could I never learn?

Well, actually, yes, I *had* learned. I had learned that I could cope, could extricate myself, could, eventually, make that move, knowing I would get it right. And so, after about ten attempts, I did finally brace my nerves for that long step, descend safely and find an alternative route, less steep and oozy, up the side of the buttress.

And then I was away, padding up gorgeous slabs of Harlech grit, thrilling again to that sensuous contact between skin and stone, solving the puzzle, searching out the cracks and edges and wrinkled rugosities, savouring the growing space beneath my feet. This was *so* good – this untrammelled fluency, alone with the rock and the heather and the sky – and it was all over too soon. But there was still the grassy pleasure of the summit – that same summit where I had lain so contentedly when I was twelve. No kestrel this time, just the comic surprise of a lone ewe ruminating beside the cairn, getting reluctantly to her feet and shuffling off in disgust at the unexpected intruder.

Like the great pre-war Himalayan explorer, Bill Tilman, I thought that no proper mountain day was complete without a swim. So, after racing down the other side of the mountain I pulled off my clothes and plunged into the icy blue of Llyn Hywel. Then I hurried on, tingling, down through the heather, past the old manganese mines, heading back to the valley.

Contentment was shattered for a moment when I remembered the unpaid tax bill. And the rent we still hadn't paid for this holiday house. But then I remembered that in a week's time I would be nipping out to Switzerland, to do some filming on the Matterhorn. Paid work! And a different way of enjoying the mountains. I might no longer have the old questing urgency of back-to-back expeditions – the intense single-mindedness which had sustained me through the mid-1980s, penniless whilst everyone else seemed to be getting rich on Mrs Thatcher's property boom – but life was now, in many ways, more varied, more fulfilled. Rosie and I even managed once a year to ignore the overdraft and drive over to Sussex to see a production at my old employers, Glyndebourne. Operas I had never heard before by Britten, Puccini and, best of all, Janacek. A whole new sound world. A whole new adventure. And a gorgeous woman to enjoy it with.

She had even done a bit of climbing, enjoying the intense concentration, until Ollie was born and the mother's self-protective instinct blunted any desire to leave the ground. So, once again, I had mainly to climb with male companions. Most of the old gang were now married with children, but still found time for the hills. Some, like Lindsay and Victor, were embedded totally in the mountain world, Lindsay as a specialist writer, Victor as a mountain guide now living in Chamonix. Luke still escaped occasionally from his business, to Greenland, or Nepal, or Ladakh. Dave Wilkinson's annual migration to the greater ranges remained sacrosanct and Phil Bartlett continued to escape the madding crowd, still discussing, debating, provoking and, in *The Unknown Country*, writing one of the best-ever philosophical analyses of why people climb.

And what about the Everest family? We hardly heard from Paul these days, but I saw Robert quite often. After several years' wandering, he was back in New York, earning hyooge amounts of money in an advertising agency, and married happily to a New Zealander who had borne him two beautiful children. Mimi was married to a fellow Jewish doctor, and living most improbably in Atlanta, with two equally beautiful children. Joe was still photographing his way around the world. Kasang was now quite a man about town in Kharta, doing good business with visiting expeditions and occasionally bumping into Robert, who had returned several times to try the north side of Everest. (He eventually achieved his richly deserved summit in 2003.) Pasang's various lodges and his new water-bottling business were flourishing in Namche Bazaar. I had only done one expedition with him since Everest, but my parents and several groups of friends had stayed with him and his wife Pinzum. And what about Ed? After several post-Everest expeditions – including one in Mongolia where he helped Julian Freeman-Attwood and John Blashford-Snell save Lindsay's life – Ed had suddenly been struck by some mysterious neurological condition which had left him weak and barely able to walk. Things were now improving, but his days of hard climbing were over for the moment. However, he had found and married Lisa, the girl he first fell in love with as a teenager, and that was ample consolation for the canyon walls of Colorado. *And*, at last, he was about to publish *Snow in the Kingdom*, his magnificent account of his three Everest expeditions, culminating in our adventure on the Kangshung Face.

I still thought about that adventure nearly every day. It had become a part of who I was. At the time I had assumed that it would lead to even bigger, harder, more committing climbs – Everest had never been intended as a full stop – but actually it had freed me to do other things. I hoped that it had also, perhaps, made me a little nicer, more patient, more compassionate. But still selfish enough to run off and desert my family for a glorious morning on Rhinog Fach.

It was getting late, long past breakfast time. I hurried on down the old railway, overgrown with grass, an emerald line curving through the purple heather. Then I headed straight down the hillside, running, leaping, dodging through that little clump of wind-blown oaks, feeling again the lichenous warmth of the little grit outcrop, before striding on through a reedy bog, boulder-hopping the river and rejoining the cattle-drovers' road for the final lap back to the house.

It was already ten o'clock and both the boys were up, playing on the sheep-cropped grass. Rosie was standing in the sunny doorway in her dressing gown and I thought again how lucky I was to have this family, always there to come back to.

'We were worried,' said Rosie. 'I was starting to plan your funeral.'

'Sorry. But I just had to have a look at that buttress. And you know climbers always get back late.'

'Yes, I know. It's all right.'

Index

Bernina, Piz: Biancograt 267–8
Beyul Khembalung 285, 296, 347
Bharak 77
Bharib Khund holy lake 258
Bhasteir Tooth 147
Bheinn a Bhurd 213
Biafo Glacier 245, 246, 248
Bigo Bog, Uganda 239, 241, 333
Bilafond La 202, 205
Biner, Paula 93, 96
Biolet campsite, Chamonix 48, 50
Birmingham Polytechnic 116, 117
Bishop, Barry 326
Bitanmal, Pakistan 129
Black Canyon, Gunnison National Park, Colorado 336
Black Crag, Lake District 41
Black Cuillin 146
Blackburn, Joe 276, 288, 298, 344, 351
Blackwell, James 241
Blair, Tony 41
Blanche de Perroc, Switzerland 35–7
Blashford–Snell, Colonel John 257, 258, 259, 263, 264, 352
Boardman, Peter 122, 138, 148, 171, 186, 295–6, 322–3
Sacred Summits 211
Body, Maggie 211, 212, 232–3
Boga, Zerksis 198, 205
Boivin, Marc 64
Bolivia 159–64
Bombay 278, 279
Bonatti, Walter 31, 59, 215, 340
Bonington, Sir Chris 31, 55, 108, 139, 148, 186, 188, 197, 211, 216, 315
boots 2–3, 26, 35, 53, 60, 82, 126, 164, 270, 327, 343
Bossons Glacier 55, 65
Botterill, Frank 183
Boulder Ruckle 29, 214
Lightning Wall 214
Bouquetins 91
Bourdillon, Tom 315
Boysen, Martin 110
Bracken, Brendan 114
Brail, Switzerland 12, 14
Braldu gorge 246
Brammah 188
Brazier, Andy 46, 48
Bregaglia Range 24, 42, 43
Brenay Glacier, Haute Route 90

Brenva Ridge 50
Brimham Rocks 136
Bristol 212–13
Bristol cliff–rescue unit 40
Bristol University 198, 201, 263
British Airways 129, 139
British Embassy, Kabul 75
British Joint Services Expedition 273, 318
British Mountaineering Council 154, 182
Brittain, Vera 114
Broad Peak 205
Broad Stand, Lake District 183
Brookes, Cho 156, 158
Brouillard, Mt., France: Right–Hand Pillar 55
Brown, Joe 58
Bruce, Geoffrey 280
Brünig Pass 169
Budden, Phil 115
Budget Bus 71, 78, 80, 199
Buhl, Hermann 31, 59, 340
Buhler, Carlos 140, 141, 143, 275
Bujuku Lake 240
Bularang Sar 121
Burgess, Adrian 275
Burke, Mick 322, 323
Butler, Anthony 117
Buxton, John 42
Buzzoni, Mrs (teacher) 10

Café Verona, La Paz 160
Cairngorms 213–14
camming ascenders 290
Campa I, Peru 155
Campa Pass 154
Carreg Wasted 28
Crackstone Rib 28
Wrinkle 28
Cartwright, Julian 242
Cartwright, Katherine 242
Cartwright, Keith 242
Cartwright, Pru 242
Cartwright, Vicky 242
Cary, Joyce 6
Cary, Lucius (SV's cousin) 212, 213
Cassin, Ricardo 43
Castor, Pennine Alps 99
Ccapana 155
Central Pillar of Frêney 215–16, 340
cerebral oedema 2, 307, 308, 342
Cervinia, Italy 99